Believers Church
Bible Commentary

Elmer A. Martens and Willard M. Swartley, Editors

D1565049

BELIEVERS CHURCH BIBLE COMMENTARY

Old Testament

Genesis, by Eugene F. Roop 1987
Exodus, by Waldemar Janzen 2000
Judges, by Terry L. Brensinger 1999
Ruth, Jonah, Esther, by Eugene F. Roop 1999
Proverbs, by John W. Miller 2004
Jeremiah, by Elmer A. Martens 1986
Ezekiel, by Millard C. Lind 1996
Daniel, by Paul M. Lederach 1994
Hosea, Amos, by Allen R. Guenther 1998

New Testament

Matthew, by Richard B. Gardner 1991
Mark, by Timothy J. Geddert 2001
Acts, by Chalmer E. Faw 1993
Romans, by John E. Toews 2004
2 Corinthians, by V. George Shillington 1998
Ephesians, by Thomas R. Yoder Neufeld 2002
Colossians, Philemon, by Ernest D. Martin 1993
1-2 Thessalonians, by Jacob W. Elias 1995
1-2 Peter, Jude, by Erland Waltner and J. Daryl Charles 1999
Revelation, by John R. Yeatts 2003

OLD TESTAMENT EDITORS

Elmer A. Martens and Allen R. Guenther (for *Jeremiah*), Mennonite
Brethren Biblical Seminary, Fresno, California

NEW TESTAMENT EDITORS

Willard M. Swartley and Howard H. Charles (for *Matthew*),
Associated Mennonite Biblical Seminary, Elkhart, Indiana

EDITORIAL COUNCIL

David Baker, Brethren Church
Lydia Harder, Mennonite Church Canada
Estella B. Horning, Church of the Brethren
Robert B. Ives, Brethren in Christ Church
Gordon H. Matties, Mennonite Brethren Church
Paul M. Zehr (chair), Mennonite Church USA

Believers Church
Bible Commentary

Proverbs

John W. Miller

HERALD PRESS
Scottdale, Pennsylvania
Waterloo, Ontario

Library of Congress Cataloging-in-Publication Data
Miller, John W., 1926-
  Proverbs / John W. Miller.
        p. cm. — (Believers church Bible commentary)
  Includes bibliographical references and index.
  ISBN 0-8361-9292-3 (pbk.)
  1. Bible. O.T. Proverbs—Commentaries. I. Title. II. Series.
  BS1465.53.M55 2004
  223'.707—dc22   2004018136

BELIEVERS CHURCH BIBLE COMMENTARY: PROVERBS
Copyright © 2004 by Herald Press, Scottdale, Pa. 15683
     Released simultaneously in Canada by Herald Press,
     Waterloo, Ont. N2L 6H7. All rights reserved
Library of Congress Control Number: 2004018136
International Standard Book Number: 0-8361-9292-3
Printed in the United States of America
Cover and charts by Merrill R. Miller

12 11 10 09 08 07 06 05 04   10 9 8 7 6 5 4 3 2 1

To order or request information, please call 1-800-759-4447 (individuals); 1-800-245-7894 (trade). Website: www.heraldpress.com

For our grandchildren,
Scott, Emily, John, Jessica,
Stephanie, Matthew, Maya, Jacob,
and great-granddaughter,
Renée

Abbreviations/Symbols

*	The Text in Biblical Context (as in Contents)
+	The Text in the Life of the Church (as in Contents)
//	equal, parallel to
BCBC	*Believers Church Bible Commentary*
cf.	compare
ch/s.	chapter/s
[Modern Study]	sample reference to an appended essay
e.g.	for example(s)
et al.	and other(s)
for attaining wisdom	sample style for a quotation from Proverbs
Heb.	Hebrew text/word. Transliterations follow *The SBL Handbook of Style*, edited by P. H. Alexander et al. (Peabody, MA: Hendrickson, 1999)
KJV	King James Version
lit.	literally; literal translation by the author
LXX	Septuagint
n	note
NIV	New International Version
NJB	New Jerusalem Bible
note/s	Explanatory notes in sequence of chapters/verses
NRSV	New Revised Version
NT	New Testament
OT	Old Testament
TBC	The Text in Biblical Context
TLC	The Text in the Life of the Church
v./vv.	verse/verses

Contents

Series Foreword

The Believers Church Bible Commentary Series makes available a new tool for basic Bible study. It is published for all who seek to understand more fully the original message of Scripture and its meaning for today—Sunday school teachers, members of Bible study groups, students, pastors, or other seekers. The series is based on the conviction that God is still speaking to all who will hear him, and that the Holy Spirit makes the Word a living and authoritative guide for all who want to know and do God's will.

The desire to be of help to as wide a range of readers as possible has determined the approach of the writers. No printed biblical text has been provided so that readers might continue to use the translation with which they are most familiar. The writers of the series have used the *New Revised Standard Version,* the *Revised Standard Version,* the *New International Version,* and the *New American Standard Bible* on a comparative basis. They indicate which text they follow most closely, as well as where they have made their own translations. The writers have not worked alone, but in consultation with select counselors, the series' editors, and the Editorial Council.

Every volume illuminates the Scriptures; provides necessary theological, sociological, and ethical meanings; and in general makes "the rough places plain." Critical issues are not avoided, but neither are they moved into the foreground as debates among scholars. Each section offers explanatory notes, followed by focused articles in "The Text in Biblical Context" and "The Text in the Life of the Church." This commentary aids the interpretive process but does not try to supersede the authority of the Word and Spirit as discerned in the gathered church.

The term *believers church* has often been used in the history of

the church. Since the sixteenth century, it has frequently been applied
to the Anabaptists and later the Mennonites, as well as to the Church
of the Brethren and similar groups. As a descriptive term, it includes
more than Mennonites and Brethren. *Believers church* now repre-
sents specific theological understandings, such as believers baptism,
commitment to the Rule of Christ in Matthew 18:15-20 as crucial for
church membership, belief in the power of love in all relationships,
and willingness to follow Christ in the way of the cross. The writers
chosen for the series stand in this tradition.

Believers church people have always been known for their emphasis on obedience to the simple meaning of Scripture. Because of this,
they do not have a long history of deep historical-critical biblical scholarship. This series attempts to be faithful to the Scriptures while also
taking archaeology and current biblical studies seriously. Doing this
means that at many points the writers will not differ greatly from interpretations found in many other good commentaries. Yet basic presuppositions about Christ, the church and its mission, God and history,
human nature, the Christian life, and other doctrines do shape a
writer's interpretation of Scripture. Thus this series, like all other commentaries, stands within a specific historical church tradition.

Many in this stream of the church have expressed a need for help
in Bible study. This is justification enough to produce the Believers
Church Bible Commentary. Nevertheless, the Holy Spirit is not bound
to any tradition. May this series be an instrument in breaking down
walls between Christians in North America and around the world,
bringing new joy in obedience through a fuller understanding of the
Word.

                                                    —*The Editorial Council*

Author's Preface

The book of Proverbs is passionate about two things primarily—acquiring wisdom and trusting God. As I worked on this commentary, it only slowly dawned on me that these differing passions reflect the book's remarkable history. The passion for acquiring wisdom is justifiably attributed to Solomon, a Judean king renowned for his vast learning. It was during his reign that the book's first edition was created (1:1).

The passion for trusting God, I have come to believe, comes from "the men of Hezekiah" who two centuries later produced an enlarged second edition (25:1). Hezekiah was a Judean king renowned for his faith and religious reforms (2 Kgs 18:1-6). As it turned out, his reforms were a watershed event not just for Israel, but for the world, since writings produced in support of these reforms eventually became core books in the Scriptures of Judaism and Christianity. Not the least of these books, I hope to show in this commentary, is the "Hezekiah Edition" of Proverbs (as called in the following pages).

There are many fine commentaries on Proverbs, and each has a unique contribution to make (see Selected Resources). The uncovering of the design, purpose, and message of the Hezekiah Edition of Proverbs is a defining characteristic of this one, affording (I have found) helpful insights into the book's genesis and relevance then and now [Distinctive Approach].

This approach need not call into question the book's divine inspiration. As I understand it, the truth that "all Scripture is God-breathed" and "useful for teaching" (2 Tim 3:16) pertains not just to a book's origin but also to how it was interpreted and preserved, then read and pondered right down to the present time. We too need the Spirit's guidance as we seek to understand and apply these teachings.

The invitation to prepare this commentary came many years ago. Fortunately, I was not required to complete it sooner. After initial studies I felt I needed to put it aside until I had a better grasp of how books like Proverbs were produced and became authoritative. A decade of research on the Bible's canon history (Miller: 1994; 2004) proved to be an essential step in my recognition of Proverbs as the pedagogical masterpiece I now deem it to be.

While completing this commentary, I was exceedingly fortunate to have had the assistance of Professor Elmer Martens, editor of the OT commentaries in this series. From the beginning he welcomed its novel approach and gave generously of his time and expertise. Members of the Editorial Council were also very forthcoming with corrections and helpful counsel. At their request, Father Lawrence Boadt, Director of Paulist Press, read the manuscript in its penultimate form and also made insightful suggestions, as did S. David Garber, copy editor. I am truly grateful to all who gave of their time in this way. Despite all the help—due to the scope and complexities of this project and due to my own limitations and shortcomings—deficiencies remain, for which I am responsible.

As in previous undertakings of this kind, I owe a great deal to the love and encouragement (and innumerable editorial suggestions) of my wife, Louise. I cannot imagine how I would have completed it without her. The commentary's dedication to our grandchildren is an expression of affection and goodwill to them and their peers. They were often in our thoughts and prayers during the years this book was in progress.

—*John W. Miller, Professor Emeritus*
Conrad Grebel University College
Waterloo, Ontario

Introduction to the Book of Proverbs

The book of Proverbs is not easy to read or study. A first impression is that it is an anthology, a book to be sampled, not read straight through. This is how it is most often used—like a coffee-table book, to be dipped into for the tidbits that fall from its pages. But what in reality is it? How did this book come to be?

A Book of Poems

Proverbs is a book of poems—not proverbs in the traditional sense. We usually think of a "proverb" as a short, pithy saying. This is not what we encounter in the book of Proverbs [Genre Issues]. While many of its teachings are short, many are not, and "pithy" is not an apt description for most of them. For this reason the book's name in English is misleading. It comes from *Proverbia*, the name of this book in the Latin Bible of the Middle Ages. *Proverbia* is a translation of the first word in the Hebrew text, *mišlê*, a plural construct of *mashal* (*māšāl*). A *mashal* is a poem-like composition (either short or long) that states a truth or teaches a lesson in a picturesque, compelling manner.

Hebrew poems of this type are almost always made up of two-line verses (or couplets), in which the first line states a point one way, and the second states it another way (or presents a new thought). Each line is short, not more than four or five words (in Hebrew). The book's opening poem in 1:8-9 is an apt illustration. Line 1 states: *Listen . . . to your father's instruction*; line 2 repeats: *and do not forsake your mother's teaching*. This is followed by a second couplet: *They will be a garland to grace your head* (line 1), *and a chain to adorn your neck* (line 2). Poems like this might be as short as a single couplet—as in the case of the 375 two-line poems in the book's main collection (10:1–22:16)—or couplets might be combined to make longer poems like those in chapters 1-9.

A Book About Wisdom

A *mashal* can be a poem on almost any topic. The opening verses of Proverbs state that its "poems" have a single theme and purpose: *for attaining wisdom* (1:2). Wisdom as we think of it is also not exactly what is meant by the Hebrew term *hokmah* used here. Its nearest equivalent in English is "expertise" (Fox: 33). Two of its most often used synonyms are "knowledge" and "understanding" (also translated "discernment"). So one might say that the *wisdom* referred to is the "expertise" that results from having "knowledge" *with* "understanding" (8:12). "Knowledge" in Hebrew refers to data derived from the bodily senses: eyes, ears, nose, touch (Harris: 366). "Understanding" has to do with the way knowledge is assessed and applied. When we have factual "knowledge" and know how to understand or use it, this in general is the "wisdom" this book is talking about *[Words for Wisdom and Folly]*.

At the time it was believed that thoughtful learning of this kind occurred in the "heart," not the head, and that the wisdom thus acquired was manifest in different ways *["Heart"]*. Those with expertise in a trade are called wise (Exod 31:2-4). A king whose heart is skilled in interpreting laws and discerning good and evil is also thought to be wise (1 Kgs 3:9). Solomon is eulogized as one of the wisest kings of the time because of his knowledge of plants, animals, birds, reptiles, and fish (4:33); for his giftedness in composing thousands of songs and proverbs (4:32); and because of his insight (3:28) and breadth of understanding (4:29).

A Manual for Educating Young Men

The teachings in Proverbs represent yet another type of wisdom: the kind young people need as they approach adulthood. Aristotle in book 6 of his *Ethics* defined wisdom of this kind as "prudence," knowing "what is conducive to the good life generally" (Aristotle: 209). Something similar is said in Proverbs about its teachings. They are *for giving prudence to the simple, knowledge and discretion to the young* (1:4). In this verse the word *young* is more accurately translated as *a young man*. The book's teachings are often addressed to a *son* or *sons* (1:8; 4:1). These *sons* are not small children but young men on the verge of (or at the beginning of) adulthood, like the young man so vividly described in Proverbs 7.

This focus on "sons" gives the impression that Proverbs might have served (initially at least) as a manual of instruction for young men. This impression was confirmed in 1923 with the discovery and publication of a booklet from ancient Egypt entitled The Instruction of Amenemope (Pritchard: 421-24). Amenemope was an employee of the Egyptian government living in the twelfth century BC. His "Instructions," written initially, he informs us, for his own son to "steer him in the ways of life," were widely used in schools where young men were trained for the Egyptian civil service. It was noted right away how strikingly similar Amenemope's teachings were to those in Proverbs, especially those in 22:17–24:22 (see commentary notes). A number of teachings in both books imply a governmental setting. Many additional manuals of this kind from this ancient world have been found and published (Walton: 172-78). An initial edition of Proverbs might well have been written for a similar purpose and setting, as a manual for steering young men "in the ways of life" who were preparing to be civil servants (see the reference to "teachers" and "instructors" in Prov 5:13).

That instructions of this kind were needed in the days of Solomon is apparent from what is said in 1 Kings about his vast national enterprises. At one point, we are told, 550 officers were employed (9:23) to supervise 3,300 foremen, who were in charge of 70,000 carriers and 80,000 stonecutters (5:15-16). In "grandeur and complexity" Solomon's kingdom rivaled that of ancient Egypt (Heaton: 59). Small wonder that right at this time "the 'wisdom' of Egypt, upon which its scribal meritocracy had been nurtured for centuries, first gained entrance to Israel and began to shape its instructions, literature and intellectual life" (Heaton: 12).

Two Editions: Solomon and Hezekiah

In our Bibles the book of Proverbs is not as it was in the time of Solomon. We know this to be the case because of editorial headings interspersed throughout, seven in all (1:1; 10:1; 22:17; 24:23; 25:1; 30:1; 31:1). One of the things they do is call attention to two very different time periods when the book's teachings were compiled and published. The headings in 1:1 and 10:1 refer to the book's origins in the days of Solomon. The heading in 25:1 alludes to a supplemental block of proverbs added in the days of Hezekiah king of Judah. This implies that there were, at least, two quite distinct editions of this book: the one created in the time of King Solomon, and another enlarged edition produced two centuries later during the reign of King Hezekiah.

A thesis of this commentary is that the Hezekiah Edition of this book (as called below) was created by adding supplements reflective of the views of those who did this to an intact older version of the Solomon Edition (as called below). For the most part these supplements are readily identifiable and were inserted into all parts of the book's older edition *[Solomon Edition]*. That Proverbs might have been enlarged in this manner during Hezekiah's reign is not a totally new idea; as mentioned, the book itself indicates as much, and this too is what the rabbis of the Babylonian Talmud imply when they ascribe it to "Hezekiah and his Colleagues" (*Baba Bathra 15a*). Heretofore, however, scant attention has been paid to this aspect of the book's composition. This commentary is the first to present a detailed study of the book from this perspective *[Distinctive Approach]*.

Approaching the book in this light was for me personally a god-send that helped resolve many otherwise puzzling features of the book. Naturally, I hope others too will be helped by this approach. With this in mind I now take some first steps in introducing the Hezekiah Edition of Proverbs as I have come to understand it.

The Hezekiah Edition of Proverbs

Hezekiah's Reforms

To begin to understand the Hezekiah Edition of Proverbs, it is essential that we pay attention first of all to what is known about King Hezekiah himself. The book of 2 Kings informs us that this king was unique among the kings of Israel for his devotion to "the commands the LORD had given Moses," and for the sweeping religious reforms enacted as a consequence (2 Kgs 18:1-6). With respect to these reforms, the text says, "There was no one like him among all the kings of Judah" (18:5). In the course of his reforms, he rid Judah of the cult objects of alien gods, including "the Asherah poles" of the Canaanite mother goddess Ashtoreth (18:4). Surprisingly, a prior account in 1 Kings states that it was none other than King Solomon who first inaugurated this practice of worshipping alien gods in Israel of the kingdom period. He did this after he himself became a follower of the goddess Ashtoreth (consort of Baal, the Canaanite storm and fertility god) and of "Molech the detestable god of the Ammonites" (1 Kgs 11:5). As a consequence shrines devoted to these and "other gods" became commonplace in both Israelite kingdoms, and remained so for some two centuries, with catastrophic moral and spiritual consequences. In the eighth century Assyrian armies destroyed the northern kingdom and were threatening to do the same in Judah (2 Kgs 17). This is the context in which the books of Kings tell us of Hezekiah's reforms (2 Kgs 18).

Hezekiah's "Men"

The period of Hezekiah's reforms is increasingly recognized as a time of intense literary activity. In support of these reforms, a collection of books was produced that would over time be expanded and become the Scriptures of Judaism and Christianity [Hezekiah Reform Literature]. In this light the brief reference in Proverbs 25:1 to the men of Hezekiah producing an enlarged edition of Solomon's proverbs takes on enhanced importance. It signifies that it too was published at this time in support of these reforms.

Who were the "men" who did this? It is often thought that they were scribes or sages [Modern Study], but this is not how they are designated. In 2 Chronicles 29-31 we are told of "Levites" whom Hezekiah had "consecrated" at the beginning of his reign (29:5) and who were his associates in all aspects of his reforms. Were these the "men" referred to in Proverbs 25:1? It becomes apparent that the Levites were Hezekiah's men when we consider their history. First Kings informs us that when Solomon became king, he banished certain priests from Jerusalem because they had opposed him as successor to his father, David (2:26-27). The leader of the banished group, we are told, was Abiathar, the sole survivor of the Levites of Shiloh who traced their appointment as priests in Israel to Moses (Exod 32:29; Deut 10:8; 33:8-11). Earlier, David had installed two priesthoods in Jerusalem, one headed by Zadok, the other by Abiathar (2 Sam 8:17). So, when dismissing the priesthood headed by Abiathar, Solomon was (in effect) dismissing the Levites whom his father had appointed and whose primary loyalty was to the teachings of Moses. The Zadokite priests who remained in Jerusalem (1 Kgs 2:35) worshipped Yahweh the God of Israel, but not (at the time) to the exclusion of other gods (as taught in the Decalogue [Ten Commandments] that Moses advocated). This is why they raised no objections when Solomon permitted other gods to be worshipped (Miller 1994:40-48).

Against this background the report in 2 Chronicles 29-31 of Hezekiah's action in enlisting Levites as colleagues in his reforms is both credible and illuminating. To reverse Solomon's policies, Hezekiah needed associates who were as loyal to Moses' teachings as he was—and who would act meaningfully and decisively on his behalf. . The Levites, even though banished from the national shrines of both Judah and the northern kingdom, Israel (see 1 Kgs 12:31), still remained faithful in their respective communities to their calling as custodians of Moses' teachings. At Hezekiah's request they returned to Jerusalem and were restored to temple duties. Some of them were set apart to be devoted full time to the study of "the Law [torah or teachings] of the LORD" (2 Chr 31:4-8). This group of state-supported Levites, I suggest, were the "men of Hezekiah" who created the Hezekiah Edition of Proverbs.

Agur Son of Jakeh

Proverbs 30:1 refers to Agur son of Jakeh. That the book even mentions an individual other than Solomon is significant, but that his name appears in chapter 30 may also be important, since the editor or author of a scroll was sometimes recognized at its end (cf. Ps 72:20; Eccl 12:9-14). There are reasons for thinking that chapter 30 is the last chapter of the Hezekiah Edition, with chapter 31 being added later (see following section). Agur's name and sayings appearing at this point in the edition might well be an indication of his leadership role in creating it.

The poems of Agur that follow in 30:2-33 (the first two in particular) are fully consistent with this suggestion. The first poem (30:2-6) is termed an *oracle* or inspired message (30:2; cf. Isa 13:1). Agur thereby addresses two individuals, Ithiel and Ucal, possibly professional scribes involved in the literary productions of the time. His message to them is that despite the fact he (Agur) has *not learned wisdom* (studied it professionally as they have), there is something he *does* know about: *Knowledge of the most Holy One I know* (30:3; for this translation, see notes). Then, in language echoing that of Moses in Deuteronomy, he chides them for their futile speculations about what is in *heaven* (30:4; cf. Deut 30:11-16) and concludes with a warning not to add to God's *words* (30:6; cf. Deut 4:2; 5:22; 12:32).

From this oracle and Agur's devout prayer in 30:7-9 (where he expresses the fervent wish to remain faithful to Yahweh whatever may come), it is evident that Agur too (like the *men of Hezekiah* referred to in 25:1) was a devout Levite. He was deeply engrossed in the words of God revealed to Moses [Distinctive Approach].

Purpose and Design of the Hezekiah Edition

In Agur's oracle and prayer—seen in the light of the account of Solomon's reign in 1 Kings 2-11 and the follow-up record of Hezekiah's reforms in 2 Kings 18—there is a hint as to the underlying motive for creating a second edition of Proverbs. Agur's oracle points to the passionately held conviction that God's "words" to Moses (Prov 30:5-6) should not be subverted, replaced, or added to, something Solomon had himself done when worshipping "other gods" and permitting Israel to do the same. Hence, when "the men of Hezekiah" began to create a new edition of Proverbs, they intended to produce a book firmly linked to and consistent with the teachings of Moses in Deuteronomy.

How did they carry out this daunting project? What was the book like before they began editing? What was it like when they were finished? Details and specifics of what they did are discussed in the notes (below). The contents of the book they began with can only be surmised as one begins to understand the multiple ways in which the men of Hezekiah supplemented it [Solomon Edition]. The following are just a few introductory examples of what they did.

They Redesigned It with Meticulous Care

A first impression of Proverbs is that it is disorganized and was created in a rather haphazard manner. Studying it more closely reveals the opposite to be the case. It has three large well-defined sections: an Introductory Collection (1:1–9:18), the Main Collection (10:1–22:16), and Supplemental Collections (22:17–31:33). The Introductory Collection (1:1–9:18) and Supplemental Collections (22:17–31:33) are quite similar in size—in fact, without chapter 31 (added later) these two sections are virtually identical, with 256 verses in the introduction and 253 in the appendixes. Noteworthy too is that the Main Collection has exactly 375 proverbs. As often observed (Murphy, 1981:50), this number equals the numerical value of the Hebrew consonants of the name "Solomon" (in 10:1), which in Hebrew are: š (300), l (30), m (40), h (5).

My conjecture is that these 375 proverbs may have been arranged for study in panels of five (see notes). These five-proverb panels are in turn arranged in two equal sections, with a set of 37 five-proverb panels in section 1 (10:1–16:1) and another set of 37 five-proverb panels in section 2 (16:7–22:16), with the remaining five-proverb panel at the center of the two sections (16:2-6). Given the fact that the Main Collection is at the center of the book (with about the same number of verses before and after), these five proverbs at the center of it are at the epicenter of the Hezekiah Edition as a whole. These several observations may be diagrammed as follows:

Design of the Hezekiah Edition of Proverbs				
Part 1 Introductory Collection (256 verses)	Part 2 The Main Collection (375 verses) 10:1–22:16			Part 3 Supplemental Collections (253 verses)
1:1–9:18	37 units of five 10:1–16:1	Center five 16:2-6	37 units of five 16:7–22:16	22:17–30:33

We might wonder why the Hezekiah editors would have created a book with such a carefully crafted symmetrical form. A reason for doing so may be related to the fact that its contents were initially written on a scroll (not in a book). A scroll is a horizontal strip of papyrus or vellum, with writing in narrow perpendicular columns on one side only. When read, it was held in two hands and rolled and unrolled from both ends a little at a time. When not in use, it likely was customary to keep larger scrolls rolled up from both ends so that when opened its contents (being equidistant from that point) would be readily accessible. Thus, when opened for reading, a scroll's middle column would be the first to be seen. My suggestion is that the Hezekiah Edition of Proverbs was designed so that the five couplets in 16:2-6 would be among the first to be seen when *it* was opened for reading.

Not surprisingly, these five proverbs are unique in that—unlike any other five-proverb panel in the whole collection—every one of them mentions Yahweh, the God of Israel. Each states a theological truth that we sense is expressive of the core convictions of those who created the Hezekiah Edition of Proverbs [Middle Poems].

They Supplemented It with Specified and Unspecified Additions

To achieve the symmetrical form just described (the equal size of its first and third parts as well as the precise number of proverbs in its middle collection) required supplementing the book throughout. *Supplements in Part 3.* In Part 3 (22:17–31:31) the editors attached supplemental collections with headings explicitly informing the reader of what they were doing. The first two of these headings (22:17; 24:23) identify "sages" other than Solomon as the source of the collected teachings that follow. The third heading (25:1) indicates that these too were proverbs of Solomon (as were the earlier ones in 10:1–22:16) and that certain "men of Hezekiah" added them (25:1). The fourth heading (30:1) identifies *Agur son of Jakeh* as the source of the sayings in chapter 30.

These four headings are stylistically similar and interconnected. In each case the source of the collected sayings added is identified, followed by the sayings themselves. The fifth heading (31:1), unlike the others, names the person *to* whom the added "sayings" are addressed (*sayings for Lemuel*, not "sayings of Lemuel") before identifying their source (*which his mother taught him*). This chapter's contents are also quite unique (see notes). They most likely were added in postexilic times, when Proverbs became part of a larger collection of scrolls [*Wisdom of Proverbs*].

The *specified* supplements added in Part 3 of Proverbs were not the only additions made when the Hezekiah Edition was created. There is at least one significant instance where the contents make it clear that supplements were inserted without being so identified, such as the block of poems in Proverbs 25-29. The heading to the large supplemental collection in 25:1 identifies the poems that follow as "proverbs of Solomon." However, when we examine the contents of these five chapters more closely, it is evident this heading applies to chapters 25-27 only, not to chapters 28-29, since the poems in these latter chapters are so strikingly different (see notes).

Supplements in Part 1. A closer look at the book's Introductory Collection in 1:1–9:18 reveals that blocks of teachings were added here as well [*Solomon Edition*]. There are marked differences between the several distinctive blocks of poems in this section. To cite just one example, the poems in 4:1–5:14 are introduced in a manner clearly indicating that the person speaking is Solomon (4:3). This was likely the opening poem of the older Solomon Edition. The *sons* addressed in 4:1 are not Solomon's sons—he does not call them "my sons" (as in NIV) but simply *sons*. After saying a bit about himself

(4:3), Solomon shares several poems that he says his father taught him (4:4-27; the "son" in these poems is Solomon being addressed as such by his father). Solomon then addresses the *sons* with whom he is sharing these poems in the concluding poem of this section (5:7-14) and in doing so refers to their *teachers* (5:13). The sons are students; the implied setting is the royal schools. There is not a single reference to God in these poems (in 4:1–5:14), only to wisdom. They seem right at home in the court of Solomon and were likely part of the Solomon Edition.

Other blocks of poems in this opening section are strikingly different (1:8–3:35; 5:15–7:27). They are introduced in a way that implies that the one speaking is a "father" teaching his own "son." He addresses him not as "son" (or sons) but as *my son*, and urges him to listen to the instruction of both his father and his mother (*your father . . . and your mother*; 1:8; 6:20). The implied setting of *these* poems is the home. They are replete with references to Yahweh, the God of Israel. The son addressed is taught to put his trust in this God to direct his paths and not to rely on his own understanding (3:5). This group of poems seems right at home in the court of the reformer king Hezekiah. They were likely added by Hezekiah's men (for details, see notes).

Supplements in Part 2. Did *the men of Hezekiah* also add supplements of this kind to the book's Main Collection (10:1–22:16)? There is much to suggest they did. In its present form this section of the book has some sixty sayings about Yahweh and the fate of those who serve or reject him (see notes). Right in its center (as observed) is a panel of proverbs, each mentioning Yahweh (16:2-6): how Yahweh weighs a person's motives (16:2), how he blesses those devoted to his ways (16:3), his oversight of all that happens (16:4), his abhorrence of the proud (16:5), and how *fear of the LORD/Yahweh* helps avoid evil (16:6). This is hardly what Solomon or his schools were teaching (see above). It seems apparent that the book's Main Collection was also supplemented with proverbs reflective of the convictions of Hezekiah's men.

They Were Motivated by a Core Conviction

I want to comment yet on a core conviction of Hezekiah's men as they prepared their edition of Proverbs. When reading their supplements, it quickly becomes evident that they were troubled over one teaching in particular in the older Solomon Edition. As noted above, the opening poems of the Solomon Edition are likely those in 4:1–5:14. The very opening poem of that block states, *Wisdom is supreme* [Heb.: *rē'šît*]; *therefore get wisdom* (4:7a). In this verse the Hebrew word translated "supreme" means "first" or "beginning" (as in Gen 1:1). What this verse is saying is that "wisdom" being "first" or the "beginning" (cf. 8:22), the foremost thing to be done is to "get wisdom." In other words, wisdom being first or supreme, its acquisition takes priority over everything else in life: it is that important.

The men of Hezekiah did not reject this idea (otherwise they would have deleted it from their edition), but they were obviously not fully in agreement with it either. In 1:7a, at the forefront of their edition, they placed a statement that takes issue with it: *The fear of the LORD is the beginning* [rē'šît] *of knowledge* (1:7a). In this carefully formulated sentence, *fear of the LORD* [Yahweh] replaces acquiring *wisdom* (in the counterpart statement in 4:7a) as the *beginning*. In effect it says: It is not acquiring *wisdom* that is the *beginning*, but *fear of the LORD* that is the *beginning of knowledge*. Significantly, there is a similar sentence in 9:10: *The fear of the LORD is the beginning* [tēḥillāh] *of wisdom, and knowledge of the Holy One is understanding*. With these two strategically placed sentences (at the beginning and end of the enlarged Introductory Collection), the editors of the Hezekiah Edition of Proverbs have crafted a new conceptual framework for the entire book. The starting point for acquiring wisdom in the Solomon Edition is simply getting *wisdom* (4:1-7); the starting point for acquiring wisdom in the Hezekiah Edition is *the fear of the LORD* (1:7; 9:10b). The goal is the same: acquiring wisdom—in that sense wisdom is still supreme, but the starting point for acquiring it is different.

They Enlarged Its Audience

Finally, the way the Hezekiah Edition editors enlarged the audience of the Solomon Edition manual should be recognized. As previously observed, the Solomon Edition of Proverbs was likely designed to serve as a manual for young men preparing for civil service (Heaton: 12). Was the Hezekiah Edition meant to function in a similar way? I believe it was; this, I sense, was one of the reasons for appending the several fairly large supplemental collections (22:17–30:33). Many of the poems in these collections are about kings and those who do their bidding (see, for example, 25:1-10). Like Solomon, King Hezekiah needed reliable civil servants to oversee his endeavors and implement his reforms, and a manual like this for training them.

Yet another purpose for the Hezekiah Edition is indicated in the insertion in 1:5: it provides instruction for those who are already *wise* by virtue of their prior training. The *wise* referred to in this verse are not young men but educated teachers (see notes), but they too are urged to ponder the book's teachings and add them to *their [previously acquired] learning* (1:5a). This admonition implies that this edition of the manual presents added teachings with which even they (experienced teachers as they are) are not familiar.

The men of Hezekiah envisioned yet a third audience for their new edition of Proverbs. As noted, the blocks of poems they added in chapters 1-9 are introduced as teachings for a son by his own parents (1:8-9; 6:20). Implied is a home where parents instruct their children in the teachings of this edition of Proverbs. A similar instructional setting is presupposed in Deuteronomy, which admonishes parents to instruct their own children in the words of God revealed to Moses (Deut 6:6-9; 11:18-21). This admonition suggests that the Hezekiah reformers may have been positioning their edition of Proverbs as a companion volume to Deuteronomy in a curriculum for homeschooling. This curriculum included not just the laws revealed to Moses, but this enlarged volume of Solomon's poems about wisdom for life [*Distinctive Approach*].

For successful homeschooling, not just fathers but also mothers were expected to embrace these values and be prepared to teach them to their sons. This suggests that while this edition of Proverbs is still directed to sons, its teachings were deemed relevant for daughters as well. They too will one day marry and play a role as wives and mothers in teaching *their* sons—and their success or failure in doing so will have profound consequences for them no less than their husbands (cf. 10:1).

Why the Gender-Specific Focus

It is a serious mistake to think (as many now do) that the book of Proverbs is prejudiced against women just because it is addressed to young men. In my opinion it likewise is a disservice to the reader when translators rid the book of its gender-specific language by substituting gender-neutral nouns and pronouns [*Translation Issues*]. Obliterating its gender-specific focus in this way robs it of its "voice" as a wake-up call to parents and educators regarding the unique, specific, and often urgent needs of young men in their growing-up years. That young men *do* in fact need specific guidance and help, targeted to their special needs, is a fact of life that is recognized in a variety of ways in virtually every society (Gilmore).

Why this is the case has also become increasingly apparent through developmental studies tracking the growth of children from infancy onward. An important truth is that a boy's journey from childhood to adulthood is markedly different from that of a girl (M. Van Leeuwen: 115-16). A girl's growth to maturity involves separation from the mother and entry into an independent social status *like* that of her mother. For the boy "the task of separation and individuation carries an added burden and peril" because he must enter into a new and independent social status "distinct and opposite" from the mother's (Gilmore: 28).

Young men face very different challenges in becoming husbands and fathers than young women do in becoming wives and mothers. A woman becomes a mother when a child grows in her womb and is born of her body. From the beginning a mother's bond with her child is tangible and intimate. A man's relationship to a child is far less obvious. His knowledge that a given child is his is based upon inferences. Apart from insemination there is no tangible bond connecting him to his own child. For a male to become a father to his own children, he must be mature and responsible enough to have united with a wife who will be faithful to him and he to her, so that the children born to her are known to be his. He must be present and remain involved in the care of these children as they grow to maturity.

That young men will mature to the point where they can assume the demanding roles of husband and father (not to speak of other adult responsibilities) cannot be taken for granted. Both boys and girls need the help of fathers or father-surrogates in becoming autonomous from their mothers, but boys much more so. Without such help many simply will not make it. Due to the marginality of males in the reproductive process, fatherhood is a cultural acquisition to an extent that motherhood is not. Hence, a culture needs to support young men in becoming responsible, caring, faithful husbands and fathers through its teachings, laws, mores, symbols, models, and rituals (Miller, 1999:11), exactly what we see happening in the teachings of Proverbs.

What about young women? Girls also need help in growing up—especially today when they are being bombarded at an early age with "the junk values of mass culture" (Pipher: 23). They need to be warned against the temptations of rebellious peers and male sexual predators. They need to be encouraged to stand firm for what is right and avoid foolish actions and activities that might ruin their lives. A companion volume to the book of Proverbs is urgently needed, one that would replicate many of the values in Proverbs but in a form that addresses the specific challenges faced by maturing girls. It is no service to young women to change the book of Proverbs into a gender-neutral manual. This only weakens it as a manual for either gender. Because the needs of boys and girls in growing up are so different, guidance needs to be targeted to each.

The advice and guidance in the book of Proverbs is intended for young men, but their adherence to this advice also benefits women. I am not aware of anything in the book of Proverbs that is demeaning to women; just the opposite appears. One of the book's foremost themes is finding a wife, loving her, remaining faithful, and building a home in which she will be honored and respected for all she does for her family and the wider community. To be sure, warnings are given to young men to be on their guard against the temptations posed by a certain kind of woman [Identity of the Foreign Seductress]. Warnings of a similar kind are given regarding resisting the clever enticements of a certain kind of lawless, evil-minded man. In neither case is it implied that all women or all men are persons of this type. Nor is the fact that young men are presumed to be gullible and an easy prey to temptations of this kind meant to excuse them when they yield and bring irreparable harm to themselves and others.

This manual's sole purpose is to hold young men accountable to a high standard of conduct through warnings and teachings that will steer them away from destructive paths, not to provide them with excuses for their failures.

The Book of Proverbs in the Life of the Church

Quite possibly the chief contribution of the book of Proverbs to the life of the church through the ages has been the way it fosters an integration of faith and knowledge, revelation and reason. Nevertheless, theologians of the church have rarely taken its point of view to heart. Why this neglect? It may be that Paul's sharp contrast between the divine wisdom revealed in Christ and "man's wisdom" (1 Cor 1:25) has left its mark [Wisdom in Proverbs]. An outstanding example is the influential Latin Church theologian Augustine (354-430), who came to believe, like Paul, that human beings are unable to grasp truth, or wisdom, without divine grace and enlightenment. "This, combined with his pastoral work, . . . led to an emphasis on faith in the authority of the Church and its Scriptures, and pre-eminently, upon a humble following of Christ, which made Christianity the only, and universal, way to wisdom" (Harrison: 137).

When too sharp a contrast is drawn between revealed wisdom and human wisdom, the wisdom spoken of in the book of Proverbs tends to be viewed as an inferior type of human wisdom. A recent case in point is the vigorous debate over "natural theology" versus "revealed theology" within the field of biblical studies itself. Proverbs seems more concerned about a reasoned approach to right and wrong and says nothing about the "saving acts" of God in the exodus or at Sinai. Hence, some regarded its teachings as a type of "natural theology" (based on human experience and reasoning) and wondered whether "wisdom literature" (so called) deserves any place at all in a truly biblical theology (Murphy, 2002:121). Roland Murphy is one of a number of biblical theologians who believe the time has come to rethink these "theological prejudices," as he terms them (123). His own views are that Israel's historical narratives, which recount the revelatory "acts of God," are themselves unique in the way they reflect on the past and do not just take it for granted (123). Furthermore, "it would be a mistake," he writes, "to characterize the wisdom experience [in Israel] as a species of 'natural theology'" and see it as something inferior to "supernatural theology." On the contrary, he writes, those who produced the book of Proverbs were ardent believers in the God of Israel. Therefore, "what they learned about the Lord from creation and experience was [therefore] necessarily associated with what they learned from their historical traditions" (124).

The tensions between "revealed" wisdom and human wisdom persist to the present time. This issue in the church's theologies is difficult to resolve and remains an inhibiting factor in the way Christians approach the Bible generally and the book of Proverbs in particular. As a consequence, it affects the way they approach the explosion of knowledge in the modern world.

As I reflect on the relevance of Proverbs for the church today, this stands out as possibly one of its major contributions. The book's introductory poems state categorically and repeatedly that acquiring wisdom of the kind alluded to in its pages is the supreme challenge facing young men and their society. This may seem an exaggeration, but did not Jesus say something similar at the end of the Sermon on the Mount with his parable of the two houses (Matt 5-7)? And is John's Gospel saying anything different when it points to Jesus as the incarnate "word" (or "wisdom") of God that has been shining in the world since the dawn of time (John 1:1-5)?

While completing this commentary, I came across an interview with the British theologian David Ford (who now teaches in the United States). He was asked why the theme of "wisdom" runs through so much of his recent writings (Cunningham: 30). Some of his answers struck me as echoing the kind of synthesis between faith and wisdom testified to in the book of Proverbs. One of the purposes of the Believers Church Bible Commentary is to stimulate a conversation about the relevance of the texts being studied and the life of the church (see sections on TLC). The following brief excerpts from the interview with David Ford in which he comments on the role of "wisdom" in *his* theology may perhaps serve as a starting point for the ongoing conversations we will be having in the following pages about these and other matters. Ford writes:

> The wisdom tradition represents the self-critical side of the Hebrew Scriptures. It's thus a very good model for what theology should be doing: paying close attention to tradition while thinking through the difficult and dark questions. Wisdom demands an integration of rigorous thought with imagination and also practical concerns—how things actually work out in the living of life. Part of its fruitfulness for me has been that it acts as a check on theology's being too doctrine-centered, and not taking account of the imaginative and the practical. . . . I spend a lot of my time reminding people that you need to be at least as intelligent in your faith as in the rest of your life.

A Note About Translations

The translation used in this commentary is the New International Version (NIV). Its citations in the textual commentary are in italics rather than quotes. My choice of this translation was partly determined by its fidelity in most instances to the gendered language of Proverbs. Many modern translations seek to hide or mute the fact that Proverbs is a manual for *sons* by deliberately mistranslating the words *son* or *sons* as *child* or *children* on the assumption that a book addressed to sons is prejudicial to daughters. On the face of it, this is misleading. Hence, the NIV may be characterized as a more literal translation of Proverbs than are some others (at least so far as the translation of this book is concerned).

However, like most translations this one too is designed for public reading, not just for study. With that in mind, the book's poems are invariably rendered as complete sentences with verbs when in fact many are not such, especially those in the Main Collection. The poems of this book are generally terser and more allusive in Hebrew than in any of the English translations [*Translation Issues*]. My frequent resort to literal translations in the commentary (signified by the abbreviation "lit.") is an attempt to convey what the Hebrew text actually says, not usually a criticism of published versions.

Another related issue merits a brief comment. Following a long-standing tradition NIV uniformly substitutes "LORD" for the divine name "Yahweh." "LORD" is an honorary title; "Yahweh" is a transliteration of the sacred name of the God who spoke to Moses at the burning bush (Exod 3:15). At that time "other gods" with other names were being worshipped in this region of the world. This was also the case in Israel itself at the time the Hezekiah Edition of Proverbs was created. Seen in this context, the use of the divine name in Proverbs served as a clarion call to its readers to trust this God and no other *[Proverbs and the Birth of Ethical Monotheism]*. With this historic struggle and development in mind, I have for the most part retained the transliterated name *Yahweh* in my translations and comments.

Part 1

Introductory Collection

Proverbs 1:1—9:18

Design of the Hezekiah Edition of Proverbs			
			Later
Part 1	Part 2	Part 3	Additions
Introductory	The Main	Supplemental	
Collection	Collection	Collections	
1:1–9:18	10:1–22:16	22:17–30:33	31:1-31
(256 verses)	(375 verses)	(253 verses)	

OVERVIEW

The book of Proverbs has three major collections. The first collection (chapters 1-9) is usually thought of as the book's introduction, although in its supplemented form it is a collection in its own right. It begins with a prologue (1:1-7), followed by poems on various topics (1:8–9:18), some having to do with specific forms of conduct to be avoided or embraced, others with issues of a theological or philosophical nature related to one's worldview or cosmology. Most commentators agree that the poems in this section are from more than one source (Fox: 322) but do not agree what the sources are or when or why the sources were combined as they now are.

This commentary proposes the thesis that some of these poems were part of an initial Solomon Edition of Proverbs, to which other poems were added at the time the Hezekiah Edition was created [Distinctive Approach]. The poems that were part of the Solomon Edition are distinguished by their being addressed to sons (4:1; 5:7; 7:24), by a reference to teachers (5:13), by the way "wisdom" is personified and lauded as supreme, and by the virtual absence of refer-

ences to God. A school setting is implied (5:13). In the poems added
in the Hezekiah Edition, a father addresses his own son (*my son*) and
invites him to listen to the teachings of his father and his mother (1:8;
6:20). These poems often refer to God and imply a home setting
where mothers are present. The impression given is that the men of
Hezekiah retained intact blocks of poems from the Solomon Edition
and inserted blocks of poems between them *[Solomon Edition]*. Yet
there were also smaller inserts made in the poems of Solomon that
begin and end this Introductory Collection. A design emerges in this
part of the Hezekiah Edition of Proverbs: blocks of poems representing the views of Solomon are supplemented with poems (and inserts)
representing the views of the Hezekiah Edition editors.

OUTLINE

Original Prologue (Solomon Edition), 1:1-7
Supplemental Poems (Hezekiah Edition), 1:8—3:35
Original Poems (Solomon Edition), 4:1—5:14
Supplemental Poems (Hezekiah Edition), 5:15—7:23
Original Poems (Solomon Edition), 7:24—9:18

Proverbs 1:1-7

Original Prologue
(Solomon Edition)

The Book of Proverbs, Part 1: Introductory Collection				
Original Prologue (Solomon Edition) 1:1-7	Supplemental Poems (Hezekiah Edition) 1:8–3:35	Original Poems (Solomon Edition) 4:1–5:14	Supplemental Poems (Hezekiah Edition) 5:15–7:23	Original Poems (Solomon Edition) 7:24–9:18

PREVIEW

Prologues like this were typical of instruction manuals in ancient Egypt (for another example, see the 22:17-21 prologue to the sayings in 22:22–24:22). The Solomon Edition prologue is a single sentence (in Heb.) that identifies the collection's origins and purpose (1:1-4, 5). The Hezekiah Edition editors added two inserts, the first in 1:5 to indicate a wider readership for their new edition of the book, and the second at the end (1:7) to clarify its presuppositions.

OUTLINE
Heading, 1:1
Purpose Statement (with Insert), 1:2-6
Watchword (Insert), 1:7

EXPLANATORY NOTES

Heading 1:1
The first word of the Prologue (*proverbs*) refers to poem-like compositions (*mĕšālîm*) that were designed to teach a lesson. The poems that follow are ascribed to *Solomon son of David, King of Israel* (1:1). Solomon might well have written many of the poems in the book's initial edition; in any case, Israel's historians recount that he was renowned for his wisdom and literary output (1 Kgs 4:29-34). His role in the production of this book is also indicated in Proverbs 4:1-3, which followed the Prologue in the book's first edition *[Solomon Edition]*. There Solomon states that the teachings following in 4:4–5:6 are a verbatim report of what his father taught him when he was in his *father's house, still tender, and an only child of my mother* (4:3). Solomon follows these teachings with words of his own, in 5:7-14 (for additional comments on Solomon's role in creating the book's first edition, see notes on 4:1–5:14, the Overview to the Main Collection in 10:1–22:16, and the essay *Genre Issues*).

It is sometime said that the book of Proverbs is devoid of references to Israel *[Modern Study]*. This is true of its teachings, which like those in other manuals of this type are transcultural in their orientation (cf. 8:4). But still, the book's heading is explicit about its teachings being sponsored or perhaps authored by *Solomon son of David, king of Israel* (see also the reference to *Hezekiah king of Judah*, 25:1). The book is thereby linked to the teachings of an Israelite king whose reign is memorialized in the annals of his people as one of the most important in its history (cf. 1 Kgs 2:12–11:42).

Purpose Statement (with Insert) 1:2-6
Four of the verses that follow (1:2, 3, 4, 6) begin with infinitive verbs that connect them to each other and verse one (1:1). They state what the book's general purpose is (1:2-3a), its subject matter (1:3b), its intended audience (1:4), as well as its study methods (1:6). Its general purpose is for *attaining* (lit., *knowing*) *wisdom* and *discipline* (1:2a). *Wisdom* (*ḥokmah*) is competence and skill "in any domain" (Fox: 32); *discipline* (*mûsār*) is the educational process required for attaining

such competence. This entails *understanding words of insight* (1:2b). The verb *understanding* and the noun *insight* are related to the preposition "between" (in Heb.) and "signify the ability to draw proper distinctions" (Cohen: 1). Developing these skills enables one to acquire a *disciplined and prudent life* (1:3a; lit., "the discipline of insight," Fox). Three words in 1:3b identify the desired outcomes of such an education: doing what is *right* (*ṣedeq,* personal uprightness); upholding what is "just" (*mišpāt,* societal justice), and being fair and honest (*mēšārîm,* integrity in community relations).

The more specific goal of this manual is to give *prudence* to the *simple, knowledge and discretion* to (lit.) *a young man* (1:4b). The young man referred to is not a child, but an older youth like the one in the story recounted in chapter 7. He is not necessarily evil or rebellious. He is simply thoughtless and lacking experience (lit., *lacks heart,* 7:7b). He needs to be educated. He needs to be taught (lit., *given) prudence* (*'ormāh,* discretion), *knowledge* (*da'at*), and common sense (*mezimāh*). The *method* to be used in educating him is briefly alluded to in 1:6. It entails *understanding* diverse types of literature: a thought-provoking poem (*mashal*), a metaphorical saying (Hab 2:6), insightful *words of the wise,* enigmas or riddles (Ps 49:4-5)—in short, the kind of "words" that follow in this book *[Words for Wisdom and Folly].*

The Hezekiah Edition added verses 1:5 and 1:7. Thus 1:5 begins with an imperative that breaks the flow of infinitives (in 1:2, 3, 4, 5). It targets a second group for its teachings, the *wise* and *discerning,* and asks that they *add* [them] *to their learning* and *get guidance.* The *sayings* of these *wise* are referred to elsewhere (1:6; cf. 22:17; 24:23). Their *teaching* is characterized as a *fountain of life* (13:14). So why would they too be told to *listen* to this book's teachings and add them to *their learning*? This unusual request implies that the book contains teachings with which they are not yet familiar, precisely the case when the Hezekiah Edition was first published *[Distinctive Approach].* The Hezekiah Edition was not just directed to young men but also to the professional teachers of the time (for further on this group, see 5:13; 30:1-7; Isa 5:21).

Watchword (Insert) 1:7

The watchword in 1:7 (*The fear of the LORD is the beginning [rē'šît] of knowledge*) is one of the most important additions made to the book at the time the Hezekiah Edition was created (see Introduction, "Purpose and Design of the Hezekiah Edition"). It appears again in modified form in 9:10, forming an "enclosure" for the introductory teachings of this edition. It is repeated at the heart of the Main Collection in 15:33 but elsewhere only in Psalm 111:10 and Job 28:28 (and there in a truncated form with a different meaning). It carefully reformulates the statement that stood at the forefront of the Solomon Edition *[Solomon Edition]*, which declares (lit.), *The beginning [rē'šît] of wisdom [is]: get wisdom* (4:7). The key word *rē'šît* (beginning) in both sentences (1:7a and 4:7a) is best understood as "the temporal starting point" (Fox: 68; cf. 9:10; 15:33; Gen 1:1). In another Solomon Edition poem, *wisdom* describes herself as existing from the *beginning* (*rē'šît*) of creation (8:22-23). This is why (in the Solomon Edition poems) *wisdom* is more important than anything else (8:11), and *the beginning of wisdom is to get wisdom* (4:7). The Hezekiah Edition insert in 1:7 takes issue with this Solomon Edition watchword. There is something prior to wisdom that is the *beginning of wisdom*, namely, *fear of Yahweh*. Acquiring wisdom remains the overall objective of this new edition of Proverbs, but another starting point for acquiring it is hereby announced: *the fear of Yahweh* (1:7a). The watchword's second line (*but fools despise wisdom and discipline,* 1:7b) clarifies that this new starting point in no way modifies the book's original purpose. The book remains a manual for *attaining wisdom and discipline* as stated in 1:2a, only that *the fear of Yahweh* is the new starting point for acquiring it.

What is meant by *fear of Yahweh?* In Deuteronomy, possibly also published at this time *[Hezekiah Reform Literature],* the phrase *fear of Yahweh* is used to characterize those who honor, love, trust, and pray to the God of Israel and obey his teachings as revealed through Moses (Deut 5:29; 6:2; 8:6; 10:12-13; 31:12-13). The psalms of the Psalter's first two books (Pss 1-72, likely also published at this time) include numerous references to those who fear Yahweh. Examples are Psalm 25:14 (lit., "the secret of Yahweh is with those who fear him and his covenant for their understanding") and 33:18 ("But the eyes of the LORD are on those who fear him, on those whose hope is in his unfailing love"). Those who fear Yahweh "turn from evil and do good; seek peace and pursue it" (34:14). "The law of his God is in his heart" (37:31).

It is reasonable to think (contra Whybray, 1995:136-40) that the phrase *fear of Yahweh* in the Hezekiah Edition of Proverbs has the same meaning that it has in the other writings of the period. Here too (in Proverbs) it signifies respect for the God who revealed himself at Horeb, from whose *mouth come knowledge and understanding* (2:6). Here too (in Proverbs) the reference is to the *knowledge of God* that was the heritage of those in Israel who were faithful to the teachings of Moses—which is more or less what the corresponding version of the watchword in 9:10 makes clear. In 9:10, the first line of the saying is similar to the one in 1:7a: *The fear of the LORD is the beginning of wisdom* (9:10a); but then a second line declares, *and knowledge of the Holy One is understanding*. In this two-line statement *fear of the LORD* and *knowledge of the Holy One* are parallels, making a statement regarding the relationship of reverence for Yahweh (which equals *knowledge of the Holy One*) to the pursuit of wisdom: *knowledge* of this kind is *understanding* (9:10b). In other words, it also qualifies as knowledge of a kind that fosters wisdom for making right choices. This too is what Agur son of Jakeh declares in the only other place in the Bible where the phrase *knowledge of the Holy One* appears (cf. 30:2-6; for similar terms and message, see Hos 4:4, 6; 11:12).

THE TEXT IN BIBLICAL CONTEXT

Revelation and Reason

The *LORD* referred to in the watchword in 1:7 is the God who was revealed to Israel in a manner described in Deuteronomy 5. There we read of the Decalogue spoken in the hearing of all the people. The first commandment of the Decalogue specifies that Israel shall worship Yahweh only. The "fear of the Lord" as described in that chapter is an emotion of awe that is so great that his people will want to obey his commandments (5:28-29). In Proverbs this awe or *fear of the LORD* is viewed as the *beginning* of an educational process that includes acquiring knowledge and discernment in the thoughtful manner advocated in *the proverbs of Solomon* (1:1-4). This involves acquiring knowledge and discernment by reflecting on the words of the wise, whether those of Solomon or others. Awe for God and studying in this way are viewed as complementary and mutually enriching approaches to becoming wise. Reverence for God and his commandments is the *beginning* of wisdom, not a replacement for other kinds of study (*but fools despise wisdom and discipline*, 1:7b).

However, in the two places in the Bible outside of Proverbs where this watchword is cited (Ps 111:10; Job 28:28), we can sense other nuances emerging. In Psalm 111:10 the statement that "the fear of the LORD is the beginning of wisdom" appears at the end of a recitation of God's mighty works in redeeming Israel and establishing his "covenant forever" (111:9). In other words, in this instance the watchword stands alone in the context of God's special deeds in redeeming Israel and is no longer situated in the context of the wisdom poems of

Solomon. The conclusion drawn in Job 28 is that the "fear of the LORD" is the only place where wisdom can be found (28:28). This point is driven home in the prior verses of the poem in this chapter: no matter how hard one tries, wisdom can be found nowhere else.

At some point in Israel's postexilic experience, this regard for the "law of the LORD" emerged as the supreme and exclusive source of wisdom (cf. Ps 119:98-100). In this manner, a tension opened up between revelation and reason in biblical tradition that one does not sense exists within the teachings of Proverbs. This tension was resolved in various ways in "early Judaism" and in the Scriptures of the NT [Wisdom of Proverbs].

THE TEXT IN THE LIFE OF THE CHURCH

Reason and Revelation

Through the centuries Israel and the church have had to struggle with the revolutionary implications of new experiences and new discoveries. One such critical moment for Israel was the advent of the life and mission of Jesus Christ and the church begun in his name. Was his wisdom about life better than that of the scribes and Pharisees, as Matthew's Gospel asserts (Matt 5:20)? Was he in some sense the incarnation of the wisdom that Proverbs speaks of—a "word" that was with God from the beginning of time, as John's Gospel proclaims (John 1:1)?

A challenge of another kind was posed for the Christian church itself by the revolutionary discoveries of Copernicus and Galileo about our cosmic home. Since then, inquiring minds have uncovered one mystery after another in virtually every domain of God's universe. Perhaps the book of Proverbs has something yet to teach us about how these various "revelations" and discoveries can be embraced and unified.

In a study attempting to convey what Proverbs' contribution might be in this regard, Daniel J. Estes draws a helpful distinction between a "worldview" and a "full-blown philosophy of life." What we have in Proverbs, he implies, is not so much a "full-blown philosophy of life" as a "worldview." A worldview, he writes is made up of "the beliefs, attitudes and values that cause a person to see the world in a certain way." It asks, among other things, "What is prime reality—the really real?" "What is the nature of external reality, that is, the world around us?" (20). In his discussion of the "worldview" of Proverbs, Estes presents the thesis that its teachings are "fundamentally connected to the rest of the Hebrew Bible" and to those in particular that view God as the Creator whose control over the world is "continuing, active and personal" (26).

In other words, "the universe is not arbitrary," Estes writes, "for Yahweh has constructed it with recognizable design. Neither is the world amoral, for Yahweh's order is intimately related to his righteous character" (29). Furthermore, "the modern dichotomy between secular life and religious faith, or between the profane and the sacred, is foreign to the worldview" of this book. "In Proverbs, the juxtaposition of the routine details of daily life with reminders of Yahweh's evaluation of these activities (cf. Prov 3:27-35) reveals that all of life is regarded as a seamless fabric" (25).

Supplemental Poems (Hezekiah Edition)

The Book of Proverbs, Part 1: Introductory Collection				
Original Prologue (Solomon Edition) 1:1-7	Supplemental Poems (Hezekiah Edition) 1:8–3:35	Original Poems (Solomon Edition) 4:1–5:14	Supplemental Poems (Hezekiah Edition) 5:15–7:23	Original Poems (Solomon Edition) 7:24–9:18

PREVIEW

This is the first block of supplemental poems added when the Hezekiah Edition was created *[Distinctive Approach]*. When adding these poems, the editors displaced a block of Solomon Edition poems (4:1–5:14) from its position at the book's beginning to where it is now *[Solomon Edition]*. Both blocks of poems (those added in 1:8–3:35 and the Solomon Edition poems in 4:1–5:14) address similar issues: how urgent it is that young men do not fall in with lawless violent companions; the absolute necessity of being attentive to the voice of wisdom and heeding the counsel of one's father if one is going to have a happy and successful life; and the tremendous benefits that do in fact ensue from following wisdom's path. The poems added by the *men of Hezekiah* at this point also touch on themes that were not addressed in the Solomon Edition: trusting Yahweh to direct one's path and heeding his words. By comparing the teachings inserted by the Hezekiah editors with those in the older Solomon Edition, we can gain an understanding of the concerns that prompted the creation of the Hezekiah Edition of Proverbs.

OUTLINE

"Listen, My Son," 1:8-9
"My Son, If Sinners Entice You," 1:10-19
"Wisdom Calls Aloud in the Street," 1:20-33
"My Son, If You Accept My Words," 2:1-22
    2:1-11   "Store Up My Commands Within You"
    2:12-22   "Discretion Will Protect You"
"My Son, Do Not Forget My Teaching," 3:1-12
    3:1-4   "Keep My Commands in Your Heart"
    3:5-8   "Trust in the LORD with All Your Heart"
    3:9-12   "Honor the LORD with Your Wealth"
"Blessed Is the Man Who Finds Wisdom," 3:13-20
Concluding Poems, 3:21-35

EXPLANATORY NOTES

"Listen, My Son" 1:8-9

Proverbs 1:8-9 (Hezekiah Edition) replaces 4:1-4 (Solomon Edition) as the book's opening admonition. A *son* is here addressed, not *sons* as in 4:1. Instead of an exhortation to listen to *a father's instructions* (4:1)—which in the Solomon Edition is followed by poems (4:4–5:6) that Solomon says his father taught him when he was a youth living with his mother (4:3)—the *son* here (in 1:8-9) is told to listen to the teachings of his father *and* mother (*your father's instruction and . . . your mother's teaching*). The presumed speaker is the son's father. It is implied that his *instruction* [*mûsar*] and the *teaching* [*tôrah*] of the son's mother are those that follow in the book. In effect this opening poem authorizes parents to take on the role that *teachers* had in the royal schools (see 5:13). The Hezekiah Edition of Proverbs, like Deuteronomy, was designed to serve as a guide not just for civil servants in the royal schools, but also for homeschooling of children by their own parents (see Deut 6:5-9; 11:18-21). The poem ends with the promise of an award for the son who remains steadfast and does not forsake his parents' teachings: they (the teachings of the parents) will be like a *garland* (turban) to grace his head and a *chain* (necklace) to adorn his neck (cf. Gen 41:42). Similar imagery is used in the older Solomon Edition poem in 4:9.

"My Son, If Sinners Entice You" 1:10-19

This ten-verse poem (mostly couplets) is similar to the one in 4:14-19. Both warn against entering the *path* of evil men (1:15; 4:14); both paint a bleak picture of these men and what they do (1:11-14; 4:16-17); both highlight the self-destructive nature of their deeds (1:16-19; 4:19). But 1:10-19 is more intense. It twice repeats the address *my son* (1:10, 15) and begins with an urgent warning against being *enticed* (lit., *made a fool of*). Those being warned against are not merely *wicked* (as in 4:14), but *sinners* (*ḥaṭā'îm,* 1:10) "habitually addicted to crime" (Cohen: 4), "thugs" (cf. Ps 1:1). The poet vividly imagines what these *sinners* might say to entice the *son* (1:11-14). They boast of the prospect of lawless, cold-blooded murder (1:11), plundering (1:13), camaraderie (lit., *one purse,* 1:14). They speak audaciously of swallowing their victims *alive, like the grave* (1:12; Heb.: *šĕ'ôl*), in the imagination of the time a shadowy world beneath the earth to which departed spirits go, without any hope of return. Verse 1:16 is redundant and missing in the Greek version of the book *[Hebrew and Greek Texts].* The poem's closing admonition, *Do not set foot on their paths* (1:15), is buttressed with urgent warnings about how reckless and self-destructive these thugs actually are (1:17-19). Although rather unclear, "the most plausible interpretation of v. 17" (Whybray, 1994) is that they are being likened to greedy birds blind to a net laid out in plain sight for trapping them (1:17): *They waylay only themselves!* (1:18; cf. 4:19). *Such is the end* [lit., *ways*] *of all who go after ill-gotten gain* [lit., *all who are greedy for greed*]; *it takes away the lives* [*nepeš, life*] *of those who get it* (1:19a; cf. 10:2). That an urgent warning of this kind was placed at the forefront of the book's Hezekiah Edition implies a massive breakdown of the social order. From other sources we know that this was the case (Hos 4:2; Mic 2:1-2; Isa 1:23).

"Wisdom Calls Aloud in the Street" 1:20-33

This poem is modeled on the one in 8:1-36 (Solomon Edition). As there, *wisdom* (personified) is introduced (1:20-21; 8:1-3) and delivers a lengthy speech in two parts. First, she tells her audience (*you*) what she has done (1:22-27; cf. 8:4-31); then she states what the future holds for those (*they*) who do or do not follow her advice (1:28-33; cf. 8:34-36). However, here is where the similarity ends. The contents of the two poems are radically different. In 1:21 wisdom *calls aloud in the street* (1:21), not *on the heights* (as in 8:2)—and she addresses her words to *simple ones* and *mockers* and *fools [who] hate knowledge* (1:22), not to *all mankind* (as in 8:4). What she proclaims is also utterly different. Her message is not about *worthy things* (as in 8:6) but a lament over the deplorable manner in which those to whom she speaks have already rejected her and her message: *How long will you . . . hate knowledge?* (1:22). Wisdom summons them to change their ways: *Repent at my reproof* (1:23a, lit.). She speaks with tremendous passion: *Behold, I will pour out to you my spirit; I will make known my words to you* (22:23b, lit.). Her speech is more precisely a warning of an imminent calamity due to the fact that the *fools* she addresses have so persistently rejected her advice (1:24-25).

Wisdom's stated reaction to this calamity merits close attention. She initially (and surprisingly) proclaims, *I will mock when calamity overtakes you* (1:26-27). At this point in the poem (1:28), there is a shift from the second person (*you*) to the third person (*they*), a shift from addressing the *fools* to commenting about their fate. What wisdom says now is a somber meditation on what is going to happen to those to whom she speaks when disaster does overtake them: *They will call to me but I will not answer* (1:28). Why would wisdom not answer? Her reply is a key to the poem's total message: *Since they hated knowledge and did not choose to fear the LORD* (1:29). The opening watchword of the Hezekiah Edition states that *fear of the LORD is the beginning of knowledge* (1:7a). Here wisdom warns of the dire consequences that await those who have already rejected such *knowledge and did not choose to fear the LORD*.

In summary, what wisdom says in this poem is what certain Israelite prophets were saying at the time of Hezekiah's reforms: Because Israel had rejected *knowledge of God*, God had rejected Israel (Amos 3:1-2; Hos 4:1-7; 8:1-3). This too is the view expressed by the historians of the time who relate how the Assyrians destroyed the northern kingdom, Israel, and threatened to do the same in Judah (2 Kgs 17; 18:11-12). This happened, they state, because the northern kingdom "had not obeyed the LORD their God, but had violated his covenant—all that Moses the servant of the LORD commanded" (2 Kgs 18:12). In the final couplet of wisdom's speech in 1:20-33, she holds out a ray of hope: *But whoever listens to me will live in safety and be at ease, without fear of harm* (1:33). These words echo the hopeful words of Moses in Deuteronomy: "See, I set before you today life and prosperity, death and destruction. . . . Now choose life, so that you and your children may live" (Deut 30:15-19). Hezekiah inaugurated his reforms to help his people *choose life*. This too is the message of the poem in 1:20-33.

"My Son, If You Accept My Words" 2:1-22

This poem begins (as do those in 1:8-9 and 1:10-19) with a father speaking to his son (*my son*). Its theme encompasses the many benefits the son will experience if he accepts the father's *words* and *commands* (2:1). The first and chief benefit is that he *will understand the fear of the LORD and find the knowledge of God* (2:5). This is precisely what *wisdom* in the prior poem said was *hated* by those she addressed and why they were going to be destroyed: they had chosen *not* to fear Yahweh (1:29). This follow-up poem spells out how a son can come to a point where he will *understand the fear the LORD* and avoid this tragic fate. To *understand the fear of the LORD* entails knowing the commandments of *the LORD* and putting them into practice in daily life (see notes on 1:7).

2:1-11 "Store Up My Commands Within You"

The poem has twenty-two verses (the number of letters in the Hebrew alphabet). These verses are in two parts of eleven verses each. Part 1 (2:1-11) starts with three clauses beginning with *if* (2:1, 3, 4), followed by two clauses beginning with *then* (2:5, 9). The *if* clauses state in general what benefits will accrue to a son who heeds his father's commandments. Part 2 (2:12-22) identifies two more specific benefits of being wise in this sense (2:12-19) and concludes with a statement about the contrasting fates of upright and wicked (2:20-22). The poem assumes the son's parents are well versed in what it means to *fear the LORD* (2:5). The father speaks of this as *knowledge of God,* which comes forth from *his mouth* (2:6b). This is an allusion to the scene described in Deuteronomy 5, where Yahweh is portrayed as having spoken the Ten Commandments in a *loud voice* (5:22). The father mentions the *faithful ones* whom the LORD *protects* (Prov 2:8b), those who are faithful to the covenant with Yahweh made at that time. The father and his wife are just such people. They are the kind of parents alluded to in Deuteronomy who teach their children to love Yahweh and keep his commandments (Deut 6:6-9; 11:18-21). As stated there, if their teachings are heeded, the result will be a wise people (4:6-8). Something similar is said here: *Wisdom*

will enter your heart, and knowledge will be pleasant to your soul
(2:10). So the poem's main point is that to *understand the fear of
the Lord* and become wise, the son must heed his father's teachings
and store them *within* him, commit them to memory (2:1-5).

2:12-22 *"Discretion Will Protect You"*

The benefits that will accrue to the son who heeds his father's
teachings are momentous. He will not only come to a proper *knowledge of God* (2:5-6); he can also count on Yahweh protecting him,
*for [Yahweh] guards the course of the just and protects the way of
his faithful ones* (2:8). Furthermore, such a son will understand what
is *right and just and fair* (2:9; the stated goals of the manual, as in
1:3b). The more specific benefits (identified in stanza 2, in 2:12-22)
are that they (his father's teachings) will save him from perverse male
companions and friends (2:12-15) and, additionally, from a solicitous
woman of an especially dangerous type (2:16-19). Readers of the
book were previously warned of males of the type referred to here
(1:10-19), and they will be warned again (6:12-19; cf. 30:11-14).
This is the first time in Proverbs that we read of the dangers posed by
a seductive woman, and it will not be the last (see 5:1-14, 15-20;
6:20-35; 7:1-27).

The woman referred to in 2:16-19 is not, strictly speaking, an *adulteress* (as NIV implies), a married woman who relates sexually with
someone other than her husband. She does have a husband (and thus
is not a prostitute). Yet the Hebrew terms used to identify her (in 2:16)
are *zārāh*, "alien" or "outsider," and *nokrîyyāh*, "foreigner." What
these terms actually mean in this context is perhaps best explained by
references to a woman of this kind in Egyptian instructional literature
[Identity of the Foreign Seductress]. In one such manual, The
Instruction of Ani, she is described as "a woman from abroad who is
not known in her (own) town." This does not mean she is from a foreign country, but from another place. She is described as being "far
away from her husband." Her demeanor is bold and seductive: "'I am
sleek,' she says to thee every day." Egyptian instructional literature is
very sharp and urgent in its warnings to young men against knowing
"carnally" a woman of this kind, because, it is said, she is "a deep
water, whose windings one knows not" (Pritchard: 420).

In other words, this is a woman of a quite specific social and psychological type: married, away from home, and openly seductive.
She *has left the partner* [or companion] *of her youth and ignored
the covenant she made before God* [lit., *forgotten the covenant of
her God*]. The covenant referred to may not be one she made at her

marriage but Israel's covenant with God, which involved certain well-known commandments, one of which strictly prohibits adultery (Deut 5:18; cf. 5:18-20; Gen 2:24; Mal 2:14). In the background here are marriages formed among youth through a process that involves parental choice and consent (cf. Gen 29:21-28; Hugenberger: 250-79). The stability and durability of such marriages was severely endangered by women of the type described. In this particular poem the covenant terminology and ideals are those of the *men of Hezekiah* who crafted the teachings here as a supplement to the Solomon Edition poems in Proverbs 5:1-14 *[Distinctive Approach]*. The fate of those foolish enough to become involved with a woman like this is described in bleak images. Her whole *house* tilts or sinks toward the netherworld, and so do all those within who consort with her (2:18-19).

The poem concludes with a summary promising that the son who accepts his father's words in the manner specified in 2:1 *will walk in the ways of good men* [lit., *in the ways of the good*] (2:20). In contrast to the wicked, who *will be cut off from the land* (2:22), such an *upright* and *blameless* son will *remain* in the land (2:21). This accords with the promises in Deuteronomy 28. Through his reforms Hezekiah sought to enlist parents in teaching their children God's "words" spoken at Horeb (Deut 5:22), believing that, if they were heeded, Israel would *prosper and be kept alive* (6:24). This poem serves to introduce this vital message into the Hezekiah Edition of Proverbs.

"My Son, Do Not Forget My Teaching" 3:1-12

This is the fourth instruction that begins with a father addressing his son. Like the other three (1:8-9; 1:10-19; 2:1-22), it was composed with great care. The poem has twelve verses (or couplets) in six two-couplet (four-line) stanzas (3:1-2, 3-4, 5-6, 7-8, 9-10, 11-12). Each of the six stanzas begins with an imperative calling for a certain line of conduct, followed by a statement of the consequences of doing so. The six stanzas are further divided into three poems, each having two stanzas (3:1-4, 5-8, 9-12). Each of these three poems has a distinct theme. The first (3:1-4) is about not forgetting the father's teachings, the second (3:5-8) about putting one's wholehearted trust in Yahweh, the third (3:9-12) about honoring Yahweh with *your wealth* (3:9-10) and submitting to his fatherlike *discipline* of those he *delights in* and *loves* (3:11-12). The poems are framed by the father's personal address to his son (*my son*) at their beginning and end (3:1, 11).

3:1-4 " Keep My Commands in Your Heart"

The first of the two-stanza poems (in 3:1-4) is a fitting sequel to the one preceding it in 2:1-22. The preceding poem's appeal to the son was that he *accept* his father's teachings (2:1); here the appeal is that he *not forget* them and make sure he will *keep* his father's command in his heart (3:1, 3). The teachings to be kept in this way are described in 3:3 as *love* (*ḥesed,* affectionate fidelity) and *faithfulness* (*'ĕmet,* truth, sincerity; in 16:6 these are the qualities of those who *fear Yahweh*). Hosea laments their absence in the society of his time (4:1). The son is instructed to *bind* these *around your neck* (as a necklace) and *write them on the tablet of your heart* (3:1, 3; cf. Jer 31:33-34). This resembles what Moses said should be done with his teachings (Deut 6:6-9; 11:18-21). The poem promises that the son in this way will *win favor* [or blessing] *and a good name in the sight of God and man* (3:4; cf. Deut 28:1-14; 30:11-20).

3:5-8 "Trust in the LORD with All Your Heart"

The second two-stanza poem (3:5-8) addresses a danger posed by the son's acquiring wisdom (the book's primary goal; 1:2): he may become wise in his own eyes and not trust Yahweh with all his heart (3:7-8). That is what happened to Solomon: "Solomon did evil in the eyes of the LORD; he did not follow the LORD completely, as David his father had done" (1 Kgs 11:6). What is meant is that Solomon abandoned the teachings of Moses, failed to put his trust wholeheartedly in Yahweh, and instead worshipped other gods. Perhaps divine wisdom itself was one of those goddesses (cf. Prov 8). At the time of Hezekiah's reforms, the wisdom teachers were prone to the same mistake ("Woe to those who are wise in their own eyes and clever in their own sight," Isa 5:21). This second poem (3:5-8) is an appeal to the son *not* to be led astray by a similar inflated pride and fail to trust Yahweh with his whole heart. This poem calls for wholehearted trust and respect for Yahweh and thus echoes the teaching of Moses (Deut 4:29; 6:5) and also that of Agur son of Jakeh (see especially his prayer in 30:7-9).

3:9-12 "Honor the LORD with Your Wealth"

In the third two-stanza poem, the religious views of those who created the Hezekiah Edition of Proverbs are especially evident (3:9-12). The *son* is told to *honor* (show respect for) Yahweh by bringing to him *from your wealth and from the beginning [firstfruits] of all your increase* (3:9, lit.). These instructions echo a text in Deuteronomy that specifies what is due in support of the Levites: "You are to give them [the Levites] the first fruits [lit., beginning] of your grain, new wine and oil, and the first [beginning] wool from the shearing of your sheep" (18:4). A plenitude of blessings is promised for those who comply with God's directive: *Then your barns will be filled to overflowing* (Prov 3:10; cf. Deut 28:8, "The LORD will send a blessing on your barns and on everything you put your hand to"; see also Mal 3:10-12).

In another section of Deuteronomy, a ritual of bringing a basket filled with "the firstfruits of all that you produce from the soil of the land the LORD your God is giving you" is beautifully related (26:1-11). The basket is brought to the priest at the place God has chosen for his Name to dwell (26:2). At the end of the ritual the one bringing the basket bows down and worships (26:10). In the following verses another donation is specified: "A tenth of all your produce in the third year, the year of the tithe, you shall give to the Levite, the alien, the fatherless and the widow" (26:12). Significantly, the Proverb's text does not specify that "firstfruits" should be given to Levites, or what should be done with them. The advice in this instance, although reflective of Israelite experience, is for peoples of every culture. To express gratitude in this way to God the Creator is a universally wise and honorable thing to do.

Additionally, the *son* is told not to *despise* or *resent* Yahweh's *discipline* or *rebuke* (3:11), for that is how Yahweh educates *those he loves, even as a father the son he delights in* (3:12). Moses' teachings about God's loving guidance are along these same lines: "Know then in your heart that as a man disciplines his son, so the Lord your God disciplines you" (Deut 8:5). Hosea spoke similarly of God's compassionate training of Israel throughout its history from "when Israel was a child" in Egypt (Hos 11:1-4).

These three poems (3:1-12) say nothing about these teachings being "wisdom," and yet their inclusion indicates this is how they were regarded. It is wise to trust in Yahweh with all one's heart—and the proof is that *length of days and years of life and well-being [shalom], they will add to you* (3:2, lit.). Specific promises in these poems are attached and matched to specific admonitions: A good reputation (3:4) is promised to those who hold on to *love and faithfulness* (3:4). *Straight* paths (3:6; paths freed of obstacles) are promised those who trust Yahweh (3:5). A healthy body (3:8) is promised to those who fear Yahweh and shun evil (3:7). *Barns filled to overflowing* (3:10) are promised those who *honor the LORD with your wealth* (3:9).

"Blessed Is the Man Who Finds Wisdom" 3:13-20

I view this poem (like the one in 1:22-33) as a carefully crafted counterpart to the majestic Solomon Edition poem on this same subject in
chapter 8. It has two parts (3:13-18 and 19-20). Part one (3:13-18)
begins and ends with the word *blessed* (*'ašrê,* 3:13a, 18b, meaning
happy). Like the poem in chapter 8, it proclaims the happiness of a
human being (*'ādām*) who finds *wisdom* (3:13; cf. 8:32). The reasoning is that wisdom is worth more than silver or gold or anything
else (3:14-15; cf. 8:11, 19). However, this particular poem differs
from the one in chapter 8 in what it relates about *wisdom's ways* (in
3:17). What is said here is that wisdom's *ways* are *pleasant* and *peace*
(*shālôm;* cf. 3:2) rather than *riches and honor, enduring wealth and
prosperity* (8:18). Unique here too is the depiction of wisdom as *a
tree of life* (3:18). In Proverbs 8 wisdom is personified as a supernatural being present with Yahweh from time immemorial (8:22). By contrast, the *tree of life* image is commonplace in the ancient Near East,
occurring elsewhere in Proverbs as "one of many expressions . . .
denoting a happy outcome in life" (Whybray, 1994:67; cf. 11:30;
13:12; 15:4). Here it signifies wisdom's benefits for those who *hold
to* (rather than *embrace*) its life-giving branches (3:18). In other
words, wisdom's attributes are praised but less effusively so than in
chapter 8.

Part 2 of this poem (3:19-20) addresses a serious ambiguity in the
Solomon Edition poem in chapter 8. From wisdom's statement about
herself in 8:22-31, one might conclude that she is a divinity of some
sort (as in Egypt). The creedlike lines in 3:19-20 demystify *wisdom,*
making her an attribute of Yahweh. What this part of the poem stip-
ulates is that *wisdom* is simply the *understanding* by which Yahweh
laid the earth's foundations and *set the heavens in place* (3:19). In
other words, *wisdom* is a characteristic of Yahweh himself as Creator:
*By his knowledge the deeps were divided, and the clouds let drop
the dew* (3:20).

Concluding Poems 3:21-35

These four short poems (3:21-24, 25-26, 27-32, 33-35) bring to a
close this opening Hezekiah Edition supplement (1:8–3:35). In the
first of them (3:21-24), a father again addresses his son (*my son,*
3:21) and advises him to *preserve sound judgment and discernment*
and *not let them out of your sight;* guard them as one would a valuable treasure (Cohen: 18). Numerous benefits are promised if the son
is successful in so doing: Wisdom will be *life for you* (lit., *your soul*)

and *grace for your neck* (3:22). There will be fewer accidents (3:23). When the son goes to bed at night, he will not be afraid, and his sleep will be *sweet* (pleasant, 3:24).

Poem 2 is also about not being afraid (3:25-26), but in this case a more traumatic fear is addressed: *Have no fear of sudden disaster* (3:25a). This *sudden disaster* is characterized as *the destruction of the wicked when it comes* (3:25b, lit.). The *destruction* referred to could be that wrought by invading armies like those engulfing Israel during Hezekiah's reign (2 Kgs 18:9-16). Even in the midst of vast devastation, there is no need to fear, *for the LORD will be your confidence and will keep your foot from being snared* (3:26). This is the kind of fearlessness Hezekiah himself displayed at this juncture of Judean history (see 2 Kgs 18:5-8).

The third of these closing teachings (3:27-32) is unique. It is made up of a series of five commandments, each beginning with the imperative *Do not,* as in the Decalogue (3:27-31). The poem concludes with a statement about Yahweh's radically different relationship to the *perverse* versus the *upright* (3:32). The five imperatives are arranged in three stanzas (3:27-28, 29-30, 31-32). All pertain to conduct between *neighbors* (3:28-29), like those in part 2 of the Decalogue (Deut 5:17-21). In stanza 1 (3:27-28) the Decalogue's command not to steal (Deut 5:19) is interpreted in a surprising way. Instead of simply prohibiting stealing, it states: *Do not withhold good from its owner* (3:27a, lit.). The command is not merely "Do not steal," but means, Do not keep for yourself the *good* due its rightful *owner,* when *it is in your power to act* (3:27). The implication is that a person keeping something a neighbor desperately needs (for daily existence) is a form of stealing. This *Do not* is followed in the same stanza by a prohibition against procrastination in responding to a neighbor's need: *Do not say to your neighbor, "Come back later; I'll give it tomorrow"—when you now have it with you* (3:28). This piece of advice closely resembles the instructions in Deuteronomy about being responsible for a "brother" who is desperately poor: "If there is a poor man among your brothers in any of the towns of the land that the LORD your God is giving you, do not be hardhearted or tightfisted toward your poor brother. Rather be openhanded and freely lend him whatever he needs" (Deut 15:7-8).

While stanza 1 of this third poem is about doing *good* (3:27), stanza 2 prohibits doing *harm* to a neighbor (3:29-30), especially when he has *done you no harm* (3:30b). More specifically, the advice is not to engage in frivolous disputes: *Do not accuse a man for no reason* (3:30a; cf. 10:12; 13:10; 15:18; 17:14). In stanza 3 the following command not to *envy a violent man* (3:31-32) resembles the admonition in 1:10-19. The behavior of thugs like this is the absolute opposite of the attributes the book seeks to inculcate. *The LORD detests* such men (3:32a); they are (lit.) *an abomination of Yahweh*, an expression found elsewhere in the Bible only in Proverbs (11:1, 20; 12:22) and Deuteronomy (7:25; 12:31; 17:1; 22:5; 25:16; 27:15). By contrast, Yahweh takes those who are *upright* (*yĕšārîm*, straight, honest, those with integrity) *into his confidence;* they become *his intimates* (3:32b, lit.; cf. Ps 25:14, "The LORD confides in those who fear him; he makes his covenant known to them").

This entire opening section is concluded with a fourth poem about *the LORD's curse* and *blessing* (3:33-35). This is reminiscent of the concluding words of Moses in Deuteronomy 28, where, however, the blessings and curses pertain to Israel and are conditional on obedience to words of Yahweh revealed in the teachings of Moses. Here *the house of the wicked* or *the home of the righteous* (3:33) are either cursed or blessed as a consequence of being *mockers* and *fools* (3:34a), or *humble* and *wise* (3:34b-35a). The actual "blessings" and "curses" are also differently described. In Deuteronomy the blessings and curses are quite concrete and material (prosperity, wealth, and power, versus poverty, sickness, and servitude). What is stressed here is that Yahweh *mocks* the *proud mockers* (3:34a; cf. 1:26; 9:8), but *gives grace to the humble* (3:34b). What this means is stated in the final couplet: *The wise inherit honor [respect of others], but fools carry away shame [disgrace]* (3:35, lit.). The "blessings" and "curses" here are the evident social and emotional consequences of being wise or foolish.

THE TEXT IN BIBLICAL CONTEXT

Parents as Teachers of Wisdom

In the opening poem of this set of poems, a father invites his son to listen to his instruction and that of his mother (1:8-9). Deuteronomy 6:6-9 and 11:18-21 expresses a similar ideal so far as the teachings of Moses are concerned. In both cases parents are to give these teachings in the home. Such ideals seemingly also guided Ezra and Nehemiah centuries later, when they arranged for Judean citizens to hear Scriptures being read in a large assembly (Neh 8). Assembled on this occasion were not only "men and woman" but also children old enough to understand (8:3; 10:28).

Home-centered teaching of the Scriptures became a firm tradition in postexilic Judaism. The book of Susanna (which appears in the

Apocrypha as an addition to the book of Daniel) says that Susanna "was God-fearing, for her parents were worthy people and had instructed their daughter in the Law of Moses" (Dan 13:1-3, NJB). Home-centered teaching of the Scriptures is also implied in Paul's reminder to Timothy of how from infancy he had "known the holy Scriptures, which are able to make you wise for salvation through faith in Christ Jesus" (2 Tim 3:15).

Youth and Violence

The initial teaching of the Hezekiah Edition of Proverbs takes seriously the possibility that a young man might be strongly tempted to join a gang of peers engaged in violent crimes (1:10-18). Violence was rife at the time of the Hezekiah editors (according to contemporary prophets; cf. Hos 6:8; Amos 2:6-8; Isa 1:21). They were aware of the attractions criminality had for young men. This realistic view of human nature is reflected in the stories in Genesis. There it is said that sin and violence gradually permeated the primeval world (Gen 3-6) and persisted after the flood. Hence, God had to issue instructions to the nations that those who spill the blood of others should be restrained (9:5-6). Against this background Genesis sets forth Israel's calling to be a people who would bring blessing to the nations through "doing what is right and just" (12:1-3; 18:18-19). When the Jewish Scriptures were compiled, the book of Proverbs was recognized as a principal resource for implementing this calling [Wisdom in Proverbs].

"Wisdom" Interprets the Times

In yet another poem in this opening section of Proverbs (1:20-33), personified wisdom interprets certain catastrophic events in a way that resembles the "words of God" spoken by the prophets who appeared in Israel in the time of Hezekiah's reforms (Amos, Hosea, Isaiah, and Micah). In this way their messages are recast within the book of Proverbs as manifestations of wisdom, just as was done with God's "words" through Moses in Deuteronomy, where "decrees and laws" are acclaimed as manifestations of "wisdom and understanding" (cf. 4:5-6). In this poem wisdom interprets Israel's imminent destruction as a consequence of one simple fact: They [the people of Israel] hated knowledge and did not choose to fear the LORD (Prov 1:29). This is similar to what Hosea had said to the priests of Israel in his time: "'Because you have rejected knowledge, I also reject you as my priests; because you have ignored the law of your God, I also will ignore your children'" (4:6). Amos said something similar (7:7-9). The message of the prophets and the speech of *wisdom* in Proverbs agreed: there was little hope that the *nation* might be spared. The best to be hoped for is that *individuals* might see the folly of their ways and repent. "Seek good, not evil, that you may live," Amos prophesied. "Then the LORD God Almighty will be with you, just as you say he is. . . . Perhaps the LORD God Almighty will have mercy on the remnant of Joseph" (5:14-15). In Proverbs *wisdom* promises something similar: a remnant will be saved (cf. 1:33; 3:25-26, 33-35). Nations rise and fall (often because of foolish decisions); only a remnant survives to begin again (cf. Neh 1; Rom 11:1-6).

Wisdom "Will Save You from the Adulteress"

The long poem in Proverbs 2 reaches its climax in the promise that the wisdom the son will receive if he accepts the words of his father will save him from the seductive charms of a woman who has no compunction about leaving *the partner of her youth* (2:17). This is the first of several poems in the Hezekiah Edition of Proverbs in which warnings are given to sons against forming intimate relations with married women *[Identity of the Foreign Seductress]*. The editors of Proverbs obviously regarded it as one of the most self-destructive things a young man could do; it could ruin his life. Elsewhere in the Bible, for a man to have intimate relations with a married woman is referred to as "adultery" (Deut 5:18) and is regarded as a crime punishable by death (Lev 20:10; Deut 22:22). Jesus called in question the harshness of that punishment (John 8:3-5, 7) but also viewed adulterous behavior *and* thoughts as dangerous to body and soul (Matt 5:27-30).

Some of the Bible's notable stories shed light on *why* adultery is so destructive. One example is in 2 Samuel 11-20, the vividly told account of the moral turpitude and chaos that ensued in the household of King David in the wake of his cruel and utterly selfish affair with another man's wife. A notable example of a young man resisting such a temptation and experiencing blessings from God for doing so is the story of Joseph in Genesis 39. In his case what saves him from a woman of the type warned against in the poems in Proverbs is precisely the kind of clear-headed thinking about consequences referred to in Proverbs 2:19. Joseph realizes that yielding to an affair with his master's wife would be a severe breach of trust. "How then could I do such a wicked thing and sin against God," he tells her (Gen 39:9).

Relying on God's Wisdom

Proverbs 3:1-12 is one of the most theologically rich poems in Proverbs. At the center of this carefully crafted poem is the astonishing counsel that readers should not rely on their own wisdom but trust God to make straight (or to direct) their paths. The reason this counsel is so astonishing is that it appears in a book whose primary purpose is to promote the acquisition of wisdom! But this too is wisdom, to realize how limited is our own human wisdom. This is what the Hezekiah editors found lacking in the Solomon Edition. In their eyes neither Solomon nor his teachings were sufficiently cognizant of the need human beings have for trusting their Creator to direct their paths. Evidence abounds that fostering a personal relationship with God through prayer was one of the major goals of the Hezekiah reformers [Hezekiah Reform Literature]. For this reason an enlarged edition of the Psalter was also produced at the same time, consisting for the most part of the "prayers of David son of Jesse" (72:20). Captions were added, indicating the circumstances when David offered these prayers (Pss 3, 7, 18, 34, 51, 52, 56, 57, 59, 60, 63), as if to say to the book's readers: "You too can turn to God in similar circumstances. You too can trust God to direct your paths" (Prov 3:5-8).

The God of Wisdom

A key theological point made in the poems of this opening section is that by wisdom the LORD laid the earth's foundations (3:19). As noted, it was a statement of creedlike importance in light of the ambiguities in the Solomon Edition poem in Proverbs 8, where wisdom is personified as an entity separate from Yahweh at the time the world was created. In the sharply stated dictum in 3:19-20, the ambiguity is removed: wisdom is not an entity in itself, but an attribute of God. By his knowledge the deeps were divided, and the clouds let drop the dew (3:20).

A contemporary of the Hezekiah reformers, the prophet Isaiah son of Amoz (Isa 1:1), may have been influential in understanding God in this way. Isaiah might have been a professional sage or teacher like those whom he criticizes (Isa 5:21; Miller, 1987:97-98). This would help explain why, following his divine call when he "saw" Yahweh's radiance filling the universe (6:3) and was informed of Yahweh's "plan" for the world (6:9-13), he began thinking of God's governance of the world in ways that resembled that of the wisdom teachers of his time. Yahweh "too is wise" in his governance of nations, Isaiah declares in one of his poems (31:2), but not only in ruling the nations.

Yahweh is also the guide of ordinary human beings, as in the case of a farmer plowing and planting and harvesting his fields. God "instructs him and teaches him [the farmer] the right way" (28:26). "All this also comes from the Lord Almighty, wonderful in counsel and magnificent in wisdom" (28:29). In these and other images of God in his wisdom guiding all who trust in him (cf. 11:1-7), we sense a worldview like that in the Hezekiah Edition of Proverbs (3:5-6).

The thought-provoking poem in Jeremiah 10:1-16 may reflect the influence of this newly minted theological synthesis. Its author (perhaps Jeremiah himself) writes of the folly of the nations when creating material images of their gods in comparison with Israel's "living God" (10:3-11), who "made the earth by his power" and "founded the world by his wisdom" (10:12). The poem goes on to declare that this wise God not only is "the Maker of all things," but also "the Portion of Jacob, . . . the tribe of his inheritance" (10:16). Psalm 104 is yet another poem that seems to reflect the influence of Proverbs 3:19-20. In the midst of a detailed description of the multitudinous ways God cares for the created world, the poet exclaims: "How many are your works, O LORD! In wisdom you made them all" (Ps 104:24).

Thinking About the Decalogue

The little poem in Proverbs 3:27-32 conveys some novel thoughts about several laws of the Decalogue. For the composer of this poem, the Decalogue was not just a set of commandments carved in stone, to be recited and obeyed. These laws were insights to be pondered and interpreted. Jesus did something similar with these commandments. He did not hesitate referring to them as a sure guide to "eternal life" (Luke 18:18, 20). Yet he also felt free to interpret them, as in defense of his Sabbath healings. He declared, "The Sabbath was made for man, not man for the Sabbath" (Mark 2:27).

THE TEXT IN THE LIFE OF THE CHURCH

The "Voice" of a Certain Kind of Father

In this section of the book, we hear the "voice" of a certain kind of father. This father belongs to a people in covenant with a God who is fatherlike himself (3:12). He is one of the *faithful ones* (2:8), who is seeking to uphold the laws of this loving God. He has seen what happens to those who follow other gods and do not live by these teachings. He is convinced that these teachings are a source of life-giving wisdom. His wife shares these convictions. And now the father of this home (with the mother's assistance and backing) is trying to teach this way of wisdom to his sons—not to the exclusion of his daughters—but because he realizes they have special need for it (see Introduction, "Why the Gender-Specific Focus").

Listening to this father's "voice" raises many thoughts and questions about the kind of father I have been—and also the kinds of fathers in our churches and societies. Modern culture exhibits a growing anxiety in this regard. In many homes fathers are not present at all. In others they are only marginally present. In his book on *Bringing Up Boys*, James Dobson writes: "While children of all ages—both male and female—have an innate need for contact with their fathers, . . . boys suffer most from the absence or noninvolvement of fathers. According to the National Center for Children in Poverty, boys without fathers are twice as likely to drop out of school, twice as likely to go to jail, and nearly four times as likely to need treatment for emotional and behavioral problems as boys with fathers" (55).

The texts just looked at in this opening section of Proverbs represent the father as not being just present but as taking the time to teach his sons. In some circles there is an assumption that the training of children falls to mothers; but the book of Proverbs assumes that fathers will take a leading role. This assumption deserves renewed consideration. What forms, apart from modeling, might a father's teaching take in today's world? The following are suggestions shared with me by a reader:

> One father of a teenage son schedules a rendezvous with his son over breakfast at a restaurant once a week. The two discuss a book both are reading, or work on an agenda or project. In one home the father, after a Bible reading, recalls instances from his life illustrating or even loosely related to the reading. In instances where fathers work alongside the sons, the occasion for pertinent comments on life and life's values are frequent. Some older fathers write their memoirs for the benefit of their children and grandchildren. A father might pen an annual extended letter to his children (whether young or grown) on their birthday.

"All Her Paths Are Peace"

Wisdom's ways are provocatively described in 3:17b as *ways of pleasantness, and all her paths are peace* (NRSV). In an insightful essay Elmer Martens relates the "story of Isaac in conflict with Abimelech over wells (Gen 26:1-33) and the story of David about to come to blows over Nabal's refusal to supply food (1 Sam 25:2-42)" to this description. In a concluding synopsis he writes: "One may readily assent to the rightness of this proverb, but it is through narrative that such Wisdom sayings take on persuasive energy. The Isaac story illustrates the wise counsel, 'You can afford not to insist on your rights.' The [Nabal-]Abigail story highlights the message, 'The wise are peacemakers; vengeance is God's business'" (Martens, 2000:75, 86).

Martens adds, "Both stories also illustrate the Wisdom claims made in the New Testament" in texts such as Jesus's saying about the meek being blessed "for they will inherit the earth" (Matt 5:5), and in words like those of James: "The wisdom from above is first pure, then peaceable. . . . And a harvest of righteousness is sown in peace for those who make peace" (3:17-18, NRSV). Martens' concludes his essay as follows:

> Modern societies are marked by violence that repeatedly shatters the hope for shalom, well-being. Clearly, among the many proposed solutions to this state of affairs is the appeal to hear and appropriate the biblical message of nondefensive, even self-effacing action (Isaac) and intentional peacemaking (Abigail). Both stories can be heard in our times in the context of Wisdom literature, and for Christians, in the context of Christ, Wisdom personified, who is the peace-bringer and peacemaker par excellence. (Martens, 2000:86)

Honoring the Lord with Your Wealth

Since its inception a concern of the Christian church has been for the needs of its members and how to sustain its life as a distinct community. A radical change occurred when the church became a privileged institution within the Roman Empire. The alliances between church and state forged at that time remained intact in one form or another throughout the Middle Ages and on into the modern period. But now increasingly church and state are separated, and churches exist on their own, needing donated monies for their institutional endeavors (houses of worship, pastors, schools, special needs of its members, and charities and missions of one kind or another).

This section of Proverbs has a saying that relates to this need. It promises a special blessing on those who honor God with their wealth by bringing the firstfruits of soil and flocks to a place of worship (3:9-10). How those who formulated the teachings of this book thought young men should honor God with their wealth in their daily lives is spelled out in sayings devoted to this subject in the Main Collection (see 10:1–22:16, under the topic "Economics"). In the saying here (3:9-10), the ancient practice is alluded to of bringing firstfruits to a shrine as a sign of gratitude to God, the rightful owner of the land. In related Scriptures we learn how these donated gifts were used: for the support of priests and for the needs of the poor (Deut 18:4; 26:2, 12). The churches of the world have rightly understood this teaching as affirming its members' practice of donating a portion of their wealth during Sunday worship. For those who honor God with their wealth, the Sunday "collection" remains a deep symbol of gratitude to the One in whom "we live and move and have our being" (Acts 17:28).

Original Poems
(Solomon Edition)

The Book of Proverbs, Part 1: Introductory Collection				
Original Prologue (Solomon Edition) 1:1-7	Supplemental Poems (Hezekiah Edition) 1:8–3:35	Original Poems (Solomon Edition) 4:1–5:14	Supplemental Poems (Hezekiah Edition) 5:15–7:23	Original Poems (Solomon Edition) 7:24–9:18

PREVIEW

The dominant theme of this set of poems is the supreme importance and personal benefits of acquiring *wisdom* as opposed to recklessly destroying one's life by associating with evil men and seductive women. The section begins in 4:1-4a with personal words of Solomon himself. The poem at the end of this set (5:7-14) is his as well. In between are poems that Solomon says his father (David, king of Israel) taught him when he was still a young man (4:3-4). There is evidence for thinking this group of poems (together with 7:24–9:6, 11-18) was the introduction to the Solomon Edition *[Solomon*

Edition]. That the poems were retained when the Hezekiah Edition was created is testimony to how highly they were regarded. Written two centuries earlier, these were by now the "classics" of Israel's wisdom tradition.

OUTLINE

"He Taught Me and Said," 4:1-4a
"Get Wisdom, Get Understanding," 4:4b-9
"The Years of Your Life Will Be Many," 4:10-19
"The Heart Is the Wellspring of Life," 4:20-27
"In the End She Is Bitter as Gall," 5:1-6
"Do Not Go Near the Door of Her House," 5:7-14

EXPLANATORY NOTES

"He Taught Me and Said" 4:1-4a

Prior to the insertion of 1:7–3:35, the poem of 4:1-4a was the first in the book *[Solomon Edition]*. As such it followed right after the book's original prologue (1:1-4, 6). The "voice" is that of Solomon himself. The *sons* addressed in 4:1 are not *my sons* (as NIV translates); there is no "my" in the Hebrew text because these young men are not his personal sons but students in the royal academies (cf. 5:13, the sons' *teachers* and *instructors*). Solomon invites them to listen to *a father's instruction*. The *father* referred to is also not Solomon himself but *his* father; this becomes clear when 4:1-4a is properly translated. In Hebrew these verses are linked by the conjunction *for* (*kî*) in the following manner: *Listen, sons, to a father's instruction* [4:1a], . . . for *I give you sound learning* [4:2a]; . . . for *when I was a son to* my *father* [4:3a], . . . *he taught me and said* (4:4a). In other words Solomon is clarifying why he wants these *sons* (students) to pay attention to *a father's instruction*: because it is *sound* [lit., *good*] *learning* (4:2a) which *his* father taught him when he was a young man as they are.

Solomon also mentions his mother and a bit of personal history, that at the time his father taught him these poems, he was his mother's only child and still living under her care (lit., *tender and the only one before the face of my mother*, 4:3). The book's first readers would know of whom he was writing. His mother (Bathsheba) was almost as famous as he was. After King David's adultery with her (and the contrived execution of her husband), she became one of David's wives and an imposing figure in his court. It was she who persuaded David that Solomon should be his successor (1 Kgs 1:17). Solomon was in fact her only surviving child (4:3; cf. 2 Sam 12:18, 24). With the words in 4:4a, *He taught me and said,* Solomon sets the stage for the four following poems (4:4b-9; 4:10-19; 4:20-27; 5:1-6).

"Get Wisdom, Get Understanding" 4:4b-9

The poems that Solomon's father taught him as a young boy are presented as verbatim reports (4:4a). Solomon is passing these on to the "sons" mentioned in 4:1, but the "voice" in the poem is that of David addressing his son Solomon. Hence, the person addressed as *My son* (4:10, 20; 5:1) is Solomon. In formulating the teachings in this manner, Solomon is following literary conventions of the time for manuals of this type. "The transmission of wisdom from father to son is the setting of almost all Wisdom Literature" (Fox: 172). In the concluding poem of this set (5:7-14), Solomon again speaks in his own voice to the "sons" addressed in 4:1.

This initial poem has six couplets in two parts (4:4b-6, 7-9). In part 1 of this first poem (4:4b-6), David instructs Solomon to heed his words and *get wisdom* and *understanding,* promising that if he does, *you will live* (4:4b) and *wisdom will protect you* (4:6). Wisdom is personified as one who can *protect* and be loved and esteemed (4:6b, 8a; cf. 8:21). This is much like the role of *Yahweh* in the previous poem (2:7-8). Part 2 of this poem (4:7-9) is even more effusive about "wisdom's" importance. It begins: *Wisdom is supreme* [rē'šît, the beginning]; *therefore get* [qĕnēh] *wisdom* (4:7a; cf. 1:7; 9:10). Following this is a second line (4:7b), in which the word *get* [qĕnēh] in the previous line is repeated: *With all your getting, get discernment* (lit.; *discernment* is the chief attribute of those who are wise). In chapter 8 (a follow-up poem in the Solomon Edition) *wisdom* declares that she is what Yahweh himself got *at the beginning: Yahweh got me* [lit., for qānānî; *possessed me,* NIV] *at the beginning* [rē'šît] *of his work* (8:22a).

This opening statement expresses a core conviction of the Solomon Edition poems: wisdom is what one must get first, and those who do so (and *esteem* her) will be rewarded *with a garland of grace on your head* and *a crown of splendor* (4:9; cf. 1:9). This imagery anticipates the festive scene in 9:1-7, where *wisdom* presides like a queen at a banquet to which all who honor her are invited. The statement *The fear of the LORD is the beginning* [rē'šît] *of knowledge* (1:7a) is the watchword of the Hezekiah Edition of Proverbs; but the statement that *wisdom is supreme* [rē'šît] (4:7a) is the watchword of the Solomon Edition. This older watchword is no longer at the book's beginning but is still retained. The watchword in the Hezekiah Edition provides a new context for the pursuit of wisdom, but it does not subvert or replace the truth that wisdom is supreme.

"The Years of Your Life Will Be Many" 4:10-19

The admonition *Listen, my son* signals the beginning of a new poem (4:10). Again, the *son* being addressed is Solomon. The poem is a verbatim report to the *sons* referred to in 4:1, a report of what his father taught him (4:4a). So the "voice" in the poem is again that of King David. In this instance the poem has ten couplets arranged in three stanzas. Two of the stanzas have four couplets each (4:10-13, 14-17), followed by a two-couplet conclusion (4:18-19). Stanza 1 (1:10-13) opens with a promise that if Solomon accepts his father's teaching, the *years of your life will be many* (4:10). This happy prospect is based on the premise that his father's teaching will guide him (Solomon) *in the way of wisdom* and lead him on *straight paths* (4:11; paths that are easy to walk on). *When you walk, your steps will not be hampered,* and *when you run, you will not stumble* (4:12). For this reason the son is told to *grab hold of instruction* [*mûsār*], *do not let her go, keep her, for she* [*hî'*, referring to wisdom] *is your life* (4:13, lit.; by being wise, Solomon will live a long and trouble-free life, free from stumbling).

Stanza 2 is more specific (4:14-17). It begins with a sharply worded command: *Do not set foot on* [lit., *enter*] *the path of the wicked* (4:14; cf. 1:19). This is followed by four imperatives: *Avoid it, pass not by it, turn from it, pass on* (4:15, lit.). Next is a portrait of the wicked being warned against, one that is linked to the preceding command (not to enter their path) by the conjunction *for* (*kî*) at the beginnings of 4:16 and 17. The portrait explains *why* the son should not set foot on this path. The persons described are compulsive criminals: *They cannot sleep till they do evil* (4:16). They live off the loot of their crimes: *Eat the bread of wickedness and drink the wine of violence* (4:17).

The poem's final stanza paints a starkly contrasting picture of the outcomes in life of the two ways referred to in the prior stanzas (4:18-19). The *path of the upright* (4:18; previously termed *the way of wisdom,* 4:11) is likened (lit.) to the first *glimmer of lightness* (at dawn), which soon grows to *the standing firm of the day* (when daylight is steady and strong). By contrast, the *way of the wicked [is] as darkness—they do not know on what they stumble* (4:19, lit.). The darkness in which they travel is so great that the wicked cannot see to walk without stumbling. This poem possibly served as the model for the one in 1:10-19.

"The Heart Is the Wellspring of Life" 4:20-27

The third poem of this set is again opened with David addressing Solomon as *My son* (4:20). The first poem (4:1-9) stressed the importance of getting wisdom, and the second (4:10-19) told how wisdom will help one live a long and trouble-free life. Now the focus turns to the robust health people may expect if they follow wisdom's path (4:20-27): *for they* [referring to *my words*, 4:20b] *are life to those who find them and health to a man's whole body* (4:22). Like the previous poems, this one was composed with great care. It has eight couplets in two equal parts (4:20-23, 24-27). Part 1 (4:20-23) opens with a summons to the son: *Attend to my words, turn your ear to my sayings* (4:20, lit.). The poem then emphasizes that these words should (lit.) *not depart from your eyes*, but be kept *within your heart* (4:21). Since the claim being made is that they *are life to those who find them and health to a man's whole body* (4:22), the verse that follows affords a key to the whole poem. It explains why keeping the father's words *within your heart* is so important: *Of all that you guard, protect your heart, for out of it [come] the sources of life* (4:23, lit.). In the culture of the time, the heart (or mind) was viewed as "the central organ which conditions all man's activities and upon whose correct functioning depends the character of his living" (Cohen: 24).

Part 2 (4:24-27) of the poem amplifies the point made in part 1 by specifying actions that can be taken to protect the heart through the proper use of the *mouth, lips, eyes*, and *feet*. The first thing to be done is to *put away from you crookedness of mouth, and perverse lips put far from you* (4:24, lit.). But also the *gaze* (lit., *eyes* and *eyelids*) must be focused on the path ahead (4:25), so that the *feet* can be properly placed (4:26). And then one must be careful to walk straight forward on the chosen path, not turning off *to the right or the left* (4:27). Only so can you *keep your foot from evil* (4:27). In other words, how we use various vital parts of our body like mouth, eyes, and feet affects the *heart* (mind), and how we employ the heart (mind) is key to the health of the whole body. In this poem the *heart* is the place in the body where data from the senses is processed and from which comes the wisdom that is the *wellspring of life* (4:23). This concept has striking parallels in Egyptian literature *["Heart"]*.

"In the End She Is Bitter as Gall" 5:1-6

This is yet another of the poems Solomon tells us his father taught him (4:4). That is why, like the two preceding poems, it begins with *My son* (5:1). It has six couplets in two parts (5:1-3, 4-6; cf. 4:4b-9).

The second of David's poems for Solomon warned him against setting foot *in the way of evil men* (4:14); this one portrays the destructive wiles of a certain kind of woman (5:3). We have already met this woman in 2:16-19, although the poem here is the older of the two, being part of the Solomon Edition. As previously noted, the woman warned against is not strictly speaking an *adulteress.* The word used to identify her is *zārāh,* meaning *outsider* or *stranger* (in the sense of being a woman from another locality). A woman of this kind is also the focus of the poem that closes this section (5:7-14), and then of four poems which the *men of Hezekiah* added as supplements in this section of the book (5:15-23; 6:20-29, 30-35; 7:1-23) *[Identity of the Foreign Seductress].*

Egyptian manuals also warned young men against becoming involved with a woman of this type (see notes on 2:16-19). There she is described as a "woman from abroad who is not known in her (own) town" (The Instruction of Ani, Pritchard: 420). There too it is said that she has a husband (and hence is not a prostitute), but that she does not let this fact get in the way of her search for illicit liaisons. This background teaching from Egypt is our best clue to an understanding of what is said here about such a loose woman. Warnings to young men against becoming involved with a wanton woman of this type are a feature of the instructional manuals of the more advanced cultures of the time.

The poem itself is artfully constructed. Its first stanza (5:1-3) picks up the body language of the prior poem (*lips, mouth, feet*). The son is advised that his *lips* should *preserve knowledge,* for the *lips* of a *foreign* [outsider] *woman drip honey, and her speech* [lit., *mouth*] *is smoother than oil* (5:3), and *her feet go down to death* (5:5). The latter *end* of such a woman (5:4; lit., *her end*) is the subject of part 2 (5:4-6): it is *bitter as gall* (a noxious plant; Deut 29:18; Amos 5:7); *her steps lead to the grave* (*šĕ'ôl,* the gloomy netherworld). The final couplet in 5:6 paints a brief but telling portrait of her character. The woman is superficial: *She gives no thought to the way of life.* Also, she has no insight into the evil of her ways or compunctions about what she is doing: *Her paths are crooked, but she knows it not.* The poem ends without any explicit advice or warning; the graphic description of her character and fate is itself the warning.

"Do Not Go Near the Door of Her House" 5:7-14

In this poem Solomon speaks once again in his own "voice" (as in 4:1-4a). No longer is he relating verbatim what his father taught him (4:4b–5:6). He begins by addressing the sons referred to in the same

terms he addressed them in the opening verse of this section: not as
My sons (NIV), but saying (lit., as the Hebrew text has it), *And now
sons, listen to me* (5:7). Now the explicit advice missing in the previous poem is forthcoming. Picking up on what his father taught him,
Solomon now urgently seeks to warn the *sons* against having anything whatsoever to do with the woman described in the final poem
of his father. He does this by evoking a time to come when, if they do
get involved with such a woman, they might well bitterly lament having failed to heed his advice: *How I hated discipline!* [he imagines
them saying]. *How my heart spurned correction! I would not obey
my teachers or listen to my instructors* (5:12-13). The reference in
this verse to *teachers* and *instructors* implies a school setting. The
Solomon Edition of Proverbs appears to have been designed for use
in the royal schools (see Introduction to the Book of Proverbs).

This poem (5:7-14) is the concluding one of this set (4:1–5:14; the
poems that follow in 5:15–7:23 are yet another cluster of supplements from the Hezekiah Edition editors). It has eight couplets in two
parts (5:7-10, 11-14; cf. 4:4-9). The advice given in part 1 (5:7-10)
pertains to the *woman* referred to in the prior poem (in 5:1-6).
Solomon urges the *sons* to *listen to me* and *not turn aside from
what I say* (5:7; lit., *from words of my mouth*). His advice is quite
simple and straightforward: Stay *far from her, do not go near the
door of her house* (5:8-9; the story told in 7:6-23 portrays a "brainless" youth not following this advice). The *lest* clauses in 5:9-10 identify the *immediate* consequences of failing to heed this advice: first,
loss of *strength* (virility, as in Dan 10:8); second, *your years* [will be
lost] *to one who is cruel*; third, loss of *your wealth* (previously accumulated assets) and *toil* (current earnings) to the benefit of *another
man's house* (lit., *the household of a stranger*). In other words, his
wealth will end up in the household of the seductive woman.

Part 2 (5:11-14) of the poem portrays the long-range consequences for a young man foolish enough to get entangled with a
seductive woman of this type. The poet imagines what this youth
might say at the end of his life when he is hopelessly sick, *when your
flesh and body are spent* (5:11). The young man (now old and sick)
looks back and expresses profound regret for how rebellious he was—
how he *hated discipline*, how his *heart spurned correction*, how he
had not obeyed his teachers or listened to his instructors, and how as
a consequence he had come to such abject disgrace *in the midst of
the congregation and assembly* (5:14, lit.; his community and its judicial assemblies). There is a crescendo effect in this list of consequences; each is worse than the previous one (loss of vitality, loss of

wealth, deterioration of health, abject remorse, public disgrace). This poem has been described as "a robust man-to-man warning, . . . a sober, earthy estimate of the disastrous results which flow from this particular manifestation of indiscipline" (McKane: 312).

THE TEXT IN BIBLICAL CONTEXT

The Supremacy of Wisdom

Wisdom is supreme; therefore get wisdom (4:7a) is the opening watchword of the Solomon Edition *[Solomon Edition]*. In this edition *wisdom* is spoken of as though she were virtually a godlike reality: *Do not forsake wisdom, and she will protect you; love her, and she will watch over you* (4:6). The one who speaks in this poem is identified in the book's heading (1:1) as "Solomon son of David, king of Israel."

Solomon states that the teachings he is passing on to the students of the royal schools (cf. 5:13) are verbatim reports of what his father taught him when he was a young man (4:3a). This bit of information comes as a surprise because nothing in the legacy of David would lead us to imagine him saying anything like this to Solomon or anyone else. On the contrary, David's literary legacy (especially his prayers in the Psalter) convey a deep sense of trust and love for Yahweh (cf. Ps 37:5), not how much he loved wisdom. Furthermore, the account of Solomon's reign in 1 Kings is clear about the fact that it was Solomon, not David, who was enamored of wisdom and pursued it with a relentlessness that rivaled his father's love for Yahweh (see 1 Kgs 4:29-34; 10:1-9, 23-25). I know of no other place in the Bible where wisdom itself is eulogized as in the description of Solomon's wisdom in 1 Kings and in the Solomon Edition of Proverbs.

More typical of the approach to wisdom elsewhere in the Bible is the provocative account in Genesis 3 of the temptation of Adam and Eve. In this story the quest for wisdom is portrayed as being fraught with danger. Eve's desire to gain wisdom by eating of the "tree of the knowledge of good and evil" (2:9) has very destructive consequences for herself and Adam. The story implies that they should not have done this, at least not in the God-defiant manner in which they do. At some level Eve's desire for wisdom seems justified, for otherwise human beings would be automata, just blindly obeying what they are told and not thinking things through on their own. And yet, historical experience teaches that human beings on their own are prone to error and evil. When they trust too much in their own wisdom, they often go astray, and the consequences can be devastating.

This story thus evokes conflicting thoughts about the human condition, perhaps not unlike those had who created the Hezekiah Edition of Proverbs. They too recognized that the pursuit of wisdom was supremely important. But they also knew from their nation's history that Solomon's wisdom was not sufficient to save him or Israel from foolish and destructive behavior. That seems to be the whole point of their supplements and additions to the Solomon Edition—to emphasize the need to fear God and keep his commandments as the *beginning of wisdom* (1:7; 9:10).

But why then did they preserve the texts in the Solomon Edition that laud wisdom's supremacy? Why did they retain the poems in which Solomon personifies wisdom as a *voice* (1:20; 8:1, 4) that virtually replaces the voice of God? An important issue is at stake in how we answer this question. I think they kept Solomon's poems because of their remarkable insight that *wisdom is* in fact *supreme* (4:7a). What is said elsewhere in their supplements is not meant to change the stark truth of this assertion. The quest for wisdom is no substitute for trusting God to direct our paths; but still, the quest for wisdom *is* paramount.

The Heart as the "Wellspring of Life"

In one of the poems of this group, the *heart* is regarded as the *wellspring of life* (4:23). The terminology is not just a metaphor for feeling or emotion (as today) but refers to the bodily organ that processes thought *["Heart"]*. Those who are foolish and unwise are described in Proverbs as lacking a heart *[Words for Wisdom and Folly]*. As such, the *heart* is by far the most important organ of the body. This is the viewpoint of other biblical writers as well. For Jeremiah too, what was happening in the hearts of his people was absolutely decisive. That is why it alarmed him when he observed that the religious reforms of his time were not seemingly having any effect on that realm of their being. Instead, their perverse values seemed, as it were, "inscribed with a flint point, on the tablets of their hearts" (Jer 17:1). "The heart is deceitful above all things and beyond cure," he lamented. "Who can understand it?" (17:9). His boldest prediction was of a time to come when God would rectify this problem and write his laws on the hearts of his people (31:33).

For Jesus too the "heart" was of the utmost importance. It is not what goes in and out of the stomach that counts, he taught, but what goes in and out of the "heart" (Mark 7:20-23). For this reason he questioned the importance others in his time gave to debates over clean and unclean foods. In other teachings too he highlighted the importance of the heart: "The pure in heart . . . will see God" (Matt 5:8). "Where your treasure is, there your heart will be also" (6:21).

THE TEXT IN THE LIFE OF THE CHURCH

Proverbs and the Arts and Sciences

The assumed setting of the block of poems in 4:1–5:15 is a school with teachers and instructors (5:13). The topics broached are those educational leaders of the ancient world thought were important for preparing young men for civil service. A host of additional topics are addressed in the sayings that follow in the Main Collection (10:1–22:16). Most of the topics they identified as important ones for the schools of their time are issues facing us today. Examples are education itself (wisdom, what it is and how to get it), economics (work, money matters, investments), personal relations (sociology), matters of the heart (psychology), knowledge of the Holy One (theological and philosophical issues; see "Thematic Index for the Poems of The Main Collection").

Heaton writes that textbooks like this in ancient Israel and Egypt were designed "to communicate the fruits of past experience not only on such professional matters as . . . [personnel] management and public-speaking, but also on the kind of personal conduct which helped or hindered a man's progress in life" (Heaton: 116). All modern societies seek to provide an analogous kind of education for their youth through degree programs in the "arts and sciences" at high school, college, and/or university levels. During the past several centuries, churches of most denominations have given leadership in establishing educational enterprises of this kind. There is a model and a precedent for this endeavor within the Christian Scriptures themselves—in the book of Proverbs.

"Above All Else, Guard Your Heart"

The advice in 4:23-27 about how to guard the heart may be more sophisticated and relevant for our time than at first meets the eye. It assumes a capacity of the "heart" to be on its guard. We all know this to be true. We do have this capacity. It is one of our prize possessions as human beings. "I can look at myself and make even my inmost self the object of care, reflection, improvement, and betterment" (R. Van Leeuwen: 61). And then we can act. We can protect our inner thoughts, desires, and imagination from corrupting influences. In protecting ourselves, the advice of this poem is on target when it encourages us to examine, in this order: our heart (4:23), our words (4:24), what we look at (4:25), and where we go (4:25-26). The book of James has something similar to say when it advises against thinking that our temptations to evil come from God. No, James writes, they come when we allow evil desires to take root within us (1:13-15). This is not all there is to say on this issue, but it touches on a truth too easily brushed aside in societies sometimes awash in salacious sights and sounds.

Ancient Wisdom on Monogamous Marriage

Apart from the more general admonition to acquire wisdom, the poems of this section advise the sons of the royal schools on two things in particular: against associating with lawless violent men (4:10-19), and against becoming intimately involved with a *wayward woman* (5:1-6). It is about the dangers of the latter that Solomon writes in an especially passionate manner (5:1-6). That he should do so is a little surprising since his own conduct with regard to women was not ideal (cf. 1 Kgs 11:1-2). As noted, however, the advice in this instance reflects teachings on this subject in the instructional manuals of Egypt. Even the terms used for describing the woman to be avoided are similar to terms used for her in the older Egyptian texts. In other words, this may be an instance where the older Egyptian manuals provided models and ideals that were superior to any currently in vogue in Israelite tradition.

This is a possibility worth pondering. When reading biblical texts, we usually assume that they reflect values higher than those found elsewhere. In this case the ideals being taught may have been in advance of those generally practiced in Israel at the time of Solomon. When we turn to the Egyptian manuals themselves, we discover that this was the case regarding marriage ideals generally. The oldest of these manuals (dating to the middle of third millennium BC), written by an aged royal servant named Ptah-hotep, describes how "a man of standing" should conduct himself. Among the issues Ptah-hotep writes about is marriage. "If thou art a man of standing," he says, "thou shouldst found thy household and love thy wife at home as is fitting. . . . Make her heart glad as long as thou livest. . . . Let her heart be soothed through what may accrue to thee; it means keeping her long in thy house" (The Instruction of the Vizier Ptah-hotep, Pritchard: 413).

Elsewhere in his manual, Ptah-hotep writes of how "a man of standing" should conduct himself in his relation to women other than his wife. "If thou desirest to make friendship last in a home to which thou hast access as master, as a brother, or as a friend, into any place where thou mightest enter, beware of approaching the women. It does not go well with the place where that is done. . . . A thousand men *may be distracted from* their (own) advantage. One is made a fool by limbs of fayence, as she stands (there). . . . Do not do it—it is really an abomination—and thou shalt be free from sickness of heart every day" (413).

This is not the only evidence of these ideals in the earliest periods of Egyptian civilization. There was an ancient practice of creating life-sized family portraits in stone. These are full-sized statues of husband and wife standing lovingly side by side—in some cases with their children. One such ancient stone portrait has justifiably been described as among the greatest works of art ever produced. It depicts Pharaoh Menkaure, builder of the third pyramid at Giza in 2500 BC, with his wife at his side. Both are standing, life-size and in full view, both are strong and handsome, both are human beings in their own right, each radiating a sense of purpose and joy. Yet one senses that the wife's strength is bonded to that of her husband's. With her right arm she embraces his waist, and the fingers of her left arm rest gently on his biceps. *His* arms are at his side, not listlessly, but poised for action, with his left foot slightly forward. (I saw this sculpture, with others from the same period, when it was on temporary display at the Royal Ontario Museum in Toronto. It was discovered by the Harvard University Museum of Fine Arts Expedition, March 2, 1911, and is on display at that museum).

That a Pharaoh of the third millennium, a builder of the pyramids, wanted to memorialize himself in this way, is a notable event not just in the history of art but in the history of human civilization. An even older portrait in stone of this kind from this region and time is equally impressive. The male in this case is not a Pharaoh, but a civil servant of King Khufu. His name is Sonb, and as we learn from his portrait, he is a dwarf. Out of deference to his handicap, he and his wife are portrayed, not standing, but sitting on a stone bench, so that Sonb's torso (which is approximately the height of his wife's) can be parallel to hers. Thus they can be portrayed together in the affectionate manner shown in the stone portrait of Pharaoh Menkaure and his wife. Her right arm is around him, with the fingers of her left hand resting gently on his biceps. Sonb sits cross-legged on the stone bench, his dwarf legs tucked beneath him. Underneath, where his legs would be if he were not a dwarf, are stone replicas of the couple's two children, a boy and a girl (for a full-page photograph, see Málek: 38).

The word for wife in ancient Egypt was "female partner." This is how Eve is described in Genesis 2 (as a monogamous helpmeet and partner to Adam). This monogamous ideal is implicit in the teachings of the Decalogue when it calls for children to honor their father and mother and prohibits adultery. It is also implicit in warnings given young men in Proverbs against becoming intimate with a "foreign seductress." These marital ideals were powerfully affirmed in the teachings of Jesus (Miller, 1973) and in the churches of every generation to the present time. They are still powerful today, but under challenge as seldom before in the five thousand years that stretches from us to the time of Jesus, Solomon, Moses, and Ptah-hotep. "Make no mistake about it," a thoughtful, experienced pastor sums up, "the Christian church is riddled with immorality, among the young and the older, the single and the married, the laity and the leadership. . . . Enslaved by sexual sin in mind and body, plagued and haunted by its guilt, innumerable children of God are tragically incapacitated in their attempts to live for Christ. Nothing so hamstrings the believer's spiritual potency as sexual compromise—and never has the church in America been so compromised as now" (Alcorn: 31).

Proverbs 5:15—7:23

Supplemental Poems
(Hezekiah Edition)

The Book of Proverbs, Part 1: Introductory Collection				
Original Prologue (Solomon Edition) 1:1-7	Supplemental Poems (Hezekiah Edition) 1:8–3:35	Original Poems (Solomon Edition) 4:1–5:14	Supplemental Poems (Hezekiah Edition) 5:15–7:23	Original Poems (Solomon Edition) 7:24–9:18

PREVIEW

The content of the poems in this inserted block of supplements (5:15–7:23) is surprisingly varied. It opens and closes with some of the most insightful teachings of the Bible on marital relations. In between are thoughts about reckless loans, the stupidity of being lazy, and deplorable attributes and characters to be avoided at all cost. The number of poems added at this point in the book may be due in part to the goal that the Hezekiah Edition editors set for themselves, to have the Main Collection (10:1–22:16) in the exact middle of the scroll (see chart with Introduction).

If we want to understand why this block of poems (5:15–7:23) is designated "Hezekiah Edition Supplements" in this commentary [Distinctive Approach], we need to pay careful attention to an erroneous translation on the part of NIV in this part of the book (other translations make the same mistake). In the Hebrew text of this block of poems, there is a subtle change of "voice." The "voice" speaking in 5:15–7:23 is no longer that of Solomon addressing sons (or students) but that of a father instructing his own son (5:20; 6:1, 3, 20), just as in the earlier Hezekiah Edition supplements in 1:8–3:35 (cf. 1:8). This change of "voice" continues to the end of 7:23. At 7:24 there is another change of "voice"; here the "voice" is again that of Solomon addressing sons (or students) just as he did in 4:1–5:16. That this is the case, however, is not at all evident in the NIV translation of 7:24, where the sons addressed are said to be my sons (as though the one speaking was a father addressing his own sons). The Hebrew of 7:24 reads simply sons (just as in 4:1; 5:7; and 8:32, which NIV also mistakenly translates with my sons).

The contents of this block of poems are consistent with the concerns and theology of the Hezekiah Edition supplements, as we come to know them in the initial supplements in 1:7–3:18 and the oracle of Agur (30:1-7). God's role in human affairs is again acknowledged (5:21; 6:16), something that is totally missing in the prior Solomon Edition poems in 4:1–5:14). The teachings of this section also echo the Ten Commandments (cf. 6:25-29, 30-35); these commandments were a vital component of Hezekiah's reforms and of the knowledge of the Holy One, which Agur in his oracle refers to as God's word (30:5a). A thesis of this commentary is that Agur son of Jakeh played a key leadership role among the men of Hezekiah (25:1), who created this edition of Proverbs [Distinctive Approach]. This may be why many of the poems added at this point in the book bear a striking resemblance to those of Agur in chapter 30 (use of numbers, hyperbole, allusions to animals). The commentary that follows will highlight some of these similarities, and the notes on chapter 30 say more about Agur himself.

OUTLINE

"Rejoice in the Wife of Your Youth," 5:15-23
"My Son, If You Have Put Up Security," 6:1-5
"Go to the Ant, You Sluggard," 6:6-11
"A Base Person, a Wicked Man," 6:12-15
"There Are Six [or Seven] Things the Lord Hates," 6:16-19
"Do Not Lust in Your Heart After Another Man's Wife," 6:20-29

"A Man Who Commits Adultery Lacks Judgment," 6:30-35
"At the Window of My House," 7:1-23

EXPLANATORY NOTES

"Rejoice in the Wife of Your Youth" 5:15-23

This poem is an important supplement to the previous two (5:1-6, 7-14). It has three stanzas with three verses each (5:15-17, 18-20, 21-23). It begins with a metaphor: *Drink water from your own cistern, running water from your own well* (5:15). In the culture of the time, having a cistern was one of life's more essential and enjoyable blessings (Isa 36:16). Here the metaphor intimates the joys of marriage. A loved wife is like *running water* in a cool, refreshing well (cf. Song 4:15). The son is advised to drink *water from your own well* (have sexual intimacies with his own wife and no one else). This counsel is reinforced by the follow-up imperative: *Let your springs be dispersed outside, and streams of water in the streets* (5:16, lit.). The metaphor of *your springs* filling the streets may allude to the numerous children born to him of this relationship. Thus, it is followed by another imperative: *Let them* [your springs] *be yours alone, never to be shared with strangers* (5:17; a reference perhaps to "children of doubtful paternity"; Cohen: 28). In other words, the son is being advised to *drink water* from his own *cistern* so that his children will be numerous and known to be his.

Stanza 2 continues the theme of being faithful to one's wife, but with a new focus. It opens with a prayerlike statement: *May your fountain* [your wife] *be blessed* (5:18a). Then it continues: *And may you rejoice in the wife of your youth* (5:18b). The father prayerfully wishes his son's *fountain* to be blessed, so that he and his wife might be favored (by God) with children (Ps 127:3-5). But right away, he also encourages his son to *rejoice* in the wife with whom he began living as a youth. It was the custom of the time to marry young, with parents often assisting in the selection of partners for their children. By the words, *rejoice in,* the father means that his son is to "enjoy" or "take pleasure in" his wife (Fox: 202). Her beauty is evoked with images of a *loving doe* and *a graceful deer* (5:19a). The son is told to be *always* (lit., *at all times*) pleasured by *her breasts* (meaning *hers* and not another's) and *ever captivated by her love* (5:19b).

This frank advice sets the stage for the probing question: *Why be captivated, my son, by a stranger? Why embrace the bosom of an outsider?* (5:20, lit.). Again, the woman referred to may be the *another man's wife* and an *adulteress* (NIV), but the Hebrew term used here to identify her (*zārāh*) is the same used in the prior Solomon Edition poem and elsewhere (cf. 5:3; 2:16) [*Identity of the Foreign Seductress*]. This verse (5:20) and the previous one (5:19) are linked by the word *captivated*. This same word appears again at the end of this poem, where it is implied that the son who is *captivated* by such a woman instead of his own wife will *die for lack of discipline, led astray* [lit., *captivated*] *by his own great folly* (5:23).

Stanza 3 (5:21-23) seeks to reinforce the behavior just advocated by calling to mind that *a man's ways are in full view of the LORD* (lit., *before the eyes of Yahweh*). This does not necessarily mean that Yahweh is the one who punishes or rewards. The *evil deeds* themselves *ensnare* those who engage in them (5:22). Those who reject *discipline* (restraint) are *led astray by their great folly* (5:23). Deeds have consequences in a world in which Yahweh watches over everything that occurs.

"My Son, If You Have Put Up Security" 6:1-5

There is no apparent reason why this and the following four poems (6:1-5, 6-9, 9-11, 12-15, 16-19) are located here rather than elsewhere in the book (Fox: 226). The compilers may have just wanted to enlarge this part of the book so that it would be equal in size to the end supplements (see Preview). This first poem has two parts (6:1-3a, 3b-5) with three couplets each. Part 1 (6:1-3a) has three *if* clauses stating a hypothetical "case"; part 2 (6:3b-6) relates what should be done if something like this should in fact occur (*then do this, my son*, 6:3a). The case laws of the biblical law codes are the prototypes for this literary form (for examples, see Exod 21-22).

The hypothetical "case" presented in this instance has to do with a son who agreed (*struck hands*) to put up collateral for a loan made by a *neighbor* (6:1a) who was not well known; 6:1b identifies him as a *stranger* (not just *another*; see NRSV note). Warnings against guaranteeing this type of loan appear elsewhere in Proverbs (see 11:15; 17:18; 22:26-27). In this instance it is viewed as tantamount to falling *into your neighbors hands* (6:3b), referring to the fact that the loan's guarantor becomes liable for the stranger's debt if he fails to pay it. To put up collateral for an urgently needed loan of a friend might be a kindness, but why would one do such a thing for a *stranger*? "Remunerative surety is the likely background" (Fox: 215), collateral offered in a moment of reckless greed over an anticipated payoff if the venture would be successful (*trapped by what you said, ensnared by the words of your mouth*, 6:2). The teaching advises the son what to do if he should be foolish enough to entrap himself in this way. He should go without delay (before sleeping) to the one whose loan he guaranteed (6:3b) and (lit.) *trample on yourself* ("grovel," Fox) and *press your plea* ("rage at him," Cohen: 31) in order to *free yourself, like a gazelle or bird twists and turns to break free of a hunter* (6:5).

Is this wise advice (to grovel and beg in this manner)? Would it even work? Maybe the poem's purpose is not to say that it would, but to highlight the enormous dangers of making a mistake of this kind (Fox: 216). Like this one, the poems of Agur in chapter 30 ripple with acerbic humor and conclude on a similar note: *If you have played the fool and exalted yourself, or if you have planned evil, clap your hand over your mouth!* (30:32).

"Go to the Ant, You Sluggard" 6:6-11

This poem also has two parts with three couplets each (6:6-8, 9-11). It is tinged with humor. In part 1 a *sluggard* is addressed and told to *consider* the ways of an ant and *be wise* (learn wisdom from an ant!). The figure of the *sluggard* is comic relief in several sayings elsewhere in Proverbs (see 10:26; 19:24; 22:13; 26:13-16). Only here is the sluggard spoken to—and in ways that remind us of Agur's poem about tiny creatures (see 30:24-28), where he points out, *Ants are creatures of little strength, yet they store up their food in the summer* (30:24). The poem here in 6:6-11 says the same thing: *It* [the ant] *stores its provisions in summer* (6:8a)—but then adds that it does so without benefit of a commander or ruler (6:7), a point Agur makes about locusts in 30:27.

In part 2 the sluggard is addressed again, with a question as to why he just lies there and sleeps (6:9). The saying that follows (in 6:10-11) is identical to the saying in 24:34, a verse that is part of a poem in one of the appended collections (24:23-34). In that poem a narrator reports what he saw when he walked past the vineyard of a sluggard (24:30): it was in ruins (24:31). How it got that way is stated in a proverb (*māšāl*) composed on the spot (24:32): *A little sleep, a little slumber, a little folding of the hands to rest—and poverty will come on you like a bandit and scarcity like an armed man* (24:34). This would appear to be where this proverb of 6:10-11 originated. Its secondary use here broadens its applicability. The failure of a *sluggard* to learn foresight and initiative from an ant can have devastating consequences not just for someone in charge of a vineyard, but in any field of endeavor.

"A Base Person, a Wicked Man" 6:12-15

This poem, unlike any thus far, simply lists the features of a certain kind of man and closes with words indicating his fate. But there are two other examples in Proverbs of poems of this type: the one that immediately follows (6:16-19) and another in the collected poems of Agur (30:11-14). Agur might well have written all three. Each is a snapshot of the kind of man the Hezekiah Edition of Proverbs is earnestly trying to dissuade young men from becoming. In this instance the portrait is of a base person ['ādām], a wicked man (6:12a, lit.). His characteristics are those mentioned in a cluster of sayings in 16:27-30. He is thoroughly corrupt (bĕliyya'al); the word is used elsewhere for rapists (Judg 19:22), perjurers (1 Kgs 21:10, 13), apostates (Deut 13:14), alcoholics (1 Sam 1:16), troublemakers (1 Sam 10:27), and fools (Prov 16:27; 1 Sam 25:17, 25; Fox: 219). The poem lists four telltale physical features of such a person: He walks about with a corrupt mouth (lit., a crooked mouth; 6:12b; cf. 16:27b). He squints (lit.; winks; his eyes are shifty; 6:13a; 16:30a). He shuffles his feet (not able to stand still). And he points his fingers with malicious intent (6:13). His outer appearance reflects his perverse inner thoughts, which are preoccupied with evil plans (6:14a). As a result, wherever he goes, he sows discord (6:14b; 16:28). The poem closes with a sharp focus on his fate: He will suddenly be destroyed—without remedy (6:15).

"There Are Six [or Seven] Things the LORD Hates" 6:16-19

This poetic sequel lists many characteristics of the person just described but views them now from Yahweh's point of view (cf. 5:21). The pronouncement The LORD hates these characteristics (6:16a) is repeated in 8:13; otherwise, the terminology The LORD hates appears only in the prophets (Hos 9:15; Amos 5:21; 6:8; Zech 8:17; Mal 1:3; 2:16). Adding that Yahweh finds them detestable (tô'ăbôth, 6:16b, an abomination) underscores the intensity of his hatred (on this term, see 3:32, notes). The numerical sequence (There are six things the LORD hates, seven, 6:16) is a rhetorical device found elsewhere (cf. Job 5:19-22; Amos 1:3–2:16; "The Words of Ahiqar," Pritchard: 428), but otherwise in Proverbs only in the poems of Agur (30:15-17, 18-19, 21-23, 29-31). The list of hated characteristics begins with the eyes and proceeds downward (tongue, hands, heart, feet). What is proscribed is reminiscent of the Decalogue (Deut 5:6-21). First mentioned, haughty eyes (pride; 6:17a; cf. Agur's poem in

30:11-14) or looks are the opposite of the humility that characterizes those who *fear Yahweh* (see 15:33). Next is *a lying tongue,* a violation of the ninth commandment (Deut 5:20). *Hands that shed innocent blood* comes next, a violation of the sixth commandment (Deut 5:17). The fourth and fifth traits, *a heart that devises wicked schemes, feet that rush into evil* (Prov 6:18), are violations of the tenth commandment (*You shall not covet . . . your neighbor's house or land,* Deut 5:21). The sixth trait mentioned (*a false witness who pours out lies,* Prov 6:19a) expands on the second trait (*a lying tongue*). The seventh and final trait mentioned (Prov 6:19b) is similar to the one at the close of the prior poem: *He always stirs up dissension;* yet here it is added that he *stirs up dissension among brothers* (6:19b). The *brothers* referred to are fellow Israelites, members of the covenant community of Yahweh (see 2:8b; this usage is pervasive in Deuteronomy: 3:18; 15:2, 3, 7, 9, 11, 12; etc.).

"Do Not Lust in Your Heart After Another Man's Wife" 6:20-29

This poem is introduced with a verse almost identical to the one in 1:8. As there, a *son* is told to keep the *commandment* of his father and not forsake the *teaching* of his mother (6:20). The presumed setting is that of a young man in his own home being instructed by his parents (for this as a mark of the Hezekiah Edition, see notes on 1:8-9). In this case the verse introduces a poem that picks up on the theme of the prior supplemental poem in 5:15-23. The question posed there, *Why be captivated, my son, by a stranger?* (5:20), sets the stage for the specific issue discussed here, how to avoid being captivated by her beauty (6:25).

The poem has ten verses in two equal parts (6:20-24, 25-29). Part 1 (6:20-24) begins with a father telling his son to heed his parent's teaching, but then instructs him on how, precisely, this should be done and what the consequences will be. He is to bind the parental teaching on his heart *forever* (likely meaning that he is to memorize it) and fasten it around his neck (like an amulet, 6:21; cf. 3:3, 22). Then, *when you walk, they* [lit., *she,* referring to the wisdom of his parents' teachings] *will guide you; when you sleep, they* [*she*] *will watch over you; when you awake, they* [*she*] *will speak to you* (6:22). These instructions are similar to what Deuteronomy teaches should be done with the teachings of Moses: parents are to impress them on the hearts of their sons "when you sit at home and when you walk along the road, when you lie down and when you get up. Tie them as symbols on your hands and bind them on your foreheads" (Deut 6:7-8).

The instructions there and here (like those in 1:8–3:35) presuppose a home in which the children are being educated for life in this way (cf. 7:1-5). The additional point emphasized here (in 6:22-24) is that a son who internalizes his parents' teaching in this manner will have a reliable guide within him at all times, right in his heart (mind). This internal guide is likened to *a lamp* and *a light* that will be there to guide him in *the way to life* (6:23b). More specifically (and this is the climactic point), this guide will prevent him from becoming involved with an *immoral woman,* from being captivated by *the smoothness of the tongue of a foreigner* (6:24, lit.).

With this we come to the specific theme of this poem, how a son might escape being seduced by an immoral woman. The advice given in part 2 (6:25-29) provides the more specific answer. It reads like a poetic commentary on the version of the tenth command cited in Deuteronomy 5:21a, which begins, "You shall not lust after (*taḥmōd*) your neighbor's wife" (lit.). The poet uses the identical verb, *taḥmōd* (*lust after*) in Proverbs 6:25a, only in this instance spells out its meaning: *Do not lust in your heart after her beauty or let her captivate you with her eyes* (lit., *eyelids,* 6:25). The next comment emphasizes how tragic it is for a young man to let something like this happen. The poem draws a contrast between consorting with a harlot (lit., *a woman of harlotry),* which might well reduce a man to poverty (lit., *to a loaf of bread),* and consorting with another man's wife, which puts his very life at risk (lit., *his precious soul; nepeš).* There are huge personal risks involved in consorting with another man's wife. The poem continues with two rhetorical questions (cf. 5:20): *Can a man scoop fire into his lap and his cloths not be burned? Can a man walk on hot coals and his feet not be scorched?* (6:27-28, lit.). The questions are not so much about the dangers involved in actually sleeping *with another man's wife,* as NIV translates 6:29a. This verse is more accurately translated: *So is he who goes to the wife of his neighbor.* In other words, the issue in view is the dangerous thought of going to visit a neighbor's wife with amorous intent, with a warning: *No one who touches her will go unpunished* (6:29b).

This poem throughout is about *internalizing* the tenth command against lust for a neighbor's wife. A son who lets lust for the beauty of a neighbor's wife consume him and goes to her house in a flirtatious mood is on an exceedingly dangerous path that *will not go unpunished* (6:29). The next poem alludes to what kind of punishment might ensue from such behavior.

"A Man Who Commits Adultery Lacks Judgment" 6:30-35

If the prior poem is a commentary on the tenth commandment against lust, this one might be thought of as a meditation on the seventh commandment against adultery. It has two parts, with three verses in each part (6:30-32, 33-35). Part 1 opens with a seemingly innocent observation about the fate of a thief who *steals to satisfy his hunger when he is starving*. No one despises him for that (6:30), but even so, if caught (lit., *found out*), he must pay sevenfold, even if it involves giving up *all the wealth of his house* (6:31). The penalty mentioned (sevenfold) is excessive. The laws in Exodus 22:1, 3 require two-, four- or fivefold restitution for stolen goods. The poet stresses that stealing is a crime that can result in the total loss of one's property even if the thief's community thinks what he did was not all that bad. This observation is mere background for a consideration of the starkly contrasting fate of a man who *commits adultery* (nō'ēp, 6:32). The verb used is the same as in the seventh commandment against adultery in the Decalogue (Deut 5:18). Here, however, adultery is not prohibited (as in the Decalogue), nor is a young man who commits adultery told he has violated the law of God. Instead, he is castigated in the harshest terms for his lack of *judgment* (6:32a); the Hebrew term used is that he *lacks heart* (or *brains*; he is witless). Why? Because he cannot see that he thereby *destroys himself* (6:32b; lit., *destroys his soul*).

In other words, a thief who steals because of hunger may lose all his property while retaining his reputation; but a man who commits adultery is absolutely without *heart* or *brains* because of his failure to realize how self-destructive such behavior is. Part 2 of this poem (6:33-35) clarifies what it means that the man who commits adultery *destroys himself*. Unlike the thief who stole because he was starving and therefore retains his reputation even though losing his property, the man who commits adultery will experience lasting disgrace and a life beset with violence. *Blows and disgrace are his lot, and his shame will never be wiped away* (6:33). A reason is cited as to why this is so: the fierce *jealousy* of the offended *husband* (6:34-35). Nothing will placate him for the dishonor inflicted by the one committing adultery with his wife (6:35). He will be relentless (lit., *not be sparing*) in taking revenge. Anyone contemplating adultery had better reckon with the implacable fury of the offended husband and the dire loss of one's reputation.

"At the Window of My House"   7:1-23

This long and unique poem has two distinct parts (7:1-5, 6-23). Its
two parts are linked by the conjunction *for* (*kî*) at the beginning of its
second part (7:6a; NIV omits *for*). This implies that part 1 (7:1-5)
should be read as a five-verse introduction to part 2 (7:6-23). In part
1 a father once again urges his son to heed his words, promising that
if he does so, they will protect him from the *seductive words* of a certain kind of woman (7:5). The translation *wayward wife* (NIV) to identify her is once again misleading. The terms used specify that she is a
stranger or foreigner, an "outsider." So once again the teaching has
to do with the dangerous allurements posed for a young man by a certain kind of woman *[Identity of the Foreign Seductress]*.

Part 1 of this poem (7:1-5) resembles the one in 6:20-29. As
there, the father requests that his son (*my son*) keep his commands
and *live* (7:2). He is to guard them as *the apple [pupil] of your eye,*
the pupil being one of the most precious and vulnerable parts of the
body (cf. Deut 32:10; Ps 17:8). He is also to *bind them on your fingers, write them* [lit., *cut them*] *on the tablet of your heart* (7:3).
This may refer to a technique for memorization using the fingers. The
expression *tablet of the heart* is rare (appearing only here and in 3:3;
Jer 17:1). One is reminded of the stone tablets on which the Ten
Commandments were written (Deut 4:13; 5:22) and what Moses asks
parents to do with his teachings (Deut 6:5-9; 11:18-20).

Once the son has memorized these commandments, there is one
thing more the father wants done with them (7:4). The father asks the
son to *say to wisdom, "You are my sister," and call understanding
your kinsman* (cf. Ruth 2:1). The *wisdom* he is referring to is his own
teachings, now internalized by the son. This internalized wisdom is to
be thought of as a loving *sister* or relative that will protect him from
the wiles of a female stranger *with her seductive words* (7:5).

In prior poems the father's teachings are followed by severe warnings of the dire consequences that would ensue were the son to disregard these teachings (cf. 2:18-19; 6:25-29, 30-35; 5:1-6, 7-14). In
this instance, however, the father relates a story of something he says
he witnessed *at the window of my house* (7:6). The story told is
unique in itself; there is nothing like it elsewhere in Proverbs, perhaps
not in the Bible. "The father's report is a masterpiece" (Clifford: 84).
It has four equal parts with four couplets each (7:6-9, 10-13, 14-17,
18-21) and a six-line conclusion (7:22-23). The story begins, *For [kî]
at the window of my house . . .* (7:6a, lit.). The *for* (missing in NIV)
clarifies that the story is a continuation of the father's teachings in 7:1-
5 (and not a new and separate literary unit). The *for* also indicates why

the father is relating this story. He does so to reinforce how important it is that his son internalizes his teachings. Realistically, one wonders how the father could have seen and heard what he reports he saw as he looked out of his window. That what he is relating is just a story is immediately evident when the father comments that the young man he witnessed sauntering down the street *lacked judgment* (7:7b; lit., *lacked heart;* had no brains). From this comment we sense immediately what manner of story this is: devised to teach a lesson. As the story begins, the father informs us that this "brainless" young man was *walking along in the direction of her house, at twilight* [no less] . . . *as the dark of night set in* (7:9). The *her* refers to the seductive female *stranger* mentioned in 7:5, the very kind of woman from which the father hopes his teachings will protect his son. This is why he is telling this story, so that his son might realize how easy it is for this kind of thing to happen, and the importance of heeding his teachings and staying on guard.

The fatal first mistake this brainless young man made was that he swept caution to the winds and took a walk one evening in the direction of her house. This precisely is what the poem in 5:7-14 warns *sons not* to do. Stanza 2 begins: *And behold, a woman met him, in the attire of a harlot* (Prov 7:10, lit.). She is actually not a harlot (as we learn later) but dresses like one (perhaps with a veil of some sort to disguise herself; cf. Gen 38:14-15). Her true character is quickly sketched. She is *crafty* (7:10b; lit., *guarded of heart*), *loud* (uncouth, rowdy), *defiant* (7:11a), restless, seldom at home, and lurking at every street corner like a hunter watching for its prey (Fox: 245). Her actions match the portrait. Upon seeing the young man, *She took hold of him* [embraced him] *and kissed him and with a brazen* [lit., *hardened*] *face* she began speaking to him (7:13).

The seduction speech that follows is in two parts. Part 1 (7:14-17) is a buildup to the brazen invitation in part 2 (7:18-21). Both speeches are vivid examples of the *smooth words* so frequently warned against in prior poems (see 7:5; 6:24; 5:3; 2:16). Rather strangely (to our ears), she begins telling the young man of *peace offerings,* which she has just made that very day (7:14). That is why, she says, *"I came out to meet you, to seek your face and I have found you"* (7:15, lit.). We read of such *peace offerings* in the biblical law codes; they could be brought to the temple at virtually any time in gratitude for some special favor received from God (Lev 7:11-36). If the offering of an animal sacrifice were involved, the law specifies that a portion of the meat shall be offered to the priests and the remainder eaten by the worshipper on the following day at the latest (Lev 7:17). Thus, the woman's declaration that she had just now made such an offering might be her not-so-subtle way of telling this young man that a fine meal awaits him at her house—and not just that, but also a bed made up with the finest Egyptian-dyed linens, *perfumed . . . with myrrh, aloes, and cinnamon* (7:17).

In part 2 of her speech (7:18-21), this seductress boldly invites him to join her for a night of *love* (7:18), *for*, she adds reassuringly (referring somewhat contemptuously to her husband), *"The man is not in his house"* (7:19a, lit.). Nor is it likely that he will return soon, unexpectedly, she implies, for *he has gone on a long journey* (7:19b). She knows this to be the case, not because he told her so, but because she observed that when he left home, *"He took his purse filled with money"* (7:20). Therefore, she is confident that he *"will not be home till full moon"* (7:20b; the night being dark at the time, 7:9). This, she realizes, is vital information for this young man to know, for both of them are only too aware what the deadly outcome might be if this were not the case (see 6:30-35). *With persuasive words like this* [lit., *much instruction!*], *she led him astray; she seduced him with her smooth talk* [*lips*] (7:21).

The story is swiftly concluded in 7:22-23. Impulsively, *all at once* (7:22), this brainless young man followed along to her house, like an ox to the slaughter, like a deer into a noose (the meaning of the Hebrew text in this instance is uncertain), like a bird into a snare (7:22b-23a). The young man is totally clueless, oblivious of the fact that this seemingly innocuous action will lead to his downfall (7:23b). The story is a sobering one, although tinged with hyperbolic humor.

THE TEXT IN BIBLICAL CONTEXT

Faithfulness in Marriage

Four of the eight poems just discussed (5:15-23; 6:20-29, 30-35; 7:1-23) are about young men being faithful to their wives and resisting temptations to have a relationship with someone else's wife. These four poems plus three others in this section (2:16-19; 5:1-6, 7-14) constitute the most detailed teaching on this issue in the Bible. The attention it receives is undoubtedly related to a massive breakdown of values at the time the Hezekiah Edition of Proverbs was first published.

The prophets refer to this breakdown in their oracles, but none more explicitly than Hosea. In several oracles he characterizes his people as being in the grip of a "spirit of fornication" (4:12-14). His own wife was unfaithful to him (1:2-9). Even at the time he married her, she was already "a woman of adulteries," as he describes her (1:2, lit.), perhaps because she like other young women of her generation had been involved in cult prostitution. When she left him (after giving birth to three of his children), Hosea relates how Yahweh prompted him to buy her back from enslavement to another man (3:1-3). This experience became the lens through which Hosea viewed Israel's whole relation to God. As his wife had been unfaithful, so Israel at the time was in a condition of unfaithfulness to God because of its love affair with other gods and their corrupt and corrupting values. As Hosea had continued loving his wife and brought her back to himself after she had become enslaved to another, so, he prophesied, God still loved Israel and planned to restore his people and renew the covenant with them, which they had broken (Hos 2:14-23).

Several case laws in Deuteronomy also address this issue of fidelity in marriage from the perspective of contemporary customs and marriage laws. The most relevant to the just-discussed poems in Proverbs is the decree in Deuteronomy 22:28-29 that specifies what should be done with a young man who "lies with" (not "rapes," as in NIV) a woman of marriageable age to whom he was not betrothed, "and they are discovered" (Deut 22:28). The assumption is that in this instance the persons involved have consented to have sexual relations but have not adhered to the prescribed steps for forming a marital relationship—a case of "premarital sex" in today's parlance (Hugenberger: 258). In this instance the penalty prescribed by the law is that the young man shall give the father of the girl what must have been a large sum of money (22:29a), and "she shall be his wife, because he violated her" (22:29b, lit.). The law further specifies, "He can never divorce her as long as he lives" (22:29c). An older law dealing with a similar case stipulated that the young man must make the girl his wife, but that if the father refused his consent, the young man must pay a hefty fine (Exod 22:15-16).

That such drastic legal measures were being devised to deal with this problem speaks of the extent to which it had gotten out of hand. There were just too many instances of young men consorting with unmarried daughters and then refusing to take responsibility for the relational bonds they had created. Laws like this together with the teachings against adultery in Proverbs are attempts at addressing a common problem: the thoughtless, hurtful sexual activity on the part of young men in particular.

Marriage in the Bible

The marital ideals expressed in the poems of this section in Proverbs are not just those of Deuteronomy or the prophets but also (as noted in the previous TBC) those as well of the instruction manuals of ancient Egypt. These same ideals are also to be found in the law codes of ancient Mesopotamia, an example being the 18th-century BC Code of Hammurabi. In this famous law code (one of the oldest in the world) is a section of some sixty laws devoted to strengthening the institution of marriage and family (about a fourth of the total). For example, the penalty prescribed for the crime of adultery is severe: death by drowning. In other words, the teachings about marriage in this section of Proverbs are in harmony with those in many of the advanced nations and societies of the time.

Those who wrote about marriage in the book of Genesis were aware of this fact. That is why they located their account of this institution's origins in a period of history long before the first nations appeared. In effect, the text says, For viable human societies to exist like those we see scattered over the face of the earth (Gen 10), God first had to create a man and a woman capable of loving one another in a way that differs from that of animals. A "helper" needed to be found for Adam, one who would be his counterpart and companion. As the story relates it, God saw that Adam was lonely, so Eve was created. On first seeing her, the man exclaimed: "This is now bone of my bones and flesh of my flesh" (Gen 2:23). The text continues: "For this reason a man will leave his father and mother and be united to his wife, and they will become one flesh" (Gen 3:24).

This is the definitive statement about marriage in the Bible. It is echoed in the cryptic words of Malachi when he alludes to the oneness between a man and his wife and declares God's hatred for divorce (2:13-16). The poems of the Song of Solomon also affirm this bond; they characterize the love that draws a man and woman together in marriage as a "flame" of God (8:6-7). Jesus also spoke of the "one flesh" union of man and woman as something God created, and therefore it should not be torn apart (Mark 10:7-12). For Jesus too (as in the poems in Proverbs), the lust that leads to adultery is a serious matter (Matt 5:27-32). Through the letters of Paul this perspective on man-woman relations became a significant feature in teaching the Gentile churches to which he wrote. For Paul, the intimacies of marriage were no longer of primary importance, given his belief in the nearness of Christ's return (1 Cor 7:26-31). Yet he did recognize the importance of the marriage bond and prescribed a panoply of sensible rules for men and women in a married relationship, counsel consistent with teachings elsewhere in the Bible. A man should have only one wife and love her (as Christ loves the church). They should take time to enjoy the intimacies of their relationship and be faithful to one another as long as they both live (1 Cor 7; Eph 5).

In summary, marriage in the Bible is thought of as a man and a woman loving one another in body, mind, and spirit, delighting in each other, and being faithful to each other. Little is made of ceremonies or traditions or laws. Consent, however, is recognized as important: the consent of the woman, the consent of her parents (and/or brothers, Gen 34; Song 8:8-9). This is beautifully illustrated in the story told in Genesis 24 of finding a wife for Isaac. Both she and her parents (and brother, 24:50) agreed to the proposed relationship. But in the end, Isaac and the wife found for him were married when Isaac brought her into his mother's tent and loved her (24:67). A recent encyclopedic study of this subject sums up the marital views of the Bible: "Sexual union, [viewed] as a marriage covenant-ratifying act, is the decisive means by which an individual 'acknowledges' his or her spouse as a covenant partner" (Hugenberger: 343).

THE TEXT IN THE LIFE OF THE CHURCH

Marriage Today

Inherent in the marital relationship of a man and a woman is the deep desire to be together for as long as they both shall live. No one tells a man and woman that this is how they should feel. No one orders them to love each other in this way. This capacity for a deep bond of love between a man and a woman comes from their Creator, embedded in how human beings are created. Genesis 2 proclaims this truth, and Jesus's teachings affirm it. It is also the truth assumed by the teachings in Proverbs that encourage young men to rejoice in the wives of their youth and remain faithful to them.

The church faces a huge task in modern culture to make these insights and values comprehensible and relevant for old and young. A repudiation of traditional sexual values in North American culture in the 1960s has now entrenched itself in traditions, entertainment, and ways of educating youth. This revolution in values is now spreading worldwide. "United States Senator Daniel Patrick Moynihan was asked to identify the biggest change he had seen in his forty-year political career. Moynihan, a public intellectual who has served presidents of both parties with distinction, responded: 'The biggest change, in my judgment, is that the family structure has come apart all over the

North Atlantic world.'" This momentous transformation, Moynihan added, "had occurred in an historical instant. Something that was not imaginable forty years ago has happened" (Bennett: 1).

The challenge North Americans are facing is made especially difficult because even the language being used to talk about marriage has been so drastically changed. For example, the word "sex" was introduced as a loosely defined catchall term for "the instinct or attraction" that draws one sex toward another. There is no term quite like it in the Bible. Along with the catchall word "sex," a new way of classifying and viewing sexual experience (so-called) was created. "Premarital sex" was coined to replace an older word, "fornication," and "extramarital sex" was substituted for "adultery." With the increased availability of contraceptives, sexual manuals of the 1960s then began differentiating further between "fun-sex" (sex for pleasure), "love-sex" (sex between people who love each other), and "repro-sex" (sex for procreation). With this new classification in hand, the authors of the sex-manuals of the 1960s and 1970s seriously downplayed the importance of procreation. They began advocating the pursuit of "fun-sex" in all its forms (with proper safeguards), whether heterosexual or homosexual, whether alone, or with others (Miller, 1973:31-32).

In this context "love-sex" was seen more and more as a relationship that could be enjoyed without commitment to a lifelong relationship. As a consequence, increasing numbers of young people began relating sexually or living together in shorter or longer-term "love" relationships. Under these circumstances the meaning of marriage became unclear. What is marriage? What do the laws and rituals traditionally associated with marriage in Western culture signify? Are these laws and rituals even necessary? The wisdom of Proverbs and the Bible addresses these questions by affirming that "love-sex" is at the core of the marriage experience. They warn that the life-changing bond so formed is one that can be easily trivialized, trashed, and destroyed, and by males especially (see Introduction, "Why the Gender-Specific Focus"). The traditions, advice, celebrations, and laws that every culture has developed to prevent this from happening are as essential today as at any time in human history. "Fun-sex" is dehumanizing. "Love-sex" without a lifelong commitment is fraught with anxieties and suffering for those left behind without partners or—as in the case of children—without one or another or both parents. Marriage celebrates the enduring love a man and a woman experience when becoming "one flesh." It provides a way for them to express publicly their instinctive desire to be faithful to one another for as long as they both shall live, and to care for the children born of their relationship.

Proverbs 7:24—9:18

Original Poems
(Solomon Edition)

The Book of Proverbs, Part 1: Introductory Collection				
Original Prologue (Solomon Edition) 1:1-7	Supplemental Poems (Hezekiah Edition) 1:8–3:35	Original Poems (Solomon Edition) 4:1–5:14	Supplemental Poems (Hezekiah Edition) 5:15–7:23	Original Poems (Solomon Edition) 7:24–9:18

PREVIEW

In this block of poems, *wisdom* is evoked as a majestic power in the universe addressing the whole of humanity. These poems likely followed those in 4:1–5:14 in the original Solomon Edition. They open in 7:24 with the same words Solomon uses in 5:7 to address the *sons* of the royal school (lit., *Now then, sons, listen to me*). In the prior poems Solomon introduced teachings his father had taught him about wisdom's preeminence (4:7ff.) and then about dangers posed by a seductive woman (5:1-6). Here, he warns them again about the dangers posed by a seductive woman and then, in four majestic poems (8:1-11, 12-21, 22-31, 32-36), introduces *wisdom* herself (8:1-3), imagined now as addressing the whole world in her own voice. In chapter 9 these poems are followed by two poems depicting *Wisdom* and *Folly* as two women competing for the attention of the *simple* and those who *lack judgment* (9:1-6, 11-12; 9:13-18). A few strategically placed inserts (8:13, 17; 9:7-10) convey again the theological and pedagogical convictions of those who created the Hezekiah Edition of Proverbs.

OUTLINE
"Now Then, Sons, Listen to Me," 7:24-27
"Does Not Wisdom Call Out?" 8:1-11
"I, Wisdom, Dwell Together with Prudence" (with Inserts), 8:12-21
"The LORD Possessed Me at the Beginning of His Work," 8:22-31
"Now Then, Sons, Listen to Me," 8:32-36
"Wisdom Has Built Her House," 9:1-6, 11-12
"The Fear of the LORD Is the Beginning of Wisdom" (Insert), 9:7-10
"The Woman Folly Is Loud," 9:13-18

EXPLANATORY NOTES
"Now Then, Sons, Listen to Me" 7:24-27
The "voice" in 7:24 is not that of the poet in 7:1-23, where the poem begins, *My son, keep my words* (7:1), and the "voice" is that of a father speaking to his own son. On the other hand, the poem in 7:24-27 begins, *And now, sons, listen to me* (lit.; not *my sons,* as in NIV; *my* is not in the Hebrew text of 7:24). In this instance the "voice" is that of Solomon: this is exactly how he addresses the students in the royal schools in his climactic poem in 5:7-14 (lit., *And now, sons, listen to me,* 5:7; also in 4:1). The *sons* in Solomon's poems are students (cf. 5:12-13). In his poems Solomon never refers to these *sons* as "my sons," nor does he ever imply that he is their father. *Wisdom* also addresses the sons in this same way in chapter 8, where she is imagined speaking in her own voice (*"Now then, sons, listen to me,"* 8:32, lit.). Of course, *wisdom* is only the voice of Solomon in another guise.

Before the Hezekiah Edition editors inserted the poems in 5:15–7:23, the poems in 7:24–9:18 likely followed the poem in 5:7-14. Together with the block of Solomon Edition poems in 4:1–5:14, they functioned as the introduction to the book's first edition

[Solomon Edition]. The vocabulary of the first poem in this group (7:24-27) resembles that in 5:1-6, which warned that the feet of a seductive woman go down to death and her steps lead to the grave (5:4). This poem adds: A mighty throng . . . turn to her ways and stray into her paths and thus are brought down (7:25-26). The poem's closing verse pictures the house of this woman as a highway to the grave [lit., the ways of Sheol] leading down to the chambers of death (7:27; cf. 5:5). Grave and death evoke images of a shadowy existence after death beneath the earth, the very opposite of the life, vitality, and health of those who love wisdom (4:22). The fact that so many are her victims is startling (7:25). This is no small matter. These grim observations set the stage for the poems that follow, setting forth another way.

"Does Not Wisdom Call Out?" 8:1-11

This is the initial poem in a cluster of four "wisdom" poems (8:1-11, 12-21, 22-31, 32-38). It has two distinct parts. The poem begins with wisdom being introduced (8:1-3). Then, in its second part, wisdom herself speaks (8:4-11). The rhetorical questions introducing wisdom (Does not wisdom call out? Does not understanding raise her voice?) anticipate an exuberant "yes" as an answer. Truly, wisdom does call out, wherever people assemble, beside the gates leading into the city (8:2-3). That is where business is transacted and important decisions are made affecting the well-being of the metropolis. This is where the voice of wisdom is needed and where she makes her voice heard. Wisdom is conveyed as an awesome, dynamic presence, eager to be heard and especially so by those in positions of responsibility, rulers who make laws that are just and nobles who rule on earth (8:15-16). For this very reason Solomon, at the beginning of his reign, requested of God "a discerning heart to govern your people and to distinguish between right and wrong" (1 Kgs 3:9).

Solomon's decision to personify wisdom in the manner he does in this poem testifies to the huge importance that "she" came to have for him. She is more than an abstraction. She is a dynamic presence, even more so than the "wisdom" sometimes mentioned in the instruction books of Egypt. Her voice in these poems is more like that of the "queen of the universe" [Personification of "Wisdom"]. Wisdom's imagined message in 8:4-11 matches the exuberance of the one introducing her (8:1-3). When wisdom lifts up her voice and calls out, it is to the whole of humanity that she speaks (lit., all the sons of Adam, 8:4), those especially who need to be educated. These include the simple (those merely uneducated) and the foolish (8:5), meaning the boorish or rebellious [Words for Wisdom and Folly]. The insert in 9:7-9 questions the wisdom of "wisdom's" pedagogical optimism in this regard (see notes below). Is wisdom really able to accomplish this much? Wisdom herself is supremely confident that she can and that all who come to her school and choose her instruction (8:10) can gain prudence and understanding (8:5).

In glowing terms wisdom speaks of how worthy (lit., princely) her utterances are, how right and true and just are her teachings, and how detestable to her lips is wickedness (8:6-8). All the words of my mouth are just, she says, none of them is crooked or perverse (8:8). Wisdom is proud of herself and the message she brings. Those who are discerning and have knowledge will find her teachings faultless (or straightforward, 8:9). She urgently calls upon those who hear her voice to choose her instruction instead of silver, knowledge rather than choice gold, for wisdom is more previous than rubies, and nothing you desire can compare with her (8:10-11). The idealism of this poem is both invigorating and unsettling. In the schools of Solomon, wisdom truly was supreme, and getting it was of first and foremost importance, just as the watchword states (4:7; Solomon Edition). The supplements and inserts of the Hezekiah Edition were seeking to temper precisely this exuberant faith in "wisdom" without rejecting it.

"I, Wisdom, Dwell Together with Prudence" (with Inserts) 8:12-21

This second of Solomon's wisdom poems has ten verses in two equal parts (8:12-16, 17-21). However, verses 8:13 and 19 appear to be insertions, so that originally it had just eight verses in two equal parts (like those in 4:20-27; 5:7-14). In the original poem wisdom first proudly identifies herself (I, wisdom . . .; 8:12), then lists a number of her attributes in the enthusiastic manner exhibited in the initial poem of this group. Among these attributes are counsel and sound judgment, understanding and power (8:14), qualities similar to those "the spirit of Yahweh" bestows on the ideal Judean king (Isa 11:2, lit.). Here, however, the attributes are ascribed to personified wisdom and cited to justify her claim: "By me kings reign and rulers make laws that are just; by me princes govern and all nobles who rule on earth [lit., nobles, even all judges on earth]" (8:16). Thus, to wisdom, rather than to God, is ascribed not just the insight and clarity for making wise laws and administering them properly, but also the power to do so (8:14). We sense again how in the schools of Solomon wisdom was visualized as a being or power in her own right—in short, queen of the universe.

In the poem's second part (8:17-21) *wisdom* holds out the promise, that those who *love* her she will *love*, and those who *seek* her will find her (8:17). From this relationship (because she walks *in the way of righteousness, along the paths of justice*; 8:20) will flow *riches and honor, enduring wealth and prosperity* (8:18), *bestowing wealth on those who love me and making their treasuries full* (8:21; compare the somewhat different picture of wisdom's benefits in 3:13-18). Right at this point wisdom's self-assertions become especially vulnerable to being considered as laying claim to a role in the universe that rivals that of God. To counteract this impression, the book's Hezekiah editors inserted a reminder that *to fear the LORD is to hate evil* (8:13a), and also that Yahweh hates *pride and arrogance, evil behavior and perverse speech* (8:13b; cf. 6:16-19). These insertions disrupt the flow of the poem and the spell cast by the poem's imagery. They serve as a reminder to the book's reader that *wisdom* after all is not really a cosmic power or deity. That honor belongs to Yahweh. By contrast, wisdom is just metaphor (cf. 3:19-20), just a construct of the poetic imagination of Solomon, who authored this poem. Many think 8:19 is an insertion as well, for its point that the *fruit* of wisdom is *better than fine gold* takes issue with the assertion made in the surrounding verses that wisdom's chief reward is *enduring wealth and prosperity* (8:18). Wisdom's fruit is far better than gold or *choice silver* (8:19).

"The LORD Possessed Me at the Beginning of His Work" 8:22-31

This is the only poem in the Solomon Edition that explains the relationship between *wisdom* and *Yahweh* (the God of Israel). In the Solomon Edition poems of the Introductory Collection to this point (4:1–5:14; 7:24–8:21), Yahweh is not mentioned even once (the only exception being 8:13, which most regard as an insert). The same is true of the three-chapter collection of the poems of Solomon added in Proverbs 25-27; there too Yahweh goes unmentioned, with one exception (25:22). Here too Yahweh is only mentioned once—at the start of the poem—as a silent background figure to the story wisdom tells about herself and her origins before the world was created (8:22). Such accounts of how the world was created were commonplace in the cultures of the time. They relate how the different gods came into existence. Genesis 1 is the foremost example in the Bible of a narrative of this type, telling of the world's origins, but it differs from the others in that nothing is said about the origins of God. Instead, God is simply there at the beginning and creates the world through his word.

Against this background, wisdom's opening assertion in 8:22 that she was *possessed* (or *gotten*) by Yahweh (or as some translate, *created by him*) *at the beginning of his work* (lit., *his way*) points to her preeminent place in the universe. She was with God from the beginning, before anything else was created that now exists. Her preeminent place in the universe is further emphasized by what *wisdom* relates in the two three-verse stanzas that follow (in 6:24-26, 27-29). In the first three-verse stanza (6:24-26) wisdom simply reinforces the point made in 8:22 that she was *appointed* (or *fashioned*) by Yahweh *from eternity, from the beginning, before the world began*. To help her audience visualize this, she enumerates the stages in which the world was actually created (the oceans, the gushing springs, the mountains and hills, dry land and fields) and proclaims that long *before* each one of these was created, she had already been born (lit., *brought forth; 8:24-25*).

This description serves as a prelude for the point wisdom then makes in the second three-verse stanza (8:27-29). What is stressed here is that, having been born (or brought forth) so much earlier, she was actually *there* when *the heavens* were being set in place (8:27) and when the horizon was being marked out. And she was there too when everything else happened that happened: when *clouds* were formed, and boundaries set for the *waters* under and around the earth, and earth's *foundations* were laid (8:28-29). In other words, throughout the entire creation process, wisdom proclaims, she was *there*—and she alone was there, for only she had been created or "gotten" prior to everything else.

The poem's climactic lines in 8:30-31 make this very same point. Some translate the opening line of this final stanza (as does NIV): *Then I was the master craftsman* [*'āmôn*] *at his side* (8:30a). However, this would suggest that *wisdom* was the *master craftsman* who created the world rather than *Yahweh*, as the poem's preceding verses indicate. Others wonder, therefore, whether *master craftsman* is the correct translation of the unusual term *'āmôn* used here. A commonplace interpretation is that the Hebrew word *'āmôn* means "nursling," but the word is masculine, and this translation hardly suits the context (Clifford: 100). In these poems wisdom is not a nursling but a magisterial, queenlike figure. The translation *craftsman* or *artisan* seems preferable. It is attested in the Greek Septuagint [*Hebrew and Greek Texts*] and used with this meaning in Song of Solomon 7:1. A compelling solution to this much-discussed issue may lie in simply adhering to the Hebrew word order when translating this line (Whybray, 1994). In Hebrew the text reads, *"Then I* [*wisdom*] *was with him [the] master craftsman"* (Prov 8:30a). *Wisdom* is not saying that she was herself the *master craftsman* but that she was *with him, the master craftsman.* The point she is making simply sums up what she had said previously about being *with him* (Yahweh) all the while he was creating the world.

This too is what *wisdom*'s final words convey as she testifies to the joy she felt in being with Yahweh as he created the universe. *"I was filled with delight day after day* [lit., *day, day,* referring to the days of creation], *rejoicing always in his presence, rejoicing in his whole* [lit., *habitable] world and delighting in mankind"* (8:30-31). Wisdom rejoices in all things pertaining to the inhabited world, and especially her delight is in *mankind* (lit., *the sons of Adam*). What then in summary does this poem convey about wisdom's relation to Yahweh? Yahweh is the Creator, but wisdom is his cosmic companion, fully knowledgeable of all that God has created by virtue of being there at the very beginning of his *work* (8:22-30). Moreover, wisdom is rejoicing in the inhabited earth and taking special delight in human beings (8:31).

In this poem Yahweh himself is silent and does not speak. It is through *wisdom* that his deeds are made known. In the royal schools of Solomon, Yahweh was honored as Creator, but it was through *wisdom* that the mysteries of creation were revealed. The counterpart was the king's role in mediating wisdom to his people. The way these polarities interlock is spelled out in the leadoff saying of the poems of Solomon added by the men of Hezekiah in chapters 25-27: *It is the glory of God to conceal a matter; to search out a matter is the glory of kings* (25:2). In other words, while God's glory is manifest in the silent mystery of the universe, the glory of kings is manifest in their capacity to penetrate this mystery (cf. 25:3). In this poem Solomon gives voice to his exuberant belief in the power of wisdom to decipher the mysteries of the created world. Scholars have searched far and wide for a background against which to explain this dramatic visualization of *wisdom*'s place in the universe, but so far without success. It may have originated with the imagination of Solomon himself *[Personification of "Wisdom"].*

"Now Then, Sons, Listen to Me" 8:32-36

This is the fourth poem in which *wisdom* addresses the students of the royal schools, but it is also closely connected to the two related poems that follow (9:1-6, 13-18). Together with them it brings the introductory section of the Solomon Edition of Proverbs to a climactic close. A fifth poem in this collage (9:7-12) was inserted at the time the Hezekiah Edition was created.

This one (8:32-36) begins with a summons to the *sons*, urging them a final time to *listen* (8:32a). This summons is exactly like those in 4:1; 5:7; and 7:24, only now it is *wisdom* herself who issues it (yet Solomon is still speaking, since he wrote the poem). Those addressed are, once again, not *my sons* (NIV) but simply *sons* (students in the royal schools; cf. 5:13). The poem has five verses in three distinct parts: a two-verse invitation to study at wisdom's school (8:32-33) and a one-verse exclamatory pronouncement of blessing upon those who do so (8:34). These are followed by a two-verse rationale for this pronouncement (8:35-36). The pronouncement of blessing (8:34) is thus at the poem's center. It is directed to the *man* (*'ādām*) who not only *listens* to wisdom, but also watches daily *at her doors.* For the first time a physical locale is mentioned—there is a place where *wisdom* holds forth, and *blessed* (*'ašhrê; happy,* 3:18) is the *man* who comes to that place *daily* (*yôm yôm, day after day*), watching at wisdom's *doors* (NRSV: *gates*) and waiting at her *doorways.* The place referred to is more fully described in the next poem (see 9:1).

This poem concludes with several reasons why those who come to this place to study are happy (8:35-36). Through their studies the *sons* will find *wisdom* and *life* and escape the harm that those who fail to find *wisdom* do to themselves (8:35a, 36; cf. 4:10-19, 20-27). "Personified Wisdom has a kerygma [message]; she announces . . . 'life.' The teaching of the wise is 'a fountain of life' (13:14); . . . The symbols of fountain and tree of life are frequent: 10:11; 16:22; 3:18; 11:30; 13:12. Concretely 'life' means riches and honor (22:4), a good name (10:7; 22:1), a long existence of many years (3:16; 28:16)" (Murphy: 2002:29). A third reason given for the happiness of those who study wisdom is unique to this poem: the person who listens to and finds wisdom *receives favor from the LORD* (8:35b). In other words, Yahweh, who possessed (or created) wisdom *at the beginning of his work* (8:22) and created the universe, bestows *favor* on those who watch daily at wisdom's doors.

"Wisdom Has Built Her House" 9:1-6, 11-12

This is an eight-verse poem with two equal parts (9:1-4, 5-6, 11-12). The insertion in 9:7-10 "interrupts Wisdom's speech and is inappropriately interposed between the injunction in v 6 and its natural sequel in v 11, which gives the reason (introduced by causal *kî*) for the injunction" (Fox: 306). This and the final poem (7:13-18) are allegorical twins: in the first of them *Wisdom* is portrayed as inviting the *simple* to her home for a meal; in the second *Folly* does the same. The imagery resonates with life in a bustling city (9:3, 14).

Folly is uncouth and *loud*—her house is that of a prostitute (see below). The house of *Wisdom* was also familiar to the book's first readers. That it had seven pillars means it was commodious and welcoming. Ordinary Israelite houses had four pillars to support a roof that partially covered the inner court, where family and friends gathered for meals and other social events, but larger houses had six or seven such pillars (Lang: 90-93).

The substantial meal *Wisdom* is said to have prepared (meat and wine on a carefully set table, 9:2) is symbolic of the rich banquet of learning that awaits those who respond to wisdom's invitation (9:3, 5; cf. Isa 55:1-3). *Wisdom* and *Folly* both issue their invitations from *the highest point in the city* (9:3b, 14b), but Folly calls out to *those who* chance to *pass by* (9:15), while Wisdom sends her maids (emissaries) in search of anyone who might benefit from her banquet. The invitation conveyed on Wisdom's behalf (9:5-6, 11-12) is surprisingly indiscriminate and inclusive. To the *simple* (those who are inexperienced and uneducated) she says, *"Come in here* [lit., *turn in*]," but to those who *lack judgment* (lit., *lack heart*, 9:4), she is equally welcoming, if not even more so. To them she says, *"Come, eat my food* [lit., *my bread*] *and drink the wine I have mixed"* (9:5). Both are invited: *"Leave your simple ways and you will live; walk in the way of understanding"* (9:6). The poem concludes with the promise that *through me* [wisdom] *your days will be many* (9:11). The concluding verse clarifies what this promise means: *"If you are wise, you are wise for yourself; if you scorn* [or mock] *you alone shall bear it"* (9:12, lit.). The decision to acquire (or refuse to acquire) an education in wisdom has profound consequences for the person making this choice.

In this poem the symbolism may reflect the realities of the royal schools of the time. Wisdom's *house* may be a school building of some sort. Students might actually have assembled in commodious seven-pillared houses. Meals too may have been part of the instructional experience. While the focus was on the education of *sons*, maids too may have played a role in preparing the meal and announcing when it was ready. While serving it, they would be listening, laughing, and learning, as recitations and discussions got underway. Fox cites as parallels ancient Greek "symposia" (or banquets), which "were the setting for displays of poetry, wisdom, and erudition." "Accepting Wisdom's invitation," he comments, "does not mean a life of grim self-denial. . . . On the contrary a life of wisdom is blessed by satisfaction and happiness" (Fox: 306).

"The Fear of the LORD Is the Beginning of Wisdom" (Insert) 9:7-10

This four-verse insert is best understood as a final supplement to the introductory section of the book, an addition from the hand of those who created the Hezekiah Edition (see Preview). Its opening three lines (9:7-8a) raise questions about the exuberant inclusiveness of wisdom's invitation in 9:4-6 (and 8:5). There the invitation to become educated is extended to everyone, even those who *lack heart* (lit.; who are totally without *judgment* or common sense). Here, however, attention is called to two groups whom it is futile, even dangerous, to try to educate (or *correct*): *a mocker* and *a wicked man* (9:7). Correcting a *mocker* will only bring *insult*; rebuking a *wicked man* could incur physical harm (*abuse*). The next three lines draw a sharp contrast between *a mocker* and one who is *wise* (9:8b-9). A similar contrast is drawn at the conclusion of the Hezekiah Edition supplement in 1:7–3:35. There it is said that Yahweh *mocks proud mockers but gives grace to the humble* (3:34). Two of Agur's poems in 30:11-14 and 30:17 portray persons of this type as *pure in their own eyes,* and hence unable to see that they *are not cleansed of their filth* (30:12; cf. 6:12-15, 16-19). The mockers and wicked lack the humility necessary for self-criticism; their *eyes are ever so haughty* (30:13; 6:17). They have an *eye that mocks a father, that scorns obedience to a mother* (30:17). That is why trying to educate them is so utterly impossible.

The *wise* are just the opposite. Educating them can lead to an outpouring of affection (*he will love you*) and growth in wisdom (9:8-9). The *wise* person and the *righteous* are equated; the result of instructing him is that *he will add to his learning* (9:9b; the desired outcome for the Hezekiah Edition of this book as stated in the insert in 1:5). What he will add to his learning is summarized in the following verse: *"The fear of the LORD is the beginning of wisdom, and knowledge of the Holy One is understanding"* (9:10; cf. 1:7). One of the chief purposes of this final insert is to state again (in a new and fuller way) the truth set forth in the Hezekiah Edition watchword in 1:7.

In this new version of the watchword, line 1 states unequivocally that *the fear of the LORD is the beginning* [tĕḥillat; "essential prerequisite," Cohen] *of wisdom*. Then line 2 clarifies the point by adding: *and knowledge of the Holy One* [qĕdōšîm, a plural form meaning *most Holy One*] *is understanding* (9:10). This second line corresponds exactly to the testimony of Agur in his oracle in 30:2-6: *"I have not learned wisdom, but knowledge of the Holy One [qĕdōšîm, most Holy One] I know"* (30:3, lit.). This is the only other text in Proverbs where God is referred to as *the most Holy One* (otherwise in the Bible, only Hos 11:12). In his *oracle* Agur urges his colleagues not to add to or change *the words of God* (30:5-6), referring to the teachings revealed to Moses (see notes). One of the chief purposes of the Hezekiah Edition of Proverbs was to convey this truth: *Knowledge of the most Holy One* [Yahweh] *is understanding* and an essential starting point for acquiring wisdom of the kind represented in Solomon's proverbs *[Distinctive Approach]*.

"The Woman Folly Is Loud" 9:13-18

In the Solomon Edition of Proverbs (before the insertion of the poem in 9:7-10), this final six-verse poem followed directly on the one in 9:1-6, 11-12. It forms a counterpart to the portrait of Wisdom in 9:1-6. In it too *Folly* is personified. She too, in her own voice, issues an invitation to her house, directed to the same individuals (the *simple* and those who *lack judgment*) that Wisdom invites to her house (cf. 9:4, 16). The poem dramatizes the choices confronting young people as they start out in life. At first it might seem that the choice is a fairly easy one. The poet depicts Folly as *loud* (boisterous, uncouth, foulmouthed), *undisciplined* (simplistic) and *without knowledge* (lit., *knows not what*). *She sits* [lazily, seductively] *at the door of her house on a seat at the highest point of the city,* brazenly inviting passersby to come into her house. She is obviously a prostitute. So in what sense is her invitation at all competitive with that of Wisdom?

The poet knows the answer: there is an allure to that which is *stolen,* an excitement and attraction to *food eaten in secret* (prohibited pleasures, which for that reason must be enjoyed in secret). The poem ends with an allusion to a previously expressed warning to those who foolishly choose to enter her house: *Her house is a highway to the grave* (šĕ'ôl, 7:27). Here the poem warns: *But little do they know that the dead are there, that her guests are in the depths of the grave* (šĕ'ôl, 9:18). The poems in 7:24-27 and 9:13-18 frame this final set of Solomon Edition poems. In this edition of Proverbs, consorting with a licentious woman of the kind alluded to had come to symbolize all that was contrary to the way of wisdom.

THE TEXT IN BIBLICAL CONTEXT

Wisdom in Proverbs in Biblical Tradition (Revisited)

Wisdom in Proverbs

It is not true to say that the Solomon Edition poems were secular; they were suffused with a religious vision. At the core of that vision was *wisdom*, thought of as a dynamic presence with God from time immemorial, and available to all as a loving personal presence. Taken alone (without the Hezekiah Edition supplements and insertions), the Solomon Edition poems in Proverbs 8 and 9 are without parallel in the Bible *[Solomon Edition]*. They ascribe to wisdom a preeminence that is attributed elsewhere in the Bible to the laws of God. Here (in Prov 8) acquiring prudence and wisdom is the way one finds life and avoids death (8:35-36). Elsewhere (as in Deuteronomy) it is obedience to the words and laws of God that determines whether individuals or nations live or die (Deut 28; 30:15-20).

The *men of Hezekiah* were aware of these parallels and the conundrum they posed. Their answer was to create a book in which the quest for wisdom would still be paramount (as in the Solomon Edition) but in which wisdom would be clearly understood as an attribute of God, not as an autonomous power. It is by *Yahweh's* wisdom that the universe was created (cf. 3:19-20). *Wisdom* is that which comes forth from the mouth of God (2:6). *The fear of the LORD teaches a man wisdom* (15:33). There therefore is no categorical difference between the wisdom poems of the Solomon Edition of Proverbs and the words of God revealed through Moses in Deuteronomy. The latter too is wisdom (cf. Deut 4:6-8). Both the *words* of God and the *proverbs* of Solomon are manifestations of wisdom in the sense that both teach a person how to live wisely. Their only difference is that one is wisdom born of the face-to-face intimacy between Moses and God (Deut 34:10), and the other is a product of reflections within the human heart *["Heart"]*.

Wisdom in Biblical Tradition

However, the synthesis thus achieved between these two manifestations of wisdom is not spelled out in so many words. It emerges only through reflecting on the way the Hezekiah Edition supplemental poems intersect and interact with the older Solomon Edition poems into which they have been inserted. This provocative strategy on the part of the Hezekiah Edition editors helps to explain why a split occurred in how the wisdom theology of the book was subsequently understood *[Wisdom in Proverbs]*. In one fork of that split, the Hezekiah Edition watchword (*The fear of the LORD is the beginning of wisdom*) was taken out of its original context and viewed as not just the *beginning* of wisdom (as in Proverbs) but as the sole source of wisdom. In this view, wisdom is to be found *only* in "the precepts of the LORD" revealed in the Torah of Moses (Ps 111:10; Baruch 3:9–4:4).

There is, however, another fork or way in which the wisdom of Proverbs was understood and developed. In the book of Job, a man in the land of Uz is portrayed as living an exemplary life even though, being a foreigner, he presumably does not know about the laws of Moses. Nevertheless, Job believes in God, eschews images of God, and lives in a chaste, compassionate, intelligent way (Job 31). In this sense he typifies the exemplary man of wisdom as portrayed in the book of Proverbs. He was "the greatest man among all the people of the East" (Job 1:3). He is also presented as embroiled in a controversy with friends over why he suffered as he did; this struggle is reflective of the thoughtful, hardheaded approach to questions of this kind advocated in Proverbs. The more doctrinaire approach of Job's "friends" is roundly questioned and rejected in the book's epilogue (Job 42:7-8). Ecclesiastes is another book of this kind. It too reflects and perpetuates the outlook of Proverbs in its astute observations about what goes on under the sun, and even in its skepticism toward the pretensions of "the wise" who think they can know more than is humanly possible. Agur son of Jakeh has similar reservations about the intellectual pretensions of the two individuals to whom he addresses his *oracle* (cf. Prov 30:2-6).

The Wisdom of Solomon

It is, however, in a late first century BC writing known as the Wisdom of Solomon (a book of the Apocrypha), that the wisdom theology of Proverbs was most fully embraced and developed. Its unknown author was likely a resident of Alexandria, Egypt, at a time when the Jews living there (and elsewhere) were being hard pressed to come to terms with the philosophy and culture of Greece. Addressed to the "rulers on earth" (Wis 1:1, 6:1, NJB), the book challenges them to strive above everything else for that wisdom that "in every generation . . . passes into holy souls and makes them friends of God" (7:27, NRSV). Unlike those who viewed wisdom as only among those who fear the LORD, the book's author envisions God's wisdom as pervasive everywhere on earth. Wisdom is "a breath of the power of God, and a pure emanation of the glory of the Almighty" (7:25, NRSV). "She is a reflection of eternal light, a spotless mirror of the working of God, and an image of his goodness" (7:26, NRSV). "She reaches mightily from one end of the earth to the other, and she orders all things well" (8:1, NRSV). Being one with God (9:1-2), wisdom "knows your [God's] works, . . . what is pleasing in your eyes and what agrees with your commandments" (Wis 9:9, NJB). "In these verses the writer reaches for the most delicate terms he can find to indicate the extraordinary intimacy of Wisdom with God" (Murphy, 2003:23).

In chapter 10 the author of Wisdom of Solomon describes how God's wisdom was at work in human history from "the first-formed father of the world" (10:1, NRSV) on through to the time of Moses. In other words, not just Moses was filled with wisdom, but Adam and Noah and the first ancestors of Israel. In fact, it is only because human beings had wisdom that the human race surmounted obstacles and dangers and survived on the path that leads to "the kingdom of God" (10:10, NRSV). Speaking as though he were Solomon, the author writes that it was God in his wisdom who "gave me sure knowledge of what exists, to understand the structure of the world and the action of the elements, the beginning, end and middle of the times, . . . the natures of animals and the instincts of wild beasts, the powers of spirits and human mental processes, the varieties of plants and the medical properties of roots. And now I understand everything, hidden or visible, for Wisdom, the designer of all things, has instructed me" (Wis 7:17-21, NJB).

It is this vision of God's "Wisdom" as the pervasive and dynamic source of the coming of God's kingdom in past, present, and future that forms the linguistic and conceptual background of Jesus as teacher of wisdom in Matthew's Gospel. It also lies behind the description of Jesus in John's Gospel as the incarnate "Word" that "enlightens everyone" and "was coming into the world" (John 1:9, NRSV). It is the background for the admonition in James that any one who lacks wisdom should simply turn to God "who gives generously to all without finding fault" (1:5).

THE TEXT IN THE LIFE OF THE CHURCH

Wisdom in Proverbs in the Church Today (Revisited)

In every age the church needs to find ways of instilling in its youth a deep sense of their place in the world. Today too it is not enough for young people to know about this or that subject or issue. They need a way of seeing the totality of life in a way that makes sense and matches their own deepest sensibilities, needs, and aspirations. The book of Proverbs can be of help in this regard if we recognize afresh not just what its teachings are in specifics but what it has to say about wisdom generally. There is, strangely enough, an impediment in this regard within traditional Christian thinking. It is the tendency to draw too sharp a distinction between "revelation theology" and what some have called "natural theology" (insights acquired through reflection).

Veteran biblical scholar Roland Murphy's views on this issue have already been mentioned (see Introduction, "The Book of Proverbs in the Life of the Church") but merit being revisited. As his life drew to a close, Murphy was preoccupied with the dismissive attitudes of biblical scholars themselves toward the wisdom literature of the Bible. "The touchstone for [approaching] biblical revelation and theology," he wrote, "has long been the acts of God in Israel's history" (Murphy, 2002:123). Murphy came to believe that this emphasis was part of the problem. Those dismissive of the Bible's wisdom literature thought of it as a lesser form of "natural theology." Murphy had a growing conviction that this way of looking at the "wisdom experience" (as he called it) is a mistake that does violence to the Bible itself. In the Bible, he wrote, there is no such artificial distinction between natural and revealed theologies. The "wisdom experience" itself is a faith experience. "The shaping of Israel's views of the world, and of the activity of God behind and in it, was done in an ambience of faith, and was characterized by trust and reliance upon God." Far from being peripheral to biblical revelation, "the wisdom experience" exemplifies what revelation is all about (Murphy, 2002:125).

Murphy's reflections signal that a serious rethinking of these issues is now occurring. It is based on renewed attention to the unique witness of the Bible's wisdom literature to a wise and trustworthy God, who affirms the search for wisdom as the highest and noblest and most urgently essential thing human beings and their societies can do. The intuition that the "wisdom experience" as conveyed in Proverbs might be of special relevance to the youth of our time was recently confirmed for me in a small but personal way. A seventeen-year-old granddaughter who had just been baptized answered my question as to what this experience had meant to her by reciting Proverbs 3:5: *Trust in the LORD with all your heart and lean not on your own understanding; in all your ways acknowledge him, and he will direct your paths.* It was her favorite verse, she said. She is currently enrolled at a Canadian university, studying to become a teacher. It is gratifying to observe how her faith in God is proving to be a guiding light as she grows in body, mind, and spirit.

The Possibilities and Limits of Wisdom

In the Solomon Edition poems, *wisdom* speaks to the whole world in an exuberant voice. She proclaims the virtues of knowledge and discernment and is supremely confident in her ability to educate all who choose to come to her house day after day. In all these respects she personifies the confidence in the human capacity to acquire wisdom that was a hallmark of what some have called the "Solomonic Enlightenment" (von Rad, 1972:48-56). This was a period in Judean history of burgeoning wealth, international prestige, and power.

As suggested above, certain inserts in the Solomon Edition poems in Proverbs 8 and 9 were meant to dampen and modify somewhat these exuberant pedagogical ideals and expectations. These inserts (in 8:13, 19; 9:7-10) reflect the views of the *men of Hezekiah* (25:1), who lived two centuries later in quite different circumstances. In their time the armies of Assyria had just invaded the northern kingdom, Israel, and were threatening to invade Judah as well. There were religious, moral, and political threats that must have seemed insurmountable. Hezekiah's men were for good reasons chastened by the realization that wisdom alone had not and could not save their nation. Yet they did not reject the notion that wisdom even then was the supreme attribute needed. However, there had to be a larger concept of what wisdom is and how to acquire it. Their belief was that the best of human wisdom is not enough. We need to acknowledge the Creator God and look to him to direct our paths. That is why the Hezekiah editors were again insistent on inserting something into this introductory section of their edition of Proverbs, right at the end of Solomon's majestic poem celebrating the cosmic importance of wisdom. They added their conviction that *the fear of the LORD is the beginning of wisdom, and knowledge of the Holy One is understanding* (9:10).

In John Goldingay's *Old Testament Theology* is a paragraph that makes a similar point in the context of the modern scientific quest for an understanding of the world's origins: "In principle Christians have no vested interest in any particular scientific theory about the world's origins." Yet, he adds, the scientific theories of our time and culture often do have "theological implications that a biblical account of creation does confront. One is the idea that the world came into being by a chance process." By contrast, he comments, "Proverbs sees it [how the world came into being] as a thoughtful one." It is "the nature of a wisdom book such as Proverbs," he continues, "to see God working behind empirical processes, so that its convictions about a purposefulness visible in creation emerge from looking at creation rather than bringing a theory to it."

Goldingay sums up his reflections as follows: The book of Proverbs "starts from the conviction that it is obvious that someone designed the world. We might reckon that the world is obviously a majestic and precious place and therefore that its creator is a great artist. Proverbs might also imply the converse argument, that the creator is a great artist, and therefore the creation demands, for example, our reverence" (Goldingay: 49). In these comments Goldingay comes close to the thoughts of those who created the Hezekiah Edition of Proverbs; yet for them it was not the "creation" that evokes "reverence" but the Creator. They were also wise enough to know that the truth of this discernment requires a certain attitude (or leap of faith) that cannot be taught to everyone (9:7-10).

Proverbs 8:22-31 and Doctrinal Controversy over the Centuries

In his commentary on Proverbs, Raymond C. van Leeuwen writes that the poem in Proverbs 8:22-31, among other things, "is also significant for the role it played in doctrinal controversy over the centuries." The controversy he is referring to is one that began in the fourth century AD, with debates between "orthodox" and Arian Christians. "Using Proverbs 8:22-31," van Leeuwen states, "the Arian party argued that Christ (as Wisdom) was the first creation of God, the unique creature before all other creatures. But as created, the Arians reasoned, Christ was not God in the same sense as the Father was God."

On the other hand, van Leeuwen continues, "The orthodox party, which defined subsequent Christian dogma through the centuries, preferred to take the verb in Proverbs 8:22a as 'possessed,'" following the ancient Greek LXX version. In addition, "the orthodox took the verb ['possessed'] as meaning 'to beget,'" so in their opinion "Christ was not created, but, as in the Nicene Creed of [AD] 351, eternally 'begotten, not made.' Again, conceding the possibility that the verb meant 'to create,' Athanasius took pains to say that what was created was not Christ per se, but his position as the 'first of God's works/ways'" (R. Van Leeuwen: 98-99).

Van Leeuwen concludes by noting that "Christian tradition has thus in various ways identified Wisdom in Proverbs 8 and Christ as one." And yet, he writes, "a better move, perhaps, would be to understand Christ as the hidden reality underlying and fulfilling the cosmic and personal imagery of Wisdom in Proverbs 8, without positing a direct one-to-one correspondence in all particulars" (R. Van Leeuwen: 99).

Part 2

The Main Collection
(Themes)

Part 2 is organized thematically. To find a specific proverb by chapter and verse, see chart on pages 114-15.

Proverbs 10:1—22:16

Design of the Hezekiah Edition of Proverbs			Later Additions
Part 1 Introductory Collection 1:1–9:18 (256 verses)	Part 2 The Main Collection 10:1–22:16 (375 verses)	Part 3 Supplemental Collections 22:17–30:33 (253 verses)	31:1-31

OVERVIEW

This exceptionally large anthology of short sayings, situated right in the middle of the Hezekiah Edition of Proverbs, is marked out by a heading in 10:1a and another right after its end (22:17), introducing the first of the Supplemental Collections. All of the collection's 375 poems (with one exception, 19:7) are just two lines long, the second line supplementing the first in a variety of ways. Their primary effect is to stimulate reflection on various aspects and issues of daily life. Some are more profound than others, but all are crafted with care and worth thinking about. Though in some respects these poems are similar to proverbs (or folk sayings) in other cultures, they are also quite unique. They are compositions, not popular aphorisms: they owe their existence to "thoughts" or observations creatively expressed in a prescribed literary form, much as the process is described in Proverbs 24:30-34 *[Genre Issues]*.

Authors and Editors

There is no reason to doubt Solomon had a hand in composing many of the poems in this section (10:1), for according to 1 Kings he was a prolific poet (4:32) surrounded by an entourage who benefited from his wisdom (10:8). In the culture of the time there was a precedent for a king like Solomon to create a resource for educating young men for civil service (see Introduction, "A Manual for Educating Young Men"). The sayings of this particular collection occasionally refer to the *wise* (or sages); their teachings are said to be a *fountain of life* (13:14a; see also 10:13-14; 13:20; 14:7). This group too (possibly scribes or teachers; cf. Jer 18:18) must have had a hand in the collection's creation. As time went by and new copies were needed, one imagines that poems might have been added or deleted. It seems certain that a major enlargement of the collection occurred when the *men of Hezekiah* prepared their edition of Proverbs (25:1). It is likely they who decided it should have 375 proverbs (no more, no less), the equivalent of the numerical sum of the consonants of Solomon's name (see Introduction, "Purpose and Design of the Hezekiah Edition").

Organization

Many have noted that the collection has two rather distinct sections. In chapters 10-15 the parallel lines of the two-line poems are mostly antithetical (the second line states the opposite or antithesis to the point made in the first line), though this is not the case in 16:1–22:16. Also, where these two sections are joined, in 14:26–16:15, there appears to be a "suture" of sorts. This is indicated by duplications of proverbs that occur right here (e.g., 15:20 and 10:1; 14:27 and 13:14), as well as the more frequent use of the divine name and references to kings (Murphy, 1981:64).

Otherwise, students of this main section of the book are baffled by the seemingly random way the two-line poems are arranged. Why are they so jumbled? How were they to be studied? My own still largely untested hypothesis is that the poems are arranged for study in groups of five, the number of fingers on a hand. Fingers played a role in memorization, it seems, as indicated in a poem in the introductory part of the book, where a father asks his *son* to *bind* his words on his *fingers* and write them on *the tablet* of his *heart* (7:3). The five fingers of the right or left hand afforded a way to keep track of the father's teachings. This may be why the Decalogue consists of two sets of five precepts (one precept for each of the ten fingers). In short, the poems in this main collection may have been arranged to be pondered, discussed, and memorized five proverbs at a time. That would explain why the themes vary from poem to poem; thus each study session would offer an interesting mix of subjects. In this way too students were afforded an opportunity to reflect on how different facets of life are interrelated.

As previously noted (see Introduction, "Purpose and Design of the Hezekiah Edition"), when the 375 two-line poems of this section are divided into sets of five poems each, the result is 75 sets of five-poem units. When in turn these 75 sets are divided by two, the result is 37 sets twice, plus one additional five-poem set. If the collection is divided into two equal parts, then 37 five-poem sets are in part 1 and 37 in part 2, with an additional five-poem unit somewhere else. That additional unit, I conjecture, is right in the middle of the two parts. Since that five-poem set is right in the middle of the Main Collection, it is also right in the middle of the Hezekiah Edition as a whole, given the fact that its Introductory and Supplemental Collections are virtually equal in size. This design of the Hezekiah Edition may be diagrammed as follows:

Introductory Collection (256 verses)	The Main Collection (375 verses) 10:1-22:16			Supplemental Collections (253 verses)
1:1–9:18	37 units of five 10:1–16:1	**Center five 16:2-6**	37 units of five 16:7–22:16	22:17–30:33

As explained, this symmetrical design may be related to the fact that scrolls, when stored, were rolled up from both ends. Thus the poems in the scroll's middle columns would be seen first, each time it was opened. Possibly the editors gave special thought to these poems. This central cluster of five poems is the only one in which the divine name (Yahweh) appears in each poem. From their contents one gains the impression that these poems express some of the core theological or philosophical convictions of the Hezekiah Edition editors [Middle Poems].

Methods of Study: Thematic Approach

The poems of this Main Collection might be profitably studied just this way: five poems at a time in the present arrangement. However, to do so would require considerable time and patience. A thematic approach seems intuitively more compatible with contemporary needs and sensibilities. In determining what themes there are in this collage of 375 poems, and in what order to discuss them, the prior analysis of the composition and themes in the book's Introductory Collection (chapters 1-9) has proved helpful. There, blocks of Solomon Edition poems, mostly focused on the supreme worth of wisdom, are supplemented with Hezekiah Edition poems, many of which extol the importance of revering and trusting God. A similar contrast is apparent in the poems of the Main Collection. This contrast is especially striking in a poem stating that *the teaching of the wise is a fountain of life, turning a man from the snares of death* (13:14), followed by another poem that declares, *The fear of the LORD is a fountain of life, turning a man from the snares of death* (14:27). These two sayings are virtually identical except that in the first it is *the teaching of the wise that is a fountain of life*, and in the other it is *the fear of the LORD*.

From the Introductory Collection of the Hezekiah Edition of Proverbs, we know that the *men of Hezekiah* believed that both of these maxims were true. My assumption, however, is that most of the poems reflecting *the teaching of the wise* were part of the Solomon Edition. Then poems emphasizing how important it is to *fear Yahweh* and be upright (adhere to his laws) were added when the Hezekiah Edition was created. Of course, in this section of the book one cannot be certain about what was in each edition. The most that can be said is that both *the teaching of the wise* and teaching associated with *the fear of Yahweh* were combined as "subjects" in the agreed-upon curriculum for civil servants and for homeschooling in the period of the Hezekiah reformers. Nevertheless, we must remember the foundational conviction of Hezekiah Edition editors: *The fear of the LORD teaches a man wisdom* (15:33).

These poems are an excellent educational resource simply by virtue of their form. For the most part they present astute observations. They invite discussion. They are not written in stone. The truth of each poem can be stated in a variety of ways. The first line puts it one way, and the second line another (or broaches a related idea). The sayings are assertive but not overwhelmingly so. There *are* certain truths—there is a right and wrong way to think and act—and the choices made do make a difference, bringing good and bad consequences. A large part of being wise is looking ahead, seeing what the consequences would be for a contemplated course of actions, and then acting to produce the good result.

THEMATIC OUTLINE

The outlines and headings of the sections list references to related proverbs. To identify which section discusses a proverb in the Main Collection, see the chart below.

Wisdom: What It Is, Its Value, and How to Get It
Nationhood: Kings, Courts of Law, Civil Servants
Speech: Tongue, Lips, Mouth, and Words
Family: Husbands and Wives, Parents and Children
Economics: Wealth and Poverty
Personal Relations
Matters of the Heart
Knowledge of the Holy One

Thematic Index for the Proverbs of the Main Collection (10:1–22:16)

This index lists the 375 verses in the Main Collection, each with a code letter indicating under what topic the verse is discussed. Below the index a key shows what the code letters stand for and page numbers for the topics in part 2.

10:1 ...... F	10:24 ...... K	11:13 ...... S	12:4 .... F	12:26 ...... P	13:20 .... W
10:2 .... E	10:25 ...... K	11:14 ..... N	12:5 .... N	12:27 ...... E	13:21 ...... E
10:3 .... E	10:26 ...... E	11:15 ...... E	12:6 .... S	12:28 .. N,K	13:22 ...... E
10:4 .... E	10:27 ...... K	11:16 ...... P	12:7 .... K		13:23 ...... E
10:5 .... E	10:28 ...... K	11:17 ...... P	12:8 ...... W	13:1 .... F	
10:6 .... K	10:29 ...... K	11:18 ...... K	12:9 ...... M	13:2 .... S	13:24 ...... F
10:7 .... K	10:30 ...... K	11:19 ...... K	12:10 ...... P	13:3 .... S	13:25 ...... E
10:8 ...... W	10:31 ...... S	11:20 ...... K	12:11 ...... E	13:4 .... E	
10:9 .... K	10:32 ...... S	11:21 ...... K	12:12 ...... K	13:5 .... K	14:1 .... F
10:10 .... W		11:22 .... W	12:13 ...... S	13:6 .... K	14:2 .... K
10:11 ...... S	11:1 .... E	11:23 ...... K		13:7 .... E	14:3 .... S
10:12 ...... P	11:2 ...... W	11:24 ...... E	12:14 ...... S	13:8 .... E	14:4 .... E
10:13 .... W	11:3 .... K	11:25 ...... E	12:15 .... W	13:9 .... K	14:5 .... N
10:14 .... W	11:4 .... E	11:26 ...... E	12:16 ...... P	13:10 .... W	14:6 ...... W
10:15 ...... E	11:5 .... K	11:27 ...... P	12:17 ..... N	13:11 ...... E	14:7 ...... W
10:16 ...... E	11:6 .... K	11:28 .. N,E	12:18 ...... S	13:12 .... M	14:8 ...... W
10:17 .... W		11:29 ...... F	12:19 ...... S	13:13 .... W	14:9 ... W,P
10:18 ...... S	11:7 .... K	11:30 .... W	12:20 ...... P	13:14 .... W	14:10 .... M
10:19 ...... S	11:8 .... K	11:31 ...... K	12:21 ...... K	13:15 .... W	14:11 ...... K
10:20 ...... S	11:9 .... S		12:22 ...... K	13:16 .... W	14:12 .... M
10:21 ...... S	11:10 ..... N	12:1 .... W	12:23 ...... S	13:17 ..... N	14:13 .... M
10:22 ...... E	11:11 ...... S	12:2 .... K	12:24 ...... E	13:18 .... W	14:14 ...... K
10:23 .... W	11:12 ...... S	12:3 .... K	12:25 .... M	13:19 .... M	14:15 .... W

14:16 .... W	15:24 .... W	17:1 .... E	18:16 ...... E	20:5 ...... W	21:1 ...... N	21:17 ..... E
14:17 .... W	15:25 ..... K	17:2 .... F	18:17 ..... N	20:6 .... P	21:2 ...... K	21:18 ...... K
14:18 .... W	15:26 ..... K	17:3 .... K	18:18 ..... N	20:7 .... F	21:3 ...... K	21:19 ...... F
14:19 ..... K	15:27 ..... E	17:4 .... S	18:19 ..... P	20:8 ...... N	21:4 ...... M	21:20 ...... E
14:20 ..... E	15:28 ..... S	17:5 .... E	18:20 ..... S	20:9 ...... M	21:5 ...... E	21:21 ... P,K
14:21 C	15:29 ..... K	17:6 .... F		20:10 .... E	21:6 ...... E	21:22 .... W
14:22 ..... P	15:30 .... M	17:7 .... S	18:21 ...... S	20:11 ... F,E	21:7 ...... K	21:23 .. S,E
14:23 ..... E	15:31 ... W	17:8 .... N	18:22 ...... F	20:12 .... W	21:8 ...... N	21:24 ..W,P
14:24 ..... E	15:32 ... W	17:9 .... P	18:23 ...... E	20:13 ..... E	21:9 ...... F	21:25 ...... E
14:25 ..... N	15:33 ..... K	17:10 .... W	18:24 ...... P	20:14 ..... E	21:10 ..... P	21:26 ...... E
14:26 ..... K		17:11 ..... N		20:15 .... W	21:11 .... W	21:27 ...... K
14:27 ..... K	16:1 .... K	17:12 .... W	19:1 .... E	20:16 ..W,E		21:28 ..... N
14:28 ..... N	16:2 ..... K	17:13 ...... P	19:2 ...... W	20:17 ..... E		21:29 ...... W
14:29 ... W	16:3 .... K	17:14 ...... P	19:3 ...... M	20:18 ..... N		21:30 ...... K
14:30 .... M	16:4 .... K	17:15 .. N,P	19:4 .... E	20:19 ...... S		21:31 ...... K
14:31 ..... E	16:5 ..... K	17:16 .... W	19:5 .... N	20:20 ...... F		
14:32 ..... K	16:6 .... K	17:17 ...... P	19:6 ...... N,E	20:21 ...... E		22:1 .... E
14:33 ... W	16:7 .... K	17:18 ...... E	19:7 .... E	20:22 ...... P		22:2 .... E
14:34 ..... N	16:8 .... E	17:19 ...... P	19:8 ...... W	20:23 .. E,K		22:3 ...... W
14:35 ..... N	16:9 .... K	17:20 ...... S	19:9 .... N	20:24 ...... K		22:4 .... E
	16:10 ..... N	17:21 ...... F	19:10 ..... N	20:25 .. E,K		22:5 .... E
15:1 .... S	16:11 ...... E	17:22 .... M	19:11 ...... P	20:26 ..... N		22:6 .... F
15:2 ...... W	16:12 ..... N	17:23 .... N	19:12 ..... N	20:27 .... M	21:1 ...... N	22:7 .... E
15:3 .... K	16:13 .. N,K	17:24 .... W	19:13 ...... F	20:28 ..... N	21:2 ...... K	22:8 .... K
15:4 .... S	16:14 ..... N	17:25 ...... F	19:14 ...... F	20:29 ...... F	21:3 ...... K	22:9 .... E
15:5 .... F	16:15 ..... N	17:26 ...... N	19:15 ...... E	20:30 ...... F	21:4 ...... M	22:10 ...... P
15:6 .... E	16:16 .... W	17:27 ...... S	19:16 .... W		21:5 ...... E	22:11 .. N,S
15:7 ...... W	16:17 ...... K	17:28 ...... S	19:17 ...... K	21:1 ...... N	21:6 ...... E	22:12 ...... K
15:8 .... K	16:18 .... M		19:18 ...... F	21:2 ...... K	21:7 ...... K	22:13 ...... E
15:9 .... K	16:19 ...... E	18:1 .... P	19:19 .. N,P	21:3 ...... K	21:8 ...... N	22:14 ...... F
15:10 .... W	16:20 ...... K	18:2 ...... W	19:20 ..... W	21:4 ...... M	21:9 ...... F	22:15 ...... F
15:11 ..... K	16:21 .... W	18:3 .... K	19:21 ..... K	21:5 ...... E	21:10 ..... P	22:16 ...... E
15:12 .... W	16:22 .... W	18:4 .... W	19:22 ...... E	21:6 ...... E	21:11 .... W	
15:13 .... M	16:23 ...... S	18:5 .... N	19:23 ..W,K	21:7 ...... K		
15:14 .... W	16:24 ...... S	18:6 .... S	19:24 ...... E	21:8 ...... N		
15:15 .... M	16:25 ..W,M	18:7 .... S	19:25 ... W	21:9 ...... F		
15:16 ..... E	16:26 ...... E	18:8 .... S	19:26 ...... F	21:10 ..... P		
15:17 ..... E	16:27 ...... S	18:9 .... E	19:27 .... W	21:11 .... W		
15:18 C	16:28 ... P,S	18:10 ...... K	19:28 ..... N			
15:19 ..... E	16:29 ...... S	18:11 ...... E	19:29 ... W	21:12 .... N		
15:20 ... F,K	16:30 ...... S	18:12 .... M	20:1 ...... W	21:13 ..... K		
15:21 .... W	16:31 ..... K	18:13 ...... S	20:2 .... N	21:14 ..... E		
15:22 .... N	16:32 ...... P	18:14 .... M	20:3 .... P	21:15 ..... N		
15:23 ...... S	16:33 ..... N	18:15 .... W	20:4 .... E	21:16 .... W		

E = Economics (pp. **166-84**); **F** = Family (pp. **155-65**); **K** = Knowledge of the Holy One (pp. **206-21**); **M** = Matters of the Heart (pp. **197-205**); **N** = Nationhood (pp. **131-42**); **P** = Personal Relations (pp. **185-96**); **S** = Speech (pp. **143-54**); **W** = Wisdom (pp. **116-30**)

Proverbs 10:1—22:16

Wisdom: What It Is, Its Value, and How to Get It

The Book of Proverbs, Part 2: The Themes of the Main Collection							
Wisdom	Nation-hood	Speech	Family	Econo-mics	Personal Rela-tions	Matters of the Heart	Know-ledge of the Holy One

PREVIEW

The introductory poems in Proverbs 1-9 emphasize how important it is to be wise, but they are rather vague regarding what this concretely means or how to become wise. This is the focus of the some seventy proverbs in the main collection on this theme. I have subdivided them into three groups: (1) sayings that describe what *wisdom* essentially is, (2) proverbs that emphasize the tremendous value and importance of gaining wisdom, and (3) sayings (quite a large number) that tell how wisdom might be acquired. In brief, the wise are those who look ahead, give thought to their ways, avoid dangers, and promote education. To acquire wisdom of this kind is worth more than virtually anything else, but it does not come easily. Above all, one must embrace certain habits and attitudes and reject others [Hezekiah Reform Literature].

116

OUTLINE

Wisdom: What Is It? 13:16; 14:8, 9, 15, 16; 15:2, 7; 16:21; 18:4;
19:2; 20:1, 5; 21:24; 22:3
Wisdom: Its Value, 11:22; 12:8; 13:14, 15; 15:10, 24; 16:16, 22;
17:12; 19:8; 20:15, 16; 21:16, 22
Wisdom: How to Get It, 10:8, 10, 13, 14, 17, 23; 11:2, 30; 12:1,
15; 13:10, 13, 14, 18, 20; 14:6, 7, 17, 18, 29, 33; 15:12,
14, 21, 31, 32; 16:25; 17:10, 16, 24; 18:2, 15; 19:16, 20,
23, 25, 27, 29; 20:1, 12; 21:11, 24, 29

EXPLANATORY NOTES

**Wisdom: What Is It? 13:16; 14:8, 9, 15, 16; 15:2,
7; 16:21; 18:4; 19:2; 20:1, 5; 21:24; 22:3**

*Every Prudent Man Acts out of Knowledge, but a Fool
Exposes His Folly (13:16) 13:16; 14:8, 9, 15; 19:2*

A number of sayings in the main collection more or less define
what it means to be wise. They identify three complementary qualities
of the wise. The first of these is simply, as 14:8 puts it, the amount
of serious *thought* they devote to *their ways* (14:8). *Their ways*
(Heb.: *his way*) is a frequently used metaphor in the Bible for the path
of life (cf. 2:9-15). The Hebrew verb for *give thought* in 14:8a is
based on the same root as the preposition "between"; in other words,
the wise distinguish "between" one path and another on the basis of
knowledge. They act *out of knowledge* (13:16a). *The mouth of the
fool gushes folly* (15:2b). On the other path, *The tongue of the wise
commends* [lit., *makes good, improves*] *knowledge* (15:2a); their lips
spread [lit., *scatter*] *knowledge* (15:7a). The *knowledge* referred to is
verifiable knowledge. They know what's what and how to talk about
it. Because fools lack such knowledge, they are easily duped (13:16b;
14:8b); they do not distinguish between paths. Another thing about
fools is that once duped, *fools mock at making amends* (14:9a; NIV
adds: *for sin*); they lack the ability for self-correction. They fail to learn
from their mistakes.

The point at issue here is made with special clarity in 14:15: *The
simple believe anything, but the prudent gives thought to his steps*
(lit.). The Hebrew word for *simple* (*petî*) in this sentence is not that
used for an outright fool, but for a youth who is still untutored and
quite naive about life *[Words for Wisdom and Folly]*. Without experience or an education, such a person is gullible and vulnerable to
wrong choices; he does not yet have what it takes to distinguish wisely

between alternatives. Proverbs 19:2 sums up: *Also, as a soul without knowledge is not good, he who hastens with his feet sins [misses the mark]* (lit.). The wise have knowledge and experience to guide them as they travel life's path and thus are circumspect and move a little more slowly. Fools, lacking such knowledge, run hither and yon: this is definitely *not good*. The consequences can be tragic.

A Wise Man Fears . . . and Shuns Evil, but a Fool Is Hotheaded and Reckless (14:16) 14:16, 17; 18:1; 20:1; 22:3

These five sayings are especially important for understanding the inner world that distinguishes a wise person from a fool. They make even clearer what the wise think about as they contemplate their way. On the positive side, *A wise man fears . . . and shuns evil* (14:16a); the Hebrew text of this line does not specify that *a wise man fears the LORD,* as NIV translates; the line itself does not specify what the wise man fears, but only that he *fears and shuns evil.* Also, the *evil* that he *shuns* is not wickedness (he fears that too, of course) but harmful consequences ("misfortune," Toy). What this verse observes is that the *wise* have a healthy dread of the misfortunes that can result from taking the wrong step or following the wrong way. As a result they travel down the path of life alert to the dangers ahead, whereas the fool is overconfident (*hotheaded and reckless,* 14:16b). This key attribute of the *wise* is captured in an alliterative wordplay: *A prudent man [ʿarûm] sees [rāʾāh] danger [rāʿāh, suffering] and takes refuge, but the simple keep going and suffer for it* (22:3; repeated in 27:12). To look ahead, see danger, and avoid it: that is the mark of a man of wisdom.

Several things are identified as impairing and distorting this capacity to *see* danger and avoid it. One is being *quick-tempered* and *crafty;* such are bound to do *foolish things* and stir up hatred (14:17). Another is being too *unfriendly* (a loner) and self-centered; such attitudes lead to being defiant and contentious (18:1; the same verb *gālaʿ,* "become irritated/angry," is used here as in 17:14). Most blatantly impairing of sound judgment is an addiction to alcohol. *Wine is a mocker and beer a brawler; whoever is led astray [reels] by them, is not wise* (20:1); on this latter issue, see the vividly expressed advice in 23:29-35 (also 23:20-21).

A Wise Man's Heart Guides His Mouth, and His Lips Promote Instruction (16:23) 16:21, 23; 18:4

In addition to being alert to dangers, the wise also know how to express themselves intelligibly. Their *heart* (the organ of thought) instructs the mouth (16:23a), and then the lips *add* (NIV: *promote*) *instruction* to the fund of accepted knowledge (16:23b; cf. 1:5). The astonishing ease with which this happens among the wise appears to be the subject of 18:4. For the *mouth* of an ordinary man, words are like *deep [underground] waters* (18:4a), inaccessible and hard to come by; but the *fountain of wisdom is a bubbling brook* (18:4b), flowing from the heart to the mouth and lips. This is what gives *the wise in heart* their reputation for discernment: the fact that *the sweetness of [his] lips* (NIV: *pleasant words*) adds to the fund of knowledge (16:21, lit.). In summary, wisdom involves having knowledge and knowing how to use it in making right distinctions and decisions on the journey through life. It is especially evident in the ability to look ahead and avoid dangers, and in the gift for communicating what is seen so persuasively that it is accessible to others and can become part of the generally accepted wisdom.

Wisdom: Its Value   11:22; 12:8; 13:14, 15; 15:10, 24; 16:16, 22; 17:12; 19:8; 20:15, 16; 21:16, 22

Gold There Is, and Rubies in Abundance, but Lips That Speak Knowledge Are a Rare Jewel (20:15) 11:22; 16:16; 20:15

Proverbs 20:15 might best be translated as a continuous sentence (Toy; Cohen): *Gold there is, and rubies in abundance, and a rare jewel—such are lips of knowledge* (*lips that speak knowledge*). To have lips from which flow words that bubble up from a wise heart (18:4b) is something so valuable that only the most precious metals and jewels can compare with it. Indeed, if it were to come to a choice between the two, the choice would be clear: *How much better to get wisdom than gold, to choose understanding rather than silver!* (16:16; cf. 3:13-18). This is why it is so jarringly incongruous (like *a gold ring in a pig's snout*) when *a beautiful woman . . . shows no* [lit., *turns aside from*] *discretion* (11:22).

He Who Gets Wisdom Loves His Own Soul; He Who Cherishes Understanding Prospers (19:8) 13:15; 16:22; 19:8

Why is wisdom so fantastically valuable? Several reasons are alluded to in this group of sayings, beginning with the one identified by these three proverbs: wisdom's very *personal* value for the individual possessing it. Literally translated, 19:8 states *not* that *he who gets wisdom loves his own soul* (NIV), but that *he who gets heart*

loves his nepeš [*his person/spirit*]. To get *heart* is an idiom for being
educated (see 15:32b, lit.: *Whoever heeds correction gains heart*).
Also, what a person who gets heart gains is not primarily material
wealth (*prospers,* 19:8b) but *good* (lit.; Heb.: *tôb*): "peace of mind,
self-satisfaction, and fulfillment" (Alden). This is what makes getting
heart (getting educated) such an act of *love* for oneself (19:8). That
too is why *understanding* is viewed as a *fountain of life* (16:22a),
and why 13:15a says that *good understanding gives grace* (not *wins
favor,* as in NIV). It contributes to a quality of life that is gracious and
rewarding, while *the way* of those who give no thought to being wise
(*the unfaithful*) is *hard* (13:15).

A Man Is Praised According to His Wisdom, but Men with Warped Minds Are Despised (12:8) 12:8; 21:22

Two additional reasons for wisdom's value are alluded to in these
two sayings. Being wise is demonstrably superior to might, even in
such matters where power appears to have the upper hand, as for
example in the case of a *city of the mighty* (21:22a). Even a powerful city like this is vulnerable to attack and destruction by *a wise man*
(21:22b; see 2 Sam 5:6-8; 1 Chr 11:4-6 for a concrete example of
the truth of this saying). In short, *a wise man has great power* (24:5).
Public recognition of a wise man's power is an added reason for wisdom's value. Such individuals are held in high esteem, a reality highlighted by another saying: *A man is praised according to his wisdom*
(12:8a) and *despised* (12:8b) if his thinking is *warped* ("distorted,"
Cohen). The truly wise are both powerful and honored as such in virtually every society.

Good Understanding Wins Favor, but the Way of the Unfaithful Is Hard (13:15) 13:15; 15:10, 24; 17:12; 21:16

It is dangerous not to be wise! That is yet another reason for attaining wisdom. Failure to acquire wisdom is dangerous both for the individual and the larger society. *Good understanding* [*good sense*] *wins
favor, but the way of the unfaithful* [*reckless*] *is hard* [*harsh*] (13:15).
Indeed, *stern discipline* [*severe punishment*] *awaits him who leaves
the path; he who hates correction will die* (15:10). It is a serious thing
to be reckless and rebellious. The potential consequences are deadly
for the individual and his community. The individual *who strays from
the path of understanding* (21:16a) eventually *comes to rest in the
company of the dead* ("ghosts," Alden). The image is of depleted spirits somewhere underneath the earth (see 9:18; cf. 2:18), symbolic of
the emptiness of life without *understanding.* A *fool in his folly* may

be a serious danger to others. *Better to meet a bear robbed of her cubs, than a fool in his folly* (17:12). A bear robbed of her cubs is extremely dangerous; a human being on the loose who lacks common sense can be more dangerous still.

Wisdom: How to Get It 10:8, 10, 13, 14, 17, 23; 11:2, 30; 12:1, 15; 13:10, 13, 14, 18, 20; 14:6, 7, 17, 18, 29, 33; 15:12, 14, 21, 31, 32; 16:25; 17:10, 16, 24; 18:2, 15; 19:16, 20, 23, 25, 27, 29; 20:1, 12; 21:11, 24, 29

He Who Walks with the Wise Grows Wise, but a Companion of Fools Suffers Harm (13:20) 10:13, 14; 11:30; 13:14, 20; 14:7

If wisdom is so important, how can it be obtained? Many sayings in this collection appear to be focused on answering this question. This particular group of proverbs suggests that to become wise one needs a teacher. In this group of sayings these teachers are referred to as *the wise* (13:20), a possible reference to royally appointed sages responsible for the education of youth for civil service (cf. 5:13). In other words, to become wise was not something individuals could do on their own; they needed to *walk with the wise* (13:20a) and become their associates rather than becoming *a companion of fools* (13:20b).

What kind of teachers were these sages? *Discernment* can be *found* on their *lips* (10:13). In other words, these persons were skilled at making insightful distinctions and expressing their convictions. Also, *wise men store up knowledge* (10:14); they had an impressive fund of knowledge. This is why the *teachings of the wise* were such a *fountain of life* to their students (13:14), "a source of vitality . . . and advice, in the same way that a well supplies refreshment to them who draw its water" (Cohen: 59). Their wisdom about life helps their students escape *the snares of death,* "the pitfalls along the road of life which, if not avoided, bring one to a premature death" (Cohen: 83). Something similar is alluded to in 11:30, whose first line states that *the fruit of the righteous is a tree of life* (cf. 3:18). Then the point made is that *he who wins* [lit., *takes*] *souls is wise* (11:30b). Elsewhere in the Bible, to "take a soul" (to take a life) is an idiom for killing. But the saying's first line implies that in this instance the expression has "a benign sense" (Clifford), as in the Jewish Publication Society translation, *A wise man captivates people.* In summary, the first thing one must do to become wise is *stay away from a foolish man,* whose *lips* are void of *knowledge* (14:7), and instead walk with one truly wise, whose *teachings* are a *fountain of life* (13:14).

The Wise in Heart Accept Commands, but a Chattering Fool Comes to Ruin *(10:8) 10:8, 10; 11:2; 13:10, 18; 14:17, 29; 16:25; 18:2; 19:20, 27; 21:29*

Most of the remaining sayings on the theme of "Wisdom: How to Get It" highlight qualities of the good or bad student. This group of sayings alludes to an attitude foundational to all others: one must not be too enamored of one's own opinions. The *chattering fool* referred to in 10:8, who also *winks maliciously* (10:10), thinks he is so smart: he *delights in airing his own opinions* (as 18:2b puts it). He is utterly convinced of the rightness of his way, even though, tragically, *in the end it leads to* [a premature] *death* (16:25). Because the fool is so full of himself and his opinions, he *finds no pleasure in understanding* (18:2a; pondering the teachings of the sage). He *puts up a bold front* [lit., *hardens his face*] (21:29a). He is totally lacking in *humility* (11:2); this produces a contentious atmosphere (13:10a) in which tempers flare (14:17) due to impatience (14:29).

By contrast, the *wise in heart accept* [the sage's] *commands* (10:8a) and *take* [his] *advice* (13:10b; 12:15b). Attaching oneself to a sage with *discerning lips* is the first step in obtaining wisdom (see above), but only as one ponders the advice given and accepts it will one *in the end* become wise (19:20). The phrase *in the end* means the "latter end" of one's life. If at any point the student would *stop listening,* that could terminate the process; *you will stray from the words of knowledge* (19:27). An even worse fate awaits one who *scorns instruction* (13:13a); here the term for *instruction* is *word,* referring perhaps to God's *word* (as in 30:5-6; Deut 29:29). The word *scorns* implies outright rebellion; such will *pay for it* (be indebted to God), while the one who *respects* [lit., *fears*] *a command* [Heb.: *miṣwāh*] can anticipate being rewarded (13:13). The verse echoes the teaching of Moses in Deuteronomy. In summary, to become wise one must establish a relationship with a wise teacher and be humble and teachable. Those with *discerning* hearts actively seek *knowledge* (15:14a). As 19:16a reiterates, by heeding *instruction* (*miṣwāh*) the wise in heart preserve their *soul* (or their *life*) from an untimely death (19:16). The wise in heart know how to listen to instruction *["Heart"].*

10:17; 12:1; 13:18; 15:31, 32

A quite specific and somewhat emotional issue in becoming educated is alluded to in these verses: what one does with a *rebuke*. A *rebuke* is not simply any advice or instruction; a rebuke is advice or instruction directed to specific misbehavior that has already occurred. The priest Eli was warned of disasters that would come upon him and his family because of his failure to "rebuke" the misdeeds of his sons (1 Sam 3:13).

A rebuke requires strength on the part of teachers; they must interpose themselves into the lives of their students. For the students too this is a difficult moment in their educational experience. Some will simply shrug such a rebuke off or *ignore it* (10:17a); students like this are dangerous to their fellow students. Their cavalier attitude is proof of their capacity to *lead others astray* (10:17b). Other students, when rebuked, turn livid with *hate* (12:1); the word used is *brutish* (NIV: *stupid*).

To *hate* a rebuke is animal-like in its mindlessness. Such *hate* is diagnosed as a form of self-hatred, for it is precisely by accepting *correction* of this kind that a person acquires *understanding* [lit., *heart*] (15:32). An inner aspect of the human psyche is missing in those who do not (or are unable) to accept a rebuke. That is why a rebuke can be termed *life-giving* (15:31a); its reception is essential for being among the wise (15:31b; cf. 15:5, 10, 12; 17:10). The consequences of ignoring discipline of this kind are fateful: *He who ignores discipline comes to poverty and shame, but whoever heeds correction* [a rebuke] is honored (13:18).

Flog a Mocker, and the Simple Will Learn Prudence; Rebuke a Discerning Man, and He Will Gain Knowledge (19:25) 10:23; 14:6, 18, 33; 15:12, 14, 21; 17:10, 16, 24; 18:15; 19:23, 25, 29; 20:12; 21:11, 24

Three contrasting types of individuals and how they learn (or fail to learn) is the focus of this group of sayings *[Words for Wisdom and Folly]*. They are the *mocker* (*lēs*), *the simple* (*petî, uneducated*), and the *discerning* (*nābôn*, 19:25); sometimes a *mocker* is called a *fool* (*kĕsîl*; 10:23; 17:24). It is too much to say that the *mocker* or *fool* learns at all, for he *resents correction* (15:12a; lit., *loves it not*). *He will not consult the wise* (15:12b) and is unable to concentrate: *A fool's eyes wander to the ends of the earth* (17:24). Even if he were to seek wisdom, for these and other reasons he *finds none* (14:6b). Instead, *A fool* [*kĕsîl*] *finds pleasure* [lit., *laughter*] *in evil conduct*

(10:23a; in this line the word *evil* is very strong). His attributes are summed up as follows: *The proud and arrogant man—"Mocker" is his name; he behaves with overweening pride* (21:24). This type of person typically runs afoul of the law and suffers blows and punishments (19:25, 29).

Even then (when suffering blows), *mockers* and *fools* learn little, but their punishment does serve a purpose. It makes an impression, we are told, on a second type of individual: the *simple ones.* Out of fear that the same thing might happen to them, these simple ones *learn prudence* (*smarten up*) and *gain knowledge* (19:25). The simple ones are not hardened *mockers* but raw youth who have not yet been educated. If they were to remain uneducated, their inheritance would be *folly* (14:18a), but those who do become *prudent* [educated in how to live wisely] *are crowned with knowledge* (14:18).

For naive youth to become wise, they need to mature as individuals and gain discernment, the third type mentioned in these saying. *The heart of the discerning acquires knowledge* (*dā'at,* 18:15a; 19:25b). A *discerning heart* is constantly taking in more and more knowledge in order to have the information needed for making intelligent distinctions "between" (the root meaning of *discerning*) options and choosing well even when the lines between them are fuzzy. This process begins (as noted above) by listening (with his *ears,* 18:15b) to the *lips of the discerning* (those with a proven track record of making wise distinctions; 10:13a). Once such a teacher is found, the discerning of heart take as much pleasure in pursuing *wisdom* as mockers and fools do in pursuing perversity (10:23). That is why *knowledge comes easily to* a *discerning* person (14:6), and *wisdom* once found rests so securely *in* his *heart* (14:33). Since the goal of attaining *wisdom* is ever before the face of the *discerning* (17:24), they hold to a steady *course* in life (15:21b).

The gulf that separates this type of person from the mocker is highlighted in what is said about their contrasting responses to a *rebuke.* As noted above, receiving a *rebuke* is an especially critical moment on life's road; it has to do with the uniquely human capacity of repenting of or learning from mistakes. In the case of the discerning, *a rebuke impresses* [them] . . . *more than a hundred lashes a fool* (17:10). In this verse the verb translated *impresses* has the literal meaning of *descends*: a simple *rebuke* goes down deeper into the inner being of the discerning than the *fool* experiences when being whipped (cf. 15:14). The fool *lacks judgment,* an inner capacity for self-reflection (lit., *lacks heart*), and delights instead in folly (15:21). That is why the ironic question is posed as to why a *fool* would offer money to obtain *wisdom* when he has *no heart* (lit.; not just *no desire* but not even the *heart*) for receiving it (17:16). The discerning, on the other hand, keep to a *straight course* (15:21b) and are constantly building up their inner resources by internalizing the *knowledge* that comes through learning from their mistakes (19:25). They value their *ears* and *eyes* (the ability to see and hear and ponder the knowledge they acquire), recognizing that *the LORD has made them both* (20:12; God is the one who has given them this awesome capacity for knowledge and discernment).

THE TEXT IN BIBLICAL CONTEXT

Knowledge-Based Wisdom in Proverbs and Genesis

The sayings just surveyed emphasize that being wise means using eyes and ears and being mentally alert to the consequences of good and bad choices and actions. Being wise in this sense is hugely important. It can make the difference between life and death. In these sayings a worldview is apparent. It is one in which the human capacity for acquiring knowledge-based wisdom is prized above everything else. It is also one that is aware of the difficulties involved in acquiring such knowledge. Human beings are not naturally wise. Life is complex, and it takes time and patience to see what the consequences of a given choice or action might be. The acquisition of knowledge-based wisdom is a shared undertaking. Insights garnered in older generations need to be passed on to those who come after. To receive this wisdom the younger generation must be receptive. Attitudes come into play, either negative or positive. Some young people are more receptive than others are. These diverse attitudes must themselves be addressed, understood, and dealt with. All this (and more) is at work in the background of the insightful sayings just surveyed regarding what it means to be wise.

The worldview presupposed in these sayings is enshrined in the opening chapters of the Bible, in Genesis 1-11. Genesis portrays human beings, regardless of their national or ethnic origins, as bearing the image and likeness of the one who created them. Because of this they are assumed to have the freedom and intelligence to be able to exercise a godlike dominion and control over the other creatures. This picture of human beings corresponds to the one presupposed in the sayings just surveyed.

However, as in the sayings in Proverbs, Genesis 1-11 is aware of a darker side to the human psyche. Right after describing the majestic role human beings have been given within the world, to care for it and rule over it, the story is told of the temptation of Adam and Eve (Gen 2-3). They are commanded not to eat of the tree of the knowledge of good and evil, lest they die, but they do so anyway. The story's author believes that human beings generally speaking chafe against limits or restrictions of any kind. They don't want others to tell them how to live. They want to live just as they choose, regardless of the consequences. Subsequent stories in Genesis 4-6 reveal the consequences of this desire for a more freewheeling, uninhibited existence: the world became lawless and violent.

A partial solution is arrived at through divine decrees given in the aftermath of the flood. These authorize use of force to restrain violence and protect human life (Gen 9:6), but the deeper problem remains. How can the life of the peoples of the world, now so divided by language, be improved? How can blessings be intensified? That is how Genesis envisions God's act of calling Abraham and his descendants, the Israelites. They are to be just such a people who by doing what is right can intensify goodness and wisdom and thereby increase the blessings of God among all of the world's peoples (Gen 12:1-3; 18:18-19). In this calling education plays an important role, education like that expressed and fostered in the sayings examined in this section of Proverbs.

Knowledge-Based Thought in Job, Ecclesiastes, Jesus, and James

Job

Job is among the most erudite writings of the Bible. Its author was a literary craftsman on the order of Shakespeare, with an encyclopedic knowledge of nature and the world. His poems, in which Job is portrayed dialoguing with three friends over the reasons for his sufferings, reveal a human mind at work seeking an understanding of why there is in general so much seemingly undeserved suffering in a universe that is presumably watched over by a good God. His wife wants him to curse God and die, but Job never does. He questions, he probes, he prays, and he scornfully rejects the facile notions of his friends that he suffers because of his sins. But in the end he is brought to the point of trusting in the goodness of God even though he still does not know the answer to the questions he has posed. The book of Job is an exercise in knowledge-based thinking about some of the more intractable problems of human existence.

Ecclesiastes

The unique individual who produced the discourses and sayings in Ecclesiastes was exploring along lines somewhat similar to Job. In Ecclesiastes, however, a prime objective is to refute those who think that by knowledge-based wisdom alone human beings can construct a worldview or philosophy that would explain things from beginning to end. He very much doubts if this can be done, even if certain of the wise thought so (Eccl 8:16-17). To him, such philosophical aspirations were just "chasing after the wind" (nine times in the book, as in 1:14). For himself, wisdom was important. It was better to be wise than foolish, but there is much we do not know and likely never will know. Those who edited his book and added it to the collected works of Israel's Scriptures shared the point of view of the *men of Hezekiah*. They showed this by encouraging its readers to *fear God and keep his commandments* (12:13) and not put too much stock in their own understanding (cf. Prov 3:5).

Jesus

It is beyond the scope of this commentary to say all that might or should be said about knowledge-based thought in the life and teachings of Jesus. I only want to underscore the obvious by saying that whatever else we might affirm about his mission, death, and resurrection, he was a wise and down-to-earth teacher in the tradition of the wisdom sayings we have just explored. As noted elsewhere *[Wisdom in Proverbs]*, in the times in which he lived, the Torah of Moses had become for many of his contemporaries virtually the only recognized source of wisdom. As a consequence they thought it was of great importance that it be rightly interpreted and strictly observed. Besides, expectations were in the air of the advent of a messianic law-observing leader, who on this basis would restore Israel's kingdom as a prelude to the kingdom of God being established over all the earth. Jesus made a major contribution to the salvation of the world by creating space within this volatile, expectant Torah-centered Judaism for a knowledge-based wisdom about life that did not reject the Law or the Prophets. He freed people for fresh thinking and application, as exemplified in his parables or in Matthew's Sermon on the Mount (Miller, 1997:86-90).

Like Job and Ecclesiastes, Jesus was a realist. As with the wisdom teachers of old, his focus was mostly on down-to-earth matters. Examples are rampant divorce rates, how to break through the perfectionist thinking of the "elder sons" of the time, and how to spark more compassion (for he was sure of God's compassion) and a greater readiness to forgive. When asked about which is the greatest commandment, he had a ready answer (because he had thought about it): love God, and also love the neighbor as yourself. "What does that mean?" he was asked. He replied with a simple story that has lived on and become part of our collective memory. A priest passed a man smitten by thieves, without stopping to help him, followed by a member of a hated group, a Samaritan, who showed compassion by what he did. Jesus said, "Go and do likewise" (Luke 10:37).

Jesus respected the Torah of Moses, but he was also free to differ with it when its teachings were demonstrably deficient. To him, its teachings about hating one's enemies were demonstrably deficient, and he said as much. In support, he observed how the Creator of the world behaved in sending sun and rain on good and bad alike (Matt 5:43-48).

James

James obviously approved of his brother's manner of teaching. His book carries on the tradition of wise, down-to-earth teachings, many of them echoing the words of Jesus. "Of all the books of the New Testament," states William P. Brown, "James best reflects the ethos of the Hebrew wisdom traditions. . . . Echoing the exhortative language of Proverbs, James brings the insights of wisdom into a distinctly Christian context and community" (160). "James has much to say about wisdom itself. He echoes his predecessors by capturing the dynamic, character-based nature of wisdom [when he writes:] . . . 'The wisdom from above is first pure, then peaceable, gentle, willing to yield, full of mercy and good fruits, without a trace of partiality or hypocrisy'" (164; Jas 3:17).

THE TEXT IN THE LIFE OF THE CHURCH

Knowledge-Based Wisdom in the Teaching Mission of the Church

By isolating the poems in this section on the subject of wisdom, we can see more clearly what they are saying in their own right. They teach that unlike animals (whose behavior is determined by inherited instincts) human beings need to learn how to live. They must think about what choices they are going to make and what kind of culture they are going to have. In every generation young people need to be educated. The teachings just surveyed encourage the churches not to neglect instructing their youth in the commonsense, knowledge-based wisdom needed for living. Parents do this every time they warn their children about this or that danger or problem. But there is a place for the church to back up parents with classes in wisdom of precisely the kind spoken of in Proverbs.

In doing so, there is no need for anything other than the proverbs themselves. A Christian elementary and high school in Texas has a Bible Proverbs Project. "Students read through each chapter of Proverbs recording selected verses in ten categories. They learn what Proverbs says about friends, anger, wisdom, discipline, the tongue, money, laziness, humility, righteousness and honesty. For each topic students write and illustrate personal applications." "The testimonies given over the years, as to the value of this study in individual lives is awesome" (quotes from a project report). I have used a variation on this approach to good effect by selecting five or ten proverbs from each thematic group indicated in this part of the commentary. I write them on a sheet of paper, duplicate them, and discuss them with youth or adults (or both) on a succession of Sundays.

Truth and Consequences

Some of the most provocative proverbs in this group are those that highlight how gullible or careless we often tend to be and explain the consequences of this only too human character flaw. *A simple man believes anything*, is the way one of the sayings puts it, *but a prudent man gives thought to his steps* (Prov 14:15). We are often not thoughtful enough. Another puts the same truth in these terms: *It is not good to have zeal without knowledge, nor to be hasty and miss the way* (19:2). We simply do not do enough research before making our choices. As a proverb of our own puts it, "Haste makes waste." This applies to decisions we make as individuals, as churches, or as cultures and nations. Especially today, the decisions made are often hurried and reckless.

But even when we foresee the possible dangers that certain choices are sure to entail, we oftentimes plunge ahead anyway. It is popular to be a risk-taker. One of the most sobering proverbs of this group, for me personally, speaks to this issue: *A prudent man sees danger and takes refuge, but the simple keep going and suffer for it* (22:3). A great deal of suffering in life comes from the simple fact that we do not avoid dangers we know will result from certain actions. And yet, we wonder why we suffer. Rather than blaming ourselves, we blame God or fate or bad luck or others.

What happened during the time of Hitler in Nazi Germany is a classic case of wrong choices leading to disastrous consequences on a world scale. Many have asked why God stood by and allowed six million Jews to be massacred. A few saw what kind of man Hitler was and warned of the consequences if he were to get control of the nation. They tried to stop him but didn't succeed. Eventually he was stopped, but only after a world war in which millions of lives were lost—and only after it was too late for the millions of Jews (and others) who lost their lives in this Holocaust.

Where was God, many ask in retrospect? Theologian Paul Van Buren struggled with this question in the final years of his life. In a book published at the end of a long career, he wrote that in his opinion the question the Holocaust poses is primarily about "our responsibility for what took place and so about our responsibility for the future." Along with Dietrich Bonhoeffer, he came to sense what the Holocaust was telling us: "It is God Himself who is forcing us to live in this world as if the God of our theological tradition . . . were not there . . . to do for us what He expects us to do for ourselves and for His creation." Van Buren came to believe, "Had more Christians come to this realization earlier, perhaps millions murdered by Hitler might have been saved." The chief lesson of the Holocaust, he concluded, "is that God requires that we take unqualified responsibility before Him for His history with us" (181).

Proverbs 10:1—22:16

Nationhood: Kings, Courts of Law, Civil Servants

The Book of Proverbs, Part 2: The Themes of the Main Collection							
Wisdom	Nation-hood	Speech	Family	Econo-mics	Personal Rela-tions	Matters of the Heart	Know-ledge of the Holy One

PREVIEW

Nationhood, courts of law, and kings were closely interrelated spheres of social reality at the time this collection was created. Kings not only led the nation but were also expected to play an active role in seeing to it that the disputes of their people were settled equitably (Weinfeld, 1995). This was true not only in Israel but elsewhere in the ancient Near East, especially in Mesopotamia, where the first (known) law codes were created, like those of Hammurabi (Pritchard: 163-80). In the judicial process itself, when crimes or misdemeanors were involved, penalties were imposed that were thought to be suitable to the crime. Typical cases would then be recorded as precedents for others to follow if they should wish to do so (for examples, see the case laws in Exod 21-22). The testimony of truthful witnesses was vital to the judicial process, and for capital crimes eyewitness evidence supplied by at least "two or three witnesses" was required (Deut 17:1-7).

When the court system broke down and became corrupt, as it sometimes did (see 1 Kgs 21:8-14 for a graphic example), then a king might initiate reforms as Jehoshaphat did (see 2 Chr 19:4-7). One of the important legacies of the Bible to the modern world is that, to survive and prosper, a nation must be founded upon just laws justly administered. This includes the provision that the supreme leader of such a people, the king (or other chief executive), is himself both subject to law and responsible to see that a judicial order is in place for the fair administration of that law. The teachings on this important theme in the Main Collection both reflect and reinforce this set of values. They fall into three major categories: (1) kings and their courtiers or servants, (2) law courts and related matters, and (3) qualities that make a nation great.

OUTLINE

Kings and Their Courtiers or Servants, 13:17; 14:35; 15:22;
    16:10, 12, 13, 14, 15; 17:8, 11, 23; 19:6, 10, 12, 19; 20:2,
    8, 18, 26, 28; 21:1; 22:11
Courts of Law, 11:10; 12:5, 17, 28; 14:5, 25; 16:33; 17:15, 23,
    26; 18:5, 17, 18; 19:5, 9, 28; 21:8, 12, 28
Qualities That Make a Nation Great, 11:10, 14; 14:28, 34; 15:22;
    20:18; 21:15

EXPLANATORY NOTES

Kings and Their Courtiers or Servants 13:17; 14:35; 15:22; 16:10, 12, 13, 14, 15; 17:8, 11, 23; 19:6, 10, 12, 19; 20:2, 8, 18, 26, 28; 21:1; 22:11

A King Delights in a Wise Servant, but a Shameful Servant Incurs His Wrath (14:35) 13:17; 14:35; 17:11; 19:10; 22:11

What these five sayings have in common is their allusion to a quite specific vocational role, that of *servant* to the king. This term puts us in touch with the social and institutional setting and purpose for which many of the sayings of this collection were originally prepared. The young men who first studied these sayings were being educated for civil service. For this they had to be *wise* in the ways specified in these sayings (14:35).

Certain specific duties of such a servant are intimated: the saying in 13:17 alludes to his role as *messenger* in arbitrating disputes; 17:11 may refer to his potential role in putting down a rebellion. In the first instance, that of arbitration, what is essential, the saying suggests, is that the servant be faithful to the one who sent him (13:17b; cf. 25:13). What is called for in the second instance (putting down a rebellion) is a certain fierceness, even *merciless* action (17:11b; for a vivid example of a king's messenger skillfully functioning in both roles, see Isa 36). A servant of this kind whose motives are genuine (not self-serving) and who is able to express his thoughts gracefully (*whose speech is gracious*) may well advance to the point where he is no longer just a servant, but the king's *friend* (22:11). Even then he must be careful not to be presumptuous or assume an authority that is not rightfully his. For if *it is not fitting for a fool to live in luxury* (and it is not), *how much worse for a slave [servant] to rule over princes* (19:10).

When a King Sits on His Throne to Judge, He Winnows Out All Evil with His Eyes (20:8) 16:10, 12, 13, 14, 15; 17:8, 23; 19:6, 12, 19; 20:2, 8, 26, 28; 21:1

Anyone being prepared to serve the king in the role of a *wise servant* (14:35) needs to understand what makes a king tick—how he behaves and how those around him behave—in short, what to watch out for when serving him. This appears to be the purpose behind this group of sayings. Several allude to a mysterious, supernatural aura of the kingly office. God's power is manifestly at work within the *king's heart* (or mind); God *directs it like a watercourse* [an irrigation channel] *wherever he pleases* (21:1).

Proverbs 20:28 may refer to the pledge of enduring *love and faithfulness* which Yahweh made with the Davidic dynasty (see 2 Sam 7:12-16; 23:1-7; Pss 61:7; 89:24-37). It is this divine promise and presence that makes the king's throne *secure* (Prov 20:28) and empowers the one who occupies that office when *he sits on his throne to judge* (20:8a). *He winnows out all evil with his eyes* as a farmer winnows wheat from chaff at harvesttime (20:8b; cf. Isa 11:2). This thought is repeated in 20:26. *A wise king winnows out the wicked; he drives the threshing wheel over them*, referring perhaps to a cart used at harvesttime designed to separate wheat from chaff by means of spikes attached to the wheels (cf. Isa 28:27-28).

In actuality the king winnows the wicked when his *lips . . . speak as an oracle* (16:10a). This refers to a divinely guided decision or determination (for similar notions of the king's miraculous insights, see 2 Sam 14:17, 20; cf. 16:23); all this effort is directed to the end that justice be done (16:10b). The king is thus a figure to be regarded with awe, especially when he is functioning in his divinely appointed role of defending right against wrong, the upright against the wicked.

This is not, of course, how kings always conduct themselves. Kings do not in reality always *detest wrongdoing* (as the NIV of 16:12a suggests). A more accurate translation would be, *It is an abomination for kings to practice evil, for a throne is established by uprightness* (16:12, lit.). This is how kings *should* conduct themselves if they wish their reign to be securely established.

Kings in general do *value a man who speaks the truth* (16:13b), but kings, like everyone else, are subject to high and low moods, which a *wise man* will need to relate to and interpret (16:14b). For example, even though a king's face can be as benign as *a rain cloud in spring* (16:15a) and his favor *like dew on the grass* (19:12b), his *wrath* can be as fierce as *the roar of a lion* (19:12a), forewarning of death (16:14a). In this latter case it will be in everyone's best interest if the *wise* servant tries to *appease it* (16:14b; "pacify him," Cohen). Those who live and work in the king's entourage should also be conscious of the many pressures he is under (*Many curry favor with a ruler,* 19:6a) and how powerful are those who have wealth and use it to buy friends (19:6b; cf. 17:8). Bribery can easily pervert one of the chief tasks of royalty, to uphold *the course of justice* (17:23b).

Courts of Law 11:10; 12:5, 17, 28; 14:5, 25; 16:33; 17:15, 23, 26; 18:5, 17, 18; 19:5, 9, 28; 21:8, 12, 28

Acquitting the Guilty and Condemning the Innocent—the LORD Detests Them Both (17:15) 17:15, 26; 18:5, 17; 21:12

The sayings of this block are all related in one way or another to the process by means of which disputes were adjudicated and justice dispensed in the kingdoms of the time. It was the king's supreme duty to see that justice was done and a foremost duty of his servants to assist him in this. The specific form and dynamics of the judicial process are alluded to in 18:17. A lawsuit begins with the offended party presenting his charge (*case*) before a judge (18:17a); then *his*

neighbor (lit.; NIV: *another*) is given the opportunity to defend himself by *searching him out* (18:17b, lit.; NIV: *he questions him*). A
judge is warned against taking the side of the plaintiff before the
defendant has had a chance to present his side of the dispute (18:17).
Two *not-good* sayings stress how important it is for the judge to
be impartial and fair. One states that if *it is not good to punish* [*fine*]
an innocent man, [even more so is it wrong] *to flog officials for their
integrity* (17:26; to humiliate honest officials by having them
whipped). Another thing that is *not good* is for a judge *to lift up the
face of the wicked* (18:5a, lit.), to raise the face of a prostrate sup-
pliant as an indication that his plea has been granted (Toy). Yielding
to a wicked man's abject pleading in this manner (out of pity, perhaps)
would *deprive the innocent* [the injured party] *of justice* (18:5b).
    A similar point is made in yet another saying, although the trans-
lation is uncertain. It alludes to a *righteous one* (*ṣadîq*) showing too
much consideration for *the house of the wicked* (21:12a; the household of a guilty man) and in effect perverting *the wicked* by being too
lenient (Cohen). In summary, *Acquitting the guilty and condemning
the innocent—the LORD detests them both* (17:15; lit., *verily, both
are an abomination to Yahweh*; cf. Exod 23:6-8). For a society to be
pleasing to God, a foremost requirement is that it have just laws justly
adjudicated.

A Truthful Witness Gives Honest Testimony, but a False Witness Tells Lies (12:17) 12:5, 17; 14:5, 25; 17:23; 19:5, 9, 28; 21:8, 28

Any system designed to dispense justice must of necessity rely on the
testimony of witnesses. These ten sayings are all about the importance
of such witnesses giving truthful testimony. Two simply define what a
true and false witness is in the most basic of terms: *A truthful witness
gives honest testimony* (12:17a) and *does not deceive* (14:5a), but *a
false witness tells lies* (12:17b) and *pours out lies* (14:5b). Another
saying alludes to the beneficial consequences that follow from the
actions of a truthful witness: *A truthful witness saves lives* (14:25). A
fourth saying paints an especially graphic portrait of a totally *corrupt
witness,* who *mocks at justice* and *gulps down evil* (19:28). This person's advice is *deceitful* (12:5). Such a witness is not averse to accepting *a bribe in secret* [lit., *from the bosom*] *to pervert the course of
justice* (17:23). *Crooked is the way of a criminal* (21:8a, Cohen).
    Of special note are the three remaining sayings, which declare
confidently that *a false witness will not go unpunished* (19:5a, 9a),

will perish (19:9b; 21:28a), *will not go free* (19:5b; the Hebrew text of 21:28b is unclear). Alden's suggestion that this group of sayings should be interpreted in the light of Deuteronomy 19:15-19 is helpful (143). The point made in this text is that "one witness is not enough to convict a man accused of any crime"; the testimony of "two or three witnesses" is required (19:15). This important development in judicial procedure provided an opportunity for judges to check one witness against another and "make a thorough investigation" as to their veracity, if they contradicted one another (19:18). The witness discovered to be "giving false testimony against his brother" (19:19) could then be made liable to the fine or punishment he had sought to bring upon his neighbor by means of his false testimony (19:19; cf. the graphically told story of Susanna in the Greek version of Daniel). The sayings in Proverbs presuppose this procedure for verifying testimony by means of several witnesses and tacitly support it.

Casting the Lot Settles Disputes and Keeps Strong Opponents Apart (18:18) 16:33; 18:18

These two sayings imply the court procedures alluded to in the preceding sayings were not the only way disputes might be settled. In certain circumstances *casting the lot* might be preferred over the normal way of adjudicating disputes (18:18). Where the contenders are *strong* (each has an especially strong case to make for their point of view), it can serve to keep the contentious parties apart (keep them from perpetually contending with each other). It is essential, however, that both parties to the dispute agree to this procedure and have confidence that once *the lot is cast into the lap, its every decision is from the LORD* (16:33). This procedure is mentioned elsewhere in Scripture as the means by which priests sometimes dispensed decisions (Num 27:21; Deut 33:8). It was also how the land was apportioned at the time of settlement (Josh 14:2) and the means by which Israel's first king was selected (1 Sam 10:16-26). It may have involved posing questions for which a "yes" or "no" answer could be obtained by withdrawing one of two objects from the pouch (of a sacred garment) in *the lap* (Prov 16:33a; cf. 1 Sam 23:9-12; 30:7-8).

Qualities That Make a Nation Great 11:10, 14; 14:28, 34; 15:22; 20:18; 21:15

A theme for this section is aptly stated in 14:34: *Righteousness exalts a nation, but sin is a disgrace to any people.* What distinguishes the sayings of this subgroup is their reference to the success or failure of a people or nation. Three of the sayings emphasize how important it is—if a nation is to be successful in its various enterprises (including war)—that those leading it be open to the thoughts and opinions of *many advisers* (11:14b; 15:22b; 20:18). A major reason for a nation's failure, these sayings suggest, is too little input into the decision-making processes (lack of consultation, 15:22a; *lack of guidance,* 11:14a). Too few citizens can also be a problem (14:28; a declining birthrate?).

Three additional sayings focus on the deeper moral issues involved in national greatness or decline. The profound emotional impact of justice being rendered through a nation's courts of law is highlighted in one saying: *When justice is done, it brings joy to the righteous but terror to evildoers* (21:15; cf. Deut 19:20). How successful a nation is in this regard has implications for its international standing, as the following saying implies: *Righteousness exalts a nation* [in the eyes of other nations], *but sin* [including the miscarriage of justice] *is a disgrace to any people* (14:34). The phrase, *to any people,* underscores the relevance this saying has for every nation on earth (cf. 8:14-16). This is true as well for the world's cities: *When the righteous prosper, the city rejoices; when the wicked perish, there are shouts of joy* (11:10). When a society's laws are just and justly upheld, the wicked are curtailed, the upright are protected, and its citizens rejoice.

THE TEXT IN BIBLICAL CONTEXT

Creating a Just Society and World

This group of sayings expresses some of the national and international ideals of those who produced the Solomon and Hezekiah editions of this book. They show how wise leaders wanted a kingdom to work: with honest, courteous, prudent civil servants under the supervision of fair-minded kings, upholding just laws in an equitable manner. To this end additional teachings on this theme were attached in the supplements to the main collection (22:17–23:3; 25:1-10; 28:1–29:27). Whoever becomes acquainted with this group of sayings and others like them elsewhere in Proverbs will realize how serious the Hezekiah reformers were about creating a just society, not just in Israel but also throughout the world.

Deuteronomy

These lofty ideals for Israel and the world are also expressed in other books of the Bible published at this time *[Hezekiah Reform Literature].* A core conviction of this literature is the statement in

Deuteronomy (the constitutional foundation of these reforms) that God had created Israel for a unique role in world history (Deut 4:32-34). It was to be an upright kingdom and therefore blessed and powerful among the nations (28:1-14)—not only for its own sake but also as an example to be held in awe and emulated by other nations of the world (4:5-8). A defining goal of this kingdom-reform literature was to create a court system informed by just laws, where citizens could receive a fair settlement of their disputes (cf. 16:18-20) (McBride: 73-74).

The Prophets

This is an aspect of national life about which the prophets of the time also spoke with conviction. A prime example are the oracles of the prophet Isaiah, in many respects the architect of Hezekiah's reforms. In his famous allegory of the vineyard, he expressed his dismay over the abysmal degree to which the nation's court system had broken down (Isa 5:1-7). The alliterative words of its final line may be represented as follows: "The LORD Almighty . . . looked for 'right,' but behold 'riot'; for 'harmony,' but behold 'harm.'" But Isaiah had not lost hope. He envisioned a new leader "on David's throne," who would repair the vineyard and govern Judah in "justice and righteousness" (9:7; cf. 11:3-5). Not just Judah would be the beneficiary of such an upright reign, but also the world's other nations. So far as we know, Isaiah was the first of the prophets to envision a world without war as a result of the gradual willingness of nations to arbitrate their differences in the light of recognized laws and an established authority for adjudicating them (Isa 2:1-5). Micah 4:1-5 repeats this vision at a strategic place in his prophetic book (Miller, 2004:37-39).

Genesis 1-11

Similar hopes are expressed in the opening chapters of the Bible. In Genesis 1-11—by means of a compact sequence of theologically rich stories—we are told of the origins of the world's nations. Though sometimes read as a story of sin and despair, Genesis 1-11 can also be read as a story of hope. Sin and anarchy do threaten the world at its beginning (Gen 3-6), followed by a great flood (7-8). Yet there is a hope-filled new beginning (Gen 9), giving rise to a world inhabited by a multitude of flourishing nations and peoples (Gen 10-11). The difference between the two periods of history (the sin and anarchy before the great flood, and the rise of flourishing nations after the flood) is God's promise to bless and uphold the world (8:21-22). God implements this promise by issuing divine decrees in Genesis 9:1-6, specifying actions to be taken by the world's peoples (the sons of Noah). They must act decisively to respect and protect human life against murderous assaults and thus put an end to the sheer anarchy that had existed before the great flood. These decrees, known as the Noachide laws in Jewish tradition, are the narrator's way of signifying the God-willed worldwide existence of peoples and kingdoms that do actually protect the right to life of their citizens.

The origins and existence of the world's nations, as founded and sustained by God in this manner, provide the context in which the narrator in Genesis relates the story of Israel's own origins. In Genesis 12:1-3 we learn of God's summons to Abram/Abraham and Sarai/Sarah to be the progenitors of a people who will intensify God's blessings among all the nations and peoples whose origins are described in Genesis 1-11. This mission will be accomplished, the narrative states, as their descendants become an exemplary "kingdom of priests and a holy nation" (Exod 19:5-6). The image here is not that of Israel as a great and powerful kingdom in its own right, one that other kingdoms might fear and emulate, as in Deuteronomy. Instead, this people is to be a witness and blessing to other nations by knowing and doing what is right (cf. Gen 12:3; 18:19; Miller, 2004:40-43).

The New Testament

The NT similarly recognizes national governments and expects them to approve and support the right. Peter speaks of them as "every authority instituted among men" and urges followers of Jesus Christ to "submit yourselves" to them "for the Lord's sake: . . . whether to the king, as the supreme authority, or to governors, who are sent by him to punish those who do wrong and to commend those who do right" (1 Pet 2:13). Paul also refers to rulers as "governing authorities, . . . which God has established," and "as God's servant, an agent of wrath to bring punishment on the wrongdoer. Therefore," he writes, "it is necessary [for Christian believers] to submit to the authorities, not only because of possible punishment but also because of conscience" (Rom 13:1-5). He also explains that this is "why you pay taxes, for the authorities are God's servants, who give their full time to governing" (13:6).

In the Gospels (as in Genesis) these nations are depicted as the focus of the world mission of Jesus and his disciples. In Matthew's Gospel, Jesus commissions the disciples to make disciples of all nations (Matt 28:18-20). In Luke's Gospel, the disciples are envisioned proclaiming "repentance and forgiveness of sins to all nations" (Luke 24:45-48). Thus in both Testaments the people of God are summoned forth on a mission to bring about blessings on earth through a change for the better in the life of all nations. What that change for the better entails so far as the court systems of these nations are concerned is the subject of the sayings in Proverbs we have just looked at.

THE TEXT IN THE LIFE OF THE CHURCH

The High Calling of Good Government in the Global Village

The sayings in this section of Proverbs serve as reminders of the high calling of those responsible for devising and enforcing the laws of the various nations of the world. There was a time in North America and elsewhere when laws and the court systems that implement them were taken for granted. People assumed that if disputes arose or a court of law was needed, it would be there, and the laws would be fair and fairly interpreted and enforced. Events have changed all that: the massive breakdown of law and unspeakable crimes against humanity in powerful modern nation-states during the twentieth century, and the global wars that ensued. Wise people now are giving renewed attention worldwide to the importance of just laws being justly adjudicated as a simple necessity for the well-being of every nation on earth. Without a justly administered court system, free of corruption, a people simply cannot prosper.

It was in this context of the massive breakdown of law and order in the global village and the world wars that ensued that the United Nations was founded in 1945. Three years later, on December 10, 1948, through its auspices, the world's nations adopted without dissent a universal declaration of human rights. The UN charter holds forth the hope that after "the scourge of war, which twice in our lifetime has brought untold sorrow to mankind," another way might be found. In that way "the acceptance of principles and the institution of methods" would insure that "armed force shall not be used, save in the common interest." The entry to the UN headquarters in New York City displays the hope-filled words of Isaiah. They speak of a time to come when the nations of the world will have found a way to adjudicate their disputes in the light of God's law and will start to "beat their swords into plowshares" (Isa 2:2-4).

On March 11, 2003, another momentous step was taken. For the first time in human history, an International Criminal Court was established at The Hague, to prosecute war crimes and crimes against humanity committed by or in the eighty-nine countries that agreed to participate in this court. The court's first president, Philippe Kirsch, in a speech given at the United Nations about this court, characterized the establishment of the rule of law as a "matter of life and death." "The International Criminal Court," he said, "will have a profound effect on the lives of ordinary people. A clarion call has gone out to potential perpetrators of unspeakable atrocities that the world is not going to stand by silently and watch the commission of outrageous violations of international law, such as genocide, war crimes and crimes against humanity. The world has decided that 'enough is enough.'" We can sense in these words the same governmental idealism that reverberates again and again in the sayings in Proverbs just surveyed: *Righteousness exalts a nation, but sin is a disgrace to any people* (Prov 14:34).

The Calling of the Church in Fostering Good Government in the Global Village

Several nations of the world (including the United States) have still not signed on to the agreement that established the International Criminal Court. Unless changed, this opposition portends an ongoing debate over the rule of law in the global village. The churches' role in this momentous debate is complicated by differences over the relationship of church and state. The just-discussed sayings in Proverbs bear witness to social and governmental ideals at the heart of Israel's Scriptures. In Proverbs these ideals are cast in a form that makes them applicable not just for Israel but for every society on earth. The Christian church, as a community that shares Israel's calling to be light and blessing to all the world's nations (Isa 42:6; 49:6; Gen 12:1-3; Matt 5:14-16), is thereby reminded of its calling to foster just laws and good government at home and abroad. For this a global vision is needed.

"Human rights cannot exist simply as a set of isolated positivist demands. To be meaningful, such demands depend on a larger world view, an overarching interpretation of human nature and human existence." These words of Christopher Marshall, in his book subtitled *Human Rights in the Biblical Tradition* (47), pose the question of where such a worldview might be found. Marshal goes on to observe, "The secular human rights tradition was forged on the foundation of Christian theological assumptions and a Christian value system that encouraged respect for individual dignity." However, he adds, "the accumulated capital of that Christian ethic is now substantially depleted in Western culture, which makes consideration of a Christian perspective on human rights timely as well as legitimate" (47). The convictions expressed by Raymond Van Leeuwen in a recent essay on this subject are strikingly similar. He laments the fact that "secular society denies the objective reality of God in the world" and "tries to restrict 'god' to the subjective irrelevance of individual hearts." This poses, he believes, one of the church's foremost challenges. "Since this neopagan society overwhelmingly shapes the media and forms of our communal life, the church's most difficult spiritual battles may not concern what we do in worship or in private. Rather, it is in our public, civic existence that we Christians are prone to sin and fall short of God's glory (Rom 3:23)." Therefore, he declares, "like the godly Israelite and Christian inhabitants of the pagan empires of old, we latter-day servants of God must rediscover the more difficult spirituality of wisdom and obedience in the ordinary" (2000:210). He urges that "all our 'secular' activities must be done with a wisdom, righteousness, and love that reflect the Creator's own building of creation. It is here that the people of God especially need revival; it is here that our *spirituality* is most often lacking" (2000:209-10).

Proverbs 10:1—22:16

Speech: Tongue, Lips, Mouth and Words

The Book of Proverbs, Part 2: The Themes of the Main Collection							
Wisdom	Nation-hood	Speech	Family	Econo-mics	Personal Rela-tions	Matters of the Heart	Know-ledge of the Holy One

PREVIEW

Another subject of utmost importance to the wisdom teachers of Israel was instruction in speaking. Training on this matter was a prominent feature of the Egyptian scribal schools as well. To know how to speak appropriately and well was essential to the functioning of a civil servant not only in his professional capacities as "messenger" or envoy, but also in his personal relationships. While skill in writing was also important, the world of the time was an oral culture to an extent unknown in the world today. How a person spoke, how concisely and clearly, as well as how picturesquely and movingly (as the occasion required), was a distinguishing mark of a well-educated person. On the other hand, there were problems in this realm that needed attention. Just as a kingdom could be built up through speech, certain uses of

143

speech could also tear it down. *Death and life are in the hands of the tongue!* (18:21a, lit.).

To become wise in this regard was not easy. The world's oldest wisdom manual of this kind, the Egyptian The Instruction of the Vizier Ptah-hotep, characterizes "speaking" as "more difficult than any labor," and one who knows how to do it well as a real "craftsman" (Pritchard: 414). Another ancient manual, written by a Pharaoh (The Instruction for King Merikare), likens the well-trained tongue to "a sword" and deems its use "more valorous than any fighting" (Pritchard: 415). Yet another Egyptian manual, The Instruction of Amenemope, expresses the hope that all its teachings might provide a "mooring-stake for the tongue" at a time "when there is a whirlwind of words" (Pritchard: 422).

Some fifty sayings in the Main Collection of the book of Proverbs are about right and wrong ways of speaking, although this is not how the subject is identified in the sayings themselves. The sayings themselves refer to good and bad speech in terms of the bodily organs used in producing speech. *A wise man's heart guides his mouth* is the way speech is described in one of the sayings (16:23); the mouth, tongue, and lips, which produce the words, are the focus of most of these sayings.

I have noted four subthemes around which the proverbs on this subject cluster. First, there are sayings focusing mainly on the tremendous benefits of knowing how to speak well. The focus of another group is on the importance of being restrained and disciplined when speaking. A third surprisingly large group identifies devious ways of speaking that can harm or destroy one's neighbor or a whole community. There is, finally, a cluster of sayings that point to the healing or wounding power of certain modes of speech.

OUTLINE

Benefits of Knowing How to Speak Well, 10:10, 11, 20, 21;
    12:14; 13:2; 16:23, 24; 18:20, 21; 22:11
Disciplined, Restrained Speaking, 10:11, 19, 31, 32; 12:13, 23;
    13:3, 5; 14:3; 15:28; 16:23; 17:27, 28; 18:13; 21:23
Harmful Speech, 10:18; 11:9, 11, 12, 13, 19; 12:6, 19; 16:27,
    28, 29, 30; 17:4, 7, 20; 18:6, 7, 8; 20:19
Healing Words, Wounding Words, 12:18; 15:1, 4, 23; 16:24

EXPLANATORY NOTES

Benefits of Knowing How to Speak Well   10:10, 11, 20, 21; 12:14; 13:2; 16:23, 24; 18:20, 21; 22:11

From the Fruit of His Lips a Man Is Filled with Good Things as Surely as the Work of His Hands Rewards Him (12:14) 12:14; 13:2; 16:24; 18:20, 21

These five sayings refer to the *fruit of the lips* (12:14; 13:2; 18:20) and *tongue* (18:21) as something that a person can *eat* (18:21) and use to fill his *stomach* (18:20; 12:14)—it is just that tangible. The benefits of this *fruit* are likened to the rewards that come from manual labor (12:14). Speech like this is as vital to life as what is done with the hands; its absence is equally powerful. Because *the tongue has the power of life and death* (lit., *death and life are in the hand of the tongue!* 18:21a), *those who love it will eat its fruit* (18:21:b). When they do so, *a man's stomach is filled; with the harvest from his lips he is satisfied* (18:20). Yet another saying likens *pleasant words* to the eating of a *honeycomb, sweet to the soul* [*nepeš, spirit*] *and healing to the bones* (16:24; cf. Ps 19:10). *Pleasant words* (gracious, loving, agreeable words) have a beneficial effect (like good-tasting, nourishing food) on the whole person, body and spirit.

The Lips of the Righteous Nourish Many, but Fools Die for Lack of Judgment (10:21) 10:11, 20, 21

The sayings in the prior section focused on the personal benefits of knowing how to speak well. These three sayings note the benefits to others. The saying in 10:21 points to the way *the lips of the righteous nourish* others, *many* others. By contrast, *fools die for lack of judgment* [Heb.: *heart*] (10:21b). Fools can neither produce such nourishment for others or themselves. The word translated *nourish* in 10:21a refers to the feeding that comes from being pastured and grazed by a shepherd (see Ps 78:72; Ezek 34:2, 3, 8, 10, 23).

The *mouth of the righteous* is also described as a *fountain of life* (10:11). That the lips of the righteous *nourish many* alludes to the role of the righteous as teachers, as in Psalms 1 and 119. There, *righteous* and *wicked* designate contrasting social circles (Ps 1:6), one of students and teachers of Torah, the other of *sinners* and *mockers* (Ps 1:1-2). There is a similar contrast in the reference to *the righteous* and *the wicked* in 10:20. The *tongue of the righteous* is likened to *choice silver* and by contrast *the heart of the wicked* is said to be of *little value,* worthless metal that produces speech of little value to others (see final theme of the Main Collection, "Knowledge of the Holy One").

Disciplined, Restrained Speaking 10:11, 19, 31, 32; 12:13, 23; 13:3, 5; 14:3; 15:28; 16:23; 17:27, 28; 18:13; 21:23

When Words Are Many, Sin Is Not Absent, but He Who Holds His Tongue Is Wise (10:19) 10:11, 19, 31, 32; 12:23; 13:5; 15:28; 16:23; 17:27, 28; 18:13

A virtue universally cultivated in the schools of the time was that of a restrained, disciplined use of words. That is the subject of these ten sayings. The *words* that *are many,* referred to in 10:19a, are presumed to be thoughtless, inappropriate words and therefore bound to cause offense (*sin is not absent,* 10:19a). The basic point is that a person who is *wise* learns how to restrain his tongue (10:19b; 17:28b). The overall effect of such restraint is that a wise person generally speaks less than a foolish one (17:27), which is why it can be said, half-humorously, that *even a fool is thought wise if he keeps silent* (17:28a).

The ideal is that *the heart of the righteous,* before speaking, first *weighs* (lit., *meditates on*) what is going to be said before blurting it out; *but the mouth of the wicked gushes evil* (15:28). This trait is beautifully expressed in the saying *A wise man's heart guides his mouth* [lit., *makes his mouth wise*], *and his lips promote instruction* [lit., *adds instruction to his lips*] (16:23).

An especially annoying and unattractive habit to be avoided is to *answer before listening* (18:13). A rule of thumb to be observed is that, in general, the prudent person is much slower to speak and give advice than is the foolish one (12:23). All this explains why *the mouth of the righteous* [when it does speak] *brings forth* [lit., *buds with*] *wisdom* (10:31a) and is *a fountain of life* (10:11a). By contrast, *the mouth of the wicked conceals violence* (10:11b, lit.); the reference is to a *perverse* [*lying* or *deceiving*] *tongue that will be cut out* (10:31b). The image of a tongue being cut out is gruesome, but meant to shock. It expresses the *hate* the righteous have for *what is false* (13:5a; lit., *a false* [or *lying*] *word*); in short, a righteous man hates lying. In summary, because of their honesty and because they think before speaking, *the lips of the righteous know what is fitting* (10:32a).

*He Who Guards His Mouth and His Tongue Keeps Himself
from Calamity (21:23) 12:13; 13:3; 14:3; 21:23*

These four sayings emphasize the benefits that accrue for the life
and soul of those who learn how to restrain their tongues. They will
experience much less trouble in their lives. The connection between
the two (restraining the tongue and a less troubled life) is brought out
sharply in 21:23 by the use of the same Hebrew verb at the beginning
of both lines: *He who guards his mouth and his tongue, guards himself from calamity* (21:23, lit.). Likewise, *he who guards his lips*
[Heb.: *mouth*] *guards his soul* (13:3a). In the second line of this saying (13:3b) is an idiom (in Heb.) for the opposite of guarding one's
mouth: *but he who opens wide his lips* [*speaks rashly*] *will come to
ruin* (13:3b, lit.).

Related to this is what 14:3a says about *a fool's talk*. What this verse
actually says is not that *a fool's talk* [lit., *the mouth of the fool*] *brings
a rod to his back,* but that *in the mouth of a fool is a rod of pride*
(14:3a, lit.). This refers to the fool's tongue, which can be seen wagging
because the fool's lips are *wide open* (13:3b, lit.). By contrast, *the lips
of the wise protect them* (14:3b), that is, the wise person *guards his
soul* (13:3a). A similar point is made in the saying *An evil man is
trapped by his sinful talk* [lit., *by the transgression of his lips*], *but a
righteous man escapes trouble* (12:13). The righteous man escapes
trouble because he is more guarded and does not sin with his lips.

Harmful Speech 10:18; 11:9, 11, 12, 13, 19; 12:6, 19; 16:27, 28, 29, 30; 17:4, 7, 20; 18:6, 7, 8; 20:19

*With His Mouth the Godless Destroys His Neighbor, but
Through Knowledge the Righteous Escape (11:9) 11:9, 11;
12:6*

Three of the nineteen sayings that have as their theme "socially
harmful speech" simply call attention to the destructive power that lies
in the *mouth* of someone perverse. *With his mouth the godless
destroys his neighbor,* states 11:9a. The word *godless* refers (in Heb.)
to a *polluted* or *profane* man ("irreligious" or "alienated from God").
Such a man *destroys his neighbor* with *his mouth,* referring perhaps
to malicious gossip or false testimony (a classic example is the false
testimony of two scoundrels leading to Naboth's execution; 1 Kgs
21:13-14). Only by virtue of his *knowledge* (integrity and intelligence)
can the *righteous* possibly escape such an assault (11:9b).

A similar point is made in 12:6, where the text refers to the *words of the wicked* lurking in the shadows and seeking *blood* (perhaps plotting a murder). If the upright learn of it, *the speech of the upright rescues them* (12:6b, perhaps by warning potential victims). Malicious speech of this kind is not just a danger for individuals but also for the welfare of larger communities. This is the observation made in 11:11, that *by the mouth of the wicked* a whole *city* can be *destroyed,* just as *through the blessing of the upright* it can be *exalted.* The mouth of profane persons intent upon evil poses a danger whose destructive potential should not be disregarded or underestimated.

He Who Conceals His Hatred Has Lying Lips, and Whoever Spreads Slander Is a Fool *(10:18) 10:18; 11:12, 13; 12:19; 16:28; 17:7; 18:8; 20:19*

This group of sayings points to an especially insidious and yet commonplace form of harm that people do with their mouth—the spreading of *slander* (the Hebrew term means *whispering*) by someone with *lying lips,* who *conceals his hatred* (10:18). There is no precise equivalent in Hebrew for our English word *gossip,* often used in translating these sayings (as in NIV: 11:13a; 16:28b; 18:8a; 20:19); the Hebrew text refers to a person like this either as a *whisperer* (16:28b; 18:8a), or as one who bears *tales* (11:13a; 20:19a). A *whisperer* may pretend to be a friend, but instead of concealing intimacies reveals them (*betrays a confidence,* 11:13); such persons simply talk too much (20:19b). *Whisperers* like this may even succeed in alienating *bosom* friends (16:28, lit.; here the Hebrew word for *friend* is the same one used in 2:17 of a young wife's husband). The effect of such whispering on those disposed to listen to it is graphically portrayed in 18:8; here *the words of the whisperer* (lit.) are likened to delicious food, which enters the mouth and goes right down to the *inmost parts* of his belly.

A *trustworthy* person *keeps a secret* (11:13b; lit., *conceals a matter*) and will *avoid a man who talks too much* (20:19b; lit., *does not mix with one whose lips are wide open*). If such *arrogant* destructive talk is not suitable even for a *fool* (17:7a; *fool* here denotes an especially debased character), how much more so are *lying lips* unsuited for a *prince* (17:7b, lit., *a man of noble character*). A human being who behaves in this manner *lacks judgment* (11:12a; lit., *lacks heart*) and is totally mindless.

A Scoundrel Plots Evil, and His Speech Is like a Scorching Fire (16:27) 16:27, 29, 30; 17:4

The person in view (scoundrel) is not a "whisperer," but someone truly evil (bĕliyya'al, a base man such as the one described in 6:12-14); his speech is like a scorching fire (16:27; lit., upon his lips like a burning fire). Like the law-defiant sinners described in 1:10-19, he is out to entice his neighbor into joining him in his delinquent activities (16:29). Only one who is himself an evil person (17:4a, lit.) and a liar (17:4b) would give ear to the wicked lips (17:4a, lit.) and tongue (17:4b) of such a person. Those who decide they want nothing to do with such individuals can keep their distance, for it is easy to spot them; their body-language gives them away: He who winks with his eye is plotting perversity; he who purses his lips is bent on evil (16:30).

A Man of Perverse Heart Does Not Prosper; He Whose Tongue Is Deceitful Falls into Trouble (17:20) 12:19; 17:20; 18:6, 7

Those who misuse their lips, tongues, and mouths in this way, harming others, also harm themselves eventually. That is the truth to which these four sayings call our attention. Someone with a perverse heart (lit., crooked heart) and deceitful (lit., twisted) tongue will not prosper (lit., find good; come to a good end) but falls into trouble instead (17:20). The kind of trouble he can expect is outlined briefly in 18:6. A fool's lips lead to personal quarrels and strife (18:6a; the Hebrew term for strife can also refer to lawsuits); his mouth invites [calls for] a beating (18:6b; either by an offended party or by order of the court). In this manner a fool's mouth and lips can become a self-destructive trap (NIV: snare) leading to personal ruin (18:7). The tragedy is that those who play so fast and loose with truth do not realize the fleeting, momentary nature of their gains: A lying tongue lasts only a moment (12:19b; lit., until I move [my eyelid], Cohen), but truthful lips endure forever (12:19a).

Healing Words, Wounding Words 12:18; 15:1, 4, 23; 16:24

Reckless Words Pierce Like a Sword, but the Tongue of the Wise Brings Healing (12:18) 12:18; 15:4; 16:24

The previous sayings highlight the social consequences of right and wrong ways of speaking; these sayings focus on the psychologi-

cal consequences. *There is reckless speaking [reckless words] like the wounds of a sword*, states 12:18a (lit.), *but the tongue of the wise is healing* (12:18b, lit.; NIV: *brings healing*). *Pleasant words are . . . sweet to the soul [spirit] and healing to the bones [body]* (16:24). The effect of the tongue's healing and wounding alluded to in these verses is spelled out in 15:4: *The tongue that brings healing is a tree of life* (15:4a); it has a therapeutic or life-enhancing effect (cf. 3:18; Ezek 47:12). *But a deceitful tongue* [lit., *a twisting therein*] *crushes the spirit* (15:4b) and is emotionally devastating).

A Gentle Answer Turns Away Wrath, but a Harsh Word Stirs Up Anger (15:1) 15:1; 23

These two sayings relate to an especially tense moment in human communication, one charged with rising tension and hostility. Accusations or arguments have been presented, questions have been raised, and an answering response is required. A distinction is drawn between the results that will ensue (under such circumstances) of using a *gentle answer* versus *a harsh word* (15:1). The Hebrew word for *harsh* might be better translated *hurtful*; a word causing pain stirs up anger. The opposite of the pain-causing word is a *tender* answer (cf. 4:3; *gentle*, 15:1a, NIV) that reconciles (*turns away wrath*, 15:1a). What a *joy* it is when a person's *mouth* is able to answer in this manner; *how good is a timely word* (15:23). "The function of speech is to provide a cement for society (cf. Gen 11) and to resolve or lessen the conflicts between persons which inevitably arise in the social context" (McKane: 477).

THE TEXT IN BIBLICAL CONTEXT

Speaking the Truth in Love

The Bible is replete with stories in which good and bad ways of speaking play a vital role. At its best, speech is exemplified in the openhearted, respectful, persuasive, and disciplined speech of Abraham's servant to his hosts as he finds a wife for Isaac (Gen 24:34-49). He knows exactly when to remain silent and when to speak. He is truthful without being blunt or discourteous. Speaking at its worst is illustrated by the abrupt, thoughtless rebuff of Nabal to David's men (1 Sam 25:9-13). How to turn away wrath with a gentle answer is eloquently portrayed in the episode that follows. Nabal's wife artfully calms and diverts David's fierce anger at her husband's boorishness. The dialogues in chapter 1 of Ruth between Naomi and her daughters-in-law and in chapter 3 between Ruth and Boaz are classics of gracious, respectful dialogue.

The NT also has many examples of eloquent speech, the outstanding example being the conciseness and beauty of Jesus's words in various settings. While his parables were sometimes blunt and forceful, study of them in their oldest versions (Miller: 1981) reveals them to be powerful examples of *soft answers* (Prov 15:1, KJV) to harsh accusations, with the intention of achieving reconciliation (cf. Luke 15). Elsewhere in the NT this kind of speech is referred to as "speaking the truth in love" so that "we will in all things grow up into him who is the Head, that is, Christ" (Eph 4:15). The tremendous challenges involved in taming the tongue are the focus of a series of picturesque observations and warnings in James 3:1-12.

Let Your "Yes" Be "Yes"

One of the wisest epigrams on the subject of good and bad ways of speaking is the saying of Jesus against oath making. "Simply let your 'Yes' be 'Yes,' and your 'No,' 'No'; anything beyond this comes from the evil one" (Matt 5:37). It is an aphorism that captures the heart of various concerns addressed in this group of proverbs: those that express hatred for lying (13:5a), those that highlight the destructive effects of *whispering* behind people's backs, and those that warn against the dark, destructive plans of plotters of evil.

The saying's specific target was a habit of oath swearing that had gotten out of hand. In Matthew 23:16-22 Jesus refers to particular practices of the time. Artificial distinctions were being drawn between different kinds of oaths, all in the name of gaining a certain leeway in the sincerity or truth of one's utterances or commitments. Jesus's response calls for a total eradication of oath making in favor of simplicity and transparency of speech. James 5:12 cites Jesus's words in Matthew 5:37 as a caption for the book's closing sequence of remarks, in which James touches on several aspects of "speech in the Assembly of Faith" (Johnson: 326-27). The words "Let your 'yes' be 'yes,' and your 'no,' 'no'" were for James a model for the transparent simplicity that should characterize how Christ's followers pray and sing, and deal with their sicknesses and sins (Jas 5:13-20).

Jesus on the Subject of "Whispering"

Special attention should also be given to the way the teachings of Jesus in Matthew's Gospel pick up the admonitions in Proverbs against character assassination by "whispering" and tale-bearing. Jesus equates angry destructive speech of this kind as equivalent to murder (Matt 5:21-26) and advocates self-criticism as the antidote to an excessive criticism of others (7:1-5). Moreover, his words in 18:19 call for a direct and open meeting between the offended and offenders in the context of the congregation met in Jesus's name. Instead of criticizing a brother to others, fellow members in the church are urged to "go and show him his fault, just between the two of you. If he listens to you, you have won your brother over. But if he will not listen, take one or two others along, so that 'every matter may be established by the testimony of two or three witnesses'" (18:15-16; cf. Deut 19:15).

The additional sayings attributed to Jesus in Matthew 18:17-19 indicate how seriously issues of this kind were being taken in the communities of those who preserved these words. When they met in Jesus's name, they felt they were empowered by his presence to deal with such issues.

THE TEXT IN THE LIFE OF THE CHURCH

Taming the Tongue

In a world increasingly linked and dependent upon honest, forthright, and yet apt and skillful communication, the relevance of the values set forth in this group of sayings has never been greater. The English department of the university where I teach is paying increasing attention not just to the writing skills of its students, but also to their oral skills. All churches have a very special reason for being concerned about the quality of speech of their members. Believers churches have a special reason to pay attention to these matters. Based as they are on the consent of their members and the mutuality of their commitment, open lines of communication are essential to their survival and growth.

This topic is also very alive in conflict transformation circles. The way words can kill, the handling of disputes, the importance of reconciling modes of speech, the importance of talking through differences rather than gossiping—all these and other issues touched on in this block of proverbial sayings remain as current and important today as ever. The following is a quote from the *Mediation and Facilitation Training Manual* published by the Mennonite Conciliation Service (fourth edition): "Communication lies at the heart of all interactions. It is central to all conflict because it *causes* conflict through miscommunication and misunderstanding, it *expresses* conflict, verbally and nonverbally, and it is *a vehicle for conflict transformation,* positive or negative" (Schrock-Shenk: 131). The sayings on this theme in this section of Proverbs touch on every one of these issues.

Dealing with "Whispering"

One of the most destructive things that can happen in a congregation is "whispering"—today the word is gossip. Gossiping is not usually included with the deadly sins, but in my experience its effect is deadly to the life of a community. A number of the proverbs speak to this issue. This is also a focus of some words of Jesus quoted in Matthew 18:15-17 (see above). When we feel offended or critical of others, the human temptation is not to talk to them but to others about them. This is a form of "whispering." Why do we "whisper"? We do it because it makes us feel good; at the moment we are criticizing another, we feel superior to that other person. There is camaraderie in doing this: we feel a bond with the listener, a bond of mutual supe-riority to the person being criticized. Meanwhile, that person knows nothing of what is happening. The well of community spirit is being poisoned.

By attending more closely to the quality of speech in our congre-gations, we can purify that well. We can raise the temperature of love and goodwill and make a contribution to the wider society. Individuals in our congregations will take these values to their workplaces. Our youth will take them to school. The world is increasingly adopting a more democratic mode of governance. Successful democracies are reliant on character education that includes resolving differences in the courteous, straightforward, honest ways advocated in Proverbs and elsewhere in the Bible.

Do Not Swear at All

A lengthy article on the "Oath" in *The Mennonite Encyclopedia* describes in detail how from their beginnings in the sixteenth century and since then the Anabaptists opposed the oath administered by gov-ernments in judicial proceedings to insure the honesty of those whose witness is being adjudicated. "It is noteworthy," the article states, "that the principle of nonswearing of oaths has been and still is upheld by all Mennonite groups of whatever country, conference, or theological position, the one historic Anabaptist-Mennonite principle of which this can be said" (Neff and Bender: 5).

In further clarification of how legal oath making was and is justi-fied by others but not by the Anabaptists, the article states:

> Luther interpreted the passage in Matthew 5 as forbidding the swearing of an oath on one's own initiative or out of custom, but taught that the command of the state to render an oath must be obeyed. . . . The Heidelberg Catechism answers thus the question whether one may piously

swear an oath with the name of God: "Yes, if it is required by the authorities or in case of need to maintain and promote loyalty and truth to the
honor of God and the welfare of one's neighbor. For such swearing is
grounded in the Word of God and therefore was rightly used by the saints
of the Old and New Testaments." This is the general Protestant understanding and teaching concerning the oath down to the present time. It is
claimed that the oath is necessary even in a Christian society because of
the all too common unreliability of ordinary statements and the general
distrust of people toward each other, in short because of the imperfection
of human society. Says Martenson, "Lying and mutual distrust are with us,
and so from ancient times the oath has been used as a guarantee for truthfulness." (Neff, Bender: 3)

The reason the Anabaptists took a different position was simply
because of the command of Jesus. "The seventh article of the
Schleitheim Confession of Feb. 24, 1527, expressly refers to the prohibition of Christ 'who taught the perfection of the law and forbids
Christians all swearing.' Our speech is to be simply yes and no. This
was the general rule among the Anabaptists as is frequently attested
in the trials, disputations, and confessions extracted by torture" (Neff
and Bender: 4). In other words, in the name of Christ—as a witness
to the truthfulness and simplicity of speech that he advocated—they
refused to comply with oaths that were designed to secure truthfulness. In most countries courts of law permit those who refuse to take
oaths for this reason simply to affirm that they are telling the truth.
This gesture might seem a small thing, but it signifies how important
for the health of our communities is the simple act of letting our "yes"
be "yes," and our "no" be "no."

Proverbs 10:1—22:16

Family: Husbands and Wives, Parents and Children

The Book of Proverbs, Part 2: The Themes of the Main Collection							
Wisdom	Nation-hood	Speech	Family	Econo-mics	Personal Rela-tions	Matters of the Heart	Know-ledge of the Holy One

PREVIEW

It is significant that both the first and second major sections of Proverbs are headed by teachings on the theme of parents and children. In 1:8-9 sons are counseled to heed their parent's teachings; in 10:1 they are made aware of the emotional impact their folly or wisdom has on their parents. The placement of words such as these at the forefront of these sections is but one indication of the importance accorded parents as teachers. That other aspects of family life were also of concern is evident from the degree of attention paid in chapters 1-9 to marital discord (due to unfaithful husbands and "loose women"). In the sayings of 10:1–22:16, this particular issue is put

155

aside (with only one brief reference near the end of the collection: 22:14). However, other matters of equal importance to the family are addressed: (1) how to found a family (finding a wife and the kind of wife to look for), and (2) thoughts and advice about parent-children relations. For the editors of this collection, the nuclear family (with husband, wife, and children) was a social institution of paramount importance for the long-range well-being of their people.

OUTLINE

Husband-Wife Relations: Finding a Wife and Remaining Faithful,
    12:4; 14:1; 18:22; 19:13, 14; 21:9, 19; 22:14
Parent-Children Relations: Having Children and How to Raise
    Them, 10:1; 11:29; 13:1, 24; 15:5, 20; 17:2, 6, 21, 25;
    19:13, 18, 26; 20:7, 11, 20, 29, 30; 22:6, 15

EXPLANATORY NOTES

Finding a Wife and Remaining Faithful 12:4; 14:1; 18:22; 19:13, 14; 21:9, 19; 22:14

He Who Finds a Wife Finds What Is Good, and Receives Favor from the LORD 18:22

Wife and *good* are closely linked in this exuberant, definitive statement—to find a wife is to find what is *good.* Indeed, finding a wife is a special mark of *Yahweh's* favor. Implied in the statement is that Yahweh is intimately involved in the success of such a venture (see 19:14, below). That finding a wife is *good* seems to echo the words in the creation account: "It is not good for the man to be alone" (Gen 2:18). The thought that Yahweh is personally involved in this process also recalls that part of the creation story, where, after creating woman, Yahweh personally presents her to Adam to be his wife (2:22). For the compilers of the book of Proverbs and for the authors of the Genesis creation account, marriage is viewed as something wonderful and *good,* which Yahweh himself designed and is personally interested in bringing to fulfillment.

A Wife of Noble Character Is Her Husband's Crown, but a Disgraceful Wife Is Like Decay in His Bones (12:4) 12:4; 14:1; 19:13; 21:9, 19

These same compilers knew, of course, that marriage could also be the arena for tragedy. This group of sayings seeks to alert young men to the fateful consequences of their choices when finding a wife. The ideal wife is identified as a woman of *noble character*; the same term is used at the beginning of the acrostic poem in Proverbs 31:10-31 (also Ruth 3:11). In Proverbs 31:10, the question is raised: *A wife of noble character who can find?* A detailed portrait of such a woman follows, one whose trustworthiness, wisdom, and adeptness in the management of her household are accented. There (in 31:27, lit.) and here (in Prov 14:1), the family domain is referred to as *her house*; it is assumed that a wife has power to build it up or tear it down (14:1). As viewed by these sayings, a wife thus was not only a "one-flesh" partner to her husband and mother of his children, but also a strong companion "suitable for him" (Gen 2:18). An ideal wife was regarded as worthy of praise in her own right (Prov 31:31; Ruth 3:11), but she also brought great good and honor to her husband (Prov 12:4a; 31:12). By contrast, a wife who acts shamefully *is like decay in his bones* (12:4b). A contentious, ill-tempered woman, whose complaints (21:9, 19) are likened to the *dripping* of rain *on a rainy day* (19:13; cf. 27:15), is to be avoided. Better to live *in a desert* or *on the corner of the* [flat] *roof* than with such a woman! (21:19; 21:9; 25:24).

Houses and Wealth Are Inherited from Parents, but a Prudent Wife Is from the LORD 19:14

Whether a man finds the right kind of wife is not completely in his control. Not even parents can guarantee the right kinds of spouses for their children, this saying observes. This is why Abraham's servant prayed for a sign before choosing a wife for Isaac (Gen 24:12-14). The saying assumes that at least three persons are involved in finding a prudent wife: husband, wife, and God. According to Malachi 2:14, Yahweh is personally present as witness when a man and woman make a covenant to be husband and wife. The enormously high esteem accorded marriage and family in the book of Proverbs is nowhere more evident than in the expressed belief that God is somehow personally involved in the formation of a good marriage.

The Mouth of an Adulteress Is a Deep Pit; He Who Is Under the LORD'S Wrath Will Fall into It 22:14

The threat posed to a marriage by a "seductive stranger" (not an *adulteress,* strictly speaking) is thoroughly addressed in the poems on this subject in Proverbs 2-7 *[Identity of the Foreign Seductress].* There was no need to repeat this teaching in the Main Collection, but neither did its compilers want their readers to forget it. That appears to be the reason for this third-from-last saying, which singles out the *mouth* of this kind of women as an especially grave danger to watch out for (as in 2:16; 5:3-4; 7:14-21). Here (22:14) that *mouth* is likened to a deep pit into which a man unwittingly falls to his death! Especially sobering is the thought that a man who *falls* in this manner is *abhorred by Yahweh* (lit.), and that is why he falls (22:14b). A man who is intent on doing such a foolhardy thing has angered God (and been abandoned to his fate) even before he does it. Once again, one senses how much the compilers of this book hated adulterous affairs.

Parent-Children Relations   10:1; 11:29; 13:1, 24; 15:5, 20; 17:2, 6, 21, 25; 19:13, 18, 26; 20:7, 11, 20, 29, 30; 22:6, 15

Children's Children Are a Crown to the Aged, and Parents Are the Pride of Their Children (17:6) 17:6; 20:29

The mutual pride and joy of parents and children is beautifully captured in this saying. This is the only proverb that refers to grandparents—here spoken of as *the aged,* whose grandchildren are likened to the crown a king might wear (see 3:11). The *pride* of children (Heb.: *sons*) in their *parents* (Heb.: *fathers*) is placed in parallel to the grandchildren being the *crown* of the *aged.* In both lines of this saying, the accent falls on the dignity and respect that radiate from a loving family headed by prideworthy parents and grandparents. Young and old have beautiful attributes. *The glory of young men is their strength, gray hair the splendor of the old* (20:29; cf. 16:31).

A Wise Son Brings Joy to His Father, but a Foolish Son Grief to His Mother (10:1) 10:1; 15:20; 17:21, 25

The emotional impact of the behavior of children on both parents is the focus of this group of sayings. Teenagers and young adults are typically unaware of the depth of emotion with which their parents react to their behavior (whether good or bad). The joy a wise son brings to his father is underscored by two of these proverbs (10:1; 15:20); his utter grief and vexation over a foolish, reprobate son is the subject of two others (17:21, 25). The sayings also reflect the mother's *grief* and *bitterness* as *the one who bore* the son who became foolish (10:1b; 17:25b). This aspect of human experience needs to be pondered by youth as a part of their education. They need to know how their actions will affect the happiness of those near and dear to them. It may temper what they do and forewarn them of how their own happiness will be affected one day by *their* children's actions.

He Who Brings Trouble on His Family Will Inherit Only Wind, and the Fool Will Be Servant to the Wise (11:29) 11:29; 17:2; 19:13, 26; 20:20

Children may not only be the cause of emotional distress on the part of their parents, but also may cause them trouble in other ways. The specific *trouble* referred to in 11:29a may be that of "mismanagement or misappropriation of family resources" (McKane: 430), with resulting loss of inheritance (he *will inherit only wind, and the fool will be servant to the wise*). A son who abuses his parents may be replaced by a trustworthy *servant* (17:2). Far worse is the fate of a son who, after taking charge of the family household from his enfeebled parents, *maltreats his father and drives away his mother* (19:26, Toy). Worse still is a son who *curses his father or mother* (20:20a; cf. Exod 21:17; Lev 20:9). The consequence of this latter action is that *his lamp will be snuffed out in pitch darkness* (20:20b; cf. 20:27), an allusion perhaps to a total loss of human personhood (cf. 20:27, where the *spirit of a man* [*'ādām*] is likened to *the lamp of the LORD*).

A Wise Son Heeds a Father's Instruction, but a Mocker Does Not Listen to a Rebuke (13:1) 13:1, 24; 15:5; 19:18; 20:11, 30; 22:6, 15

What can be done to prevent children from becoming reprobates and fools and causing suffering to their parents and themselves? That is the subject of this group of sayings. In 13:1 a *wise son* and a *father's instruction* are paired (without a connecting verb in Hebrew), implying that the one (a *father's instruction*) is a key factor in the other (the son being *wise*). Traits indicative of a child's character show up early and can be readily observed, if parents put forth the effort to do so (20:11). Parental education should likewise begin early and be *according to his way* (22:6, lit.), with sensitivity to the child's potential and long-range welfare (not *in the way he should go,* as NIV and many other translations of this verse). "The task of education [alluded to in this saying] is to enable the youth to raise his capabilities to the highest pitch of effectiveness and to set him undeviatingly on the right road by disciplining his habits and enlightening his attitudes" (McKane: 364). Once trained in this manner, this text states confidently, *when*

he is old he will not turn from it (22:6b). For this educational
process to be effective, the son must not resist his father's admonitions (15:5).
   But what if he does? What is not so self-evident is what a father
should do then. The saying in 19:18 establishes the circumstances in
which an action referred to as *chastening* (NIV: *discipline*) may be
necessary. In Hebrew the word for *chasten* is related to the word for
educational discipline *(mûsār)*. To *chasten* a son is viewed not as punishment, but as a form of pedagogy (see Deut 8:5; Hos 7:15, Heb.).
A father should never lose hope (19:18a) or wish his son's destruction
(19:18b). There is still something that can be done, even when a son
appears to be delinquent. The compilers of this book observed that
symbolically wounding a son severely enough to leave a mark (20:30a)
could have a therapeutic effect: *Purge the inmost being* (20:30b);
Drive [folly] far from him (22:15b). It should not be avoided in the
particular cases where *folly is bound up in the heart of a child*
(22:15a). This is why these editors speak of the *rod* used to inflict such
a symbolic wound as the *rod of* [educational] *discipline (mûsār)*. They
regard fathers who neglect using such a rod as not really loving their
sons, but actually hating them (13:24).

THE TEXT IN BIBLICAL CONTEXT

"He Who Finds a Wife Finds What Is Good" (18:22)

The positive attitude toward "finding a wife" that comes to expression
in the above sayings epitomizes the teachings of the OT on this subject (see Gen 1:27; 2:4b-25; Mal 2:13-16; Ruth; Song of Solomon).
The Genesis creation account is foundational for biblical thought on
this matter. Implied in that account is the uniqueness and universality
of the man-woman relationship in a bond that the text refers to as
"one flesh" (Gen 2:24). There are analogies in the animal world but
nothing to compare with the way a man and woman can form a deep
psychosomatic relationship, which (until recently) we have termed
marriage (Miller, 1973:35-42; see notes on 2:17, *covenant;* and on
5:15-23).
   We find comparable NT teachings on husbands and wives. Jesus
speaks definitive words (based on the Genesis creation stories) regarding the oneness willed by God for marital partners (Mark 10:2-9). Paul
concludes that even though it may be "good for a man not to marry"
under certain circumstances, yet as a general rule "each man should
have his own wife, and each woman her own husband" (1 Cor 7:1-
2). In addition, there is the beautiful encouragement given to husbands

and wives in Colossians 3:18-19 and Ephesians 5:22-33 to love and respect one another. Texts such as these reinforce the judgment expressed in Proverbs 18:22 that it is "good" for a man to find a wife. However, the teachings elsewhere highlight the wife's role as companion, sexual partner, and mother. But what is more at the forefront of the proverbs just studied is the wife's strength, nobility, and competence as wise manager of *her house* (14:1). Eulogized in these texts is the *prudent wife* (19:14), one like the woman described in the final chapter of Proverbs (31:10-31).

Parents and Children

Unique too are the observations in this group of sayings on parental responsibility for the training of children. The joy and sorrow children cause their parents is the theme of several biblical stories (see 1 Sam 1-3; 2 Sam 13-18; Luke 15:11-32). But nowhere else are parental emotions so explicitly identified as a reality to be reckoned with in the choices made. Also, other texts stress how important it is that parents teach their children (Exod 12:25-27; Deut 6:4-9; 11:18-21; Ps 78:5-8; Eph 6:4), but with less attention given to how this should be done. Only here is the use of the rod mentioned, although it might be assumed from an offhand remark in Hebrews 12:7b ("For what son is not disciplined by his father?") that a father's discipline of his child was commonplace among Jews. There is also the advice in Ephesians 6:4 and Colossians 3:21, cautioning fathers against being too severe in their discipline lest their children lose heart or are provoked to anger. The need for this advice becomes apparent when reading the disciplinary advice of a renowned second BC Jewish teacher, Jesus ben Sira. In Ecclesiasticus 30:1-13 (NRSV) he counsels a father who loves his son to avoid playing with him (30:9-10), but rather to "whip him often" (30:1) and "beat his sides while he is young" (30:12). "Discipline your son and make his yoke heavy, so that you may not be offended by his shamelessness" (30:13).

THE TEXT IN THE LIFE OF THE CHURCH

Family Values

The sayings just surveyed provide the most explicit words in the Bible on such crucial issues as marriage, choosing marital partners, the joys and sorrows of having children, and how to raise them to be wise and good. Hence, they deserve a place of honor in any community that treasures the family values enshrined in scriptural tradition. This does not mean blindly accepting every truth put forth here. It is the nature of sayings of this kind to invite discussion, explanation, refinement, and defense. Their only claim to our attention is the degree to which they do in fact touch upon realities that we neglect to our own hurt. How do these sayings measure up in this regard?

The topics themselves are obviously important ones. For a young man to find a wife who will be right for him during the remaining days of his life is still, obviously, one of life's major challenges. Some readers may be offended by the focus in these sayings on the ideal *wife's* qualities, rather than the qualities the *man* should bring to a marriage. It should be kept in mind, however, that virtually all the advice of this book is directed to the reproof of men. They were the exclusive target of some specific vocational and marital advice in the book's opening chapters (e.g., being upright and wise, trusting in Yahweh, avoiding lawless men and seductive women, and being loving husbands who delight in the wives of their youth). Also the emphasis in these sayings on the ideal wife being a woman of character is a "wisdom" worth pondering by men and women alike in an age when the physical beauty of women is being exploited and promoted as seldom before. It remains true today that *charm is deceptive, and beauty is fleeting; but a woman who fears the LORD is to be praised* (31:30).

Educating Children

On the matter of educating children, people today are as aware as ever of the pain and joy that comes with having children. Yet they appear to be much less confident than were the editors of Proverbs about having the power as parents to determine the character or future of their children. Faced by the inrush of mass communication and the breakup of extended and primary families, parents look to others to do for their children what they feel increasingly inept and uncertain about doing themselves. We may be in danger of grossly underestimating the impact of the family as a major force for good or ill. Even where families retreat from their custodial and educational responsibilities, an education of sorts may be taking place—an education for disaster. Families do have a profound impact on their children, whether they want to or not. The issue is not, therefore, whether or not families educate, but what kind of education is given.

Fathers especially are addressed by these sayings and asked to take a second look at what they are doing (see the Introduction, "Why the Gender-Specific Focus"). Their role as pedagogues in the family should begin early with an assessment of the gifts and tendencies of each child, these sayings suggest. The advice given to them to use the *rod of discipline* (Prov. 22:15) as an educational resource where called for is the subject of an ongoing debate regarding the kind of parental firmness and direction most appropriate for what age period. As noted, to chastise, discipline, and educate are closely related words in Hebrew. The issue is not how to punish, but how to instruct. A father's passivity and failure to take positive action in the face of a son's delinquency may be evidence of a destructive *lack* of love (or even hatred). That is a truth especially worth pondering in an age when lack of involvement (rather than a too severe discipline) appears often to be the greater danger. Even worse would be the church's silent complicity to such paternal passivity in a time when juvenile delinquency is a worrisome problem.

It is instructive to recall that one of the founders of the believers church tradition, Menno Simons, was greatly concerned about this very issue. He had observed firsthand the failure of many parents at teaching, restraining, or disciplining their children. In his role of shepherding the churches, Menno (with some trepidation about the response) wrote a pastoral tract on "The Nurture of Children" and asked that it be read in every congregation for which he was responsible (947-52). Its title translated from Dutch is "Doctrine as to How All Pious Parents Are, According to Scriptures, Required to Govern, Chastise and Educate Their Children." On its title page were four sayings about child discipline taken from Proverbs (23:13, 14; 29:15, 17).

In the tract itself Menno advocated daily instruction of children with "the Word of the Lord" and where needed "constraint and punishment with discretion and moderation, without anger or bitterness, lest they be discouraged" (951). In his ministry he had seen too much "bad love" of parents toward children, love so blinded by the natural affection of parents for their children that "they can neither see nor perceive any evil, error, or defect in them at all." This happens despite the fact that these children are "disobedient to father and mother, lie right and left, quarrel and fight with other people's children, and mock people as they pass by, crying after them and calling them names" (952).

It was not only Menno among the sixteenth-century founders of the believers church who felt the importance of matters such as these. In a little known Swiss Anabaptist confession of faith, written in 1578, four whole sections are devoted to the subject of parents and children. In these it is also stated as "doctrine" that parents should instruct their children and "with every haste and urgency" chastise them, if necessary, in order "to turn them from their lack of uprightness" (Franz: document 187). The weight accorded such teachings in a confession of faith should give us food for thought. Do contemporary doctrinal and confessional considerations need some amplification and repair at this point?

What Kind of Discipline Should Be Used?

Present in the biblical portrait of disciplining children is an ambivalence that has lent itself to a variety of interpretations and cultural expressions. More specifically, pedagogical severity may be garnered from certain texts (Prov 22:15; Heb 12:7-11), while a more relaxed, compassionate parenting can be gleaned from others (Ps 103:13; Eph 6:4). The place of corporal punishment in the education of children is a prime example of the issues at stake. Several biblical passages advise a generous use of the *rod* in educating sons in particular, but without specifying what kind of rod, how generous the use, at what age, or under what circumstances (Prov 22:15; 23:13; 29:15). A contemporary Jewish manual on the subject advises:

> According to the [Jewish] Talmud, parents and teachers should be most patient with children until the age of twelve years, but after that age, since the child's cognitive abilities are more developed, they can be more severe. . . . However, corporal punishment may be used only with inattentive or stubborn children. Even then, it is forbidden to strike a child so as to hurt him. . . . With older adolescents, it was forbidden to employ corporal punishment as a means of discipline, in order not to provoke the student to strike back and commit a sin. . . . In all cases, the teacher (and the parent) must feel and display warmth and fondness for children in order to create an environment for learning based on good relationships and trust. (Matzner-Bekerman: 244-45)

The issues remain contentious in modern societies. Thomas Millar, a Canadian child psychiatrist (deceased in 2002 at 79) wrote a popular child-rearing guide, in which he argued that children needed discipline as much as love. In his book, *The Omnipotent Child,* he wrote that children needed to be weaned from a baby's understandably selfish behavior. "The omnipotent child," he wrote, "is a very common customer in these difficult times. He is willful. . . . He is very self-centered so has problems keeping friends. . . . Every lively two-year-old is a bit like this, but when they're eight, and still this way, it's time for a little remedial parenting." Millar felt a lack of family discipline was to blame for an increase in selfish behavior. This led him to be an opponent of what he called "an anti-spanking cabal" (quoted from his obituary in *The Globe and Mail,* Aug. 26, 2002).

The controversies over child discipline in Canada reached such a peak that the Supreme Court of Canada became involved. Some citizens wanted to repeal Section 43 of the Criminal Code that allows parents and teachers to physically discipline children in their care by using "reasonable" force. In its decision (Fri., Jan. 30, 2004) the Court ruled in favor of those who believe that "reasonable corrective force" is sometimes necessary. But they specified that such force can be used only against children between the ages of two and twelve years old and that "reasonable limits" had to be observed. The court specified that it was unacceptable to hit a child with an object, like a belt or paddle, and that blows and slaps to the child's head would also be unacceptable. "For corporal punishment to be legally acceptable," the court ruled, "it must involve only 'minor corrective force of a transitory and trifling nature.'" The search for wisdom in this important matter continues.

Proverbs 10—22:16

Economics: Wealth and Poverty

The Book of Proverbs, Part 2: The Themes of the Main Collection							
Wisdom	Nation-hood	Speech	Family	Econo-mics	Personal Rela-tions	Matters of the Heart	Know-ledge of the Holy One

PREVIEW

The sheer number of sayings on the theme of "wealth and poverty" in the Main Collection (some seventy in all) testifies to its importance to those who compiled this volume. Wealth and poverty were obviously stark realities in the world of the time. Some were wealthy, very wealthy, and others were poor, very poor. The various terms for rich and poor in Proverbs have been carefully studied (Whybray: 1990), but a prophet's story evokes the realities to which they point in a single simple picture. The story begins: "There were two men in a certain town, one rich and the other poor. The rich man had a very large number of sheep and cattle, but the poor man had nothing except one little ewe lamb he had bought" (2 Sam 12:1-2).

Wealth and poverty are related to what today is called "econom-

166

ics," the production, distribution, and use of income, wealth, and commodities. How people thought about these realities—and how they should think about them—was obviously a matter of great concern both for the teachers of the time and their students. For the teachers, the sayings gathered here are the thoughts and ideals they wanted their students to ponder and espouse. That they were intent upon them doing so implies a societal need. The economic practices of the time were in disarray. The youth of their society needed to ponder and embrace these values if they and their society were to live and not die.

A hint of the importance the teachers assigned to this topic is implied by the position it has in the collection. If it is significant (as noted before) that parts 1 and 2 of Proverbs begin with teachings about parents and children, it may be equally significant that the next teachings in each part are about wealth and poverty. In 1:10-19 (in part 1), right after being warned to heed their parents' teachings, sons are admonished not to get involved with thugs bent upon enriching themselves with other people's property. At the beginning of 10:1–22:16 (part 2)—also right after an opening saying about parents and children—there is a saying that epitomizes the lesson taught in 1:10-19: *Ill-gotten treasures are of no value* (10:2). This is followed by sayings on the theme of wealth and poverty (10:3-5).

The large number of sayings on this theme can be subdivided into several subthemes. A few have to do with core economic values. Others focus on the way being rich compares to other life experiences. A third group of sayings assures those who are upright of Yahweh's care and blessing. A fourth category (by far the largest) are thoughts worth pondering about making a living. A final group of sayings are random observations on the foibles of those engaged in commerce of one type or another.

OUTLINE

Core Economic Values, 10:2, 15; 11:1; 13:8, 23; 14:20, 24, 31; 15:27; 16:11; 17:5; 18:16, 23; 19:4, 6, 7; 20:10, 23, 25; 21:6, 14; 22:7, 9
Values of Greater Worth than Wealth, 11:4; 15:16, 17; 16:8, 19; 17:1; 19:1, 22; 22:1, 2
The Faith of Those Who Do Right, 10:3, 16, 22; 11:4; 13:21, 22, 25; 15:6; 22:4, 5
Thoughts About Making a Living, 10:4, 5, 26; 11:15, 24, 25, 26, 28; 12:11, 24, 27; 13:4, 11; 14:4, 23, 31; 15:19, 27; 17:18; 18:9, 11; 19:15, 24; 20:4, 11, 13, 16, 17, 21; 21:5, 14, 17,

20, 25-26; 22:2, 13, 16
Random Observations, 13:7; 16:26; 20:14

EXPLANATORY NOTES

**Core Economic Values   10:2, 15; 11:1; 13:8, 23;
14:20, 24, 31; 15:27; 16:11; 17:5; 18:16, 23; 19:4,
6, 7; 20:10, 23, 25; 21:6, 14; 22:7, 9**

*Ill-gotten Treasures Are of No Value, but Righteousness
Delivers from Death   (10:2) 10:2; 15:27; 21:6*

In the Hebrew of 10:2, the words *of no value* stand at the beginning of the sentence, giving the sense, *Of no enduring value is a fortune acquired by evil means!* Here is a foundational principle, put forward at the forefront of this collection. It relates to an aspect of human existence notoriously fraught with temptations to dishonesty and corruption. It is only *uprightness* that can guide a person safely through the dangerous shoals and *deliver from death* (10:2b, lit.; cf. 11:4b; 15:27). The same point is made even more forcefully in a saying near the end of this Main Collection: *The acquisition of a fortune by means of a lying tongue is a vacuous vapor—such are seekers of death* (21:6, lit.). Those who seek to become wealthy by devious means court their own death.

*The LORD Abhors Dishonest Scales, but Accurate Weights
Are His Delight   (11:1) 11:1; 16:11; 20:10, 23*

The most flagrant example of a dishonest means for acquiring wealth in the cultures of the period was the falsification of scales and weights. This might involve having "two differing weights in your bag—one heavy, one light," or having "two differing measures in your house—one large, one small" (Deut 25:13-14). These laws refer to the medium of exchange in commercial transactions. Weights and measures were important for commercial transactions in that culture. Minted coinage was not widespread in Asia Minor before the Persian and Greek Empires. The earlier units of currency were precious metals. Deceptive weights or measures were equivalent to counterfeit money in our economy. In three of the four sayings in Proverbs where this practice is mentioned (11:1; 20:10, 23)—as in the teaching on this subject in Deuteronomy (25:16)—it is classified as *an abomination of Yahweh* (lit.; NIV: *the LORD abhors/detests*). The word *abomination* (found occasionally in Egyptian wisdom literature) occurs often in Deuteronomy and Proverbs as a characterization of conduct that is exceptionally abhorrent (Weinfeld, 1972:267-69).

How seriously this issue of honesty was viewed is indicated by the notification in Deuteronomy: "Accurate and honest weights and measures" are a condition for the people to "live long in the land the LORD your God is giving you" (25:15). According to the prophet Amos, "dishonest scales" (8:5) were one of the reasons for Israel losing its land at the time of the Assyrian invasions (8:1-14). The conviction stated negatively elsewhere (*the LORD abhors dishonest scales,* 11:1) is also expressed in a positive manner: *Honest scales and balances are from the LORD; all the weights in the bag are of his making* (16:11). God himself is on the side of a monetary system that is credible and honest.

The Wealth of the Wise Is Their Crown, but the Folly of Fools Yields Folly (14:24) 10:15; 13:8, 23; 14:20, 24; 18:16, 23; 19:4, 6, 7; 21:14; 22:7

While dishonest means of acquiring wealth were roundly condemned, the acquisition of wealth was not. Indeed, what a *crown* is to a king, *wealth* is to the wise (14:24). *Crown* is a favorite metaphor in Proverbs for the conferring of honor and esteem (4:9; 12:4; 16:31; 17:6). One of the clear advantages of being wealthy is the protection and security it affords. *The wealth of the rich is their fortified city* (10:15). The authors of these proverbs do not regard being poor as in any sense meritorious or desirable. Just the opposite! *Poverty is the ruin of the poor* (10:15b). Poverty exposes people to misfortunes and sufferings. *The rich rule over the poor, and the borrower is servant to the lender* (22:7). The poor are extremely vulnerable to exploitation (13:23) and abusive attitudes (18:23). By contrast, the rich are able to protect themselves with conciliatory gifts (21:14) that open doors to people in power (18:16; 19:6b).

The protective power of wealth is also alluded to in 13:8a: *A man's riches may ransom his life.* Wealth is useful in escaping trouble of one sort or another. However, the second line of this saying is puzzling and may be translated: *But the poor does not hear a rebuke* (13:8b, lit.). Are the poor being criticized (exactly the same thing is said about *a mocker* in 13:1b)? Or is this a scribal error, as many think (the unwitting repetition of 13:1b in 13:8b)? Another advantage of being wealthy, these sayings observe, is that the rich have more friends than the poor (19:4). Indeed, it is sometimes the case that not just a poor man's friends *avoid him* (19:7b; lit., *go far from him*), but he *is shunned* [lit., *hated*] *by all his relatives* (19:7a). This saying's third line (19:7c, Heb.; 19:7c-d, NIV) is odd and more than likely "a fragment of a separate proverb the other part of which is lost." "This is the only verse in the central section of Proverbs which has three clauses and the sentence is complete without these words" (Cohen). Summing up, wealth honestly acquired is honorable and advantageous in various ways.

If a Man Shuts His Ears to the Cry of the Poor, He Too Will Cry Out and Not Be Answered (21:13) 14:31; 17:5; 20:25; 21:13; 22:9

Although being wealthy is affirmed, it is perilous to ignore the needs of the *poor* (*dāl*), as the warning in 21:13 implies: *Who shuts his ear at the cry of the poor, he too shall call and not be heard* (lit.). The *poor* referred to are the helpless, oppressed poor (Whybray, 1990:20). The person who ignores their cry is forewarned that the same thing will happen to him. He too will be helpless and oppressed, and his pleas for help will not be answered. "The callousness he displayed will be remembered against him" (Cohen). Even worse than ignoring the cry of the poor is to *mock* them (17:5a) and *gloat* at their calamity (17:5b). The person who does this *shows contempt for their Maker and . . . will not go unpunished* (17:5b; cf. 14:31; 16:5). Despising the defenseless poor is dangerous for the despisers because it offends the God who created them (cf. 14:31). The saying implies a strong sense of being part of a human family created in the image of God (Gen 1:27).

These sayings serve as a warning to those well-off to avoid becoming distant and aloof from the rights and needs of others less fortunate than themselves. What they should cultivate instead is what 22:9 calls *a good eye*. The proverb states: *A good eye will be blessed, for he gives of his bread to the poor* (22:9, lit.). The *good eye* is one that sees the desperate needs of others who suffer through no fault of their own and responds generously. The blessing of God rests on those who do this. On the other hand, there is a caution in the saying in 20:25 against being too rash about vows or sacred pledges. *It is a trap for a man [*'ādām, person*] to dedicate something [make a vow] rashly [impulsively], and only later to consider his vows* (20:25; see Lev 27). "Such an impulse is a *snare* since it may carry a man too far, and later he will regret his impulsive action" (Cohen; cf. Eccl 5:4). "What is said of vows applies also to human promises generally" (Clifford: 186).

Values of Greater Worth than Wealth 11:4; 15:16, 17; 16:8, 19; 17:1; 19:1, 22; 22:1, 2

Better a Little with the Fear of the LORD than Great Wealth with Turmoil (15:16) 11:4; 15:16; 16:8, 19; 19:1, 22

The sayings of this group reinforce the point made in the proverbs just examined: wealth is good but only when other values are in play as well. In fact, certain values or attributes or experiences exceed by far the worth of wealth. The customary way of translating these sayings into English is to use a *better . . . than . . .* clause, but this may give the impression that both are good, only one is better. In Hebrew the contrast is starker: the one is declared to be *good* (*tôb*) instead of the other. Thus, to *fear the LORD* is *good* (as stated in 15:16a) even if it means being poor. By contrast (as stated in 15:16b), enjoying *wealth with turmoil* (wealth obtained by fraud or force) is not good at all; on the meaning of the word *turmoil* in this saying, see Amos 3:9. Proverbs makes the same point elsewhere, as in 16:8: *Good is a little with uprightness, rather than large revenues with no justice* (lit.). Indeed, it is even *good* to be among the humiliated oppressed (*lowly in spirit*), rather than to share in the wealth of a proud elite who exploits others (16:19). One reason is that *wealth* [obtained in this corrupt manner] *is worthless in the day of wrath, but righteousness delivers from death* (11:4). The phrase *day of wrath* is used by the prophets to refer to national and international judgment because of sin (Zeph 1:18; Ezek 7:19; cf. Isa 10:3). On a day of judgment like that, the worthlessness of wealth becomes evident: *Neither their silver nor their gold will be able to save them on the day of the LORD'S wrath* (Zeph 1:18). What counts then is *righteousness* (being honest and upright, not profiting from ill-gotten wealth; cf. Prov 10:2). In 11:4 there is an implicit confidence in God's protection of those who do right. These sayings also show an implicit awareness that those who fear God and do what is right will not always have it easy or be wealthy (*Better to be poor than a liar*, 19:22b).

Better a Meal of Vegetables Where There Is Love than a Fattened Calf with Hatred (15:17) 15:17; 17:1

Wealth as such is not evil. However, even when rightly secured, there are values whose worth is so great it would be foolish to forfeit them for the pleasures wealth might afford. Two of these sayings make this point by means of brief, sharply contrasting characterizations of mealtimes. In the culture of that period, meals with family and friends were the high point of life (Eccl 2:24). Having meat to eat at such meals was a much-sought-after luxury only the wealthy could afford (see Amos 6:4). Yet *a dry crust* of bread (17:1) or *herbs* (NIV: *vegetables*, 15:17a) with *peace and quiet* (17:1a) or *love* (15:17a) among those gathered at table should be desired over a *house full of feasting, with strife* (17:1b; or a "stalled" *fattened calf* and *hatred* with it, 15:17b). The *feasting, with strife* mentioned in 17:1b is literally *sacrifices of strife*, referring, perhaps, to a festive occasion in which an animal was slain for a sacrifice and then parts of it eaten by those making the sacrifice (cf. Prov 7:14).

A Good Name Is More Desirable than Great Riches; to Be Esteemed Is Better than Silver or Gold 22:1

There is yet a third value to be desired over great wealth and that is having a *name* or good reputation (22:1). The adjective *good* (NIV: *good name*) is implied but actually missing in the Hebrew text. Literally translated, this verse reads: *A name [reputation] is to be chosen rather than great riches and rather than silver or gold, favor [a favorable reputation] is good* (22:1). In this saying the word *good* comes at the end of the Hebrew sentence (rather than at the beginning as in the other examples of this sentence form), giving finality to this particular declaration. Wealth does bring a certain prestige to those having it, but to have a *name* that is respected because of one's character is what is really *good!*

The Faith of Those Who Do Right 10:3, 16, 22; 11:4; 13:21, 22, 25; 15:6; 22:4, 5

The Blessing of the LORD Brings Wealth, and He Adds No Trouble to It (10:22) 10:22; 22:4

The sayings in this group are reflective of the faith dimension of those who created the Hezekiah Edition of Proverbs *[Distinctive Approach]*. They were thoughtful worshippers of Yahweh, the God of Israel. They believed that when God's wise decrees are observed, then blessings will follow (cf. Deut 28:1-14). However, the Hebrew of Proverbs 22:4 is not as straightforward about this being the case, as the NIV translation suggests. The point made in this verse is not exactly that *humility and the fear of the LORD bring wealth and honor and life*, but that *the reward of humility [is] the fear of Yahweh, riches and honor and life* (22:4, lit.). In other words *humility* is rewarded by *fear of Yahweh*, and then *riches and honor and life* follow. Still, that the *blessing of Yahweh* is the key factor in this sequence (and not anything we do or do not do) is forcefully stated in the Hebrew of 10:22, the first line of which has a pronoun *it* after the words, *blessing of the LORD.* This serves to emphasize that it is truly the *blessing of the LORD* that brings wealth, not something else (*the blessing of Yahweh, it brings wealth*). Also, in the second line of this saying, if *toil* were substituted for the word *trouble* (NIV)—*toil* being the other meaning of the Hebrew word used here—then this saying would read: *The blessing of Yahweh, it brings wealth, and toil adds nothing to it* (10:22b). In other words, it is only a right relation to Yahweh and his will that brings blessing, and it is only that which ultimately brings wealth, not anything human beings can do (cf. Ps 127:1-2). This is similar to what several sayings in Proverbs say about victory in war: regardless of the plans and preparations, the final outcome is in the hands of Yahweh (see 21:30-31).

The LORD Does Not Let the Righteous Go Hungry but He Thwarts the Craving of the Wicked (10:3) 10:3, 16; 11:4; 13:21, 22, 25; 15:6

The confidence that Yahweh's blessing brings wealth extends to the economic welfare of all who are upright. They may not be blessed with wealth, but they can count on being cared for by God (11:4). What is observed is that the upright seldom go hungry (10:3), and they eat better (13:25) than their *wicked* counterparts because God watches over them. They put their wages or earnings to more productive use (10:16), which *brings them life* rather than *sin* (lit.; NIV: *punishment*). They have better furnished houses (15:6) and are more successful in passing on an inheritance to their *children's children* (13:22). In summary, *misfortune pursues the sinner, but prosperity is the reward of the righteous* (13:21). Observations such as these are based partly on life experience (see Ps 37:25-26, 35-36), but also reflect deeply held convictions about God's blessings on those who do right and curses upon those who do wrong, as revealed in the words of Moses (Deut 27-28; cf. Lev 26). Later authors raised serious questions about the across-the-board-applicability of such theologically based convictions (as in the protest of Job against the judgment of his friends that he suffered because he had sinned; see also the thoughts of Qoheleth/Teacher in Eccl 4).

Thoughts About Making a Living 10:4, 5, 26; 11:15, 24, 25, 26, 28; 12:11, 24, 27; 13:4, 11; 14:4, 23, 31; 15:19, 27; 17:18; 18:9, 11; 19:15, 24; 20:4, 11, 13, 16, 17, 21; 21:5, 14, 17, 20, 25-26; 22:2, 13, 16

Lazy Hands Make a Man Poor, but Diligent Hands Bring Wealth (10:4) 10:4, 5, 26; 12:11, 24, 27; 13:4, 11; 14:4, 23; 15:19; 18:9, 11; 19:15, 24; 20:4, 13, 21; 21:5, 25-26; 22:13

The belief that the *blessing of Yahweh* is what really brings wealth did not mean that one could be careless about making a living. More than half of the 75 sayings on "wealth and poverty" are about work-related matters. Of these, 17 are devoted to the issue of diligence versus laziness, a subject already touched on in 6:6-11. *Slack hands* and *diligent hands* are sharply juxtaposed in the very first saying of the Main Collection on this theme (10:4, lit.); the first are identified as a chief cause for poverty, the other as a chief prerequisite for wealth. Elsewhere laziness is also said to lead to *nothing* (13:4), demeaning servitude (12:24, *deep sleep* and *hunger* (19:15), or even death (21:25). Psychological dimensions of the problem are alluded to in 21:25-26 (one continuous sentence in Hebrew). It is not the *sluggard's craving* that kills him (21:25a), but his desires and appetites combined with his determination not to work (*because his hands refuse to work*, 21:25b) while *all day long he craves for more* (21:26a).

Social dimensions of the problem being addressed are alluded to in many of these sayings. The setting is rural, rather than urban. The one slack in his work is characterized as *brother* [kindred] *to one who destroys* (18:9; lit., *an owner destroying*). In other words, poor work habits can destroy a person's livelihood in exactly the same way as a landowner destroys his property by neglecting it (Cohen). The alternative vocational ideal put forward is of someone *who works his land* diligently (12:11), *plows* in winter (20:4), and *gathers crops in summer* (10:5). Thus he accumulates *money little by little* (13:11b) and manages in time to purchase oxen to help him with his work (14:4) in plowing and threshing (Deut 22:10; 25:4). Wealth gotten any other way is more than likely to disappear.

So it is with *dishonest money* (money come by suddenly through risky speculations); it will just as quickly dwindle away (13:11a). So it is also with *an inheritance quickly gained at the beginning* (perhaps through the death of parents); it *will not be blessed at the end* (20:21). Only the steady acquisition of the abilities needed for acquiring wealth in the first place will enable a person to retain it. This is precisely what the person characterized in these sayings does not or cannot do. He is slack when it comes to work (18:9a), merely *talks* (14:23b), craves many things (21:25), and *chases fantasies* (12:11) of getting rich fast by some other means (21:5b). In pursuit of these fantasies, he devises *worthless* (not *dishonest,* NIV) schemes (13:11). Even the dirty work of hunting or roasting game is beneath him (12:27; however, the verb's meaning in this instance is uncertain).

An especially egregious example of a person lacking in these abilities is the *sluggard* (or *laziness,* 19:15; a Hebrew word used fourteen times in Proverbs and only once elsewhere, Eccl 10:18, "lazy"). The sluggard is so ludicrously lethargic that when at mealtime he reaches into the common dish for food (eaten without utensils), he leaves his hand there (19:24; cf. 26:15)! His excuses for not working are more laughable still: *The sluggard says, "There is a lion outside!" or, "I will be murdered in the streets!"* (22:13). His thorn-covered fields (the result of his laziness) are an apt metaphor for his course in life: his way is, as it were, *blocked with thorns,* while the path of his more industrious, upright neighbor is clear and smooth (*a highway,* 15:19). Those unfortunate enough to have a person like this as an employee are in for a rude awakening: *As vinegar to the teeth and smoke to the eyes, so is a sluggard to those who send him* (on this or that assignment; 10:26).

Do not love sleep or you will grow poor; stay awake and you will have food to spare (20:13; cf. 6:9-11; 19:15). *All hard work [painful toil] brings a profit, but mere talk leads only to poverty* (14:23). These convictions, which epitomize the concerns of this group of sayings, echo the harsh realism of the word spoken to Adam, "Cursed is the ground because of you; through painful toil you will eat of it all the days of your life" (Gen 3:17). Steady painful tillage of the soil is man's lot in life and a prerequisite for escaping destitution and poverty.

He Who Puts Up Security for Another Will Surely Suffer; but Whoever Refuses to Strike Hands in Pledge Is Safe (11:15) 11:15; 17:18; 20:16

These three sayings relate to a type of get-rich-quick scheme that was especially tempting, it seems, to the lazier type (for a fuller discussion of such "rash pledges," see 6:1-5; cf. 22:26-27). The refer-

ence to *another* in 11:15a is actually to a *stranger* (cf. 6:1); the same
Hebrew word appears in 20:16a. The action being warned against is
that of guaranteeing a loan of money made by an out-of-town entre-
preneur, whether man or woman (20:16b). A similar warning is given
in 17:18 against putting up *security* for a *neighbor* (17:18a). The
guarantor's pledge was sealed through *striking hands* (17:18a). The
guarantor was then obligated to pay the loan this neighbor or outsider
was making if the borrower defaulted in repaying it. The motive for
guaranteeing such a risky venture was no doubt the prospect of having a share in the profits of whatever venture the borrowed money
was financing. The counsel previously given in Proverbs 6:1-5 was
that if someone were foolish enough (in a rash moment) to do a crazy
thing like this, he should at once do everything in his power to get out
of it. Here those who even consider doing something like this are
branded as *lacking judgment* (17:18; lit., *lacking heart*) and warned
of the dire consequences (11:15a) *["Heart"]*.

A Generous Man Will Prosper; He Who Refreshes Others Will Himself Be Refreshed (11:25) 11:24, 25, 26, 28; 14:31; 18:11; 19:11; 20:11, 17; 21:14, 17, 20, 26; 22:2, 16

How then might one legitimately become and remain rich, apart
from hard work? Most of the observations and advice in this group of
sayings appear to be related to this question. The first three (11:24,
25, 26) establish as a basic principle that one should not be too tightfisted with what one has. Three quite distinct alternatives are envisioned. The paradox is presented of a person *scattering* (lit.) yet
increasing, while another holds tight to what he has (*withholds
unduly*, NIV) and experiences poverty (11:24). *Scatter* in this verse
does not necessarily mean giving "gifts" (as in Ps 112:9). At issue,
rather, is the distinction between appropriate and inappropriate
spending. The man who prospers is one who does not hold on to his
wealth too tightly, but finds constructive uses for it (cf. 21:14). A particular instance of this is the example of withholding corn from the
market in a time of scarcity to drive up the price (11:26). If a person
were to hoard in this manner, people would *curse* him; but if he were
less tightfisted with his money and sell, a *blessing* would come (from
God) upon his head (11:26b). Just such a *person of blessing* who
waters others (NIV: *refreshes*) through his generous actions is the
kind of person who will *be watered* (by God) and thereby prosper
(11:25, lit.; cf. 21:26b, *the righteous give without sparing*).

Another danger to bear in mind in gaining and retaining wealth is overindulgence, especially in *wine and oil* (21:17). "Wine that gladdens the heart of man, oil to make his face shine" (Ps 104:15)—at that time these were among the coveted luxuries. The household of the wealthy (referred to as the *house of the wise,* 21:10) will have these amenities, as well as other desirable things (not only *choice food,* 21:20, NIV). But unlike those who are *foolish,* those who are wise will enjoy them in moderation (21:20b).

Yet another danger to avoid is that of becoming so aggressive in the cut and thrust of commerce that fraud creeps in. Even though a victory might taste sweet at the time, later (if there was any deception) it will leave a distinctly bad taste in the mouth (20:17). The wealthy must also constantly be on the alert not to oppress the poor (22:16a) or become overly involved and solicitous of one's wealthier social class (22:16b). Social classes are seemingly inescapable realities, but the wealthy should never forget that whether rich or poor, every human being is a creature of God: *The LORD is the Maker of them all* (22:2; cf. Job 31:15). Anyone, therefore, *who oppresses the poor shows contempt for their* [the poor's] *Maker, but whoever is kind to the needy honors God* [Heb.: *him*] (14:31), a truth powerfully amplified by Jesus in his depiction of the judgment of nations (Matt 25:31-46).

A final danger noted in these sayings is that of overconfidence in one's wealth. In this regard 18:11 affords an interesting variation on 10:15. The saying in 10:15 states without qualification that *the rich man's wealth is his fortified city* (lit.); but 18:11 adds that this is what *they* [the rich] *imagine* to be true. The point is that such overconfidence (as in other aspects of life; see 11:2) can easily lead to a fall. *Whoever trusts in his riches will fall* (11:28a).

Random Observations 13:7; 16:26; 20:14

"It's No Good, It's No Good!" Says the Buyer; Then Off He Goes and Boasts About His Purchase (20:14) 13:7; 15:26; 20:14

These three proverbs simply highlight the hidden and not-so-hidden foibles of those engaged in commercial activities of one kind or another. Their purpose is not, I think, to draw any serious lessons, but just to say, This is how people behave. Buyers love a bargain; then (and today) they find it exciting to haggle over the price. When buying something, they invariably play down its value; once purchased, they boast of how ridiculously low was the price they actually paid for it. Rich and poor play games about what they actually have by way of possessions. *One man pretends to be rich, yet has nothing; another pretends to be poor, yet has great wealth* (13:7). Another pretense is alluded to in the cryptic saying in 16:26 (lit.): *The soul [nepeš] of the worker works for him, for his mouth drives him on,* meaning that his appetite is what keeps him toiling away at his job. Here again, the saying simply states a fact. Many work simply because they must if they and their families are going to eat.

THE TEXT IN BIBLICAL CONTEXT

Economic Reforms

In seeking to relate this group of proverbs to the teachings on poverty and wealth elsewhere in the Bible, we need to keep in mind the different reasons people are poor. The two most often used Hebrew words for *poor* in the sayings just surveyed are *dal* (or *dāl*) and *rāš*. In most cases these terms are synonymous, but occasionally *dal* connotes "poverty" resulting from the person involved being exploited or oppressed (Whybray, 1990:20). Different expressions for the *poor* are also used: a poor person is *one who lacks bread* (12:9, lit.), is hungry and destitute (20:13), has virtually *nothing* (13:4, 7; 20:4), is in debt (22:7). The reason a person is poor is not made evident in each saying, but various factors are touched on. Some are poor because of personal tragedies or unjust exploitation; others may have experienced crop failures due to natural disasters. Yet others are poor because of poor work habits, or poor judgment.

The author of a study on poverty and wealth in Proverbs concludes (wrongly, I think) that "the existence of poverty is taken for granted," and that "no where is any possibility of eliminating it envisaged. There is no notion that it is due to a flaw in the organization of society, which could be corrected, nor any perception that impoverished individuals might be helped in such a way as to restore them to prosperity and to a proper place in the life of the community. The notion of social reform was apparently not conceivable" (Whybray, 1990:113). This assessment is not credible. First of all, quite a few sayings in this Main Collection are aimed at preventing the kind of poverty that results from laziness, poor work habits, risky business ventures, and the like. Likewise, a number of sayings are addressed toward alleviating destitution resulting from unforeseen disasters—drought, diseases, illness, injury, death of a breadwinner, or the loss of crops. It is assumed that the fortunate are obligated to share the necessities of life with those who have been deprived of them through no fault of their own.

The kind of poverty that results from crime and the breakdown of law and order is also recognized. There is a sense in which the opening teachings in both the Introductory Collection and the Main Collection address this issue by challenging young men to do everything in their power to resist the temptation to become part of gangs preying upon others (see 1:10-19; 10:2). There are also teachings regarding corrupt monetary practices, such as the thrice-repeated saying that *the LORD abhors dishonest scales* (11:1; 20:10, 23). These proverbs are directed not just to individuals, but also to those in government who have it within their power to do something about violations of this kind. A related issue of importance is the one addressed in a command at the forefront of the first Supplemental Collection to the Main Collection (22:17–24:22): *Do not move an ancient boundary stone* (22:28). A few verses earlier it is stated: *Do not exploit the poor because they are poor and do not crush the needy in court* (22:22). Teachings of this kind call for the protection of private property against the manipulative greed of the wealthy or the arbitrary incursions of corrupt governments, protections that are a bedrock of a prosperous society (see below).

It needs to be kept in mind that these sayings are in a manual designed to impart both personal and civic values to upcoming civil servants vested with the responsibility of implementing Hezekiah's social and religious reforms. The sayings as such are setting the tone and establishing the standards for the operation of an entire kingdom. When interpreting this particular group of sayings, it is especially important to keep in mind that the Hezekiah Edition of Proverbs was only one of several volumes published at this time to foster the goals of Hezekiah's reforms [Hezekiah Reform Literature]. Also published at this time was a newly edited version of the words of Moses in Deuteronomy. This will explain why many of the same economic issues are addressed there as in Proverbs. Examples are not moving a boundary stone (Deut 19:14), the need for those who have to share with those who are destitute (as in 26:12), and matters pertaining to fairness in the courts (as in 19:15-21). In addition, Deuteronomy makes proposals for seriously ameliorating poverty by having debts cancelled every seventh year (Deut 15:1-11).

The economic focus of both books is echoed in the economic views of the prophets of this period who also called for sweeping socioeconomic reforms (Isa 3:13-15; 5:1-7; 58:3-4; Amos 6:1-7; Mic 3:1-4). The words of Amos are especially sharp and passionate. He had come to believe that Israel was doomed because its conduct in this regard was so out of line with God's will (7:7-9). His challenge to the people of his generation is that they should let justice roll down like a steady stream (Amos 5:14-15, 21-24). Taken together, the literature of Hezekiah's reforms marks an epoch making transition in the thinking of Israelite leaders about the socioeconomic ideals that should guide its only surviving kingdom (the kingdom of Judah) if it was to meet the standards God had set for it and survive. In Proverbs, these ideals are enunciated as wisdom, not just for Judah to ponder and act on, but also for the whole world.

Economic Reforms in the Teachings of Jesus

The times and social setting of Jesus and his disciples were very different from those of the Hezekiah Edition of Proverbs, which was created during the kingdom period of Israelite history. In the days of Jesus the Jewish people no longer had a kingdom of their own, a condition that had existed ever since the Israelite kingdoms were destroyed some six centuries earlier. When they were restored to their homeland a generation later, their temple was restored, but the Jewish kingdom was never reestablished as it was before (except for a brief period in 142-63 BC). So during these centuries Israel had to rethink its whole relation to the nations of the world. It did so by redefining its God-given role in history as that of being, not an exemplary kingdom, but a people of covenant loyalty who thereby would bear witness to their God and his ways in the midst of the kingdoms of the world [Wisdom in Proverbs].

Jesus intensified that witness to the nations through his proclamation of the nearness of God's coming kingdom (Mark 1:14-15; Matt 28:16-20). His teachings in general need to be seen in the light of this proclamation and the Law and the Prophets, which he came to fulfill (Matt 5:13-20). He was not seeking to construct a comprehensive code of wisdom or laws for the governance of a nation or nations. That had already been attempted in the laws of Moses and the teachings of Proverbs. Nor were his disciples being trained as civil servants in a reformed kingdom. Israel's mission had been defined for a long time in other terms, to be a light and witness to the world's nations. It was to this mission that Jesus called his disciples, to proclaim the good news of the nearness of God's dawning kingdom among those nations (Miller, 2004:110-14).

In this context Jesus's teachings on wealth and commerce may be understood as supplements to those in Proverbs. He did not come to destroy or replace them, but to fulfill them. His teachings highlight how wealth and money matters can become totally consuming worries and preoccupations where there is (as was often the case among the Gentiles) no proper understanding of God. In the Sermon on the Mount, Matthew records Jesus saying, "You cannot serve both God and Money" (6:24b). Therefore: "Do not store up for yourselves treasures on earth. . . . But store up for yourselves treasures in heaven. . . . For where your treasure is, there your heart will be also" (Matt 6:19-21). Storing up "treasure in heaven" is a metaphor for good deeds, or acts of kindness and charity to the poor (Mark 10:21).

Many other memorable sayings and incidents reinforce this teaching of Jesus in Matthew's Gospel. He tells a wealthy young man who wanted to follow him first to go and give his possessions to the poor and only then come and follow him (Mark 10:17-26). Jesus portrays the last judgment, in which the nations of the world are envisioned being judged on how they treated those in need (Matt 25:31-46). The rest of the NT echoes these teachings. In Luke, Jesus instructs a man worried about getting his share of an inheritance: "Watch out! Be on your guard against all kinds of greed; [for] a man's life does not consist in the abundance of his possessions" (Luke 12:13-14). The book of James has especially harsh words for those who are wealthy and who do not show compassion for the poor. James defines true religion as that of taking care of the widow and orphan (1:27). In the spirit of Jesus's teachings and practice (cf. Luke 8:3; John 13:29), the early church adopted a form of communalism. The wealthy literally did what Jesus advocated: all shared in the wealth of all and "gave to anyone as he had need" (Acts 2:45; cf. 4:32; 6:1-4).

Paul reflects these same values in his personal life as a self-sacrificing missionary to the nations, pouring out his life for others. He demonstrates these concerns in his climactic project of gathering a collection from the Gentile churches he had founded for those who were in need because of a famine in Judea. The ideal, he wrote, was "that there might be equality. At the present time your plenty will supply what they need, so that in turn their plenty will supply what you need. Then there will be equality" (2 Cor 8:13-14). These and other teachings in the NT adapt and apply in fresh ways the sayings of Proverbs emphasizing the relative importance of wealth and the need for those who have to share with those who are poor.

THE TEXT IN THE LIFE OF THE CHURCH

Wealth and Poverty in the Church

The church continues the mission of Jesus to the nations: it continues to bear witness to the dawning kingdom of God in the whole world. Even though that kingdom did not come in its fullness as soon as many expected, it is still the church's hope that God's kingdom will come on earth as in heaven.

The church today is in a similar relationship to the kingdoms of the world as were the Jewish people in the postexilic period and as were Jesus and his first disciples. The Christian church exists today as a people within the nations, not as a national power in its own right. There was a time when this was not the case, beginning with the Roman emperor Constantine in the fourth century and continuing on down to recent times, until (as in the American Constitution) church and state were separated. Now all churches are more or less believers churches rather than state churches.

For this reason—when considering how the proverbs on wealth and poverty have been and might be relevant for the life and mission of the church, it is important to distinguish between church and state. The two communities are closely intertwined. The church exists as a community unto itself in various lands and under various governments. In the current situation, state governments no longer underwrite the needs of the institutional church as they once did when church and state were more closely allied. So the institutional church must be supported by the donated wealth of its members as seldom before. None of the teachings just looked at address this specific issue, although it is touched on in Proverbs 3:9-10 (see its TLC).

This need of the church for institutional support from its members can at times become the preoccupying economic issue. The church can also become too focused on *charitable* uses of wealth while neglecting issues related to the rights and wrongs in the *acquisition* and *use* of wealth. At this point it might be helpful to pay close attention to a cluster of teachings like those just surveyed. They clarify something that is not often touched on in the NT, the understanding that wealth itself is not evil. Wealth rightly obtained and rightly used is a blessing from God. There can be no charity without it.

Poverty and Wealth in the World

As a people called to be a light to the world, the church is deeply concerned in all aspects of the world's life. One of the greatest problems now facing the whole world is the huge disparity of wealth and poverty. It is estimated that 250 years ago the difference in wealth between the richest and poorest countries was perhaps 5 to 1, whereas today the difference in income is about 400 to 1 (Landes: p. xx). Why is this?

One of the surprising conclusions drawn in a study of this subject by the Harvard history professor David Landes is that the greater wealth of Western nations in recent centuries is partly to be explained by the inculcation of certain civic values through the church in medieval Europe. "Sometimes," he writes, "it [a person's house or land] was seized by force, just as today someone might be mugged and robbed. But the principle never died: property was a right, and confiscation, no more than plunder, could not change that" (34). This relative security of individual persons provided the basis for human initiatives and inventions. Landes notes that in China and elsewhere this was not the case (35). This medieval development, writes Landes, was the precursor to the industrial revolution in England, which rapidly became the front-runner in fashioning an "industrial society" that has changed the world (231).

Why did this industrial revolution occur in Great Britain and not elsewhere? Once again, Landes points to the existence of governmental values inculcated and supported by the church, laws protecting a person's security against tyranny (218). England was not a perfect society, he states, but from the time of the Magna Carta in 1215, political and civil freedoms won first for the nobles "were extended by . . . law to the common folk" (220). Relief agencies of the churches are seeking to carry out the mission of the church in poverty-stricken countries. As they do so, they are increasingly aware of how hopeless it is to make any real progress out of poverty apart from the emergence of peoples and governments that embrace human rights and civic virtues such as those enunciated in the proverbs just surveyed (Hoksbergen and Ewert).

The Church and Bribery

An especially disabling form of corruption still rampant in the modern world is bribery. Indeed, some have argued that bribery is "one of the foremost problems in the developing nations," although wealthy corporations too are not immune from this practice (Montgomery: 143). The author of an essay that probes into what the Bible has to say about bribery concludes with these challenging words:

> We must remember that Scripture has nothing good to say about bribery. Its statements are either explicitly or implicitly negative. Bribery offends God, and by participating in it or giving tacit approval to it, we misrepresent the character of God. By perpetuating the practice, those who bribe may be guilty of unwittingly oppressing the poor and weak.
>
> Extortion is a particularly odious form of bribery. Often victims will have no option but to submit. Recurring extortion and racketeering needs to be opposed vehemently by the church. Individuals cannot tackle this evil on their own. The church must become the community of creative

alternatives. We need to create a counter-cultural environment in which Christian businesspeople, bureaucrats, politicians, professionals, blue-collar workers, and others in the service industries can use and develop their gifts within a framework of honesty and integrity. Such idealism may be criticized as impractical and naïve, but the alternatives are worse: continued corruption, hopelessness, crime, economic underdevelopment, oppression, unequal distribution of resources, and privatized (hence, socially impotent) faith. (Montgomery: 144)

Proverbs 10:1–22:16

Personal Relations

The Book of Proverbs, Part 2: The Themes of the Main Collection							
Wisdom	Nation-hood	Speech	Family	Econo-mics	Personal Rela-tions	Matters of the Heart	Know-ledge of the Holy One

PREVIEW

A good society is not just one that is built on the foundations of just laws justly adjudicated, nor are the affairs of commerce all important. Neither does the realm of husband and wife, parents and children exhaust what is involved in the personal relations of those living in such a society. There are additional relationships of a personal kind that contribute significantly to human happiness. These include inter-actions between neighbors and friends—and animals. Some of these are intimate personal friendships, others more like chance encounters. Animals too are part of this community.

There is no one word in Hebrew to designate this vitally important realm. The closest, perhaps, is the verb rā'āh, meaning "to associate with," from which the nouns rē'a or rē'eh are derived, which can be translated "friend," "intimate," "companion," "fellow-citizen," or "neighbor," depending on the context. For purposes of discussion, I

185

have grouped this set of proverbs under four subthemes: (1) relations among brothers and friends, (2) relations among neighbors, (3) relations in the wider community, and (4) treatment of animals.

OUTLINE

Relations Among Friends and Brothers, 10:12; 12:26; 16:28; 17:9,
    13, 14, 17; 18:1, 19, 24; 20:6, 22; 21:10
Relations Among Neighbors, 11:16, 17, 27; 12:10; 14:21
Relations in the Wider Community, 12:16, 20; 14:9, 22; 15:18;
    16:32; 17:13, 14, 15, 19; 19:11, 19; 20:3, 22; 21:10, 21,
    24; 22:10
Treatment of Animals, 12:10

EXPLANATORY NOTES

Relations Among Friends and Brothers 10:12; 12:26; 16:28; 17:9, 13, 14, 17; 18:1, 19, 24; 20:6, 22; 21:10

A Friend Loves at All Times, and a Brother Is Born for Adversity (17:17) 10:12; 12:26; 16:28; 17:13, 17; 18:1, 19, 24; 20:6

This group of sayings probes the dynamics of personal relations among close friends and brothers. A distinguishing characteristic of the true friend is the constancy of *love. A friend loves at all times* (17:17a). In this sentence the word *friend* has a definite article, *the friend*, signifying that what is being commented on is not this or that friend but the nature of friendship. Since the defining quality of a true *friend* is constancy, the second line of this sentence, *and a brother . . . born for adversity* (17:17b), is probably best interpreted as a reinforcement of this point, not its qualification. It means that the true friend who *loves at all times* is (like) a *brother born for adversity* (17:17b). Here the word *brother* is a synonym for *friend,* as when David spoke of Jonathan as "my brother" (2 Sam 1:26). The second line of the saying in 18:24 also refers to a *friend who sticks closer than a brother* (18:24b). The word translated *friend* in this line means, literally, *one who loves.* A true friend, this saying implies, is a *companion* who will be more loving than a blood brother and closer in times of need than a host of fair-weather *companions,* who look the other way when trouble comes (18:24a) or only pretend to be friends (the meaning of the verb in this line is uncertain).

With blood brothers one must also bear in mind that offenses and contentions can arise that are virtually impossible to resolve (18:19). This is not as likely with friends, but even a *close friend ('allûp, bosom companion;* cf. 2:17) can be separated by *gossip* (16:28; lit., a *whisperer*), or by an offense between them that is repeatedly brought up as an issue (17:9b). However, if *covered over* and forgotten, unlike with brothers, the *love* between them can be restored (17:9a). Indeed, the *love* (caring) that unites friends is capable of *covering over all wrongs* (10:12b), if *hatred* (petty animosity) is nipped in the bud and not allowed to take over (10:12a).

One can look to friends like this for guidance, the possible meaning of 12:26, the first line of which can be translated, *Let a righteous man search out* [his way] *from his friend* (12:26a, Cohen). Because of the tremendous benefits of friendships like this, it must be said that *an unfriendly man* [lit., *he who separates himself*] *pursues selfish ends* [does not make friends]; *he defies all sound judgment* (18:1). Cultivating friendships is the mark of a person of wisdom (cf. 27:10). At the same time, a word of caution is needed. Many will profess to be caring, loving persons, *but a* [truly] *faithful man* [friend] *who can find?* (20:6b). A lasting friendship is rare. On the other hand, there is no reason for despair. *He who loves a pure heart and whose speech is gracious will have the king for his friend* (22:11). This is not advice on how to climb the social ladder, but a statement about the qualities needed for being a good friend. If an individual has these two virtues in particular, sincerity and grace, then so far as friendship is concerned, anything is possible, even friendship with the king.

Relations Among Neighbors 11:16, 17, 27; 12:10; 14:21

He who despises his neighbor sins, and blessed is he who is kind to the needy (14:21). The relationship alluded to here is not between "bosom friends" or "brothers" but between *neighbors,* people living side by side within the same walled village. Those addressed are presumed to be better off than others in the community are. For them to look down on their less fortunate neighbor and feel contempt is not just unwise, it is sinful (a violation of God's law, 14:21a), for the law specifies that neighbors should "love" (care for) one another (Lev 19:18). In line 2 the word in Hebrew for *blessed* means *happy* (14:21b, lit.): *Happy is he who is kind to the needy.* So the opposite of showing contempt for one's less fortunate neighbor is to be *kind* and gracious to him (14:21b), and he who does that will be *happy.*

The remaining three sayings of this group emphasize why such a person is happy. A person who is *kind* may also be described as someone who seeks his neighbor's *good*. The one who does that *finds good will* (wins the favor and love of his neighbors, 11:27a). By contrast, *evil [trouble] comes to him who searches for it* (11:27b). It is in this sense that *a kind man benefits himself, but a cruel man brings himself harm* (11:17). One of the specific *benefits* that accrues to the person who is kind is their neighbor's esteem. *A kind-hearted woman* [lit., *a woman of graciousness*] *gains respect, but ruthless* [*strong* is more accurate] *men gain wealth* (11:16). This is the only saying in the book that compares a woman with men. It highlights the goodwill among neighbors created by a gracious women as compared to the *wealth* accumulated by strong men.

Relations in the Wider Community 12:16, 20; 14:9, 22; 15:18; 16:32; 17:13, 14, 15, 19; 19:11, 19; 20:3, 22; 21:10, 21, 24; 22:10

A Fool Shows His Annoyance at Once, but a Prudent Man Overlooks an Insult (12:16) 12:16; 15:18; 16:32; 19:11, 19; 20:22; 21:10, 24

These sayings draw a distinction between two types of reactions to the insults and offenses that inevitably arise, among men in particular, in the give and take of the wider world (such as commercial transactions and the like). The one reaction, as described in 12:16a, is an immediate display of anger (lit., *on the* [same] *day*)—this is the way the *fool* reacts. The other reaction is that of the *prudent man* (or man of *intelligence*; cf. 1:4): he *overlooks* [lit., *hides*] *an insult* (12:16b). The type of man displays his anger at once is elsewhere called a *hot-tempered man* (15:18a; 19:19a; lit., *man of heat* or *anger*). The other is characterized as a *man slow to anger* (15:18b, lit.; 19:11a, lit.; *he restrains his anger*); this man *controls his temper* (16:32b; lit., *rules his spirit*). These sayings give no support for the *hot-tempered man*, as though there were some manly virtue or honor in that. On the contrary, it is the ability of a *human being* [*'ādām*] *to overlook an offense* and be *slow to anger* that is the mark of a man's honor and wisdom, the saying in 19:11 (lit.) unequivocally declares. Indeed, such a man is much more to be admired than the bravado of a warrior, even one who succeeds at such an arduous undertaking as that of capturing a (fortified, walled) *city* (16:32). *A patient man* [someone *slow to anger*] *calms a quarrel* (15:18b), reducing the need for warriors and wars in the first place. However, this is not possible in every case, the saying in 19:19

seems to imply. In some instances, a *hot-tempered man* [lit., *a man of great wrath*] *must pay the penalty; if you rescue him* [intervene], *you will have to do it again.* The verse appears to advise discretion in dealings with men predisposed to *great anger* (19:19a, lit.). Even *slow-to-anger* people intent upon calming a quarrel (15:18b) should keep in mind that there are limits to what can be done under certain circumstances.

Starting a Quarrel Is like Breaching a Dam; so Drop the Matter Before a Dispute Breaks Out (17:14) 17:14, 19; 20:3; 22:10

What these four sayings have in common is a focus on *quarrels* or disputes of one kind or another. There is a kind of person who actually relishes (*loves*) a *quarrel*, 17:19 implies; this individual also *loves sin* in the sense of being a rebel (17:19a). The word for the high *gate* that he *builds* (17:19b) means literally *opening* and could refer either to the door of his house or even his mouth. That he enlarges it (*builds it high*) could mean he has built himself a really large and ostentatious house or is a braggart (Alden). Fools such as this are characterized by a verb that means *snarling* (*quick to quarrel*, 20:3b). If a community could be rid of them, it would be rid of quarrels as well, and strife and *insults* would be *ended* (22:10). *Drive out the mocker, and out goes strife* (22:10); *he behaves with overweening pride* (21:24).

By contrast, the person to be honored is the one who avoids strife (20:3a). And the way to do this (*avoid strife*), 17:14b indicates, is to *drop* it *before* [emphasized in Heb.] a [lit., *the*] *dispute breaks out* [*bursts forth*]. Letting a quarrel start is like letting a small leak in a dam get started (17:14a); at first the water coming through is a mere trickle, but before long it becomes an unstoppable flood.

Do Not Say, "I'll Pay Back for This Wrong!" Wait for the LORD, and He Will Deliver You (20:22) 17:13; 20:22; 21:10

A quite specific instance of community discord is addressed by these sayings: one where harm against another is being contemplated in retaliation for some known or imagined hurt. It is difficult to imagine anyone paying back *evil for good,* as does the saying in 17:13, but sometimes events or motives are grossly misinterpreted and it does happen. There are those in every society on the lookout for a fight. *The wicked man craves evil,* the saying in 21:10 observes; *his neighbor gets no mercy from him.* The consequences for the individual perpetrating such mayhem are devastating and long-lasting

(17:13b)—not just for the person himself, but also for *his house* (17:13b; his family, his heritage).

On the other hand, even under normal circumstances when wrongs have been inflicted, the impulse to retaliate is often strong. The admonition not to do so, in 20:22, has parallels in Egyptian wisdom literature, where the saying's counsel to trust in God to take care of the matter (20:22b) is also part of the advice: "Sit thou down at the hands of the god, And thy silence will cast them down" (The Instruction of Amenemope, Pritchard: 424). The admonition to *wait for* (or *hope* or *trust* in) *Yahweh*, in 20:22b, is similar. The sense of security derived from the promise that *he* [Yahweh] *will deliver you* (God will see to it that you are protected and cared for) replaces the impulse to pay back evil with evil. The saying in 25:21 takes this teaching a step further when it advocates not retaliating, and not just that, but also helping an enemy with food and drink (quoted by Paul in Rom 12:19-21).

He Who Pursues Righteousness and Love Finds Life, Prosperity and Honor (21:21) 12:20; 14:22; 21:21

These sayings might be thought of as terse summaries of the basic outlook and attitudes underlying the social ideal expressed in the above sayings. They draw a contrast between those who *plot evil* (12:20; 14:22), who take an essentially negative, exploitive attitude toward their social world; and those who *plot good* (lit.; *plan what is good,* 14:22), who take an essentially constructive attitude toward their social world. Their course in life is a study in contrasts. Those who *plot evil go astray* (14:22a); those who *plot good* end up *finding love and faithfulness* (14:22b; appreciation and respect). In the contrast drawn in 12:20, we read again of *those who plot evil,* but in this instance the focus is on what is in their heart: *deceit* (12:20a). Their opposites are *those who promote peace* (lit., *counselors of peace* [shālôm]), who contribute to the well-being of the community. Again, the focus is on what is within them: *joy* (12:20b). The contrasting inner condition of these two groups (*deceit* versus *joy*) is a reflection of their contrasting attitudes and actions within their society. Those who build up the community are far happier than those who do not.

The social ideals of the entire collection are summed up in the third of these sayings: *He who pursues righteousness* [ṣĕdāqāh] *and love* [ḥesed] *finds life, prosperity* [ṣĕdāqāh] *and honor* (21:21). The saying does not ascribe perfection to this individual, but only that he *pursues* (or *follows after*) *righteousness* (right ways of living) and *love* (kindness, helpfulness). His reward is threefold: *life* (fullness of life), *righteousness* (not *prosperity* but the *uprightness* that was the object of his pursuit), and *honor* (*kābôd,* a certain honor or reputation). One is reminded of the saying of Jesus: "Seek first the kingdom of God and its righteousness, and all these things will be given to you as well" (Matt 6:33, lit.; cf. NIV; NRSV, note).

Treatment of Animals 12:10

A righteous man cares for the needs of his animal, but the kindest acts of the wicked are cruel (12:10). An upright man is not only kind to his neighbors but also to his animals. *A righteous man* not only takes care of them (*cares for the needs of his animal*), but, more literally, *knows the soul* [*nepeš*] *of his animal* (12:10a). He has an intuitive understanding of how they feel and what their needs are. The same phrase ("knows the soul of") also occurs in Exodus 23:9, "where it means to know how it feels to be a sojourner" (Clifford: 131). A *wicked* person lacks this capacity. The second line of this text (12:10b) does not refer to the *acts of the wicked* (NIV) but to his *compassions,* the "seat of his emotions" (Cohen). The emotions of the wicked *are cruel* (12:10b)—by implication, his actions toward animals are also cruel.

This is the only place in Proverbs where ideals for the treatment of animals are broached. Yet respect for their wisdom and beauty is an outstanding feature of the poems of Agur (30:24-28, 29-31), as is sympathetic regard for their needs in the law codes (cf. Exod 23:12; Deut 25:4).

THE TEXT IN BIBLICAL CONTEXT

Friendship in the Bible

A number of sayings in this group are very positive about the value of human friendships. They are seen as generally more reliable and life-sustaining than those between siblings. Is this high estimate of friendship shared by other writings in the Bible? A little thought indicates that it is. First, there are some compelling depictions of friendship elsewhere. The account of the friendship of David and Jonathan in 1 Samuel (18-23) is one of the most memorable illustrations of the "beloved" companion who sticks closer than a brother (Prov 18:24). Jonathan's father, Saul, was intent on killing David at the very time Jonathan's love for David was growing. Their friendship was a decisive factor in David's escape from the court of Saul.

There is another beautiful depiction of friendship in the book of Ruth. In this case it is that between a mother and her daughter-in-law.

Ruth is not only honored for the fidelity she showed to her deceased husband, but also for how loyal she was to her deceased husband's mother, Naomi. They were more than relatives; they were friends. Another example of friendship is that between Jeremiah and his scribe, Baruch. This was obviously more than a professional relationship. They both suffered much together and at one point hid out together (36:19, 26). At this point Jeremiah had a sobering "word" for his faithful companion that must have been difficult for both of them to bear (Jer 45). It is hard to imagine how Jeremiah's prophetic ministry could have unfolded as it did without Baruch's steadfast friendship.

In the Synoptic Gospels Jesus is spoken of pejoratively by his critics as "a glutton and a drunkard, a friend of tax collector's and 'sinners'" (Luke 7:34). It was meant as a harsh criticism, but today we cherish it as a treasured depiction of his character: he extended friendship to those whom others thought were undeserving. In John's Gospel Jesus uses the word "friend" to characterize the relationship he wants to have with his disciples. He wants them to relate to him not as "servants" but as "friends" (John 15:14-15). There was an unnamed disciple whom he especially loved, and the same is said about his relationship to Lazarus, Mary, and Martha (11:5). When he paused outside Lazarus's tomb at the time of his death, we are told, "Jesus wept" (John 11:35). This is remembered as the shortest verse in the English Bible. It is also a powerful statement about the deep meaning friendship had for Jesus.

Personal and Civic Ideals

The ideals expressed in these sayings for how neighbors should relate are realistic, but exceptionally lofty. Ideally, they suggest, one should be temperate and not easily provoked by the wrongs of others. Even when personally wronged, the advice is not to retaliate. Rather, one should be a peacemaker, overlook insults, and generally be a person of goodwill. Such teachings definitely do appear elsewhere in the Bible.

These are the ideals inculcated in the law codes. In Deuteronomy, for example, God's people are pictured as a brotherhood, "bound together," Wolff writes, "above all on the basis of their common salvation history and Yahweh's proclamation of his will (Josh 24)." This understanding of the Israelites "as a nation of brothers had results for the mutual relationships of its individual members. . . . It is noticeable," Wolff explains, "that Deuteronomy does not take over older regulations from the Book of the Covenant [Exod 21-23] without in each case expressly calling the fellow-Israelite involved 'brother' [cf. Exod 21:2 with Deut 15:12, KJV; Exod 21:16 with Deut 24:7; Exod 22:25 with Deut 23:19-20]" (Wolff: 187). In this instance (in Deuteronomy), "brother" takes on the connotation of "caring brother" or good neighbor, as in the famous saying in Leviticus 19:17-18. This advice is directly parallel to many of the sayings just surveyed on this theme in Main Collection of Proverbs, but here in the biblical law codes, it is stated as a command: "Do not hate your brother in your heart. Rebuke your neighbor frankly so you will not share in his guilt. Do not seek revenge or bear a grudge against one of your people, but love your neighbor as yourself. I am the LORD."

This latter command to "love your neighbor as yourself" (19:18) sums up the civic attitudes and duties inculcated in these codes. And then a few verses later this command is repeated: "When an alien lives with you in your land, do not mistreat him. The alien living with you must be treated as one of your native-born. Love him as yourself, for you were aliens in Egypt. I am the LORD your God" (19:34). When asked what were the greatest of all the commandments, Jesus replied that the greatest is to love God with heart, soul, and mind, and there is another commandment like it, to "love your neighbor as yourself" (Matt 22:37-38). When asked to specify who the "neighbor" is, Jesus replied with his famous parable of the Good Samaritan, in which a despised Samaritan shows this kind of neighborly compassion to a nameless man who was beaten and robbed (Luke 10:29-37).

The teachings of Jesus assembled in Matthew's Sermon on the Mount have near the close a famous version of the dictum known as the golden rule. It reads (Matt 7:12, lit.): "Therefore, in everything, as you would have others do to you, so do to them, for this is the law and the prophets." The Law and the Prophets in this sentence is a reference to the Scriptures of Judaism. The sum total of what they teach, this verse implies, can be summarized in this brief word of wisdom. In order to know how to treat someone, pause to think about how you would like to be treated, and let this be your guide.

The Joy of Those Who Promote Peace

The happiness of those who are *counselors of peace* (12:20, lit.) bridges over to the NT and Jesus's glad proclamation: "Blessed are the peacemakers, for they shall be called sons of God" (Matt 5:9). The sayings of Proverbs give advice on dampening anger and cultivating patience, about overlooking offenses and nipping disputes in the bud. They remind one of analogous NT teachings about anger with a brother being tantamount to murder (Matt 5:21-22) and not letting the sun go down on one's wrath (Eph 4:26). Jesus says you should go quickly to the person whom you may have offended (Matt 5:23-26) or may have sinned against you (18:15-22) and seek reconciliation before proceeding to worship.

In other words, a deep harmony seems to exist between the ideals here and the noblest and best teachings of the Bible elsewhere on these topics. At one point, it seems, the NT writings (influenced by the teaching and example of Jesus) have gone a step further in their emphasis on covering over (Jas 5:20) the faults of others through an excess of love (Matt 5:43-47). Jesus's act of laying down his life for his friends (and even his enemies) set in motion a "love" dynamic that envelops NT social teaching and "fulfills" (5:17) and enriches (but does not necessarily replace) these more explicit, down-to-earth teachings about social relations in Proverbs. "On two different occasions—again in dispute with the Pharisees—he cites Hosea 6:6: 'I desire mercy, . . . not sacrifice' (Matt 9:13; 12:7)" (Hays, 1996:99).

Regard for the Needs and Rights of Animals

The saying in Proverbs on this subject is unique in the Bible, not so much for what it says, but for how it says it. It makes explicit that the upright person has a sympathetic understanding and regard for the *soul* of his animal, which the wicked person does not (12:10). The focus here is on the inner attitude toward animals, knowing what they need and how they feel, and treating them accordingly. Perhaps the stipulations in Genesis 9:4, that an animal may be killed for food but not with its lifeblood still in it, may reflect similar sensibilities. Rabbinic tradition took this command to be a prohibition against treating animals cruelly by cutting off the flesh or limb or taking blood from a living animal (Montefiore and Loewe: 556). There may be a similar reasoning behind the prohibition against destroying a "bird's nest beside the road," where "the mother is sitting on the young or on the eggs" (Deut 22:6).

There is also respect shown for the "soul" or feelings of animals in several stipulations. They too should rest on the Sabbath (Exod 20:10; Deut 5:14), a donkey "fallen down under its load" should be rescued (Exod 23:5), and an ox treading out the grain should not be muzzled (Deut 25:4). Also, from the promise that if Israel is faithful, God "will provide grass in the fields for your cattle, and you will eat and be satisfied" (Deut 11:13-15), the rabbis deduced the regulation that "a man must feed his animals before feeding himself" (Cohen: 75). "Cruelty to animals was given a special term by the Rabbis, . . . which literally means: 'Afflicting anything possessed of life'" (Montefiore and Loewe:

47). This abhorrence for the mistreatment of animals is also reflected in the actions of a council called in the early years of the Christian movement to decide whether Gentile Christian converts needed to be circumcised. The council decided that circumcision would not be required, but that the inquiring churches "should" be vigilant to "abstain from food polluted by idols, from sexual immorality, [and] from [eating] meat of strangled animals and from blood" (Acts 15:20).

THE TEXT IN THE LIFE OF THE CHURCH

Friendship in the Believers Churches

In its concern about "big" issues, the church may at times neglect the "small" nitty-gritty issues involved in the more intimate social relations of daily life. Reading through this provocative group of poems about those relations is a reminder of the different strands in the fabric of a good or not-so-good community. Believers churches are rightly concerned about the quality of these relationships in their congregations. They can make or break their morale and cloud or brighten their witness. My sense is that this group of poems might be another neglected but valuable resource. Taken individually and together, they provoke thought about relational issues that are as relevant today as ever. Offenses between neighbors still arise and need to be processed and dealt with. Quarrels still threaten to break out and disrupt. There is relevant advice in these poems for how to regard insults, snobbery, and elitism.

The subject of friendship touched on here is one seldom dealt with in our churches. God has created us not just with this powerful capacity to bond in marriage, but also to bond with friends. This bond with friends is sometimes viewed with suspicion. It is true that all should be our friends, but this ideal need not diminish the bond of special friendships or the enrichment they bring. The insights of these sayings on aspects of human relations might well be the focus of a helpful study.

Church and World

The church rightly seeks to embody these teachings in its own congregations. To do so has been an especially strong impulse in the believers church tradition. In his article on the "Church" in *The Mennonite Encyclopedia*, church historian Harold Bender writes: "The original Anabaptist movement rejected the idea of an invisible church." Instead, it insisted that the Christian community is as visible as its members and "that its Christian character must be 'in evidence'" (Bender: 597). Earlier in his essay he lists the "marks of the true church": "(1) unadulterated pure doctrine; (2) Scriptural use of baptism and the Lord's Supper; (3) obedience to the Word of God; (4) unfeigned brotherly love; (5) candid confession of God and Christ; (6) persecution and tribulation for the sake of the Word of the Lord" (595-96). The emphasis on "brotherly love" led to the notion of the church as a "brotherhood," which Bender states had an impact on the "hierarchical emphasis" on office but also led to "mutual aid in economic life" (596).

But increasingly the churches are part of the larger world, since congregations no longer exist as enclaves. New media of communication exercise a powerful hold on our imagination and culture. Christians must pay attention to this as never before and fight for civility not just within church, but also in the culture at large. Christians may lament their powerlessness. Who can change Hollywood? Who can do anything about the manners and morals of the endless stream of television shows? But yet, each in our own place, in accordance with our own voice and talents, inevitably plays a role in an evolution toward more civility in human relations or the opposite. This can begin to happen in our homes, in the way we settle disputes and train our children. It may be that God will place us, like Joseph, in places of responsibility where more can be done.

One of the great heroes of Canadian national life is Tommy Douglas, a man of God who became a Baptist pastor, then a member of the Canadian Parliament, and following that premier of Saskatchewan. This was at a time when the availability of health care for all Canadians was being debated. Douglas had a deep conviction that it was the neighborly thing to do to make health care available for all Canadian residents. From his convictions and advocacy came the national health system of Canada, one of the most humane in the world. As a relative newcomer to Canada who has benefited from this act of civility, I am deeply grateful. Canada has benefited from the spirit of goodwill and neighborliness of many, among them Mennonites, who were among the first Europeans to settle the Canadian heartland in Ontario.

Proverbs 10:1--22:16

Matters of the Heart

The Book of Proverbs, Part 2: The Themes of the Main Collection							
Wisdom	Nation-hood	Speech	Family	Econo-mics	Personal Rela-tions	Matters of the Heart	Know-ledge of the Holy One

PREVIEW

Just as there are things a wise person should know about relationships in the wider world, so there are truths about the inner world worth contemplating as well. Today terms like "mind" or "emotions" are used to identify a realm the Bible refers to as the "heart," "soul," or "spirit" (Wolff: 40-58). Then as now, this inner world was a realm of mystery that could not be directly observed by anyone except the one possessing it. Yet experiences can be shared, talked about, and pondered ["Heart"]. The thoughts within are also known not just through speech; they also display themselves on our faces, in our demeanor. From observation one can learn that certain emotions affect people's health and their success or failure in what they attempt to do. In the Main Collection are some fifteen sayings that probe these "matters of the heart."

OUTLINE

The Mystery of the Heart, 14:10, 13; 20:27
The Heart's Impact on Health, 12:25; 13:12, 19; 14:30; 15:13,
   15, 30; 17:22; 18:14
A Proud, Self-Righteous Heart, 14:12; 16:18, 25; 18:12; 19:3;
   20:9; 21:4

EXPLANATORY NOTES

The Mystery of the Heart 14:10, 13; 20:27

*Each Heart Knows Its Own Bitterness, and No One Else
Can Share Its Joy (14:10) 14:10, 13*

Here is a literal translation of the saying in 14:10: *The heart
knows the bitterness of its soul, and its joy cannot be fathomed by
an outsider.* The joys and sorrows in our hearts are fully known only
to our *heart* and to no one else. In this sense we are all strangers. No
one else but ourselves fully knows or can know what we are experiencing. The emotions of the *heart* are also complex and elusive: *Even
in laughter the heart may ache, and joy may end in grief* (14:13).
This alludes to the well-known fact that things are not always what
they seem, even to the *heart* itself. The joy felt in one moment may
be tinged with sadness and quickly turn to depression. There is a sense
in which the "secrets of the heart" are known only to God, a point
made in several proverbs (17:3; 21:2; 24:12) and psalms (Ps 44:21;
139:23-24).

*The Spirit of Man Is the LORD'S Lamp; It Searches Out
His Inmost Being (NIV note) 20:27*

This unusual saying refers to an inner capacity for self-transcen-
dence: there is a *spirit* within us, which is able to *search out all the
inward parts* (*his inmost being,* NIV). This capacity is here identified
as *the spirit of a human being* [*'ādām*].The word translated *spirit*
(*nišmat*) is used elsewhere of the breath of life breathed by God into
"Adam's" nostrils (Gen 2:7; 7:22; Job 34:14; 36:14), but only here
is this breath characterized as a *lamp of Yahweh* (20:27a). The NIV
preferred translation of the first line of this poem, *The lamp of the
LORD searches the spirit of a man,* seems contrived, since the verb
searches is not found in the poem's first line, but only in its second
line. In the poem's first line, the phrases *lamp of the LORD* and *spirit
of man* are simply juxtaposed (20:27a), implying that *lamp of the
LORD* is a metaphor for *spirit of man.* It is this (*the spirit of man*

likened to *the lamp of the LORD*) that *searches out his inmost being* (20:27b). The human capacity for thought and self-reflection (*spirit of man*) is thereby recognized and characterized as a divine gift; God himself has placed this awesome *lamp* (light of consciousness) within the human heart.

The Heart's Impact on Health 12:25; 13:12, 19; 14:30; 15:13, 15, 30; 17:22; 18:14

A Man's Spirit Sustains Him in Sickness, but a Crushed Spirit Who Can Bear? (18:14) 17:22; 18:14

The strength or dominance of certain closely related emotions and the impact they have on the body's health are the subject of these two sayings. *A man's spirit sustains in his sickness* is a literal translation of the first line of 18:14a, *but a crushed* [or *broken*] *spirit who can bear?* (18:14b). The basic meaning of the word *spirit* in this poem (Heb.: *rûaḥ*) is *wind*. Living human beings breath in and out. When they die, they no longer have breath. When they are strong or determined or excited, it shows in the way they breathe. So by analogy *rûaḥ* is used to refer to a person's emotional, mental, or spiritual condition. The implied answer to the question posed in 18:14b (*but a crushed spirit who can bear?*) is "no one." No one can survive a broken spirit because it *dries up the bones* (17:22b); the whole body shrivels up.

A Heart at Peace Gives Life to the Body, but Envy Rots the Bones (14:30) 12:25; 13:12, 19; 14:30; 15:13, 15, 30

What distinguishes an inner life that *sustains* (18:14a) from one that is *broken* (18:14b, lit.)? It has something to do with *hope deferred* versus *longing fulfilled,* according to the insight shared in another poem. *Hope deferred* [drawn out] *makes the heart sick, but a longing* [desire] *fulfilled is a tree of life* (13:12). Moreover, *a longing fulfilled is sweet* [pleasant] *to the soul* [nepeš, the whole person] (13:19a). The related insight, *but fools detest* [lit., *it is an abomination to fools*] *turning from evil* indicates that by *longing fulfilled* is meant one's inner desires for an upright, meaningful, and essentially good and successful life (13:19b). When hope for success in life is deferred or drawn out too long, hope dies and the whole body sickens. When, on the other hand, even glimmers of success appear, it is as though the "sap" of life has been restored. Then one has *a heart at peace* (14:30); the inner life is more tranquil, even tempered

(Cohen) rather than being agitated (full of *envy,* which *rots the bones*); serenity like this is also conducive to health (*gives life to the body,* 14:30a).

Three additional proverbs say something quite similar. One of them implies that even though *the days of the oppressed* [lit., *all the days of the poor*] *are wretched* [*evil*], with a *cheerful heart* [lit., *good heart*; "an instructed mind," Clifford] there can be, as it were, *a continual feast* (15:15). How might one be cheerful under circumstances of poverty? "Being wise makes impoverishment not only bearable, but even joyful, like the joy of feast days" (Clifford: 153). One of these sayings alludes to the power of *a kind word* (lit., *good word*) to cheer someone burdened by *an anxious heart* (lit., *care in the heart of a man,* 12:25). Simply *a cheerful look* [lit., *the light of the eyes*) can also, by itself, bring *joy to the heart,* even as *good news gives health to the bones* [lit., *makes the bones fat*] (15:30). What therefore is especially conducive to good health is a *happy heart* (15:13, 15, 30; 17:22). It is uncertain, however, whether a cheerful heart is good *medicine,* as the final word of 17:22a is often translated. The Hebrew word translated *medicine* is found only here in the Bible. The word might mean *face* (based on 15:13, which is similar to this verse; Alden). If that is the case, this saying would sum up the effect of inner peace on the body and might be translated as follows: *A cheerful heart makes a happy face, but an anxious spirit dries up the bones* (Clifford).

A Proud Self-Righteous Heart   14:12; 16:18, 25; 18:12; 19:3; 20:9; 21:4

There Is a Way That Seems Right to a Man, but in the End It Leads to Death (14:12; 16:25) 14:12; 16:25; 19:3; 20:9; 21:4

The crucial insight of this group of sayings is expressed in a poem that appears twice in the collection: *There is a way that seems right to a man, but in the end it leads to death* (14:12; 16:25). The mental condition signified is self-righteousness: the person involved is totally convinced that he is right. Another poem in this group alludes to a similar state of mind by posing a rhetorical question: *Who can say, "I have kept my heart pure; I am pure and without sin"?* (20:9). The implied answer is "No one," but that the question is posed at all implies the asker's conviction that human beings have a strong tendency toward believing in their own perfection. This too may be the *heart* condition referred to in yet another saying: *A man's own folly ruins his life, yet his heart rages against the LORD* (19:3). The *man* referred to is clinging to a self-righteous self-understanding, even though the choices he has made have proven to be self-destructive and foolish. Instead of taking stock of his life and changing course, he rages against Yahweh for the mess his life has turned out to be.

Before His Downfall a Man's Heart Is Proud, but Humility Comes Before Honor (18:12) 12:9; 16:18; 18:12; 21:4

Three of these poems diagnose the source of the *heart* problem just mentioned as the result of a prior condition termed *pride*—which is further characterized as a *haughty* [or *lifted up*] *spirit* (16:18). The opposite of *pride* is *humility* (18:12). The humble are referred to as those *lowly in spirit* (16:19). The terminology *lifted up* and *lowly* points to the essential issue at stake here. A prideful person thinks too highly of himself (has an exaggerated or inflated picture of his attributes or abilities); a humble person is open to the reality of who he is and what his abilities are. This is why *pride goes before destruction, a haughty spirit before a fall* (16:18; lit., *before the face of destruction* [is] *pride; before the face of a fall* [is] *a haughty spirit*). This too is why *before his downfall a man's heart is proud, but humility comes before honor* (18:12; lit., *before the face of destruction, the heart of a man* [is] *haughty, and before the face of honor* [is] *humility*). Pride distorts reality; to be receptive to knowledge and wisdom of a kind that helps one live within the world as it really is requires humility. The humorous saying in 12:9 reinforces this point: *Better to be a nobody* [lit., *one despised*] *and yet have a servant than pretend to be somebody* [lit., *self-honoring*] *and have no food* (12:9). Prideful pretensions create a world of illusion that leads to poverty.

THE TEXT IN BIBLICAL CONTEXT

Conflicted and Transformed Hearts

The texts here reflect an anthropology not unlike that portrayed in the creation accounts in Genesis 1-3. Human beings are creatures distinguished from plants and animals by virtue of being created in the image and likeness of God. When God created the first man, he breathed into his nostrils and he became a living being with a capacity for "naming" the animals and exercising a dominion over them. However, his subsequent choices, though seemingly right in his own eyes, have had deadly consequences (Gen 3). Still, a *lamp of Yahweh* shines within him, searching the inward parts (Prov 20:27). A longing and hope for a right and better way propels human beings onward, which, when fulfilled, *is sweet to the soul* (Prov 13:19a).

Jeremiah (who may have received an education based on the book of Proverbs) has similar ideas. He too experienced the heart as a mystery, "deceitful above all things. . . . Who can understand it?" Jeremiah felt that in his generation at least it was "beyond cure" (17:9) because "Judah's sin" had been too deeply engraved on it as "with an iron tool" (17:1). His hope was that a time would come when this would be changed, and his people would humble themselves, seek Yahweh with all their heart (29:13), and again become a teachable people with Yahweh's laws written "on their hearts" (31:33). That hope for the purification of the human heart—so that "the house of Israel" might sincerely do God's will—is echoed in the prophecies of Ezekiel (36:24-27). It appears again with the actions of Ezra and Nehemiah in their reforms, when they assembled Israel's sacred Scriptures for reading, study, and decision-making (Neh 8-10). It was to renew the inner life of Israel that these Scriptures were assembled— and now they included a slightly enlarged book of Proverbs as part of their end-section called "the Writings" [Wisdom in Proverbs].

Conditions of the heart were also a core concern of the mission of Jesus and those first apostles who carried his mission forward into the wider world with the Holy Spirit's help. Indeed, at that time in Israel the hearts of too many were (for many reasons) showing signs of the kind of self-righteousness that the sayings we have just looked at highlight. It was just this alternative attitude alluded to here that Jesus in his wisdom (and in his own unique way) again brought forward. No one is "good" but God alone, he replied to a certain over-exuberant disciple who addressed him adoringly as "Good teacher" (Mark 10:17-19). He too was profoundly aware, as was Jeremiah, of the potential for evil in the human heart (7:21-23). Even the best of us (if we truly understand our hearts) have much to repent of, he pointed out in his little portrait of two men at prayer: a Pharisee and a tax collector (Luke 18:9-14). Jesus's whole mission, seen within the messianic expectations of the time, was one of divesting Israel of its grandiose futuristic dreams in favor of a humbler vision of a world filled with down-to-earth kindness, wisdom, and love of a kind most people can realistically aspire to and realize.

THE TEXT IN THE LIFE OF THE CHURCH

Cure of Souls Through the Centuries

In his classic *History of the Cure of Souls,* John T. McNeill shows how the aspirations for a renewed and transformed heart in the teachings of Jesus are summarized in the NT book of James. There the "highest approval is bestowed upon the earnest believer who feels impelled to seek a lapsed and wandering member, and to bring him back from the error of his way, saving his soul from death" (5:19; McNeill: 86). Jesus's words in Matthew 18:15-18 evoke a similar mutuality of concern among believers. A core thesis of McNeill's book is that it was primarily because of the degree to which Christians faithfully adhered to these ideals of mutual edification and correction (or "cure of souls") "that the Church emerged as a firmly knit organization. It was because they shared in these ways and perpetuated by sharing, a new life in Christ, and effectively revealed it in their lives, that the Roman world failed to smother the Christian groups in its mass or crush them by its power. . . . It finally turned to the Church for deliverance from its own political chaos" (87).

However, this practice of "mutual edification and correction" was hard to maintain. In the "Patristic Age" (second to fifth centuries), McNeill writes, "the pursuit of holiness took the form of ascetic discipline, wherein a few attained a high spirituality but the majority were earnestly engaged in a perpetual warfare with their besetting sins. Something had been lost of the liberating power of the Gospel, and medieval doctrines of sacramental grace were still not far developed" (111). What was lost at this time, McNeill observes, was not regained during the medieval period through the practice of confessing long lists of sins and seeking absolution through the confessional and acts of penance and indulgences.

As this practice gradually died out in the Reformation period, it was replaced by a more personal involvement of pastors through personal conversations and home visitations. But this was only sporadically successful. According to McNeill, what is potentially the most important contribution of the Reformation period to the "cure of souls" was "the cultivation . . . of the mutual cure of souls on the part of laymen. Each man was his brother's keeper in a spiritual fellowship. *'Seelsorge aller an allen'* (the care of all for the souls of all) aptly expresses this principle. This is the implementation of the doctrine of the spiritual priesthood of all Christians—a doctrine often erroneously interpreted in an individualistic sense."

It is McNeill's conviction (what apparently compelled him to undertake this study) that "there are still undisclosed possibilities in the application of this principle in the Church, both in the direction of brotherly correction and of mutual enrichment. The principle of mutual guidance and spiritual stimulation is as old as the New Testament; in some sense, as old as religion. It rests upon the belief that the gifts of the Spirit move through the whole membership of the

Church, and that, in no merely theoretic sense, all Christians are functioning members of one living body, exercising toward one another a
spiritual or priestly office" (190).

Matters of the Heart Today

Reading the little poems of this group is a chastening experience for
anyone who thinks we are much more knowledgeable about things of
the mind and spirit than those who lived in far-off times and places.
Long before the rise of modern medicine, people intuited that our attitudes and emotions have a huge impact on our health. They also
knew how profoundly influenced we are by our successes and failures,
and the words of affirmation or kindness we receive from others.
Above all, they were sensitive to the issues of pride and self-righteousness and how deeply prone human beings are to such attitudes.

It must be recognized, however, that this side of our human experience continues to be probed and studied. Insights that we now more
or less take for granted about the human "heart" were not known in
biblical times. There are distinct differences, for example, between
human pride and an appropriate self-esteem. An appropriate self-
esteem emerges from a realistic understanding of one's gifts and calling. Low self-esteem may be rooted in prideful, unrealistic
expectations, but pride and unrealistic expectations may be affected
by factors beyond our control such as traumatic experiences in early
childhood or our genetic make-up.

We are still prone to self-righteousness, find it difficult to acknowledge our faults, and tend to blame others. But here again, many factors may be in play. Children, who for no fault of their own may not
have had a mother's love during crucial periods of the trust-bonding
stage, may suffer a lack of trust or confidence later in life. Children
without a father present in the home may be too mother-dependent.
Children suffering with "trust deprivations" earlier in life may move
from friend to friend or spouse to spouse in an endless search for what
is lacking. In compensation for the loss of a father's presence and
love, boys may take on compensatory identities in which hyper-mas-
culinity plays a role.

Psychologists and philosophers alike are still hard pressed to
explain the mystery of human consciousness. Within us is a light of
awareness that is "godlike" in its capacity to reflect and search out the
inward parts (20:27). This light is not God, as many now think (claim-
ing divinity for our inner being). We have this capacity as a gift from
our Creator. It is the gift of thought, of reflection, of study and decision-making, of weighing our options and making the choices that we

deem best. It is the gift of freedom. With it comes the gift of responsibility and the burden of suffering the consequences of the decisions
we make for good or ill.

Taking into account all the insights of which modern studies make
us aware, I still think it would be beneficial for the churches to make
greater use of the wise sayings in Proverbs about "matters of the
heart." This can be done by simply selecting ten or so of the above-
cited sayings, putting them on a piece of paper, and starting a conversation.

Proverbs 10:1–22:16

Knowledge of the Holy One

The Book of Proverbs, Part 2: The Themes of the Main Collection							
Wisdom	Nation-hood	Speech	Family	Econo-mics	Personal Rela-tions	Matters of the Heart	Knowl-edge of the Holy One

PREVIEW

Only a handful of the 275 couplets of the Main Collection examined thus far mention the divine name *Yahweh* (the God of Israel), who is twice referred to in Proverbs as *the Holy One* (9:10b; 30:3). If we would conclude our study of this section of Proverbs at this point, we might imagine that those who compiled it were rather unconcerned about what their students believed about God. To come to such a conclusion, however, would be seriously mistaken and necessitate ignoring some seventy-five sayings of this Main Collection still remaining to be investigated. Virtually all of these are either about Yahweh and his ways, or about the character and fate of those who do or do not revere or serve the God so named *[Middle Poems]*.

Over twenty-five of these sayings speak explicitly of Yahweh. They mention his sovereign awareness of all that goes on in the universe, right down to the depths of each individual's consciousness. They speak of his sovereign power and involvement in all aspects of the universe, of his passionate likes and dislikes, and of the great benefits that accrue to those who fear him, trust him, and give heed to his word. Another cluster of sayings paint a general picture of the character of the *upright* and *wicked* (those who do or do not believe in and follow God) and of their contrasting future destinies.

For purposes of discussion, I have subdivided this group of sayings into two major subunits. Some twenty-five sayings in the first subunit refer by name to Yahweh (a few sayings of this type have already been studied in connection with earlier themes). These speak quite explicitly and forcefully of God's omniscience and power, of his "loves" and "hates." The remaining block of about fifty sayings, which speak of the fate of those who do or do not serve him (the *upright* and *wicked*), constitute the second subunit.

OUTLINE

God's All-Seeing Providence and Power, His "Loves" and "Hates,"
11:20; 12:2, 22; 15:8, 9, 25, 26, 29; 14:2; 15:3, 11, 20, 25, 33; 16:1, 2, 3, 4, 5, 7, 9; 17:3; 19:17, 21; 20:23, 24, 25; 21:2, 3, 7, 13, 27, 30, 31; 22:12

The Contrasting Fate of Those Who Do or Do Not Serve God (the Upright and Wicked), 10:6, 7, 9, 24, 25, 27, 28, 29, 30; 11:3, 5, 6, 7, 8, 18, 19, 21, 23, 31; 12:3, 5, 7, 12, 21, 28; 13:6, 9; 14:11, 14, 19, 26, 27, 32; 16:6, 13, 17, 20, 31; 18:3, 10; 19:23; 21:7, 18, 21; 22:8

EXPLANATORY NOTES

God's All-Seeing Providence and Power, His "Loves" and "Hates" 11:20; 12:2, 22; 15:8, 9, 25, 26, 29; 14:2; 15:3, 11, 20, 25, 33; 16:1, 2, 3, 4, 5, 7, 9; 17:3; 19:17, 21; 20:23, 24, 25; 21:2, 3, 7, 13, 27, 30, 31; 22:12

The Eyes of the LORD Are Everywhere, Keeping Watch on the Wicked and the Good (15:3) 15:3, 22:12

This first group of sayings is especially important for grasping how the final editors of this collection linked their belief in the personal reality of God to the world of wisdom. For them, Yahweh was not only

Israel's God, but also sovereign over the whole world. In the sentence *The eyes of the LORD are everywhere* (15:3a), the word *everywhere* (lit., *in every place*) stands at the forefront of the sentence (*In every place, the eyes of Yahweh*). The expression *the eyes of the LORD* is found elsewhere in the literature of Hezekiah's reforms (Deut 11:12; 13:18; 1 Kgs 8:29, 52), but not as here with the emphasis on *everywhere*. Such a comprehensive emphasis also does not appear in the words of the Chronicler: "The eyes of the LORD range throughout the earth to strengthen those whose hearts are fully committed to him" (2 Chr 16:9). Here *eyes* of God are everywhere *keeping watch on the wicked and the good* (15:3b); the implication is that the fate of *wicked and good* is not just the outcome of natural causes alone. God too is involved somehow. This should not be taken to mean, however, that the truth about the world, which can be observed by those who have eyes and ears, is of no importance. God's watchfulness encompasses not only matters of morality. *The eyes of the LORD keep watch over knowledge* as well, but *he frustrates the words of the unfaithful* (22:12), subverts [*overturns*] *the words of the devious* (lit.). Thus, "where knowledge of the true and the good exists, there does it stand under the protection of God" (Delitzsch). These sayings unite in a single image the world of knowledge and wisdom and the world of faith in the living God, as those who formulated them understood him.

Death and Destruction Lie Open Before the LORD [Yahweh]—How Much More the Hearts of Men! (15:11) 15:11; 16:2; 17:3; 21:2

God's all-knowing sovereignty is not only worldwide; it also encompasses the inner world of the human *heart* (mind), these four sayings declare. If *Death and Destruction* [Sheol and Abbadon, the underworld domains of the dead] *lie open before the LORD—how much more the hearts of men* [lit., *sons of 'ādām*] (15:11). God sees the hidden depths of the earth and likewise the hidden inner world of human beings. This knowledge enables him to *test the heart* as a burning hot *furnace* tests gold or silver (17:3), separating out the "spurious from the genuine and ascertaining what a man is as opposed to what he professes to be" (McKane: 511).

That this testing process may reveal a state of mind different from a person's self-righteous appraisal of himself might have him believing is stated twice in almost identical words (16:2; 21:2). In 16:2 it is observed that *all a man's ways* [*every way of a man*, 21:2a] *seem innocent to him* [*seem right to him*, 21:2a], *but motives* [lit., *spirits*, 16:2b; *heart*, 21:2b] *are weighed by the LORD.* The Hebrew word translated *innocent* in 16:2a is used of pure, uncontaminated olive oil (Exod 27:20); here it refers to the "seeming" purity (16:2a) or rightness (21:2a) of one's motives. Both texts put in contrast what this individual's inner world looks like "in his own eyes" with how it measures up when *weighed* by Yahweh. The person who *fears the LORD* is profoundly aware that human beings are prone to think they are right but that this predisposition may be false. In the end what counts is not so much what he thinks as what God sees and knows his inner world to be. For the classic expression of this awareness, see Psalm 139.

There Is No Wisdom, No Insight, No Plan That Can Succeed Against the LORD (21:30) 16:1, 3, 4, 7, 9; 19:21; 20:24, 25, 30; 21:30, 31

God is not only all-knowing but also all-powerful and providentially involved in all that transpires on earth. This is the theme of these eleven proverbs, the first three of which are in the five-proverb collection (16:2-6) at the center of the Main Collection (and hence also at the center of the Hezekiah Edition). In them (as in 8:22-31) wisdom itself is explicitly subordinated to the personal rule of God, which manifests itself in the most intimate details of a person's life [*Middle Poems*]. The thoughts and plans of a person's heart are referred to in five of these sayings (16:1, 3, 9; 19:21; 20:24). They make the point that it is not necessarily a person's thoughts and plans that will prevail, but rather that which is determined by Yahweh (16:1, 3, 9b; 19:21). In the creative gap between the thought and its formulation in speech (16:1), between the plan and its execution (16:3, 9; 19:21) Yahweh's sovereign power is at work determining the outcome. *How then can anyone* ['*ādām*, a human being] *understand his own way?* (20:24)—the implied answer is: "No one can!" A total management of one's life by means of reason or the powers of the mind is impossible. *There is no wisdom, no insight, no plan that can succeed against the LORD* (21:30). That too is why *it is a trap for a man to dedicate something rashly*, thinking that this will secure a desired outcome (20:25; cf. Judg 11:29-40; 1 Sam 14:24-46; Eccl 5:3-4). The outcome of someone's life is ultimately in the hands of God, as yet another metaphorical epigram makes clear: *The horse is made ready for the day of battle, but the victory rests with the LORD* (21:31; meant to apply to more than warfare).

Those who are truly wise will recognize that wisdom itself has limitations, and ultimately it is only the purpose of God that will prevail. *The LORD works out everything for his* [or *its*] *own ends—even the wicked for a day of disaster* (16:4). This is the saying that the *men of Hezekiah* (25:1) placed at the very center of their edition of Solomon's proverbs (see Overview to the Main Collection). The idea expressed is not that everything that happens is a manifestation of God's will, but that God is a divine presence or providence everywhere in the universe. God sees to it that *everything* unfolds in accordance with his plans and purposes, and that includes *the wicked for a day of disaster*. This universe is not simply the outworking of cause and effect. Their experience was that *when a man's ways are pleasing to the LORD, he makes even his enemies live at peace with him* (16:7). This emphasis on Yahweh's sovereignty at the heart of the collection is not meant to subvert the teachings elsewhere that are equally passionate about the importance of human foresight and planning, but to encourage an approach to life that incorporates both planning and trust in the Lord.

The LORD Detests the Way of the Wicked, but He Loves Those Who Pursue Righteousness (15:9) 11:20; 12:2, 22; 14:2; 15:8, 9, 25, 26, 29; 16:5; 19:17; 20:23; 21:3, 27

What manner of God is this sovereign Yahweh? These fourteen sayings speak of his passionate loves and hates, that which is an *abomination* to him (NIV: *detest* or *detestable*), versus what he *loves*. What is said to be abominable to Yahweh are *men of perverse* [*crooked*] *heart* (11:20), *lying lips* (12:22), *the sacrifice of the wicked* (15:8; 21:27), *the way of the wicked* (15:9), *the thoughts* [*schemes*] *of the wicked* (15:26), *all the proud of heart* (16:5), *the proud man's house* (15:25), *differing weights and dishonest scales* (20:23).

By contrast Yahweh *delights in* and *loves those whose ways are blameless* (11:20) and *who pursue* [*follow after*] *righteousness* (15:9). To follow after righteousness means to obey Yahweh's will as represented by a code like the Decalogue. Those who embrace God's ways by keeping his laws are declared to be *righteous* or *upright* and shall "surely live" (Ezek 18:9; cf. Prov 4:4; 7:2; 15:27). The words of such persons (*the pure*) are characterized as *pleasing* (lit., *words of friendliness*) to Yahweh in contrast to the schemes of *the wicked* (15:26b). Twice the *prayer* of these upright ones is mentioned, and Yahweh is said to be pleased by it (15:8b) and to *hear* it (15:29b).

Indeed, the *prayer* of the upright is more acceptable to God than the *sacrifice* offering *of the wicked* (15:8), for *the LORD is far from the wicked, but he hears the prayer of the righteous* (15:29). The person *whose walk is upright* is one who simply *fears* [*reveres*] *the LORD* rather than despising him as do those *whose ways are devious* (14:2).

Sacrifice as such is not rejected but is radically devalued (as in Deuteronomy [e.g., 6:4-9] and the oracles of the Prophets [e.g., Isa 1:11; Jer 7:21-26]). What counts more with Yahweh is doing *what is right and just; this is more acceptable to the LORD than sacrifice* (Prov 21:3). What brings atonement is summed up in the saying in 12:2: *A good man* [Heb.: *the good*] *obtains favor from the LORD, but the LORD condemns a crafty man* [*a man of wicked devices*] (cf. Amos 5:14; Hos 8:2-3). A specific instance of this interplay between human goodness and the *favor of the LORD* is formulated as follows: *He who is kind to the poor lends to the LORD, and he will reward him for what he has done* (19:17). Like Jesus on this same theme (Matt 25:31-46), this and other sayings of this group encourage a life of generosity and prayer rather than religious formalities such as animal sacrifice.

The Name of the LORD Is a Strong Tower; the Righteous Run to It and Are Safe (18:10) 10:27, 29; 14:2, 26, 27; 15:9, 33; 16:6, 20; 18:10; 19:23

These eleven sayings foster loyalty to God by summarizing some of the basic benefits that accrue to those who *fear the LORD*, take refuge in his *name*, and follow in his way (18:10). Walking uprightly and fearing God are intimately interrelated: the one naturally leads to the other. *He whose walk is upright fears the LORD, but he whose ways are devious despises him* (14:2; cf. Deut 5:29). From this *walk* follow certain tangible and highly desirable consequences. Respect for God, trusting in his *name* (18:10), and giving heed to his *word* (*instruction*, 16:20a, NIV) not only *adds length to life* (10:27), but also enriches the quality of life: it is a *fountain of life* (14:27). Those who walk in Yahweh's way are *content, untouched by trouble* (19:23), kept safe from harm (10:29; 18:10). Such obedience leads to all manner of *good* (Heb.: *tôb;* one *prospers,* 16:20) and happiness (*blessed* [*happy*] *is he who trusts in the LORD,* 16:20b). These sayings reflect and to some extent synopsize the promises made in Deuteronomy to those who are loyal to God's covenant-creating "word" and "law" (e.g., Deut 28; 30:1-10).

Situated close to the center of the 375 sayings of the Main Collection is an especially important saying that states, *Fear of Yahweh [is] instruction [mûsar] in wisdom, and before honor, humility* (15:33a, lit.). This saying clarifies a point presupposed throughout the Hezekiah Edition of Proverbs: those humble enough to revere and obey Yahweh (the God of Israel, who spoke to Moses, as in Exod 3:15) are becoming educated in wisdom. In other words, *fear of the LORD* (and all that this involves) is of first importance in becoming wise in the ways that will lead to fullness of life (cf. 1:7; 9:10).

Something similar is said in Deuteronomy. There Moses declares one of the reasons Israel should observe his teachings: "This will show your wisdom and understanding to the nations, who will hear about all these decrees and say, 'Surely this great nation is a wise and understanding people'" (4:6). A comparison of the sayings in Proverbs 13:14 and 14:27 underscores the same point. The first states, *The teaching of the wise is a fountain of life, turning a man from the snares of death* (13:14); the second states, *The fear of the LORD is a fountain of life, turning a man from the snares of death* (14:27). The two statements are identical except that the second, 14:27, replaces the phrase, *teaching of the wise* with *the fear of the LORD.* The point of repeating the same sentence with a different subject is not to equate the two, as though the teaching resulting from *fear of Yahweh* were identical with *the teaching of the wise.* Instead, the repetition indicates that each (*fear of Yahweh* and *the teaching of the wise*) has its unique contribution to make to the same end: fullness of life and avoidance of those things that result in disorder and death.

Other sayings also allude to the way these two spheres (*fear of Yahweh* and *teachings of the wise*) complement and enrich each other. One of these states, *He who acts wisely according to the word shall find good* (16:20a, lit.); the second line declares, *And blessed is he who trusts in the LORD* (16:20b). The *word* referred to in the first line of this saying (NIV: *instruction*) may be a reference to the *word of God* revealed to Moses (30:5; Deut 30:14). The saying implies that it is an act of wisdom to obey this *word,* and that doing so will enable one to *find good* (the good path in life) and thus experience the blessings that come to those who trust in God. Another saying in 13:13 illuminates the meaning of this rare reference to the *word* in 16:20a: *He who scorns the word shall suffer for it, but he who fears the commandment shall be rewarded* (13:13, lit.). In this sentence *the word* (NIV: *instruction*) for which its scorners shall suffer is synonymous with *the commandment* (*miṣwāh*), which brings

reward to those who *fear* (NIV: *respects*) it. The terminology is again
similar to that used in Deuteronomy for the commands and word of
God (30:10, 15). The theology of yet another saying (Prov 16:6) may
be interpreted in this light. It declares that it is by means of *love*
(*ḥesed, covenant loyalty*) and *faithfulness* (*'emet*) that *sin is atoned
for* (guilt is expiated or covered, 16:6a; cf. Hos 6:6), and *through fear
of the LORD* that *a man avoids evil* (lit., *turns from evil*, 16:6b).

These ideas are fully in accord with the theological outlook of
Deuteronomy, which sees the spiritual renewal of Israel as primarily a
matter of heartfelt love and obedience to Yahweh and his commandments. This is more effective than the rituals of atonement at the temple (e.g., Deut 30:4-5; see the discussion of Prov 15:8; 21:27 under
"The LORD Detests . . . , but He Loves," above). Thus the poem in
14:2 seems to be saying that the essential character of one who *fears
the LORD* is not all that different from the essential character of those
who become wise. In both instances, what counts is that their *walk is
upright* [*straight, honest*] and not *devious* [*dishonest, crooked*]
(14:2; cf. 15:19b).

The Contrasting Fate of Those Who Do or Do Not Serve God (the Upright and Wicked) 10:6, 7, 9, 24, 25, 27, 28, 29, 30; 11:3, 5, 6, 7, 8, 18, 19, 21, 23, 31; 12:3, 5, 7, 12, 21, 28; 13:6, 9; 14:11, 14, 19, 26, 27, 32; 16:6, 13, 17, 20, 31; 18:3, 10; 19:23; 21:7, 18, 21; 22:8

*Blessings Crown the Head of the Righteous, but Violence
Overwhelms the Mouth of the Wicked (10:6) 10:6, 7, 9,
24, 25, 30; 11:7, 19; 12:3, 7, 12, 21, 28; 14:11, 19;
16:13; 19:16; 21:7, 21; 22:8*

A substantial number of proverbs in the Main Collection reinforce
the importance of serving God and following in his way by highlighting the contrasting fates of the *righteous* (*ṣadîq*) and *wicked* (*rāšā'*).
These terms are descriptive of those who are for or against God and
his way. As such, they refer more to commitment than to character:
both righteous and wicked are ordinary human beings with the usual
faults and foibles, but the righteous (in contrast to the wicked) have
covenanted to serve God. As a consequence they *pursue righteousness and* [*covenant*] *fidelity* [*ḥesed*] (21:21, lit.), observe the *law*
(*miṣwāh*, 19:16, lit.), and turn from evil (16:17a). Their *plans* (or
designs) are *just*, whereas those of the wicked are *deceitful* (12:5).

What is declared regarding their future is therefore not unlike the "blessings and curses" of Leviticus 26 and Deuteronomy 28, which spell out the consequences of keeping or forsaking Yahweh's covenant law. Only here the subject is explored from different angles in a more thought-provoking way.

As in the law codes, the benefits accruing to the *righteous* are referred to as *blessings (běrākôt): Blessings crown* [lit., *to*] *the head of the righteous* (Prov 10:6). Indeed, even after they have died, the *remembrance of the righteous* lives on as a *blessing* (as a power and influence for good) in the memories of those who admired them during their lifetimes (10:7a, lit.). But *the name of the wicked will rot* (be forgotten and perish, 10:7), a point underscored by yet another saying: *When a wicked man dies, his hope perishes, all he expected from his power comes to nothing* (11:7). What it more concretely meant to experience *blessing* is alluded to several times in the expression that those who are *truly righteous* are heading toward *life* (11:19a; 12:28a), while those who *pursue evil* are heading toward *death* (11:19b; 19:16b). Here and elsewhere in Hebrew Scripture, dying and living refer to actual life and death.

To *live* means to live long and fully ("many years in the land," Deut 30:20b; prolonged life and prosperity, Prov 3:2, 16, 18, 22; 4:22); to *die* means to suffer and die prematurely. Thus, the gray hair of the aged who have had a long and satisfying life can be described as *a crown of splendor, . . . attained* [in old age by following] *in the way of righteousness* (16:31, lit.; 20:29). There is as yet no teaching regarding what happens to a person after death. The NIV translation of 12:28 is thus misleading: *In the way of righteousness there is life; along that path is immortality* (lit., *no-death*, a hyphenated phrase in Hebrew). The text's second line simply repeats the point made in its first line: *In the path of righteousness there is life* and *not death*—meaning death before the time normally allotted for a human being (cf. Ps 90:10).

The Righteous Will Never Be Uprooted, but the Wicked Will Not Remain in the Land (10:30) 10:9, 25, 30; 12:3, 7, 12; 14:11, 19; 21:7; 22:8

These ten sayings have been grouped together because they all allude to a quite special blessing those are said to enjoy who walk uprightly: the confidence of being able to *remain in the land* (10:30b; cf. 2:21-22). Through bitter experience Israel learned that the durability of a people in their homeland was highly dependent on their moral and spiritual commitments and condition. This group of sayings summarizes the core teaching of Deuteronomy and related histories (Joshua, Judges, Samuel, Kings) to the effect that those who depart from Yahweh's commandments will *not* live long in their land (see Deut 30:15-18). It is only *the righteous* (those covenanted to serve God) who will *never be uprooted* (Prov 10:30a); the *wicked will not remain in the land* (10:30b). Disasters there may be, but *the righteous stand firm forever* (10:25), they *walk securely* (10:9a), their *house* endures (12:7), their *root* remains (12:3), their *tent* (even though fragile by comparison with the *house of the wicked*) *will flourish* (14:11). Those who are *good* will eventually triumph over those who are evil: *Evil men will bow down in the presence [before the face] of the good, and the wicked at the gates of the righteous* (14:19): this is the deeply felt conviction that comes to expression in these sayings.

Be Sure of This: The Wicked Will Not Go Unpunished, but Those Who Are Righteous Will Go Free (11:21) 10:24, 28; 11:21, 23, 31; 12:21; 14:32; 21:21

That the *righteous* are on a path leading to *life* does not mean that they have no troubles. They too, like the wicked, may be brought down to the point of death by calamities. *When calamity comes, the wicked are brought down, but even in death* [lit., *in his death*], *the righteous have a refuge* (14:32). Nor are the righteous regarded as faultless (cf. Eccl 7:20) or undeserving of such troubles: *If the righteous receive their due on earth, how much more the ungodly [wicked] and the sinner!* (Prov 11:31, implying that the righteous also suffer as a consequence of their sins). Rather, the point stressed is that *the righteous have a refuge* in their troubles (14:32b; cf. Pss 37; 73), while in their *misfortune* (NIV: *calamity*), *the wicked are brought down* (Prov 14:32a). Thus, *what the wicked dreads will* [eventually] *overtake him; what the righteous desire will* [ultimately] *be granted* (10:24). The conviction that this is the case is forcefully expressed by means of a Hebrew idiom. *Be sure of this* [lit., *hand to hand*, as in striking a bargain]: *The wicked will not go unpunished, but those who are righteous* [lit., *the seed of the righteous*] *will go free [escape troubles]* (11:21).

Several sayings indicate that the focus in this group of sayings is on the general outcomes of the deep aspirations and character of these two groups, not moralistic superficialities. Thus, one of these sayings refers to *the desire of the righteous* and *the hope of the wicked* (11:23), and another to someone *who pursues righteousness* (21:21a). It is these fundamentally differing attitudes, pursuits, and commitments that result in radically differing outcomes. The aspirations of the *righteous* lead to *good* (11:23a), summarized in 21:21 as *life, prosperity* [*ṣĕdāqāh,* usually meaning "righteousness" but here the rewards of righteousness] *and honor*—and *joy* (10:28a). Meanwhile, the *hopes of the wicked,* because they *come to nothing* (10:28b), result in frustrated *wrath* (11:23b). This affords an explanation of why *no iniquity befalls the righteous, but the wicked are full of evil* (12:21, lit.). The aspirations of the righteous are tangibly leading somewhere, while those of the wicked are not. In summary, the contrast drawn by these sayings has to do with the essential goals and commitments of the two groups and the consequences resulting from these over the course of a lifetime. The insights disclosed are that those loyal to the morally upright way of Yahweh experience, overall, a longer, better, happier, and more fulfilling life than those not so committed.

The Righteousness of the Upright Delivers Them, but the Unfaithful Are Trapped by Evil Desires (11:6) 11:3, 5, 6, 8, 18; 13:6, 9; 14:14; 18:3; 21:7, 18, 21; 22:8

Another thirteen sayings seek in several ways to call attention to the same truth, that the differing fates of the righteous and the wicked are not externally or arbitrarily imposed but result from natural consequences. It is the inner condition of the wicked that leads step by step to the harsh sufferings they experience: *When wickedness comes, so does contempt, and with shame* [*disdain*] *comes disgrace* [*provocation,* Cohen] (18:3). The wicked are entrapped by their own wickedness, but the integrity of the righteous guides them on a *straight way* that leads to their deliverance (11:3, 5, 6). A concrete example of this is somewhat vaguely alluded to in a saying that seemingly refers to a legal suit in which an innocent party is falsely accused. As it works out, however (when the truth comes to light), *the righteous man* [innocent person] *is rescued from trouble, and it comes on the wicked* [the one making the false accusation] *instead* (11:8; cf. 21:18). Thus it can be said that *the wicked become a ransom for the righteous, and the unfaithful for the upright* (21:18).

Another example of natural consequences is the "violence" of the wicked, which over time escalates and becomes self-destructive: *The violence of the wicked will drag them away* (21:7). Several metaphors are used to describe this kind of natural link that so obviously exists between a person's conduct and the consequences: Wickedness has *wages* (11:18a). Righteousness is *sown* by the upright and brings forth *a sure reward* (11:18b); the wicked *sow wickedness and reap trouble* (22:8). *Righteousness guards the man of integrity* (13:6). *The light of the righteous shines brightly* (13:9). *He who pursues righteousness and love finds life, prosperity and honor* (21:21). Those who compiled these sayings were deeply conscious of God as a personal sovereign who protected and rewarded the good and judged the evil on earth. Yet they were equally aware of the way right and wrong conduct brings about its own fateful consequences, and they wanted their students to be conscious of this as well.

THE TEXT IN BIBLICAL CONTEXT

The Birth of Ethical Monotheism

Taken together, these sayings are as rich and full a distillation of thought about faith in God as we encounter anywhere in the Bible. What is their source? How might we explain the presence of such a large block of sayings on these themes in a book of teachings purportedly about *attaining wisdom and discipline* (1:2)? These questions are addressed in the introduction to this commentary. The goal of the reforms for which the Hezekiah Edition of Proverbs was created was to put an end to the worship of other gods in Judah and to restore fidelity to Yahweh alone as prescribed in the first commandment of the Decalogue. For this reason the point of view reflected in this group of sayings is similar to that in Deuteronomy, a collection of Moses' words also (in all likelihood) compiled at this time and published as the nation's constitutional guide *[Hezekiah Reform Literature]*. Both there (in Deuteronomy) and here (in the Main Collection) the expression *fear of the LORD* is used for characterizing those who belong to the people of the covenant. Both there and here those who are in awe of *the LORD* are said to walk uprightly. Both there and here being upright carries with it the promise of long life in the land God promised his people if they obey his teachings.

At two points, however, the sayings in Proverbs affirming *fear of the LORD* go beyond the laws and traditions encoded in Deuteronomy. First, in Proverbs fearing the LORD and pursuing wisdom are viewed as overlapping and complementary pursuits. *Fear of the Lord is the beginning of wisdom* (9:10a). In Deuteronomy fearing God and serving him contribute to being wise (4:6), but the book does not say what wisdom is nor how fearing the Lord is but the first step toward a wider study of wisdom. This issue is spelled out in

Proverbs. In the saying *the fear of the LORD is the beginning of wisdom* (9:10), a connection is forged with the teachings of Moses in Deuteronomy and the pursuit of wisdom more broadly (cf. Prov 15:33).

God himself is now viewed in this light. In Proverbs the primary attribute of God is wisdom. *Wisdom* was with him from the dawn of time (8:1, 22). *By wisdom* he created the universe (3:19-20). These observations point to a second way in which the sayings in the book of Proverbs affirming *fear of the LORD* go beyond Deuteronomy. In these sayings *the Holy One* (Yahweh) is not just the only God to be worshipped, but simply God. In Deuteronomy there is still a view of the world that some have called henotheism (one true God among many gods). The first commandment specifies that Israel shall have no other gods besides Yahweh; this suggests that there *are* other gods but that in Israel only one God is to be worshipped, not these others. The sayings in Proverbs on this theme are quite different. There is no suggestion of other gods. The sayings assert not just that Yahweh is to be honored but that no other divine power is at work in the universe (16:4). "The Lord [in Proverbs] is not merely 'the God of Israel,' but quite simply 'God'—the divine Being whose power completely fills the divine realm" (Clements, 1992:157). As such these sayings mark a first clear enunciation of what some have termed "ethical monotheism" *[Proverbs and the Birth of Ethical Monotheism]*.

Godly Wisdom in the Bible

In this group of sayings the *men of Hezekiah* (25:1) articulate their theology of wisdom. At its core is an awareness of the all-seeing sovereignty of Yahweh and of the moral dimensions of his rule of the whole world. The religious outlook of these sayings is that of people loyal to God, named and understood in a certain way. The God referred to, *Yahweh*, is *the Holy One* whom Moses met at the burning bush (Exod 3:1-15)—the God who forged a covenant with Israel, in which this people promised to live in accordance with the values specified and summarized in the Decalogue (Exod 19-20). These values define what is good in terms of a reverent attitude toward God and human conduct respectful toward others.

The conviction is deep and repetitiously stated (in the proverbs just looked at) that those who honor Yahweh in this manner are wise and will be blessed with fullness of life, and those who do not are on a path that leads to destruction. There is thus a profound synergy between what is wise and good and what God's sovereign will and purposes are for each and every human being. What these sayings aim at is faith in

God coupled with a "pursuit" of what is wise, good, and right in every aspect of life (cf. Prov 15:9; 21:21). This pursuit of God and *good* is seen as a universal phenomenon. It is the challenge facing human beings everywhere in every culture and religion. It is a challenge that lies beneath and beyond the rituals and beliefs of given religions, even that of Israel itself. The God encountered in this pursuit is the Creator of the heavens and the earth.

This theology permeates the whole Bible. It is the theology that finds expression on the very first pages of the Bible, in Genesis 1. Just like the wisdom theology of Proverbs, Genesis 1 pictures every human being in every nation and culture as created in the image and likeness of God. They therefore are capable not only of exercising an extraordinary godlike care over the world but also of communicating and being in a relationship with the Creator (*the Holy One*). It is this vision of the world that manifests itself in Psalm 104, where the psalmist exclaims: "How many are your works, O LORD! In wisdom you made them all; the earth is full of your creatures" (104:24). It is also that of Job as he struggled with the inequities in life but did not abandon the God who revealed himself through his awesome handiwork. It is the theology of the psalmist who wrote Psalm 73 as he struggled in a similar way, but eventually came to see that God was "the rock of my heart and my portion for *ever*" (73:26, lit.).

It is also the theology of Jesus's teachings in the Sermon on the Mount, where he speaks of God's watchful care over all aspects of his creation and encourages his disciples to commune with him through times alone in prayer. It is the theology of the prayer Jesus taught his disciples, whose opening petition is that God's name be hallowed and his will be done throughout the earth, but also that "bread" be given for today, and forgiveness, and protection from going down a wrong or evil path. Thus the godly wisdom of Proverbs can serve as a window into the spirituality of the whole Bible.

THE TEXT IN THE LIFE OF THE CHURCH

A Journey into Immediacy with God

For secular societies the religious dimensions of Israelite wisdom pose a special challenge. What Judaism and Christianity have contributed to the formation of Western culture was not only a deep respect for wisdom but also respect for the reality of "the Holy One," who created all things. However, the legislated separation of church and state in our time, valuable as it is, has brought with it an unprecedented degree of silence about "God." Not only has prayer been banished from public schools, but also events in the "public square" are increasingly bereft of any acknowledgment of God. Many in the modern world are agnostic or atheist, which may explain the growing attraction in the West for Buddhism.

Under these circumstances the chief agency for perpetuating that unique understanding of God in biblical tradition has devolved to the synagogues, churches, and mosques. How will they respond to this challenge? Can Proverbs be of help? It has not generally been regarded as a sourcebook for renewed faith in God. In his book on *The Contemplative Face of Old Testament Wisdom,* biblical scholar John Eaton writes: "In modern times the wisdom books have been undervalued. Theologians have passed over them rather quickly as offering little for a systematic theology of sin, grace and redemption. Philosophers have found here nothing akin to modern philosophy. The moral teachings were treated as mere advice for a prosperous life. The religious sentiments were regarded as only an afterthought of later compilers" (3).

But now, Eaton adds, "after a period of relative neglect the Old Testament wisdom books are gaining more attention. There is growing awareness that they may have particular value for the spiritual quest of our time" (3). Eaton himself seeks to foster a renewed appreciation for the contribution Proverbs might make in this regard by noting in detail the "contemplative themes" it shares with the quest for godly wisdom in various religious and philosophical traditions. Examples are the need (in such a quest) for a spiritual director, for discipline, attentiveness, humility, honesty, work, and trust. The theme of trust, he writes, is an especially prominent one in Proverbs. "It is a matter of being alive toward God: sensitive, open, aware towards him, and so delivered from the illusion of self-reliance and vanity" (76). The several themes are "woven into one texture—a pattern of life lived with quiet and receptive awe before God, the Lord of the mysterious and marvelous universal order" (90). "The whole quest for wisdom," Eaton sums up, "becomes a journey into immediacy with God. Wisdom herself, God's Thought underlying all that exists, takes the pilgrim into a loving divine friendship" (91).

The two focal points of this spirituality are prayer and wisdom. Prayer is the lifeblood of any relationship with God. It is becoming aware of the reality of God and living in that light. "He wakens me morning by morning, wakens my ear to listen like one being taught" (Isa 50:6). Prayer is a wager: once made it calls for repeated acts of choice: "Trust [and keep on trusting] in the LORD with all your heart and rely not on your own understanding" (Prov 3:5). A wisdom-based spirituality involves our minds as well. It means loving the LORD our God with our hearts, souls, and minds (Mark 12:30).

Meister Eckhart: "To Take God Evenly in All Things"

To my knowledge there are few spiritual guides who saw or expressed the unity of prayer and wisdom (hence the spirituality of Proverbs) more clearly than did the celebrated fourteenth-century scholastic Meister Eckhart. The following are a few excerpts from talks he gave on this subject to "some of his spiritual children, who asked him about many things as they sat together at collation" (Blakney: 3):

> [Meister Eckhart:] One ought to keep hold of God in everything, and accustom his mind to retain God always among his feelings, thoughts, and loves. Take care how you think of God. As you think of him in church or closet, think of him everywhere. Take him with you among the crowds and turmoil of the alien world. As I have said so often, speaking of uniformity, we do not mean that one should regard all deeds, places, and people as interchangeable. That would be a great mistake; for it is better to pray than to spin and the church ranks above the street. You should, however, maintain the same mind, the same trust, and the same earnestness toward God in all your doings. Believe me, if you keep this kind of evenness, nothing can separate you from God-consciousness. (8)
> [Meister Eckhart:] In all his work, and on every occasion, a man should make clear use of his reason and have a conscious insight into himself and his spirituality and distinguish God to the highest possible degree in everything. One should be, as our Lord said, 'Like people always on the watch, expecting their Lord.' Expectant people are watchful, always looking for him they expect, always ready to find him in whatever comes along; however strange it may be, they always think he might be in it. This is what awareness of the Lord is to be like and it requires diligence that taxes a man's senses and powers to the utmost, if he is to achieve it and to take God evenly in all things—if he is to find God as much in one thing as in another.
> In this regard, one kind of work does indeed differ from another but if one takes the same attitude toward each of his various occupations, then they will be all alike to him. Thus being on the right track and God meaning this to him, he will shine, as clear in worldly things as heavenly. To be sure, one must not of himself behave intemperately or as being worldly, but whatever happens to him from without, whatever he sees or hears, let him refer it to God. The man to whom God is ever present, and who controls and uses his mind to the highest degree—that man alone knows what peace is and he has the Kingdom of Heaven within him. (10-11)

Part 3

Supplemental Collections

Proverbs 22:17—31:31

Design of the Hezekiah Edition of Proverbs			
			Later
Part 1	Part 2	Part 3	Additions
Introductory	The Main	Supplemental	
Collection	Collection	Collections	
1:1–9:18	10:1–22:16	22:17–30:33	31:1-31
(256 verses)	(375 verses)	(253 verses)	

OVERVIEW

Part 3 of Proverbs contains five distinct supplemental collections that were added by the *men of Hezekiah* referred to in 25:1 *[Distinctive Approach]*. Four of these five supplemental collections are clearly marked as such by their headings (22:17; 24:23; 25:1; 30:1); a fifth collection (chs. 28-29) has no heading but can be readily identified as such by its content and form (see chart below). It is the viewpoint of this commentary that the additional poems in chapter 31 were added still later, in the postexilic period *[Wisdom in Proverbs]*.

The headings to the first three collections (22:17; 24:23; 25:1) are in sequence; these, plus the one in 30:1, are stylistically alike in that all four identify the source of the collection, followed by the collection itself. The heading to the additions in 31:1 differs from the previous four in that the name of the person *for whom* the first addition was created is mentioned first and then its source. There are other differences in these final poems (in ch. 31) indicative of the later period when they were added (see notes). These six supplemental collections may be charted as follows:

The Book of Proverbs, Part 3: Supplemental Collections					
"Words of the Wise" 22:17–24:22	"Also Words of the Wise" 24:23-34	"Also Proverbs of Solomon, Copied by the Men of Hezekiah" 25:1–27:27	Hezekiah Reform Manual 28:1–29:27	"Words of Agur Son of Jakeh" 30:1-33	Later Additions 31:1-31

It appears that these collections were added to enrich the overall collection. Some issues are revisited, such as alcoholism, how best to discipline children, concern for the poor, fearing God, finding a wife. Some new topics are addressed, such as the conduct of civil servants at court, caring for domestic animals, pain relief, issues affecting a nation's greatness. The person named in the heading to the fifth collection, *Agur son of Jakeh*, seems to have played a prominent role in the production of the Hezekiah Edition of Proverbs. That is probably why his sayings are located at the end of that edition, for it was customary at the time to identify a book's editor or author in this way (see Deut 34; Ps 72:20; Eccl 12:9-10).

OUTLINE
"Words of the Wise," 22:17–24:22
"Also Words of the Wise," 24:23-34
"Also Proverbs of Solomon," 25:1–27:27
Hezekiah Reform Manual, 28:1–29:27
"Words of Agur Son of Jakeh," 30:1-33
Later Additions, 31:1-31

Proverbs 22:17—24:22

"Words of the Wise"

The Book of Proverbs, Part 3: Supplemental Collections					
"Words of the Wise" 22:17–24:22	"Also Words of the Wise" 24:23-34	"Also Proverbs of Solomon" 25:1–27:27	Hezekiah Reform Manual 28:1–29:27	"Words of Agur Son of Jakeh" 30:1-33	Later Additions 31:1-31

PREVIEW

This first block of added sayings is clearly marked at its beginning and end. It opens with a heading, *Listen to the sayings of the wise* (22:17a), and ends just prior to a new heading in 24:23a, which introduces a second small supplemental collection (24:23b-34). When turning from the sayings of the Main Collection to this first block of added teachings, the reader is at once aware of differences in form and content. Rather than a repetitious string of two-line observations, most of the poems are admonitions in the imperative. Allusions to duties of those who serve kings (as messengers, 22:21; handling disputes, 22:22, 28; 23:10; 24:23b-24; keeping records, 22:29; attending banquets, 23:1-3) suggest that this collection was first compiled for use in training young men for civil service. If so, then the *wise* referred to in the heading (22:17a; cf. 24:23) were teachers in the royal schools (cf. 5:13).

An additional reason for thinking that admonitions such as these were for men training for civil service came to light in 1923 with the publication of The Instruction of Amenemope, an Egyptian manual for training civil servants from the twelfth century BC. It turned out to be so remarkably like the instructions in this Proverbs' supplement that many now regard this Egyptian manual as the prototype of the collection here in Proverbs (Washington: 135-45). Indeed, in the New American Bible (Roman Catholic translation) the biblical collection is explicitly identified as such "through a slight emendation in verse 22:19b," so that it reads: *That your trust may be in the LORD, I make known to you the words of Amenemope* (Boadt: 78).

When comparing the two, not only are the similarities of content especially striking, but also in both instances the instructions are divided into thirty units or chapters (22:20). However, the commonality of themes in the two collections extends only to the prologue of the biblical collection (22:17-21) and its first ten teachings (22:22–23:11). The twenty teachings that follow (23:12–24:22) are all unique (Ruffle). Noticeable too is that a new heading or preface (Cohen: 154) is placed right at the point where the twenty teachings begin (23:12; cf. 22:17); from that point onward, the teachings are directed to a more diverse group of students, not just those preparing for civil service.

Thus, the teachings of this first supplemental collection may be divided into two sections: a first block of ten teachings that are of special relevance for young men in training to be royal servants (22:17–23:11); then a second block of twenty teachings of relevance to a more diverse group of young men (23:12–24:22). The impression given is that an older textbook designed for use in the royal schools of Egypt has been adapted for use in Israel in the period of Hezekiah's reforms, with the needs of a more diverse range of students in mind.

OUTLINE

Title and Prologue, 22:17-21
For Civil Servants (the Initial Ten Teachings), 22:22–23:11
22:22–23:11	Organization
22:22–23:11	The Yahweh Dimension
22:22–23:11	Repeated Admonitions
22:22–23:11	New Topics

For a Wider Audience (the Remaining Twenty Teachings), 23:12–24:22

23:13-14, 22-25	Duties of Parents and Children
23:26-28	Avoiding Seductive Women
24:3-4, 5-6, 7, 13-14	Wisdom's Great Worth
23:17-18; 24:1-2, 8-9	Fearing the LORD; Avoiding Sinners
19-22	
23:19-21, 29-35	Dangers of Drinking Too Much Wine and Eating Too Much Meat
24:10, 11-12, 15-16 17-18	Being Strong and Charitable in Times of Persecution

EXPLANATORY NOTES

Title and Prologue 22:17-21

The title of this addition is embedded in its opening sentence: *Pay attention* [lit., *turn your ear*] *and listen to the sayings* [*words*] *of the wise* (22:17a). The language is personal and concrete—a teacher ("*I*," 22:19a) is addressing a specific student (*even you*, 22:19b). The student is told that *it is pleasing when you keep them* [the sayings of the wise] *in your heart* [lit., *within you*; memorize them] (22:18a); then they will be *ready on your lips* (22:18b). The importance of memorizing such teachings is also stressed in the Egyptian Instruction of Amenemope: "Let them rest in the casket of thy belly," then "at a time when there is a whirlwind of words, they shall be a mooring-stake for thy tongue" (Pritchard: 421-22). The significance of the word *thirty* in 22:20 was uncertain until the above-mentioned Egyptian instruction manual came to light. In it are thirty "chapters"; there are also thirty "teachings" in 22:22–24:22, even though the teachings are not explicitly numbered as they are in Amenemope's collection.

The stated purpose of the Egyptian and Israelite collections is similar in part as well. In his opening words Amenemope, an Egyptian official in charge of land management, writes that his teachings are "for intercourse with elders, the rules for courtiers, to know how to return an answer to him who said it, and to direct a report to one who has sent him" (The Instruction of Amenemope, Pritchard: 421). What is first said about the purpose of the biblical collection is strikingly similar: *to make you know the certainty of the words of truth* [so that you will be able] *to bring back words of truth to him who sent you* (22:21, lit.). However, at this point an additional goal unique to the biblical collection is specified: *so that your trust may be in the*

LORD, I teach you today, even you (22:19). In Hebrew the words *in the LORD* are strongly emphasized by being placed first (*so that* in the LORD [Yahweh] *may be your trust*). Also the word *today* stands out (*I make known to you* today, *even you,* 22:19b). What this sentence seems to stress is that, whatever the *earlier* objectives of this document might have been, *today* (in this edition) it is being dedicated to the objective of training students to put their *trust* in Yahweh. This means to learn how to *trust* Yahweh and keep his commandments (a key characteristic and conviction of Hezekiah's reforms; cf. 2 Kgs 18:5-6).

For Civil Servants (the Initial Ten Teachings) 22:22–23:11

22:22–23:11 Organization

As noted above, the "thirty teachings" that follow the prologue are in two blocks. The first consists of ten teachings of special relevance for royal servants or courtiers (22:22–23:11). Nine of these have parallels in The Instruction of Amenemope (the one exception is the warning against striking hands in pledge, 22:26). The first four begin with admonitions not to do certain things: *Do not exploit the poor* (22:22-23). *Do not make friends with a hot-tempered man* (22:24-25). *Do not be a man who strikes hands in pledge* (22:26-27). *Do not move an ancient boundary stone* (22:28). These are then followed by two instructions on a more positive note: *Do you see a man skilled in his work? He will serve before kings* (22:29). *When you sit to dine with a ruler, note well what is before you* (23:1-3). Then come four more admonitions about what *not* to do: *Do not wear yourself out to get rich* (23:4). *Do not eat the food of a stingy man* (23:6-8). *Do not speak to a fool* (23:9). *Do not move an ancient boundary stone* (23:10-11).

The commands of the Decalogue (Exod 20:2-17) have the same pattern: first come four commands in the negative; next, two positive commands; last, four in the negative. Perhaps this (Prov 22:22–23:11) was a Decalogue for civil servants. Thus, at the beginning (22:22-23), middle (22:28), and end (23:10-11) of this Decalogue are stern admonitions against exploiting the weak through abusing the court system (22:22b) or changing boundary stones (22:28; 23:10). Protecting the "rights" of the poor and vulnerable is here regarded as a foremost duty of those in royal service.

22:22–23:11 The Yahweh Dimension

Teachings of this kind are not new to this book (see 21:13;
22:16), but only here is there a stern warning that, if wronged,
Yahweh himself will take up the cause of the poor (22:23) and
become their *Defender* (23:11). *Defender* (gō'ēl) is the term used in
Leviticus 25:25 to refer to the responsibility of a next of kin to buy
back family property lost through impoverishment. Those who *crush
the poor* by neglecting their rights (22:22) should be warned that
Yahweh will take up their cause: He will *plunder those who plunder
them* (22:23; cf. Amos 5:10, 12, 15). The twice-repeated admonition
not to *move an ancient boundary stone set up by your forefathers*
(22:28; 23:10) is also new to the book. Dishonest officials could easily move such markers with devastating consequences (cf. Deut 19:14;
27:17). Orphans were especially defenseless against crimes such as
this, lacking fathers to speak up on their behalf (Prov 23:10b). The
Instruction of Amenemope also warns young officials against crimes
of this nature.

22:22–23:11 Repeated Admonitions

Three remaining admonitions of this section touch on themes
addressed elsewhere in the book of Proverbs: a warning against making friends of a *hot-tempered man* (22:24-25), striking hands in
pledge (22:26-27), or becoming obsessed with wealth (23:4-5).
However, there are nuances here that enrich the earlier teachings.
Thus, 22:24 warns not just against *being* a hot-tempered man (as
15:18), but also to avoid *friendship* with such a person, lest one
become like him (22:25). Also, the danger involved in *striking hands
in pledge* (22:26-27) is more precisely spelled out than in previous
teachings (cf. 6:1-3; 11:15; 17:18; 20:16). What is emphasized here
is the danger of making a pledge *if you lack the means to pay,* for
then you could become destitute, losing the *very bed* you sleep on
(22:27)! Finally, not only are unjustly gained riches declared to be *of
no value* (as in 10:2), but also, wealth obsessively acquired to the
detriment of one's health (23:4) is extremely ephemeral as well. On a
moment's notice acquisitions can fly away *like an eagle* (23:5b).

22:22–23:11 New Topics

The four remaining teachings of this section (22:29; 23:1-3; 23:6-
8; 23:9) are on subjects not mentioned elsewhere in the book thus far.
The first calls attention to the bright future that awaits *a man skilled
in his work* (22:29a). The term translated *skilled* is used elsewhere in

the Bible of professional scribes (Ps 45:1; Ezra 7:6). Such is its connotation here too, for the follow-up line states that a man like this *will serve before kings* (22:29b). The conduct befitting such public officials is indicated by two additional instructions (23:1-3, 6-8). The first advises how to conduct oneself at a banquet when dining with a *ruler* (23:1a). On occasions like this it is important to be content with your food (23:1b) and not let your appetite get the better of you, craving *his delicacies* (23:3a). An interesting parallel in chapter 23 of Amenemope's booklet counsels young men: "Look at the cup which is before thee, And let it serve thy needs" (Pritchard: 424). Anything else is *deceptive food,* states 23:3b, meaning, perhaps, that in overeating one might betray a weakness for gluttony, which could prove fatal to the servant's career. *Put a knife to your throat* if so tempted, the *wise* half-humorously suggests (23:2, in hyperbole).

Similarly, young men are advised on how they should relate to a host who is *stingy* (23:6-8; Heb.: *has an evil eye*). In this instance one should avoid taking a meal with him at all, even though invited to do so (23:7c), for deep down *his heart is not with you* (23:7d). As a consequence the occasion will undoubtedly prove to be unpleasant and a waste of time. *You will vomit up the little you have eaten and will have wasted your compliments* (23:8). Skilled public servants need to be aware of subtleties of this nature if they are to succeed in their work. For similar pragmatic reasons, talking to a *fool* should be avoided as well, since all one can hope to get from it is his *scorn* or derision (23:9).

For a Wider Audience (the Remaining Twenty Teachings) 23:12–24:22

A new admonition to *apply your heart* (23:12; cf. 22:17b) opens the second section of this collection. The twenty teachings that follow are characterized as *instruction* and *words of knowledge* (23:12) rather than *words of the wise* (22:17). This appears to be a signal to the reader that the more specialized instruction of the first section is now ended. The remaining twenty units are as follows (McKane): verses in chapter 23: (1) 12, (2) 13-14, (3) 15-16, (4) 17-18, (5) 19-21, (6) 22-25, (7) 26-28, (8) 29-35; verses in chapter 24: (9) 1-2, (10) 3-4, (11) 5-6, (12) 7, (13) 8-9, (14) 24:10, (15) 11-12, (16) 13-14, (17) 15-16, (18) 17-18, (19) 19-20, (20) 21-22. In this part of the manual, the teachings are less specific to royal servants and of general interest to those just wanting to be faithful to Yahweh (see 23:17-18; 24:19-20).

The twenty teachings cluster around *six themes*, four prominent elsewhere in the book, the remaining two unique to this collection. The four themes prominent elsewhere are (1) duties of parents and children (23:13-16, 22-28), (2) avoiding seductive women (23:26-28), (3) the superiority of wisdom over folly (24:3-7), (4) the importance of fearing the LORD and avoiding sinners (23:17-18; 24:1-2, 15-16, 21-22). The two themes unique to this collection are (1) the dangers of overeating and excessive drinking (23:19-21, 29-35), and (2) and the need to remain strong *and* charitable in troubled times (24:10, 11-12, 17-18). One senses a good bit of social turmoil in the background of these latter teachings. My further comments will follow the thematic sequence just indicated.

23:13-14, 22-25 Duties of Parents and Children

The priority given to teachings about parents and children in this part of the collection (23:13-14, 22-25) follows the pattern of the two earlier collections (see 1:8-9; 10:1). This emphasis is consistent with the thesis that the book as a whole (as now edited) was designed not just for preparing civil servants, but also as a resource for home-schooling. Hence, the appeals to respect parents—*Listen* to *your father, who gave you life* (Heb.: *begot you*); *Do not despise your mother when she is old* (23:22)—can be immediately followed by an admonition to *buy the truth and do not sell it; get wisdom, discipline and understanding* (23:23). The presumed instructors are parents, and the goal of their teaching is an upright, *wise son* (23:24), not just a royal servant *skilled in his work* (22:29). It is this, being a *wise son,* that is said to bring such tremendous joy to father and mother (23:25; cf. 10:1), but to the father especially: *Greatly rejoices the father of a righteous one; he who begets a wise one will be glad in him* (23:24, lit.; cf. 23:15-16).

An issue of importance to the *wise* of the time is addressed right at the beginning of this section: whether or not to use a *rod* in a son's *discipline* or training (23:13-14). Although touched on earlier (13:24; 22:15), this was apparently a matter of continuing debate, for here the advice is directed to those who have chosen to *withhold discipline* (23:13a). Such are challenged in no uncertain terms not to persist in this neglectful passivity. Educating a young man (*na'ar*) by striking him with a stick or switch when necessary will not cause his death, it is half-humorously said (23:13b). The strong follow-up admonition is virtually a command addressed presumably to the father of the son: *You* [emphasized] *switch him with a stick and deliver his* soul [*nepeš*] *from death* [*šĕ'ôl, underworld*] (23:14b, lit.). Here again, a judicious use of a switch or rod is advanced in the belief that it might save a young man from the kind of folly that could end in personal tragedy (cf. 19:18; 20:30; 22:15).

23:26-28 Avoiding Seductive Women

Once again in the poem in 23:26-28, the topic of the seductive woman is broached (as in 2:16-19; 5:1-23; 6:20–7:23; 22:14) *[Identity of the Foreign Seductress].* Here in 23:26-28 this *wayward wife* (*nokrîyyāh, outsider,* 23:27b) is paired with a *prostitute* (23:27a). She herself is not a prostitute but is an unfaithful wife away from home, or her husband is away from home (cf. 7:19). The fatal consequence of young men becoming involved with women of this kind is graphically emphasized through the image of two wells or pits. The *prostitute* is likened to a *deep pit* from which one might with great difficulty escape. The *wayward wife,* however, is likened to a *narrow well* from which escape is virtually impossible (she is also compared with a *bandit* who secretly *lies in wait* to attack; 23:28a). Becoming involved with either of these women is deadly. What is especially new in this warning is the observation that a woman of this kind *multiplies the unfaithful among men* (23:28b). By making it easy for men to have affairs, marital fidelity is weakened in the whole culture. Knowing the potential dangers, a concerned father urgently warns his son of the dangers involved to him and others: *My son, give me your heart and let your eyes keep to my ways* (23:26).

24:3-4, 5-6, 7, 13-14 Wisdom's Great Worth

In this group a third theme (also familiar) is that of wisdom's unsurpassed worth. The first poem on this subject (24:3-4) echoes the message implied in earlier sayings (9:1; 14:1). Once again it declares that *wisdom* and *understanding* are the essentials by which a house (or household) is built and established. Unique here is the additional thought that it is *through knowledge* that such a house is furnished with *rare and beautiful treasures* (24:4). The inner *strength* that comes from being wise is the theme of 24:5, something that needs to be clearly understood when waging war (24:6), where brute strength is often thought to be the decisive factor. On the contrary, *for waging war you need guidance* [cf. 20:18], *and for victory many advisers* (24:6; cf. 11:14). The *fool* is not wise and also fails to grasp the importance of *wisdom* (Heb.: *wisdoms,* fullness of wisdom). It is simply *too high* for him (24:7a, *out of his reach*). That is why he is speechless before his peers *in the assembly at the gate,* where leaders gather to deal with community affairs (24:7b). As *honey is both good* (24:13a) and *sweet to the taste* (24:13b), so also *wisdom is sweet to your soul* (24:13). "The law of the LORD" is similarly spoken of in Psalm 19:7-10, and the "promises" of Yahweh in 119:103. Finding *wisdom* and *fearing the LORD* lead to the same end: *There is a future hope for you, and your hope will not be cut off* (24:14b; cf. 23:17-18). Here as elsewhere in the Hezekiah Edition, pursuing wisdom and being faithful to Yahweh are seen as two sides of the same reality.

23:17-18; 24:1-2, 8-9, 19-22 Fearing the LORD; Avoiding Sinners

Four times in this collection—close to the beginning (23:17), in the middle (24:1), and twice at the very end (24:19, 21b)—a strongly worded admonition is given not to be envious of men who are *sinners, wicked, evil,* or *rebellious.* These men are identified in 24:21 and characterized as *rebellious* against Yahweh and the king. Then 24:8-9 and 15 add that they plot *evil* and scheme (24:8) *like an outlaw* against a righteous man's house and *raid his dwelling place* (24:15). These sayings allude to a chaotic social situation, one in which a lawless sector of society is preying on those who are God-fearing and law-abiding (cf. the poems in chs. 28-29). These latter (the God-fearing and law-abiding) are encouraged not to waver, but *always* [lit., *all the day*] *be zealous for the fear of the LORD* (23:17b).

The final admonition of the collection adds, *Fear the LORD, my son, and the king* (24:21, lit.). In 23:17 this same strong admonition is followed in 23:18 by an equally forceful motive clause emphasizing that those who do so will *surely* have a *future hope,* which will not be cut off (cf. 24:14). By contrast, the two concluding motive clauses (24:20, 22) declare: *The evil man has no future,* for *the lamp of the wicked will be snuffed out* (24:20). This will happen when *sudden destruction [comes] upon them* due to *calamities* brought about by Yahweh and the king (24:22). *For those two* [Yahweh and the king] *will send sudden destruction upon them, and who knows what calamities they can bring?* (24:22). This closing couplet in the collection of the thirty sayings leaves no doubt about the social and religious milieu of these teachings. They belong to a religious and social world in which God and king are revered and feared, but with serious opposition. The challenges facing King Hezekiah and his colleagues in their reform efforts are especially palpable.

These quite serious admonitions in 23:17 and 24:21 form an enclosure for 18 of the 20 teachings in this second section of these 30 teachings and link this collection of wise teachings to the covenant traditions of Moses. *Always be zealous for the fear of the LORD,* as stated in 23:17b (lit., *be in the fear of Yahweh all the day*), is a quite specific emphasis in Moses' teachings assembled in Deuteronomy (see 5:29; 6:24; 10:12; 14:23). There too the promise is made that it will go well with those who do revere God in this strong and steady way, but those who do not do so will suffer for it (as in Deut 28). That this is the case is observable and experientially verifiable, as yet another couplet states: *For though a righteous man falls seven times, he rises again, but the wicked are brought down by calamity* (24:16).

23:19-21, 29-35 Dangers of Drinking Too Much Wine and Eating Too Much Meat

Thus far the teachings were on themes touched on earlier in the book. With the teachings about drunkards and gluttons, an altogether new subject is addressed (23:19-21). An especially earnest appeal to the *son* to take heed, *be wise,* and keep to the right path opens this set of teachings (23:19). This is a serious matter; a related text in the teachings of Moses identifies drunkenness and gluttony as character-istics of a rebellious son who is beyond reform (Deut 21:20; cf. Luke 7:34). Drinking wine was not regarded as wrong in itself, but exces-sive drinking and eating were perceived to be serious dangers, to be avoided at all cost. To persist in them would result in being incapaci-tated (induce *drowsiness,* 23:21b) and subjected to poverty (23:21a).

The debilitating personal effects of excessive wine drinking is the focus of a second teaching on this subject (23:29-35). First comes a rapid-fire series of six questions (lit., *To whom woe, to whom sorrow, to whom strife, to whom complaints, to whom needless bruises, to whom bloodshot eyes?*). Then the answer is given: those who spend *endless* time drinking wine and go about (from place to place) sam-pling *mixed wine* (wine mixed with spices, 23:30; cf. 9:2). The fol-lowing admonition advises youth against being enticed by the red sparkle or smooth taste of wine—not even to look at it. A wordplay links admonition and consequences: those who linger *endlessly* (23:30, lit.) over wine will in the *end* (23:32) experience it biting them like a poisonous viper (cobra). The hallucinations and addictive conse-quences of alcoholism are vividly described (23:33-35). Most tragic of all is the compulsive desire for sobriety only for the purpose of begin-ning another cycle of drunkenness (23:35b). "The realism of the picture drawn in these verses is a measure of the disgust which the average Hebrew felt with the addict to strong drink who, under its influence, lost all semblance of man created in the image of God" (Cohen: 157). For evidence of an acute problem with alcoholism in the period of Hezekiah's reforms, see Isaiah 5:22; Amos 4:1-3; 6:6.

24:10, 11-12, 15-16, 17-18 Being Strong and Charitable in Times of Persecution

The terse statement in 24:10 epitomizes the theme of this little group of teachings: *If you falter in times of trouble* [ṣārāh], *how small* [ṣar] *is your strength* (a pun that plays on the root meanings of ṣar: "narrowness," "confinement," "restriction"). In other words, *If in times of* restriction [trouble] *you falter, how* restricted [small] *is your strength.*

Three examples of "troubled times" are alluded to in 24:11-12, 15-16, and 17-18; all serve to illuminate the kind of *strength* needed to survive in such times. The challenge is to be resolute at rescuing certain persons *being led away* to execution (unjustly so, 24:11). The all-too-human excuse of lack of knowledge about what is happening is countered with a vigorous reminder of Yahweh's knowledge of all that transpires in the *heart* (and of the consequences that must inevitably flow from this; 14:12). In other words, lack of courage in helping another unjustly condemned to death should not be papered over with lame excuses, lest a similar fate befall the one looking on (for a comparable teaching, see 3:27-28). For the same reason one must avoid provocations or plots against one's neighbor when there is no just reason for doing so (23:15-16; 3:29-30: *when he has done you no harm*). A similar cluster of thoughts is combined to support the admonition in 24:17-18 not to *gloat* or *rejoice* when your enemy *stumbles* or *falls*. Such gloating is known to the all-seeing Yahweh and is not approved of (24:18a). The additional warning that such gloating might result in Yahweh not punishing the enemy (24:18b) puts the all-too-human desire for vengeance to work in the service of restraining the human tendency to delight in another's disaster (even if deserved).

THE TEXT IN BIBLICAL CONTEXT

Implementing Justice

The initial ten teachings of this collection seem to have been taken from an instruction manual of Egypt. The editors obviously intended to form a code for civil servants, a code that would prepare them for working within the realities of the Israelite kingdom in such a way that they could bring about true justice for the poor and vulnerable. It is one thing to criticize the conduct of the state, as do the prophets of the period of Hezekiah's reforms; it is another thing to bring about a reformation of that state so that justice is in fact done. It is one thing to fashion good laws and another to ensure that those laws are implemented. The first ten of these supplemental instructions are designed for educating civil servants so that they will put these laws into practice as part of their daily work. In this respect they are unique in the Bible, not for the values espoused, but for the goals envisioned. The vision was to create a professional guild who would work on the front lines of implementing the values of the prophets and lawgivers in the daily life of a kingdom.

Becoming Responsible, God-Fearing, Law-Abiding Citizens

It was the core conviction of the compilers of this first appendix to the Main Collection that teachings of the varied kinds assembled here were essential for equipping young men not simply for success as royal servants, but also for becoming law-abiding God-fearing citizens. The passion that inspires this collection is not just that Judah or Israel be a great nation, but that the nations of the world might come to know the God of Israel and his teachings. The compilers hoped that eventually the whole world might come to live in accord with these values and thereby find a way out of the misery and wars that now ravage it (cf. Isa 2:1-5).

There is a remarkable compatibility between the themes identified here and the teachings on these themes in other biblical compilations such as law codes in Leviticus 19-20 or Deuteronomy, or the Sermon on the Mount (Matt 5-7). All emphasize the importance of being zealous for justice and insuring the basic rights of all, especially those who are weak and vulnerable to abuse. All call for marital fidelity. Many challenge parents to educate their children. All seek to restrain the human bent toward vengeance. All seek to rein in the excessive desire for wealth. All counsel against being hot-tempered. All seek to foster an openness toward God.

Unique here is the specificity of the counsel to fathers to reconsider their decision to withhold the *rod* when disciplining their sons. Also unique are the explicit counsels regarding the dangers of excessive eating and drinking, and the importance of risk-taking for others in times of persecution. Here again, the closest parallels are the teachings of the prophets and lawgivers. Amos and Isaiah were especially livid against those upper-class people in their time who had lavish banquets with wine and meat, while so many were in poverty (Isa 5; Amos 2:8; 4:1-3; 6:1-6). But it is one thing to criticize, another to educate a citizenry to do otherwise. In these teachings we can sense the struggle involved in doing just that—even the resulting dissensions and sufferings. That too is a theme that recurs in the teachings of Jesus, who pronounced his disciples blessed when they suffered abuse for righteousness' sake. The kingdom of heaven is theirs, he said (Matt 5:10-12).

THE TEXT IN THE LIFE OF THE CHURCH

Egypt and the Bible

The section of Proverbs just surveyed affords an occasion for revisiting the issue of what is meant by "revelation." Some have taken the position that the world's non-Christian religions are without merit. Others advocate that certain values in those religions can comport with the traditions of faith in the Bible. This latter appears to be the point of view of the *men of Hezekiah* as they approached the instructions of Amenemope and adapted and added them to the Hezekiah Edition of Proverbs (25:1). The author of the book of Hebrews (in the NT) expresses an analogous point of view: God spoke of old "at many times and in various ways," but in "these last days he has spoken to us by his Son" (1:1). This implies (as in Heb 11) that "revelation" or "faith" (like wisdom) is unfolding and progressive.

It came as a surprise to students of the Bible when the first Egyptian manuals of instruction were discovered and published. The oldest of these date from the middle of the third millennium BC and provide an illuminating background for understanding the teachings of Proverbs in general and the proverbs of the section just studied in particular. We now realize that many of the finest ideals of the Bible had precedents in ancient Egypt, as with the family values taught in the oldest Egyptian instruction booklets. Just as in Proverbs, the manuals from Egypt instruct young men about being loving husbands and caring fathers, and warn them not to become intimately involved with women other than their wives. Their teachings on wealth and poverty are also remarkable in their advocacy on behalf of the poor (Washington: 205).

A few of these Egyptian booklets are surprisingly religious as well. The outstanding case in point is The Instructions of Amenemope. There are frequent references to "god" in Amenemope's teachings (Oesterley: 12-18), so many in fact that biblical scholar Lawrence

Boadt has conjectured that this may be one of the reasons "why Israel valued this foreign work so highly." It exhibited a "particular sensitivity . . . toward human dependence on the gods," which Israel's sages felt "would help deepen their own understanding of Yahweh's action in the world" (Boadt: 77).

Teaching These Values Today

It is sobering to realize how many of the issues touched on in this thirty-item collection are still of concern to teachers and parents today as they struggle with educating their children. We too must contend with abuse of food and alcohol, and now also addiction to drugs. Fathers are still sometimes neglectful of their children and fail to discipline them properly. Sexual problems are with us too, as are lawlessness and social discord. In the midst of it all, we too sometimes falter in our faith and need to be encouraged. This little manual is one of the few places in the Bible that highlights the importance of young men being skillful and socially intelligent so they can advance professionally. The focus of this manual is the education of sons; yet most would apply to daughters as well (see Introduction, "Why the Gender-Specific Focus"). These thirty teachings could be read and discussed with profit, just as they are, in almost any young adult Sunday school class.

Proverbs 24:23–34

"Also Words of the Wise"

The Book of Proverbs, Part 3: Supplemental Collections					
"Words of the Wise" 22:17–24:22	"Also Words of the Wise" 24:23-34	"Also Proverbs of Solomon" 25:1–27:27	Hezekiah Reform Manual 28:1–29:27	"Words of Agur Son of Jakeh" 30:1-33	Later Additions 31:1-31

PREVIEW

There are just five short poems in this brief supplement, three of·them having to do with procedures for settling disputes (24:23b-25; 26, 28-29) and two with making a living (24:27, 30-34). The subject matter is not totally new but is dealt with in a new way. As such, the poems supplement and reinforce earlier teachings on issues deemed important for young men starting out in life.

Literally translated, the opening words introduce this short collection: *Also these are sayings [words] of the wise* (24:23a). The first word of this new heading (*also*) refers back to the previous heading (22:17, *sayings of the wise*), indicating that the sayings here are *also sayings of the wise* like those in the previous collection. At the same time, these two headings distinguish the source of these two collec-

240

tions from the collected *proverbs of Solomon* preceding them (10:1) and following them (25:1). The contents here and in the previous collection are not from Solomon but from two distinct groups of nameless *wise* or teachers.

OUTLINE
Advice on Settling Disputes, 24:23b-25, 26, 28-29
Rules for Making a Living, 24:27, 30-34

EXPLANATORY NOTES

Advice on Settling Disputes 24:23b-25, 26, 28-29
The first of these sayings is addressed to young men who might one day need to assist in the adjudication of disputes. The qualifications for men of this type are cited in Deuteronomy 1:9-17, the first being fairness: "Do not show partiality in judging" (1:17). The counsel here is similar, stated not as an imperative not to do so and so, but as a solemn assessment of what showing partiality in judging is in the scheme of things. *To show partiality* [lit., *to respect faces*] *in judging is not good* (Prov 24:23b; cf. 18:5; 28:21). As explained in the Torah, it more often than not is bribery that leads to partiality in judgment. There, judges are warned in no uncertain terms: "Do not accept a bribe, for a bribe blinds the eyes of the wise and twists the words of the righteous" (Deut 16:18-20). Both Deuteronomy and the teaching here emphasize how utterly important this issue is for the well-being of a community. A man who fails to be fair in adjudicating disputes should be in no doubt as to what the response will be: *Peoples will curse him and nations denounce him* (24:24b). On the other hand, *rich blessing will come upon* those who are fair in their judgments (24:25; cf. Deut 16:20).

Two additional teachings on this theme emphasize how utterly important truthful speech is in handling judicial matters (24:26, 28-29; cf. 12:17; 19:5, 28; 21:28). In a provocative epigram (not easily translated), *an honest answer* (or *testimony*) is likened to a *kiss on the lips* (an emotional pledge of affection, trust, commitment; 24:26). Some reasons why persons in court proceedings resort to false testimony are mentioned in the poem in 24:28-29. To the admonition *Do not testify against your neighbor without cause or use your lips to deceive* (24:28a) is added a sharp rebuke against harboring a grudge: *Do not say, "I'll do to him as he has done to me; I'll pay that man back for what he did"* (24:29).

Rules for Making a Living 24:27, 30-34

The advice given in the first of these two teachings is that one should *finish your outdoor work and get your fields ready* before building *your house* (24:27). This points to the importance of fields being prepared and prepared for cultivation and husbandry before building a dwelling. In other words, young men are counseled to establish a basis for supporting a family before beginning one. The second of these teachings (24:30-34) revisits the issue of laziness (see the many sayings on this subject in the Main Collection, e.g., 10:4, 5; 12:11, 24, 27; 13:4). In fact, the teaching here (24:30-34) may have been the source of the poem cited in 6:10-11. The poem was born, we are told, when its author walked by *the field of a sluggard, past the vineyard of the man who lacks judgment [lacks heart]* (24:30). The vineyard was overgrown *with weeds; its wall was in ruins* (24:31). The poet then reports that he paused, applied his mind to what he observed (24:32a), and *learned a lesson* (*mûsār*) from what he saw (24:32b). *A little sleep, a little slumber, a little folding of the hands to rest—and poverty will come on you like a bandit and scarcity like an armed man* (24:33-34). What this poem is advocating is not just the lesson learned, but also how it was learned: through looking and applying one's mind. Overall, that is what this manual is about.

THE TEXT IN BIBLICAL CONTEXT

Proverbs and Jesus

This little collection highlights values that are central not only to the book of Proverbs but also throughout the Scriptures. Of high importance in the teachings of Deuteronomy, for example, is a fair and honest judicial system (just laws, justly implemented; see Deut 1:13-17; 16:18-20). For such a system to work, there must be honesty. "Let your 'Yes' be 'Yes,' and your 'No,' 'No,'" Jesus taught (Matt 5:37).

Similarly important are the values associated with building a home (family). The economic foundations of a family are essential. This requires planning ahead and being careful with money. Without these, it is foolish to begin building a home. Jesus is usually thought of as emphasizing the need to trust God for the future and not be worried about things of this nature. This is true. But there are also teachings in the Gospels that stress planning. One is the parable of the builder who wanted to construct a tower but did not plan ahead (Luke 14:30). Another is Jesus's parable about two houses, one built on sand and the other on rock (Matt 7:24-27).

It is important to keep in mind that Jesus spent his adulthood before his public mission at "about thirty" (Luke 3:23) in the same trade as his father, that of carpentry (Mark 6:3; Matt 13:55). At that time carpenters were among the most skilled people of the village. Some think, with justification, that he was more like a contractor, building on a larger scale. There are also reasons for thinking Joseph may have died during Jesus's teenage years, leaving him as the eldest son (Luke 2:7) in charge of a family that included at least four younger brothers and an unspecified number of sisters (Mark 6:3; Matt 13:55-56). Some of the wisdom shown during his public mission may have been acquired during these challenging years when he was a house-holder himself and responsible for his deceased father's family (Miller, 1997:98).

THE TEXT IN THE LIFE OF THE CHURCH

Cultivating Civic and Domestic Virtues

The three values taught in the poems just surveyed—fairness in settling disputes, establishing a livelihood before establishing a family, being diligent in one's work or profession—are presupposed throughout the Bible but articulated here in fresh, memorable ways. In its mission in the world, the church is called to be a light and blessing. In few areas is this more important than in perpetuating the civic and domestic virtues highlighted in these poems.

The judicial system in most Western countries is mostly taken for granted. This is because it was established over a long period of time—and yet it can be quickly lost if there is not a citizenry that values it. For a citizenry to value it, there must be an agency that highlights its value and communities that exemplify it.

Not the least of the reasons for the economic troubles of many countries of the world is the failure to establish just processes for settling disputes. Bribery is rampant and corrupts everything. When this is the case, wealth gets siphoned off into the hands of those in charge of the corrupt system. Again, for these systems to be reformed, there must be people trained for functioning with integrity as lawyers and judges.

Such people are nourished in homes and churches where these values are taught (as here in these verses) and exemplified. That requires the building of such homes and churches. This in turn requires the cultivation of a pragmatic and industrious attitude toward making a living—a value espoused and cultivated in most families and churches. The poems just surveyed support them in this. These values are not old-fashioned; they are as essential today for a happy and successful life and society as ever. At the end of his erudite study of *The Wealth and Poverty of Nations*, the Harvard professor David Landes summed up the situation: "Some people find it easier and more agreeable to take than to make. This temptation marks all societies, and only moral training and vigilance can hold it in check" (522).

Proverbs 25:1—27:27

"Also Proverbs of Solomon"

The Book of Proverbs, Part 3: Supplemental Collections					
"Words of the Wise" 22:17–24:22	"Also Words of the Wise" 24:23-34	"Also Proverbs of Solomon" 25:1–27:27	Hezekiah Reform Manual 28:1–29:27	"Words of Agur Son of Jakeh" 30:1-33	Later Additions 31:1-31

PREVIEW

Solomon was remembered as a prolific poet who composed some 3,000 proverbs and 1,005 songs (1 Kgs 4:32). I see no reason to doubt that this was the case—nor that the poetic insights assembled in these chapters (25-27) are examples of his prolific output. In chapter 25 the poems are grouped thematically. The first are about God and king, and the behavior appropriate for those in the king's service (25:1-7). These are followed by sayings on speech, social problems, strife, fools, sluggards, and various other topics. Some of the remaining poems are also arranged in small topical groups. The collection as a whole is capped with down-to-earth advice on how to run a farm in

245

economically uncertain times (27:23-27).

Literally translated, the heading identifies this new collection: *Also these are proverbs of Solomon* (25:1). With the words *also these*, a major new supplemental collection is begun that extends ostensibly to the end of chapter 29. In Hebrew the heading in 25:1 begins exactly as does the one in 24:23 (with the words *also these*), but in 25:1 the word *also* refers back not to the previous heading (as is the case in 24:23), but to the heading in 10:1. The point is that these too (the sayings that follow) are *proverbs of Solomon* just like those in the Main Collection. On closer inspection, however, it becomes apparent that this heading applies only to the sayings in chapters 25-27, not to those in chapters 28-29, for the sayings in these latter chapters are strikingly different from those of Solomon. The *proverbs of Solomon* in Proverbs 25-27 are rich in imagery; *God* is seldom referred to (25:2), and his name (*Yahweh*) is mentioned only once (25:22). Avoiding *folly* and being *wise* are emphasized rather than avoiding *evil* and being *righteous*. This block of poems fits right into what is otherwise known about the court of Solomon (1 Kgs 3-11). The poems that follow in Proverbs 28-29 are quite different: they are less artistic, more intense, more God-centered, and mention the law several times. A number of poems name what makes a nation great and happy. This block of poems fits right into what is otherwise known of the reforms of King Hezekiah (for further insights into the nature and message of these chapters, see next section). The present focus is on chapters 25-27 only.

OUTLINE

EXPLANATORY NOTES

Heading 25:1

The point being made in the opening words of this heading is not that *these are more proverbs of Solomon* but that these too (lit., *also these*) are *proverbs of Solomon* like those in the main collection (10:1). The heading in 25:1 also relates the fact that it was *the men of Hezekiah king of Judah* who *copied* these proverbs (25:1b). The verb translated *copied* means literally *to remove* (Toy), implying they performed this task by transferring them from a larger archive of Solomon's proverbs (cf. 1 Kgs 4:32). Other than being associates of Hezekiah, the *men* who performed this task are not otherwise identified. Many believe they were professional scribes or sages. A more likely possibility is indicated in the account of Hezekiah's reforms in 2 Chronicles 29-30, where the "men" who assisted the king in his reforms are identified as "Levites." For the history of this remarkable group of men and why King Hezekiah turned to them for help at the very beginning of his reign (2 Chr 29:5), see Introduction, "The Hezekiah Edition of Proverbs."

Kings and Courtiers 25:2-10

At the beginning of this added collection of Solomon's *proverbs* are five carefully crafted four-line poems (25:2-3, 4-5, 6-7, 8, 9-10). They are of special relevance to young men who might one day be serving *in the king's presence* (25:6a; lit., *before the king's face*). The first three poems have to do with attitudes and conduct becoming to such an elite group. Two others relate to their future role in the settlement of disputes both judicial and personal (25:8, 9-10).

The first of these poems (25:2-3) contains a rare reference in Proverbs to the more general term for *God* ('ĕlōhîm) in Hebrew Scriptures. Rarer still is what is said about God: *It is the glory of God* ['ĕlōhîm] *to conceal a matter* [lit., *to conceal a word*], whereas *to search out a matter* [lit., *word*] *is the glory of kings.* "'Glory' here means 'action worthy of glory'" (Clifford). The core theology or philosophy of the schools of Solomon is apparently stated here: (1) God's glory is manifest in the impenetrable mystery of the created world. But (2) it is the glory of kings to make the mystery of the universe known through their inquiring intelligence and lucid insights (cf. 8:22-36). "God's world is full of conundrums and puzzles beyond the capacity of ordinary people [was the belief of the times in the ancient Near East], but the king is there to unravel them and lead people to serve the gods" (Clifford). The poem's second couplet underscores this contrast by comparing the unfathomable heart of kings with the heavens for height and the earth for depths (25:3).

The second poem in this group (25:4-5) identifies an additional task of a king who wishes his rule (or throne) to be *established through righteousness* (25:5b). As dross must be removed from silver before anything beautiful can be done with it, so *the wicked (rāšā', rebel, lawless one)* must be removed from the king's presence. The third poem in this group (25:6-7) is about the deportment required of those deemed fit to remain *in the king's presence.* Even in their case it is not wise for them to be too ambitious *and claim a place among great men* [lit., *the great*]. Rather, they are counseled to position themselves below their rank, for to be demoted in such prestigious company is far worse than to be at a lower rank and then be invited up (for Jesus's adaptation of this teaching, see Luke 14:7-11).

Both of the two additional poems of this group (25:8, 9-10) have to do with procedures for settling disputes. The first (25:8) warns against bringing charges against (or starting a quarrel with) a neighbor too quickly after first witnessing something amiss. The word *court* (25:8b, NIV) is actually not in the text. The poem warns against initiating a dispute with a neighbor without first doing careful research, lest the accused neighbor shames the accuser (when it turns out that the accusations are false). The second of these poems (25:9-10) counsels both parties in a dispute to settle it amicably: *You should settle a dispute with your neighbor* (25:9a, lit.). In other words, do not let it drag on or take it to court, but instead resolve it. However, when settling a dispute, be careful *not* to *betray* the *confidence* (or *secret*) of another (25:9b), for this might lead to countercharges and irreparable loss of reputation (25:10). Both admonitions favor settlement of disputes by means of direct, discreet conversations between the persons involved (for an adaptation of this advice in the teachings of Jesus, see Matt 18:15).

Apt and Inept Speech 25:11-20

Most of these nine poems are about good and bad ways of speaking. Also, most are metaphors (oblique undesignated comparisons, provoking wide-ranging thoughts), not similes (specified comparisons using "like" or "as") as in most of the NIV translations of these verses (only 25:13 merits being so translated). In every instance, an object of some sort is cited first, followed by one kind of speech or another. The first puts *apples of gold in settings of silver* side by side with *a word aptly spoken* (25:11). *Apples of gold* may refer to an exquisite ornament of some kind but not to *apples* as we know them, since apples "had not been introduced into Palestine in Old Testament times" (Whybray, 1994:364). An example of a *word aptly spoken* is alluded to in the next saying, which compares *an earring of gold or an ornament of fine gold* to *a wise man's rebuke to a listening ear* (25:12). A wise rebuke to a listening ear is just that valuable.

Pleasant, too, *like the coolness of snow at harvest time* are the words of a *trustworthy messenger* to the one sending him (25:13; cf. 10:26; 13:17). At the time, before the days of electronic communication, people in positions of responsibility were more dependent on trusted *messengers* for conducting the affairs of government. The added line, *He refreshes the spirit of his masters* (25:13c), may be an explanatory note by a later reader, but an apt one.

All but one of the seven sayings that follow (in 25:14-20), are about inept or bad speech. The first pinpoints *a man who boasts of gifts he does not give* (25:14b) and likens him to *clouds and wind without rain* (25:14a). He presumptuously "poses as a great benefactor" when he actually lacks the resources to give what he has promised (McKane). The saying that follows is the sole example of "apt" or "good" speech in this cluster: *Through patience a ruler can be persuaded, and a gentle tongue can break a bone* (25:15; can overcome stubborn opposition, Cohen). On the other hand, when visiting (or talking to) neighbors (25:17), one should not overdo the matter, as when eating honey: *Eat just enough—too much of it, and you will vomit* (25:16). Eating honey (which requires some thought about what is enough and yet not too much) is an apt metaphor for the discernment needed in many of life's more subtle and demanding circumstances (cf. 25:27). An especially cruel or hurtful use of words (*like a club or sword or a sharp arrow*) is to bring false witness against a neighbor (25:18; cf. Deut 5:20). Not quite as bad, but bad enough (*a bad tooth or a lame foot*), are the empty promises of an unreliable man in a time of trouble (25:19). Contrived or poorly timed mirth or song is the final example of inept speech (*one who sings songs to a heavy heart*). This is likened to having one's garment taken on a cold day or the fizzle of *vinegar poured on soda* (25:20).

An Assortment of Teachings 25:21-28

Between teachings about speech (25:11-20) and about fools (26:1-12) are seven sayings on a variety of topics. The first (25:21-22) advises giving *your enemy* (lit., *someone who hates you*) food or drink if he is hungry or thirsty, promising that if you do, *you will heap burning coals on his head* ("arouse remorse for his enmity," Cohen), and *the LORD [Yahweh] will reward you* (25:21-22). Advice of this nature "was not uncommon in ancient wisdom literature" (Clifford: 226). An example in the Babylonian Counsels of Wisdom (Pritchard: 426): "Unto your opponent do no evil; Your evildoer recompense with good; Unto your enemy let justice [be done]. . . . Give food to eat, give date wine to drink. . . . This is pleasing unto the god Shamash, he rewards it with good." The advice here (25:21-22) is remarkably similar (cf. Lev 19:18; Rom 12:20; Matt 5:43-44).

Alternate translations of the first line of the next proverb have been proposed since *a north wind* (in Canaan) does not usually bring *rain* (west winds from the Mediterranean do that; 25:23). Sometimes, however, the rains do blow in from the northwest, and when they do are cold and dreary, a fitting metaphor for the effects, *angry looks,* of a slanderous blowhard (*a sly tongue,* 25:23b). The next saying in 25:24 (repeating 21:9; cf. 21:19) is also about the chilling effect of certain kinds of speech: that of a *quarrelsome [complaining] wife.* Better for a man to have a tiny spot on the roof than to share a house with a woman like that.

The next two sayings begin with water metaphors, the first one positive (*cold water*), the second one negative (*muddied spring* or *well* water; 25:25-26). Good news from a distant land is likened to the first (cool, refreshing water); *a righteous man who gives way to [totters before] the wicked* is likened to brackish, muddied undrinkable well water. Elsewhere it is said that the righteous *will never be uprooted* (10:30; 12:3); therefore, for the *righteous* to *totter* or *give way* before the wicked is profoundly disturbing and distasteful. Something equally disturbing is alluded to in the next poem: *It is not good to eat too much honey* (25:27a; cf. 25:16). Likewise, *searching their glory* [is not] *glory* (25:27b, lit.; NIV: it is not *honorable to seek one's own honor*). The poem's precise meaning is uncertain, but it may refer to the nauseating effect on others (like having swallowed too much honey) of individuals bragging about their own achievements. Yet another disturbing type of man is identified in 25:28: *Like a city whose walls are broken down is a man who lacks self-control* (lit., *a man who is without restraint in his spirit*). Such a person's *spirit* is defenseless against temptations to wrongdoing.

Fools 26:1-12

With one exception the next twelve proverbs are about *fools.* The exception may also be about something only a fool would do: utter a *baseless* [NIV: *undeserved*] *curse.* Such a curse need not be feared, the poem states, since it is ineffective (26:2). If this poem is counted among them, then the first five proverbs of this set are about relating to a fool (26:1-5), the next five about what to do if unfortunate enough to have a fool (kĕsîl) as an employee [Words for Wisdom and Folly]. In the first category (how to relate to a fool), it is not appropriate to honor a fool (it is as incongruous as snow in summer or rain in harvest, 26:1). Nor need one fear his disapproval or curse, for like a fluttering sparrow or a darting swallow, it never comes to rest (26:2). Physical punishment may be called for (as a horse needs a whip and a donkey needs a halter, 26:3). When addressing a fool, one must be careful not to come down to his level: Do not answer a fool according to his folly (26:4). At the same time, one must be blunt and specific in countering a fool's foolish thinking: Answer a fool according to his folly, or he will be wise in his own eyes (26:5).

As to what to do with a foolish employee, first be sure not to elevate him to the position of a messenger; the results could be devastating: Like cutting off one's feet or drinking violence (26:6). And above all do not even consider using him as a teacher, for a proverb [māšāl, poem] in the mouth of a fool is utterly useless (like a lame man's legs that hang limp, 26:7) and self-defeating (like a thorn bush in a drunkard's hand, 26:9). He will not know at all how to interpret a proverb, and his attempts at doing so will be wild and essentially useless (compare what is said of the "words of the wise" in Eccl 12:11).

If a fool is of no use as a messenger or teacher, what is he good for? The final three proverbs (26:10-12) seemingly warn against hiring a fool for any kind of job, although the meaning of the first of these sayings is uncertain. I favor the following conjectural translation of its first line: A master workman [rav] performs everything (26:10a; some can do virtually any kind of job); the second line (26:10b) compares one who hires a fool to someone who hires any passerby or transient without regard for his competence. In other words, do not hire a fool, for you have no idea what his competencies are. And don't allow yourself to imagine that a fool, once hired, can be trained or upgraded for the job you have in mind for him. As a dog returns to its vomit, so a fool repeats his folly (26:11); a fool simply doesn't learn from his mistakes. And yet there is more hope for a fool than a man wise in his own eyes (26:12). This saying is directed to the students for whom this entire cluster of sayings is meant. There is more hope for a fool than for them if they fail to heed the advice being given due to their feeling too sure of themselves and their own opinions.

Sluggards 26:13-16

The next four proverbs are about a species of *fool*—the *sluggard*. Two of these sayings appeared earlier in the book (26:13 echoes 22:13, and 26:15 echoes 19:24), but now they are together and paired with two more on the same theme. This produces a collective portrait that is both humorous and incisive. The traits of the sluggard are universal: he makes absurd excuses for not getting on with his life (*There is a lion in the road, a fierce lion roaming the streets!*). He sticks to his bed, tossing and turning *as a door turns on its hinges,* rather than getting up and facing the world. When up, he is too lazy even to eat properly (26:15). But he does talk—and talk a lot. Lacking contact with reality, he fantasizes that he is wiser *than seven men who answer discreetly* (26:16). Thus, this and the prior group of proverbs turn the spotlight on a humorously pathetic character puffed up with his wisdom and importance. Adolescents especially can be like this. These sayings seem to be a way of easing them through this stage in their lives by opening the issue up for discussion.

Quarrels 26:17-28

The next ten proverbs cluster around the theme of disputes and quarrels between neighbors. The focus is on the things that lead to such quarrels. For the most part, therefore, this is a list of things to be avoided for the sake of community harmony and happiness. First, as a mere *passer-by,* one should avoid becoming involved *in a quarrel not his own* (this is likened to someone who on the spur of the moment grabs *a dog by the ears* and thus surely provokes the dog to bite him; 26:17). Second, one should avoid playing "practical jokes" (26:18). Though the intent is benign, the consequences can be deadly (like a crazy man shooting off *firebrands* or *deadly arrows*).

The remaining proverbs in this group are all about the role malicious speech plays in fomenting disputes and quarrels. A *malicious whisperer* (26:20a, lit.) is the first example cited (NIV: *gossip*; the word *whisperer* [*nirgān*] is unique to Proverbs; cf. 16:28; 18:8; 26:22). Nothing provokes a quarrel and keeps it going more than malicious gossip. So when a person like this is no longer present, *a quarrel dies down* (as does *a fire without wood*). It follows that when such a contentious person *is* present, strife flares up again (*as charcoal to embers and as wood to fire,* 26:21). The proverb that follows explains why the *whisperer* has such power: his words are like delicious tidbits, greedily swallowed right down *to a man's inmost parts* (26:22). The evil intent of the gossip's words is difficult to discern because *fervent* [*persuasive*] *lips* know how to hide the *evil heart* (evil intentions) *like a coating of glaze* painted on an *earthenware* jar (26:23). The thought here is elaborated in the next two couplets (26:24-25), culminating in an urgent warning not to *believe* such a man (26:25a), even though *his speech is charming* (lit., even though *he shows graciousness with his voice,* 26:25). *A malicious man* [lit., *he who hates*] *disguises himself with his lips, but in his heart* (lit., *his inner being*] *he harbors deceit* (26:24). In reality, filling his heart are *seven abominations* (an excess of evil, 26:25b).

The next two proverbs (26:26, 27) afford some hope that with patience the deceit of such a person will come to light and be dealt with, be revealed to *the assembly* (*qāhāl*, public forum; see 5:14) and adjudicated. But even if that is not the outcome, life itself has a way of rectifying matters. Often, it seems, the one who digs a pit for others falls into it, and *if a man rolls a stone, it will roll back on him* (26:27). This section of teachings closes with an epigram on the origins and effects of a *lying tongue* and a *flattering mouth* (lit., *smooth mouth*). A *lying tongue* originates in sheer hate; its effects are *hurt* and *ruin: A lying tongue hates those it hurts* (26:28a).

An Assortment of Teachings 27:1-27

27:1-2 Boasting

From this point to the end of this chapter, the poems touch on a variety of topics. The first two are admonitions (in the imperative) about boasting. The first advises against boasting about tomorrow, because no one knows what the future holds: *You do not know what a day may bring forth* (27:1; cf. Matt 6:34; Jas 4:13-16). The second is against boasting about oneself (27:2). The counsel is to let *another praise you* [if you are worthy of such], *and not your own mouth.* Implied (but not stated) is that self-adulation is unseemly.

27:3-6 Hurtful Human Relations

Next come four aphorisms on the more hurtful aspects of human relations. Two are about being mistreated by a *fool* (27:3) and someone jealous (27:4). The *provocation* of a *fool* is extremely hard to take (heavier than *stone* or *sand*), but far more so is *jealousy,* which is even worse than experiencing *fierce fury or overflowing anger* (27:4, lit.). Two other sayings are about *the wounds of a friend* (27:6). It is better for someone who loves us to rebuke us directly and discreetly (cf. 25:9-10) for wrong things we may have done than to remain silent (17:6b). *Better reproof revealed than love concealed*

(27:5, lit.). The *wounds* (reproofs) of a friend are *faithful* (expressive of loyalty and solidarity) and are to be carefully distinguished from the *profuse* (possibly: *deceptive*) *kisses* of an enemy (lit., *someone who hates*, 27:6).

27:7-11 Neighborhood and Friends

The next five proverbs cluster about the importance of having a solid neighborhood of family and friends (27:7-11). On the surface, the first is about appetite (lit., *A satiated appetite [nepeš, soul] deplores honey, but to a famished appetite [soul] every bitter thing is sweet*). This commonplace observation may be a metaphor for the individual described in the following saying, someone *who strays from his place [māqôm, neighborhood]* (27:8, lit.). At home he does not appreciate what he has (*deplores honey*, 27:7a, lit.), but when elsewhere he is so hungry for what is missing that he eats anything (loses his values). He is *like a bird that strays from its nest* ("the malaise of rootlessness," McKane; 27:8a).

The next two poems comment on the virtues of friendship (27:9) and *a neighbor nearby* (27:10c). The personal advice of a friend, *his earnest counsel*, is likened to the wafting sweetness of *perfume and incense* (27:9). It follows that one should not move away from the neighborhood where one was born (27:10a), forsaking *your friend and the friend of your father* (old, solid, intergenerational relationships). Surprisingly, the admonition in 27:10 goes on to advise that one should not contemplate a move like this (away from one's neighborhood) even to take refuge in *your brother's house when disaster strikes you*. After all, it is *better* to have *a neighbor nearby than a brother far away* (27:10b; cf. 18:24). In other words, the *neighbor nearby* is generally better known and more trustworthy than a *brother far away*, with whom contact may be tenuous and relationships strained.

In the fifth of these sayings, a "father" addresses a personal word to his son. He asks him to respect the advice being given (not to move away): *Be wise, my son, and bring joy to my heart*, he says. For if the son remains and cultivates not just his own friends but also his father's older friends, then he (the father) will have an answer for *anyone who treats me with contempt* (27:11). The advice in this cluster of sayings puts a premium on building solid and lasting intergenerational communities made up of families and friends.

27:12-16 Being Alert to Troubles Ahead!

The next four proverbs (27:12-16) also seem to have a common theme: being alert to dangers or troubles ahead and taking appropriate action. The first is virtually a repetition of 22:3: *The prudent* ['ārûm] *see danger* [rā'āh rā'āh] *and take refuge, but the simple keep going and suffer for it* (27:12). The chief distinction between those who are *prudent* (smart, wise, educated; cf. 1:4) and those who are not is explained. The prudent see what lies ahead (are able to discern consequences) and take action, but those who are inexperienced plunge thoughtlessly ahead and suffer the consequences.

The next admonition (duplicating 20:16) cites a concrete example of precisely this kind of danger or evil to be avoided at all cost: putting up security (being the guarantor for a loan) for someone who in turn *puts up security for a stranger* (17:13; cf. 6:1-4; 17:18; 22:26). Before doing something so rash, the person is advised to be certain of having a tangible pledge, such as a costly garment (27:13a). Another danger of which to be wary is a neighbor who *early in the morning* (27:14) is too loud with his blessings (greetings). Instead of taking these greetings at face value, the neighbor saluted in this manner is half-humorously advised to regard such insincere greetings as a "curse" (Cohen: 182).

Still another danger of which to be aware is a *quarrelsome wife,* likened to the *constant dripping on a rainy day* (27:15-16; cf. 19:13). Elsewhere (21:9; 25:24), living with such a woman is said to be intolerable. Here it is said that her contentious bickering is not only irritating, but also that nothing can be done about it. Restraining her is as impossible as stopping *the wind* or *grasping* hold of *oil* (27:16). The implicit advice is that young men should avoid getting married to women of this kind, but if they do, it is a problem that cannot be rectified.

27:17-22 Personal Growth

Six more proverbs focus on personal growth. The first calls attention to the way social interaction facilitates growth: *As iron sharpens iron, so one man sharpens another* (lit., *sharpens the face of his friend,* 27:17b). This could refer to the sharpening of wits or character that comes through the frank and open interaction of friends. Another example of personal growth is the way someone who *looks after* [interacts helpfully with] *his master will be honored,* as surely as one *who tends a fig tree will eat its fruit* (27:18). In reality, however, it is not the interaction itself that produces the personal growth, but something going on in the person's *heart* (27:19). Literally translated, this unusual aphorism reads, *As water [reflects] the face to the face, so the heart [reflects] the person [hā'ādām] to the person ['ādām]* (27:19). This calls attention to the powers of introspection that are such a unique feature of the human mind (cf. 20:27), suggesting that "it is through introspection, through self-examination in depth, that a man acquires self-knowledge" (McKane: 616).

Another attribute of the human person (*hā'ādām*) is the phenomenon of *eyes* (27:20b) that are as insatiable as *Death* (*šě'ôl*) and *Destruction* (27:20a). This relentless curiosity is not being criticized but is simply identified as a truth about human beings. In their searching, however, human beings assess differently what is good and bad, as the following aphorism implies. *The crucible for* [refining] *silver and the furnace for* [refining] *gold* (27:21a), so is *man according to the mouth of his praise* (27:21b, lit.). What a man's mouth praises (after a process of testing) is what the man becomes, whether *gold* or *silver* or something else (cf. 17:3, where God is said to play a role in refining). This capacity for reflection and discernment is what is lacking in the *fool,* the subject of the final saying of this group (27:22). No matter how much you *grind* him, even if you pound him *with a pestle—* as one might pound grain to remove its husks and reduce it to flour—even drastic action like that would not succeed in separating a fool (*'ěwîl*) from his folly [Words for Wisdom and Folly]. The fool is just too self-assured and resistant to change (27:22; cf. 26:3, 11, 12).

27:23-27 Take Care of Your Flocks

A five-couplet teaching (27:23-27) on the importance of taking care of one's domestic animals (such as goats and sheep) brings this section of *proverbs of Solomon* (25:1) to a close. One should *know* for certain (lit., *knowing know*) what their *condition* (their *face*) is (27:23a) by devoting to them the *careful attention* they deserve (27:23b; lit., *setting your heart* on them). The reasoning behind this advice is indicated by two observations: first, the fleeting quality of *riches* (27:24a; accumulated material wealth); and second, the instability of the *crown* (the kingdom), through one king's reign to another (27:24b). Neither wealth nor the political conditions that support it are totally reliable over time (*for all generations*). So one must be careful to provide a steady income that is as much as possible impervious to economic swings of this kind.

A third rationale for the advice given (to care for one's domestic animals) is the idyllic picture sketched of what happens year after year when flocks are in fact well cared for (27:25-27). Then, when food for the animals is gathered in from land and hills, the lambs and goats will not only provide clothing, but also surplus income from which a field can be bought. And all the while there will be plenty of goats' milk to feed the whole family, including *your servant girls* (27:27). In other words, pay attention to what provides a steady supply of food, clothing, and money, rather than accumulated wealth, which may quickly lose its value.

THE TEXT IN BIBLICAL CONTEXT

Secular Wisdom

In this section of Proverbs, we have proverbs that *the men of Hezekiah* gleaned from a larger collection of Solomon's proverbs for enriching their expanded edition. As noted, there is virtually nothing here about God, except for the opening statement about God's glory being manifest in the manner in which he may *conceal a matter*, whereas the glory of kings is on display in the way they *search out a matter* (25:2). When we consider that the *men of Hezekiah* were colleagues of Hezekiah in his reforms (reforms intent on fostering *fear of Yahweh* as *the beginning of wisdom*, 9:10), this opening verse is surprising, as is the secularity of the sayings in general. What is going on? Why were Hezekiah's *men* devoted to the teachings of Moses so enamored with the *proverbs of Solomon* that they went to the trouble to add many more of them to their edition of his book?

There may be a clue to this conundrum in a verse in Deuteronomy that also refers to "things hidden" so far as God is concerned (as does Prov 25:2). The verse in Deuteronomy, however, alludes as well to things revealed: "The secret things belong to the Lord our God, but the things revealed belong to us and to our children forever, that we may follow all the words of this law" (29:29). This verse draws a distinction between things concealed and revealed. A similar distinction is presupposed in the *words of Agur* (Prov 30:1a, lit.) in chapter 30, where he writes of the *word of God,* to which additions must not be made (30:5-6). But then he adds his own thought-provoking prayers and insight-poems (30:7-33). It would appear that Agur and his colleagues were open to two forms of wisdom—humanly derived wisdom and also the wisdom of God's "word"—and saw no essential conflict between them.

It was not Solomon's wisdom that they objected to; they did not even object to Solomon's notion of a God who *conceals* (25:2). Their only objection was to his neglect or rejection of a God who "speaks" through prophets like Moses (Deut 18:17-20). It was their conviction that when Solomon "turned away from the LORD" for the worship of "other gods" (1 Kgs 11:4-11), he had cut himself and his people off from a vital source of wisdom (see Introduction, "Purpose and Design of the Hezekiah Edition").

Metaphorical Truth

In many of the picturesque *proverbs* added in this section, the word *like* is missing, even though often added by translators *[Translation Issues]*. They are metaphors (not similes). In a metaphor two things are juxtaposed without any indication that a comparison is being made. A metaphor does not announce itself. *Clouds and wind without rain—a man who boasts of gifts he does not give* (25:14) is the way this sentence reads in Hebrew. There is no word *like* at the beginning of the sentence, proclaiming what is going on (as in NIV). A metaphor is a riddle: the reader is in the dark until an "aha" experience occurs and all of a sudden one "sees" that it is a comparison and what it means. Clouds and wind without rain and a braggart who boasts of gifts he does not give—they truly are alike!

In this manner metaphors surprise, or shock and provoke. They create a surplus of meaning that is difficult to grasp or express in any other way. A metaphor cannot be summarized and then dispensed with; the truth is bound up with the metaphor. Biblical literature is exceptionally rich in metaphorical sayings and stories. Nathan told a metaphorical story to David when he wanted him to see how heinously he had sinned (2 Sam 12:1-10). The truth, when it dawned on him, hit him like a ton of bricks. Isaiah recited a carefully contrived metaphorical poem when he wanted to convey how heinously he believed his fellow Judeans had sinned (Isa 5:1-7). Hosea resorted to drastic metaphorical actions to convey his burning insights into what was wrong and what it would take to set it right (Hos 1-3). Longer stories and books of the Bible (Jonah, Ruth) may resonate with metaphorical meaning if we had the eyes to see it. Biblical names for God are "deep metaphors" drawn from our most profound human experiences (Miller, 1999).

It was a breakthrough event in modern study of the Bible when scholars realized that many if not all of Jesus's parables were provocative metaphorical stories, just like the one Nathan told to David (Miller, 1981:4-6). "At its simplest," writes C. H. Dodd, "the parable is a metaphor or simile drawn from nature or common life, arresting the hearer by its vividness or strangeness, and leaving the mind in sufficient doubt about its precise application to tease it into active thought" (Dodd, 1961). If we are not aware of the Bible's metaphorical riches, we miss a great deal when reading and studying the Scripture.

The Bible on Treating Enemies Humanely

Among the *proverbs of Solomon* that *the men of Hezekiah* added to those in the earlier edition is one that calls for treating enemies humanely, offering them food and drink if hungry and thirsty (Prov 25:21-22). There are similar teachings in the literature of the time (see notes). The law codes also present analogous teachings, the outstanding example stating: "Do not hate your brother in your heart. . . . Do not seek revenge or bear a grudge against one of your people, but love your neighbor as yourself" (Lev 19:17-18). This particular law is not, strictly speaking, about the humane treatment of enemies but about showing love to "one of your people" instead of bearing a grudge or taking vengeance if wronged or offended.

The *proverb* of Solomon in 25:21-22 is more specific. It has to do with enemies who are in a vulnerable situation of needing food and water (such as prisoners of war; cf. 2 Kgs 6:21-23). The saying of Solomon is also unique in establishing a motive for treating an enemy in this manner: *In doing this, you will heap burning coals on his head, and the LORD will reward you* (25:22). The image of live coals being heaped on the enemy's head through kindliness is puzzling, but most interpret it as referring to the "painful [but therapeutic] effect" such an action might have (Cohen: 170). When quoting this saying, the apostle Paul seems to agree when he adds: "Do not be overcome by evil, but overcome evil with good" (Rom 12:20-21).

In the well-known words of Jesus on this theme, the command to love the neighbor as one's self is enlarged to include the "enemies" (Matt 5:44; cf. Luke 10:27-37). Jesus thus conflates the advice given in the law code (Lev 19:18) with the advice given in the proverb of Solomon (Prov 25:21-22). In other words, the enemy too (any enemy) is to be regarded as a neighbor and loved as oneself. However, as a rationale for doing so, Jesus does not refer to the effect this might have on the enemy (*coals on his head*, 25:22) but to the way God acts toward enemies. When acting in this way, one becomes a son or daughter of God, who "causes his sun to rise on the evil and the good, and sends rain on the righteous and the unrighteous" (Matt 5:45).

These words of Jesus echo yet another text in the Bible, the passage in Genesis that relates how God, after the great flood, determined that "as long as the earth endures, seedtime and harvest, cold and heat, summer and winter, day and night will never cease" (Gen 8:22). This text, promising to good and bad alike the benefits of a livable world, is followed by yet another that authorizes the peoples and nations of the world to restrain those who violate the right to life of another human being (9:5-6). This divine decree lies in the background as Paul and Peter describe the role of "governing authorities" in Roman 13 and 1 Peter 2:13-17. As Jews, they understood that Jesus did not ground his word about loving enemies on the effect such love will have on enemies, nor on this pattern being the only way God relates to evildoers. Instead, loving enemies is founded on God's generosity toward the world in giving sun and rain to good and bad alike (Matt 5:48).

THE TEXT IN THE LIFE OF THE CHURCH

The Church Treating Enemies Humanely

Treatment of enemies remains a burning issue. In the historical peace churches, the teachings of Jesus on this issue have been interpreted to mean not just treating enemies more humanely but also abstaining from war and rejecting military service. Article 14 of the Anabaptist Confession of Faith adopted in 1632 at Dordrecht, the Netherlands, spelled out the convictions of those who interpreted the words of Jesus in this way:

> With regard to revenge and resistance to enemies with the sword, we believe and confess that our Lord Christ as well as his disciples and followers have forbidden and taught against all revenge. We have been commanded to recompense no man with evil for evil, not to return curse for cursing, but to put the sword into its sheath or in the words of the prophet beat the swords into plowshares. From this we understand that following the example, life, and doctrine of Christ, we may not cause offense or suffering but should instead seek to promote the welfare and happiness of others. If necessary for the Lord's sake, we should flee from one city or country to another; we should suffer the loss of goods rather than bring harm to another. If we are slapped, we should turn the other cheek rather than take revenge or strike back. In addition, we should pray for our enemies and, if they are hungry or thirsty, feed and refresh them and thus assure them of our good will and desire to overcome evil with good. In short, we ought to do good, commending ourselves to every man's and woman's conscience, and according to the law of Christ do unto others as we would wish them to do unto us. (Horst: 33)

These ideals were promulgated with sober awareness that "the Office of Civil Government" had a quite different (but complementary) role to play in maintaining the good order of society. In the preceding article 13 of the same confession, they wrote about the role of the state:

> We also believe and confess that God instituted civil government for the punishment of evil and the protection of the good as well as to govern the world and to provide good regulations and policies in cities and countries. Therefore, we may not resist, despise, or condemn the state. We should

recognize it as a minister of God. Further we ought to honor and obey it and be ready to perform good works in its behalf insofar as it is not in conflict with God's law and commandment. (Horst: 32)

This emphasis on differing but complementary roles for church and state has made a contribution to the separation of church and state in the United States and elsewhere. It also has led to a host of initiatives on the part of the churches in accord with the example and teachings of Christ himself in his time on earth. Among these are world relief and service programs that seek to minister to friend and foe alike "in the name of Christ."

The State Treating Enemies Humanely

A first attempt at encoding the humane treatment of enemies into international law was made at the Geneva Convention of 1864. Rule 4 of this convention states: "Prisoners of war must be humanely treated and protected from violence. Prisoners cannot be beaten or used for propaganda purposes." The guidelines adopted at that time turned out to be insufficient for the wars of the twentieth century. Therefore, a greatly expanded set of rules for the treatment of prisoners of war was adopted on August 12, 1949, at the third Geneva Convention. It stated (among other things) that "in all circumstances" prisoners of war shall be treated humanely, not only by providing them with necessities of life, but also, "outrages upon [a prisoner's] personal dignity, in particular, humiliating and degrading treatment," are strictly forbidden. It also specified that the "wounded and sick shall be collected and cared for" with the assistance of "an impartial humanitarian body" (such as the Red Cross). Amid the wars and rumors of wars that continue to afflict the nations of the world, it is heartening to realize that the world's nations have spelled out ideals such as these and are striving to embrace and implement them (however imperfectly).

The Universality of Wisdom

The bold manner in which *the men of Hezekiah* embraced Solomon's secular wisdom (as exemplified in Prov 25-27) can perhaps be an example for the church in relating the faith traditions of the Bible to wisdom about life in the world at large. As explained, it is remarkable that these additional *proverbs* were added when we consider the reforming faith of those who added them (see above). And yet, one must assume that their openness to Solomon's proverbs had limits. Their immersion in the teachings of Moses must have sensitized

them on what to include and what to reject. One assumes as well that
the needs and challenges of the moment guided them. They were also
adding these additional sayings to a collection on which they had put
their theological imprint. Christians today go through a similar process
whenever they relate their faith to that of other peoples and religions.

Proverbs 28:1—29:27

Hezekiah Reform Manual

The Book of Proverbs, Part 3: Supplemental Collections					
"Words of the Wise" 22:17–24:22	"Also Words of the Wise" 24:23-34	"Also Proverbs of Solomon" 25:1–27:27	Hezekiah Reform Manual 28:1–29:27	"Words of Agur Son of Jakeh" 30:1-33	Later Addi- tions 31:1-31

PREVIEW

The form and content of the sayings in these two chapters (28-29) are strikingly different from the *proverbs of Solomon* in the preceding three chapters (25-27). Solomon's proverbs are picturesque and mostly secular. God is thought of as gloriously mysterious (25:1); the king searches out wisdom (25:2). Major issues are court etiquette, fools, and sluggards. In chapters 28-29, the poems are more straight-forward and serious. Weighty matters of national significance are addressed. Religious issues such as trusting Yahweh are front and cen-ter; keeping the *law* is singled out as the key distinguishing mark of a *discerning son* (28:7a). Again and again we hear echoes of the teachings of Moses in Deuteronomy.

One senses an intense struggle going on in the background that is related somehow to Hezekiah's reforms. I have come to see this collection of sayings as a first attempt during the early days of these reforms at fashioning a manual for civil servants. At that point yet, the more ambitious undertaking that resulted in the Hezekiah Edition of Proverbs had not yet begun. When it was, this initial smaller manual was included as the next to the last of the supplemental collections. It thus had an initial existence as an independent collection in its own right.

Others too have characterized it as a once-independent manual of some sort related to the duties of monarchs. One scholar believes there are four strategically placed couplets (28:12, 28; 29:2, 16) that highlight the joy a nation feels when "the righteous come to power" (28:28b; 29:2a); he dubs it a "Manual for Monarchs" (Malchow: 355). However, the issues addressed are of relevance not just for monarchs but also for their entourage and courtiers. Hence, this manual is exactly like the instruction booklets of Egypt that were designed for educating civil servants. It is, so to speak, a miniversion of the book of Proverbs. This is the case in another sense as well. The proverbs of this collection are short two-line poems or couplets exactly like those in the Main Collection. Also like them, they appear to be grouped in clusters of five for study purposes (see Preview to the Main Collection).

The collection here and the Main Collection are similar in yet another way. As noted, the 375 poems of the Main Collection (10:1–22:16) are grouped in sets of five proverbs each. These sets are arranged in two equal parts: 37 five-proverb clusters in part 1, and 37 five-proverb clusters in part 2, and a cluster of five proverbs at the exact center. The poems of this shorter manual (chs. 28-29) seem to have been arranged in the same way; in this case, however, there are just 55 poems in all. These 55 divided by five make 11, so in this case there are eleven sets of five-proverbs each. These 11 sets are arranged in two equal parts: five sets of five proverbs in part 1 (28:1-25) and five sets of five proverbs in part 2 (29:3-27), with a single five-proverb set in the exact middle (28:26–29:2). This may be diagrammed as follows:

Early Training Manual for Civil servants Involved in Hezekiah's Reforms		
Part 1	Middle Panel	Part 2
Five Sets of Five Proverbs	Five Proverbs	Five Sets of Five Proverbs
28:1-25	28:26–29:2	29:3-27

As previously noted, the purpose of a symmetrical design like this was related to the way scrolls were stored, rolled up from both ends (see Introduction, "Purpose and Design of the Hezekiah Edition"). Thus, when a scroll was opened, the first words to be seen would be its middle column, and from there one would have easy access to other parts of the scroll. The symmetrical design of the poems in these chapters would therefore be an additional indication that they were published first as an independent scroll before being added to the Hezekiah Edition of Proverbs.

Because the proverbs of the Main Collection were so numerous, it seemed best to group them in *thematic* clusters and not approach them in their present sequential arrangement. The collection here is much smaller, and its five-proverb sets are thematically more coherent. Hence, I decided to study them five sayings at a time in the sequence in which they appear. First, however, a brief overview of the themes touched on in *this* collection may be helpful. Among them are the following:

- The qualities that distinguish the righteous from the wicked, the evil from the good, those who *seek the LORD* from those who do not (28:1, 5, 13, 14, 25; 29:7, 10, 24, 27)
- The contrasting fate of the evil and the upright, those who *fear the LORD* and those who do not (28:10, 14, 18; 29:6, 16, 25)
- The qualities and benefits that distinguish those who *keep the law* from those who do not (28:4, 7, 9; 29:18)
- The qualities that distinguish good and bad rulers (28:2, 3, 15, 16, 21; 29:4, 12) and the essential differences between good and bad governments (28:12, 28; 29:2)
- Being poor but upright versus being wealthy but perverse (28:6, 8, 11, 19, 20, 22, 24, 27; 29:13, 14)

OUTLINE

"The Righteous Are Bold as a Lion," 28:1-5
"He Who Keeps the Law Is a Discerning Son," 28:6-10
"When the Righteous Triumph, There Is Great Elation," 28:11-15
"A Faithful Man Will Be Richly Blessed," 28:16-20
"A Greedy Man Stirs Up Dissension," 28:21-25
"When the Righteous Thrive, the People Rejoice," 28:26–29:2
"The Righteous Care About Justice for the Poor," 29:3-7
"Mockers Stir Up a City, but Wise Men Turn Away Anger," 29:8-12
"The Rod of Correction Imparts Wisdom," 29:13-17
"Blessed Is He Who Keeps the Law," 29:18-22
"Whoever Trusts in the LORD Is Kept Safe," 29:23-27

EXPLANATORY NOTES

"The Righteous Are Bold as a Lion" 28:1-5

These first five poems touch on themes central to the Hezekiah reforms (see 2 Kgs 18:1-8). The first (28:1) highlights the boldness in battle of those who are *righteous* (*ṣadîqîm*, loyal to Yahweh and his covenant law; cf. 28:4-5), as contrasted with the cowardice of the *wicked* (those disloyal to Yahweh and his covenant law). The latter *flees though no one pursues.* The same phrase is used in Leviticus 26:17, 36 to describe "flight that continues even when the enemy has ceased pursuing; the terror is so profound that one cannot stop running" (Clifford). With such *lion*-like boldness (Prov 28:1b), Hezekiah "rebelled against the king of Assyria and did not serve him." That also led to his success in the wars he fought at this time with the "Philistines, as far as Gaza and its territory" (2 Kgs 18:7-8).

The second poem in this group paints a contrast between the *many rulers* (anarchy) that exist when a *country* [*'ereṣ*, land] *is rebellious,* and the *order* that prevails when *a man* [*'ādām*] *of understanding and knowledge* (28:2) leads it. King Hezekiah aspired to be that kind of ruler through espousing and promoting "the commands the LORD had given Moses" (2 Kgs 18:6). However, not everyone followed his example. The third saying in 28:3 refers to one such exception. They are the *poor* (there is no support for the NIV translation *ruler*) who though themselves *poor* still do not hesitate to oppress those weaker than themselves (28:3a). Such are said to be like *driving rain that leaves no crops* (devastating in their effect on the community, 28:3b). Others *forsake the law* [and openly] *praise the wicked* (28:4a), but thankfully there are those as well *who keep the law* [*tôrāh*] *and resist them* (28:4b). This verse in particular seems to reflect the fight Hezekiah and his co-workers had on their hands in trying to implement their reforms. The final saying in this group sums up their teaching: *Evil men do not understand justice, but those who seek the LORD understand it fully* (28:5, lit.). The reason *those who seek the LORD* have such a profound understanding of what justice entails is because they are informed and motivated by the words of Moses on precisely these matters (cf. Deut 16:18-20).

"He Who Keeps the Law Is a Discerning Son" 28:6-10

This group of five poems begins (28:6) and ends (28:10) with statements about those who are *blameless* (meaning "complete" or "wholehearted" in regard to the law; see 1 Kgs 9:4-5). It is *better to be a poor man who walks in his blamelessness* (completeness, integrity) *than a rich man whose ways are perverse* (28:6, lit.; cf. 19:1). The second poem in this group draws a contrast between a son who *keeps the law* and for that reason is *a discerning son,* and a son who is *a companion of gluttons* and for that reason *disgraces his father* (28:7). This mirrors the legislation in Deuteronomy 21:18-21, where a "rebellious son" is characterized as a "glutton" (21:20, NRSV) who will not listen to his parents. The next proverb pertains to increasing one's wealth through *interest and increase* on loans, a practice forbidden in biblical law (28:8, lit.; see Lev 25:36; Deut 23:20). The proverb observes that a son who acquires money in this manner *amasses it for another, who will be kind to the poor* (28:8b); in other words, it will be of no lasting personal benefit, for God will see to it that it is returned to the poor. This and the next two poems (28:9, 10) make a similar point: turning *a deaf ear to the law* (*tôrāh*), is hazardous. Anyone who does so cannot count on God's help; *even his prayers are detestable,* 28:9; cf. 15:8). Indeed, anyone *who leads the upright along an evil path will fall into his own trap* (28:10). Only those who are *blameless* (wholehearted in obedience to the law) can expect to inherit *good* (the "blessings" mentioned in Deut 28:1-14).

"When the Righteous Triumph, There Is Great Elation" 28:11-15

These five proverbs focus on a number of challenges involved in creating a good society. The first provides a vivid snapshot of the struggle between wealthy and poor (28:11). *A rich man may be wise in his eyes but a poor man who has discernment sees through him* (sees and exposes his devious motives and posturing). To be *wise in one's own eyes* (28:11a), as the wealthy sometimes are, is a sign of folly and imminent demise (3:7; 26:5, 12). The second poem (28:12) paints a verbal contrast between the joy that erupts when *the righteous triumph,* and what happens when *the wicked rise to power*— then *men* ['*ādām*] *go into hiding* (28:12). The challenge posed in the third poem is *not* to conceal *sin* (transgressions, or rebellions), but to confess and renounce it—for those who conceal it will *not prosper* (thrive), but *whoever confesses and renounces their sins finds mercy* (28:13). This is the only verse in Proverbs that refers to God's forgiveness of a repentant individual. The piety that informs this teaching is evident in the fourth proverb (28:14). Here the individual who is *blessed* (happy) is one *who always fears the LORD* (Yahweh), with the emphasis being on *always* (see also 23:17; Deut 5:29: "Oh, that their hearts would be inclined to fear me and keep all my commands always, so that it might go well with them and their children forever!"). The last proverb of the set paints yet another picture of *a helpless people* demoralized by a wicked, oppressive ruler (28:15). A king of this stripe is aptly likened to *a roaring lion or a charging bear.* This is just the opposite of the kind of king Hezekiah was striving to be.

"A Faithful Man Will Be Richly Blessed" 28:16-20

This group of five proverbs highlights certain vices and virtues of different strata in society and what the consequences are for them and their community. The first states that *a ruler [prince] who lacks discernment is a great oppressor* (28:16a, lit.), whereas *he who hates unjust gain will prolong his days* (28:16b). The implication is that rulers who lack discernment become brutal tyrants who fail to see the consequences of their actions, the hatred of their people. But a ruler who abhors *unjust gain* wins his people's respect and thereby enjoys *a long life* (28:16b). The second poem in this group is also about an oppressor—someone with *blood* on his hands (28:17a, lit.). Although the text is difficult, it may be translated as follows: *A man pressed down with the blood of a person* [a man who committed murder] *to the pit shall flee* [will be holed up in some hiding place and die there or be caught]; *do not support him* (28:17).

The next three poems portray opposite kinds of people (persons of good character) by first showing the good that happens to them, and then the bad that happens to those who have just the opposite qualities. The first of these sayings draws a contrast between those whose walk is *blameless* and those whose ways are *perverse* (28:18). Those whose *walk is blameless* are *kept safe;* those whose ways are perverse *suddenly fall.* This may allude to the tumultuous events of Hezekiah's period (cf. 2 Kgs 18:9-12). The second of these sayings draws a contrast between a man who *works his land* and one who pursues vanities (vain pursuits of wealth; cf. Amos 5:11); the former will have an abundance of bread, the latter an abundance of *poverty* (28:19; cf. 12:11). The third of these couplets singles out a *faithful man* (one who is steadfast) and contrasts him with someone in a hurry to get rich (28:20). The first will experience blessings in abundance; the second will not go unpunished. With these proverbs young men are trained to value a society in which king and commoner alike curb their greed and lawlessness and are content with living honest, industrious lives. The confidence expressed is that those who do this will be *richly blessed* (by God).

"A Greedy Man Stirs Up Dissension" 28:21-25

These five couplets continue warning about the evils of greed. The first (28:21) warns against *partiality* (lit., *to regard faces*) in dispensing justice, even in the case of a man who steals a *piece of bread*; this is resoundingly declared to be *not good* (Cohen); even the *poor* need to be held accountable for stealing (cf. Exod 23:3; Prov 24:23). The second warns against a *stingy man* (lit., *a man of evil eye*; consumed by greed; 28:22; cf. 23:6) who hastens after riches (cf. 28:20). The tragedy is that he does not know that what he will likely get is *poverty* (cf. 28:19). The third saying commends the person who rebukes another over one who fawns (is greedy for favors), for in the end the straightforward man will gain more favor (28:23). The fourth strongly condemns the greed of someone who thinks there is nothing wrong with defrauding his father and mother, because their wealth will be his anyway some day (*"It's not wrong,"* he says; 28:24). On the contrary, such a person *is partner to him who destroys.* By this grossly irreverent and criminal act, he destroys the social bonds that make for a humane society.

The fifth couplet summarizes the insights of the previous four by drawing a contrast between a *greedy man* (lit., *a man of large appetite*) with someone who *trusts in the LORD* (28:25). The former *stirs up dissension* with his greed and ambition. The latter is less driven and more relaxed and caring; ironically, he is the one who is said to *prosper* (lit., *be made fat*; cf. 11:25). Not just to *fear the LORD* (1:7; 9:10) but to *trust* him is advanced here and elsewhere in Proverbs as a core ideal of Hezekiah's reforms (3:5-6; 16:20; 22:19; 29:25). A characteristic of King Hezekiah was that he *trusted in the LORD, the God of Israel* like no Israelite king before or after him (cf. 2 Kgs 18:5).

"When the Righteous Thrive, the People Rejoice" 28:26–29:2

This group of five sayings is the center panel of the compendium of fifty-five poems in chapters 28-29. From the analogous arrangement of sayings in 10:1–22:16, in which there is also a similar center panel of five core sayings (see Preview to that collection), one expects that it will articulate core values of the Hezekiah reforms. This appears to be the case. The poem at the very middle states: *When the wicked ascend* [to power], *a human being* ['ādām] *hides himself, but when they perish, righteous ones increase* (28:28, lit.). The goal of the Hezekiah reforms was to diminish the power of the wicked and increase the numbers of the *righteous*, those faithful to God and his laws. When that happens and the upright do in fact increase, then *the people rejoice,* states the final saying of this group, whereas under a *wicked* ruler *the people groan* (29:2).

The struggles involved in implementing these reforms are reflected in the fourth poem of this group: *A man of reproofs* [someone often reproved] *who hardens his neck, suddenly will be broken and without healing* (29:1, lit.). Two key attributes of the upright are mentioned in the first two poems: their humility (28:26) and generosity (28:27). *He who trusts in himself* [lit., *trusts his heart*] *is a fool* [lit., *he is a fool*], *but he who walks in wisdom* [of the kind being set forth in these sayings, keeping the law; 28:7] *is kept safe* [lit., *he shall escape;* he shall survive in the midst of the perils of the time; 28:26b; cf. 3:25-26]. To be wary of one's own understanding and to trust Yahweh instead—this was at the heart of Hezekiah's reforms (3:5-7). Another central theme was that of being generous to those in abject poverty. *He who gives to the poor will lack nothing, but he who closes his eyes to them will receive many curses* (28:27). Those in a position to help become the target of justified anger and curses when they simply shut their eyes and close their hearts to the needs around them. On the other hand, *he who gives to the poor will lack nothing* (28:27a; lit., *does not lack*; Yahweh will repay him; cf. 19:17).

"The Righteous Care About Justice for the Poor" 29:3-7

This is yet another collage of key values espoused by Hezekiah's reforms. Most are variations on themes already raised. The first underscores the point just made in 28:26 (about the importance of walking in *wisdom*) by drawing attention to the impact a son who *loves wisdom* has on *his father*: his father rejoices (29:3). The second reiterates a core value of Deuteronomy with respect to the duties of a king. A king establishes a *country* (*land*) by implementing *justice,* but a man *greedy for bribes* [or "one who levels extortionate taxation," Whybray, 1995:399) *tears it down* (29:4). Repeated here is the warning given against a man who flatters his neighbor with intent to deceive and entice him to follow a wrong path (29:5; cf. 28:10; 27:14). Such a man *is spreading a net for his feet* (lit., *his steps;* trips him up). The poem that follows generalizes this warning: *In the transgression of an evil man* [there is always] *a snare* (something malicious), *whereas an upright man sings and rejoices* (29:6, lit.); he has a song on his lips and is happy.

The final proverb of this group draws attention once more to the contrasting attitudes of upright and wicked toward the helpless *poor* (*dal*, 29:7; cf. 22:22). What is emphasized here is the contrasting *knowledge* each has of this underclass. *The righteous care about* [lit., *know about*] *justice for the poor*, whereas *the wicked have no such concern* (lit., *do not perceive knowledge*); they have no insight or empathy for the conditions of the poor (29:7).

"Mockers Stir Up a City, but Wise Men Turn Away Anger" 29:8-12

The first of this group of proverbs pertains to what agitates and, by contrast, what calms the life of a *city*. *Mockers* [lit., *men of scorn*] *stir up a city* [lit., *blow a city; fan discontent*], *but wise men turn away anger* (29:8). The next poem states, however, that it is useless for a wise man to argue with a foolish man (29:9a). For whatever the fool might do (whether shake with anger or laugh), in the end there will be no resolution (NIV: *peace*; better: *calm*; 29:9b). The poem is not necessarily about going to *court* with such a man (NIV; the word *court* does not appear in the Hebrew text) but about arguing with him. This is a cautionary note for the wise about the futility of arguing with fools.

The harsh turmoil and conflict of city life is reflected in the third poem of this group. It alludes to *bloodthirsty men* (*men of blood*; criminal types) who *hate a man of integrity and seek to kill the upright* (lit., *seek his soul*, 29:10). Another factor to be reckoned with in a city's turmoil is the way a *fool* gives *full vent to his anger* (lit., *all his spirit* or emotions), while *the wise man keeps himself under control* (lit., *in holding back he quiets it*; 29:11). The last of these proverbs (29:12) highlights the disastrous consequences of a gullible ruler who listens to *lies* (lit., *a word of deception*). When this happens, *all his officials become wicked* (29:12b). The well-being of a city depends on a ruler having men of wisdom and integrity around him who can stand firm against those who are foolish and corrupt (cf. 25:5).

"The Rod of Correction Imparts Wisdom" 29:13-17

Common to these five proverbs is an essentially hopeful outlook in the midst of life's difficulties, a hope inspired by a sense of God's oversight and sovereignty. The opening poem (29:13) observes that *the poor man and the oppressor* (lit., *a man of oppressions*; someone unscrupulously rich; cf. 22:2), *have this in common* (lit., *meet together*; have a chance encounter). The observation that follows,

The LORD gives sight [light] to the eyes of both (29:13b), brings a new perspective to their chance "meeting." They are not as different as one might think. The saying evokes a sense that both the poor and the rich are creatures of God, made in his image (cf. Gen 1:27), before whom both are accountable. This awareness of Yahweh's all-sustaining providence is also reflected in the second poem: A king who judges the weak with integrity [because Yahweh is with him in this], his throne will forever be established (29:14, lit.).

The third (29:15) and fifth poems (29:17) commend and challenge fathers to be proactive in using rod and reproof (NIV: discipline) to impart wisdom to their sons, rather than neglecting them. A child left to itself [lit., a youth (na'ar) let go] disgraces his mother (29:15). A rare imperative is employed in yet another saying on this theme: Correct your son and you will have rest [you will be able to relax]; it will give delight to your spirit (28:17, lit.; cf. 23:24-25). Like similar sayings in the Main Collection (13:24; 19:18; 20:30; 22:15), these two poems express confidence in a judicious use of the rod as a way of reproving and educating sons. The essential optimism of this whole manual is summed up in the final saying of this group: When the wicked thrive, so does sin, but the righteous will see their downfall (29:16). In the end it is those who do right who will survive and succeed.

"Blessed Is He Who Keeps the Law" 29:18-22

The five proverbs of this unit may be thought of as random concluding insights, some of great importance, others addressed to issues not touched on before. The first (in 29:18) summarizes a key conviction of the Hezekiah reformers in a new way. Without revelation [ḥāzôn, vision, meaning divinely inspired teaching like that of the prophet Moses], the people cast off restraint [cf. Exod 32:25], but blessed [happy] is he who keeps the law [tôrāh] (Prov 29:18; cf. 28:4, 7, 9). The law referred to is what Moses set before the Israelites (Deut 4:44), beginning with the Decalogue (Deut 5:1-21). Without that law to guide them in the period from Solomon onward, the Israelite kingdoms cast off restraint and worshipped other gods with other values, bringing devastating consequences (cf. 2 Kgs 17). King Hezekiah's lifelong endeavor was to hold fast to Yahweh: "He kept the commands the LORD had given Moses. And the LORD was with him; he was successful in whatever he undertook" (2 Kgs 18:6-7). This couplet (Prov 29:18) states as simply and clearly as any in the entire Hezekiah Edition of Proverbs what motivated the Hezekiah reformers and the production of reform literature of this period (see

Introduction, "Purpose and Design of the Hezekiah Edition").

Two additional proverbs in this group address a matter not previously dealt with: how best to discipline or train a servant. In many instances mere words are not enough, the saying advises, for even though the words are understood, the servant may not respond (29:19). Implied is that the relation of master and servant is not an especially cordial one, and that forceful actions may be needed to keep a servant in line. Nor should a servant be pampered, especially not when young, or *in the end* there will be *grief* (29:21); however, the meaning of the word translated *grief* is uncertain since it appears only here in ancient sources. The social status of the slave is simply taken for granted, although the law of Moses in Deuteronomy specifies that Hebrew slaves should be given an opportunity to "go free" after six years of service (male and female alike), with generous provisions for their future (Deut 15:12-18).

The two remaining proverbs have to do with disorders of temperament. The first profiles the folly of *a man who speaks in haste* (29:20); the second is about the devastating communal and personal consequences of a *hot-tempered* man (29:22). For the man who speaks in haste, *there is more hope for a fool than for him* (29:20b). And those prone to anger. create *dissension* in the community and *many sins* (lit., *many offenses;* 29:22). Numerous sayings in the Main Collection address these same topics, but these are apt summaries of the observations there.

"Whoever Trusts in the LORD Is Kept Safe" 29:23-27

These are additional poems on a variety of subjects, some old, some new. In the first of these sayings (29:23), the Hebrew word for *pride* means *swelling up, rising* (cf. Ps 46:3, "surging"), being "puffed up," we might say. *Puffed-up* people will be brought low, the proverb states, while a *man of lowly spirit gains honor* (29:23; cf. 11:16, saying something similar about a gracious woman). The next poem singles out *the accomplice of a thief* (29:24) and warns him of the penalty he incurs for himself personally if he does not testify to what he has seen or done. In the background here is the situation described in Leviticus 5:1: "If a person sins because he does not speak up when he hears a public charge to testify regarding something he has seen or learned about, he will be held responsible [by God]."

The middle poem of this group of sayings highlights a core value of the book's Hezekiah Edition: *Fear of man* ['ādām, *a human being*] *will prove to be a snare, but whoever trusts in the LORD is kept safe* [lit., *will be set on high*] (29:25). In the swiftly moving events of

Hezekiah's regency, there were many competing voices calling for trust in this or that nation or power. Isaiah (a contemporary of Hezekiah's reforms) proclaimed something similar to what is said here: "Do not call conspiracy everything that these people call conspiracy; do not fear what they fear, and do not dread it. The LORD Almighty is the one you are to regard as holy, he is the one you are to fear, he is the one you are to dread" (Isa 8:12-13; cf. 30:15). It was Isaiah's counsel to trust in Yahweh in the midst of the Assyrian invasions that saved the nation (2 Kgs 19).

The poem that follows is also about Yahweh's sovereignty in human affairs: *Many seek an audience with* [lit., *seek the face of*] *a ruler, but it is from the LORD that man gets justice* (29:26). Yahweh is the ultimate guarantor of human rights, and it is to him therefore that people should always look. The final poem of this manual is more forceful in Hebrew than in translation (29:27). Both lines begin with the emotionally charged word *tôʿăbat*, meaning *abomination* (abhorrent): *Abhorrent to the upright, a man of perversity; abhorrent to the wicked, the straight way* (29:27, lit.). The word *abhorrent* (*abomination*) is often used to express what is utterly unacceptable to God; here it characterizes "the 'either-or' quality of moral life" (Clifford: 256). The upright and wicked are on two radically different paths. Jesus concluded his teaching in the Sermon on the Mount in a similar way. There are two paths, two ways of building a house, on sand or on rock (Matt 7:13-14, 24-27).

THE TEXT IN BIBLICAL CONTEXT

God's Kingdom

This little manual (Prov 28-29) reflects the energy and spirit of the Hezekiah reformers and enshrines some of their most cherished goals. It is directed not only to the conduct of the king (as some have suggested), but also to that of soldiers, landowners, and people of wealth and responsibility throughout the society. It issues a stirring call to be bold as a lion, generous to the poor, lawful and good. It gives an appeal to intensify goodness and make it possible for good people to flourish. It is a call to righteousness. It speaks sharply against those who mock at what is being attempted, against those who are too proud to seek Yahweh and try to uphold his law. It is even-tempered. It is not fanatic. It does not foster haste or anger. It is not idealistic. It speaks to the conduct of life as it really is.

This in itself is remarkable: how sober and down to earth it is. It urges the young men of the society to have as their ideal not exorbitant wealth, but a modest and honest life, one that will provide a livelihood for themselves and their families. Then they can be generous toward those less fortunate than themselves. Its core ideal is uprightness, honesty, and fidelity to God. A verse in Micah echoed by Jesus summarizes its goals perfectly: "And what does the LORD require of you? To act justly and to love mercy and to walk humbly with your God" (6:8). Jesus put the ideal similarly: "Seek first the kingdom of God and its righteousness, and all these things will be given to you as well" (Matt 6:33, lit.; cf. NIV; NRSV, note).

The Need for Divine Revelation

This part of Proverbs reveals what is presupposed throughout the Hezekiah Edition of Proverbs: the need for and priority of divine revelation in the human quest for a wise and upright existence on earth. As a key verse of this manual puts it, *Where there is no [divine] vision, the people cast off restraint, but he who keeps the law is happy* (29:18, lit.). The statement is an observation, not a command. This is the way life is, the way nations are. Without a divine *vision* (NIV: *revelation*; NRSV: *prophecy*), human beings tend toward rebellion. They tend to be too proud and self-sufficient; they tend to rely too much on their own wisdom, which can only go so far.

This perspective on the life of a people or nation is reinforced by a large part of the biblical narrative and teaching. It is inscribed in the Genesis 1-11 account of the creation of the world's nations in the first place. Early on in the history of humanity, there was manifest a rebellious spirit that led to a violent self-destructive existence (Gen 6:5-6). God intervened with a great flood and then yet again, in its aftermath, with decrees and promises; only thus was ongoing human existence possible (9:1-17).

The story of the calling of Israel is about a people tutored by God in the ways of wisdom, through prophets like Moses. Even so, Israel needed to keep listening and learning and revising what it heard God saying. So revelation itself is progressive, as is wisdom. Christians regard the teachings of Jesus, and Jesus himself in his person and bearing, as a manifestation of divine wisdom. But here too, finality eludes us, for this teaching must be interpreted. According to John's Gospel, Jesus promised that his disciples would be led in an ongoing way by "the Spirit of truth" (16:13). Throughout the Bible there thus is an ongoing interplay between revelation and reason, wisdom and vision. We need to search things out and also, at the same time, look to God, who is source of all wisdom (Jas 1:5; 3:17).

THE TEXT IN THE LIFE OF THE CHURCH

Nation Building

These two chapters of Proverbs come down to the church from a time of intense struggle within the Israelite kingdom founded by David, as it sought to renew itself in accordance with the ideals represented by the teachings of Moses. In recent times there have been many examples of nations attempting to renew themselves. The need to do so is apparent. The greatest sufferings of the twentieth century were due to great nations descending into corruption, deceit, and terror. Still in too many nations, peoples are suffering under corrupt governments and brutal leaders. One of the great challenges of our age is in the realm of what is sometimes called nation building.

Not all think of the church as having a vital role in nation building. The believers churches especially have seen their primary role as that of building the church through seeding an expanding network of witnessing congregations. This is unquestionably one of their most vital tasks, for without doing that they would cease to exist. But the church does not live only for itself. By virtue of its founding and calling, the church is oriented to a reality greater than itself, the conversion of the nations (Matt 5:13-16; 28:16-20). It exists to be leaven and light in the whole world, helping the world's peoples open themselves to the dawning of the "kingdom of God on earth as it is in heaven" (Matt 6:9-10).

Does that mission encompass nation building? Is nation building not also a concern for which to pray and contribute? The texts we have just looked at prod us to consider that Christians do have a vital role to play in nation building. They speak of the joy a nation feels when righteous rulers ascend to the throne, and the agony they feel when that is not the case. They speak of the values that any nation on earth will need to embrace if its citizens are to be at peace and prosper. They call for an energetic response on the part of a nation's citizens in the struggle to enshrine those values in every aspect of its national life.

A Man's Pride Brings Him Low

I have written (above) of the sobriety and humility of this reform document. In this regard, it is not at all like *The Communist Manifesto* (1848). It is more like Plato's *The Republic* in its awareness that reforming the various facets of a society will be truly difficult, and even so, perfection is not possible—simply improvement. But Proverbs 28-29 differs vastly from Plato's reformist writings as well. Plato was exceedingly speculative in some of his proposals, such as his idea that the state should replace the family as the responsible agent for care and education of children. No one today seeks to implement these ideals; indeed, most thoughtful people agree that even trying to do so would be a disaster. Yet virtually everything advocated in Proverbs seems sane and applicable to virtually anybody and any society. Of course, even here are points on which people might differ, such as, for example, the advice regarding discipline of children. But even this provides an occasion for thinking about a real problem: how to deal with rebellious youth. Is incarcerating them in the manner practiced today any better solution?

One of the most surprising features of the Hezekiah Reform movement's manifesto is its modesty. This stems in part from its profound sense of a need for God. We are not as wise as we think we are. We make mistakes. When we make mistakes, we should not hide them, but confess them, for when we do so we find mercy. We need to walk with God, and those who refuse to do so are in trouble. Modern nations and leaders tend to be too nationalistic, too proud. It is surprising to see powerful nations with large Christian populations displaying so much arrogance. It is a dangerous sign when the leaders of nations boast about what they are going to do or not do.

One of the more needful things the book of Proverbs may have to offer church and world is the modesty of its tone. It is passionate about goodness and about justice, but quite humble in tone. It realizes how small human beings are and how much they need God. This is one of its greatest achievements, in my judgment. There was an individual, I have concluded, who brought this combination of zeal for goodness with humility to the fore in this book and saw to it that it would be maintained throughout the collection. It is the person to whose words we turn next, Agur son of Jakeh (30:1).

Proverbs 30:1–33

"Words of Agur Son of Jakeh"

The Book of Proverbs, Part 3: Supplemental Collections					
"Words of the Wise" 22:17–24:22	"Also Words of the Wise" 24:23-34	"Also Proverbs of Solomon" 25:1–27:27	Hezekiah Reform Manual 28:1–29:27	"Words of Agur Son of Jakeh" 30:1-33	Later Additions 31:1-31

PREVIEW

Who was *Agur son of Jakeh?* Why would his words be attached as the final chapter of a book of poems attributed to the renowned King Solomon? The mystery deepens as we note the varied *sayings* assembled under his name: an *oracle* (30:1-6), a highly personal prayer (30:7-9), followed by ten poems on a variety of topics (30:10-33). A core thesis of this commentary *[Distinctive Approach]* is that Agur was not a skeptic (as often thought) but a devout believer in God (Yahweh) and a leading member of the guild of *men* who prepared the Hezekiah Edition of Proverbs (25:1). Prior supplements were attributed to anonymous *wise* ones (22:17; 24:23) or to *Solomon* (25:1).

For the first time in Proverbs, this chapter adds *sayings* (lit., *words*) from a named person other than Solomon. That his name and words are located at the end of the Hezekiah Edition accords with the custom of the time of sometimes identifying the person responsible for a scroll's contents in its closing sentences (cf. Eccl 12:9-10; Ps 72:20; Deut 34:10-12).

The extent of Agur's words is clearly indicated by the new heading in 31:1. That heading, unlike those preceding it (22:17; 24:23; 25:1; 30:1), identifies the person *to whom* the words that follow are addressed, only then identifying the person whose words these are. This slight variation is but one of several reasons for thinking chapter 31 was added later and that the Hezekiah Edition of Proverbs was concluded with the words of Agur son of Jakeh. As the book's editor in chief, his name, oracle, and sayings were accorded the honor of being that edition's final word, so to speak.

OUTLINE

Heading, 30:1a
Agur's Oracle, 30:1b-6

30:2-3	Opening Introduction of Himself
30:4	Series of Questions
30:5-6	Statement of Principle

Agur's Prayer, 30:7-9
Agur's Poems, 30:10-33

30:10	Beware of Slandering a Servant to His Master
30:11-14	"Those Who Curse Their Fathers"
30:15-16	Three or Four That Never Say, "Enough!"
30:17	"The Eye That Mocks a Father"
30:18-19	"The Way of a Man with a Maiden"
30:20	"The Way of an Adulteress"
30:21-23	Three or Four Under Which the Earth Trembles
30:24-28	Four That Are Small but Extraordinarily Wise
30:29-31	Three or Four Pompous in Their Bearing
30:32-33	"If You Have Played the Fool"

EXPLANATORY NOTES

Heading 30:1a

In Hebrew the heading consists of three words only: *Words [of] Agur bin-Yaqeh [son-of-Jakeh]*. The fourth word, *the-oracle*, is best understood as the title for Agur's initial "word." With this heading we are told the source of the various *words* that follow in this chapter. The prior two headings begin with the word *also* (*also words of the wise*, 24:23, lit.; *also proverbs of Solomon*, 25:1, lit.). The word *also* is notably missing in this heading. The *words of Agur* are not like any other but stand alone as the Hezekiah Edition's final words. The attribution of these words to a named individual is further evidence of the chapter's finality and importance. The person so named is given no title: he is simply identified as *this man* (lit., *the man*; Heb.: *ha-geber*, referring to a man of exceptional strength and insight, such as Balaam, Num 24:3; David, 2 Sam 23:1). Who might he have been? In Hebrew, names have meanings. *Agur* means "assembler"; his father's name, *Yaqeh* (NIV, *Jakeh*), is thought to mean "obedient" or "pious" (Toy: 519). Agur's oracle and prayer express deep devotion to *Yahweh* (30:7-8), to *every word of God* (30:5-6), the latter referring to the divine word received by Moses (see below). Levite guilds deeply loyal to the instructional heritage of Moses assisted Hezekiah with his reforms (see 2 Chr 29-31). These were *the men of Hezekiah* (25:1) who brought out a new edition of Proverbs. It appears that Agur son of Jakeh belonged to this guild of men loyal to Moses.

Agur's Oracle 30:1b-6

The first of Agur's poems is introduced as *an oracle* (lit., *the oracle*, 1:1b). The word *oracle* (*maśśā'*) means "burden" but is used elsewhere to identify divinely inspired utterances (Isa 13:1; 15:1; Jer 23:33-40). Its use here sets this initial poem apart—no other poem in Proverbs is so designated. The inspired nature of his oracle is also indicated by its introductory words. The expression, *This man declared* (lit., *says the man*), followed by the identification of those to whom he spoke, is traditional language for introducing a prophetic oracle (cf. Amos 1:1-2).

Agur's oracle was initially spoken to two men named Ithiel and Ucal (30:1b). Some regard these names as verbs, which slightly altered can be translated: *I am weary, O God, I am weary, O God. How can I prevail?* As such, they would suggest that Agur was in despair, which accords with how many interpret his oracle's words in 30:3. This rendering, however, is highly conjectural and unnecessary. The name *Ithiel* appears in Nehemiah 11:7; *Ucal* resembles the name of a sage mentioned in 1 Kings 4:31 ("Calcol"). From the oracle itself we can infer that these two men were professional scribes who collaborated in producing the Hezekiah Edition of Proverbs.

Agur's oracle has three distinct parts: an opening introduction of himself (30:2-3), a series of questions (30:4), and a statement of principle (30:5-6).

30:2-3 Opening Introduction of Himself

Agur begins with self-deprecating statements about himself, introduced with the Hebrew conjunction *kî* (*for*): *For I am the most ignorant of men* (30:2a, lit.), suggesting that "something preceded the verse" (Cohen), perhaps some statement of the two men to whom he speaks. Right off, he admits to being *brutish* (NIV: *ignorant*, as a beast; cf. Ps 73:21-22), unlike *a man* (30:2a), and lacking in the discernment typical of a human being ('*ādām*, 30:2b). What he is referring to, more concretely, is stated in line 3 (30:3a): he reveals that he has not *learned wisdom*, as presumably have Ithiel and Ucal, to whom he addresses the oracle. If Agur has not *learned wisdom*, then who is he? And what gives him the right to utter an oracle to two men who in all probability *had* studied wisdom as professional sages?

The final line of this self-revelation (30:3b) is Agur's answer and the essence of his oracle. Most translate this textual line, as does NIV: *Nor have I knowledge of the Holy One.* However, there is no negative word meaning *nor* or "not" in the Hebrew of this line as in the previous two lines. It is linked to the previous line by a simple conjunction consisting of a single letter (*wāw*) that can be translated either as "and" or "but." In this instance this conjunctive *wāw* should be translated *but* (not "and") because Agur is drawing a strong contrast between what he does *not* know (as stated in 30:2-3a) and what he does know (as stated in 30:3b). Agur is admitting to Ithiel and Ucal that his knowledge of wisdom may be limited since he has not *learned* or studied wisdom (professionally), *but* there is something he does know—*knowledge of the Holy One I know* (30:3b, lit.).

To what *knowledge* is Agur referring? Who is the *Holy One* to whom he refers? The Hebrew word translated *Holy One,* as used here (*qĕdōšîm*), is a plural of majesty meaning *the Most Holy One* and is found only two other places in the Hebrew Scriptures. One is in Hosea 11:12; the other, significantly, is in a key saying at the end of the introductory section of the Hezekiah Edition of Proverbs: *Fear of the LORD* [Yahweh] *is the beginning of wisdom, and knowledge of the Holy One is understanding* (9:10). In this verse (a variation on the watchword in 1:7) the term *Holy One* is parallel with *Yahweh*. Yahweh is *the Holy One*, and to fear him is the beginning of wisdom and knowledge. The *knowledge of the Holy One,* which Agur states he knows, is knowledge derived from fearing and knowing Yahweh.

30:4 Series of Questions

Agur is a devout worshipper of the God of Israel. This is movingly reflected in his prayer in 30:7-9, but also in the questions he addresses to Ithiel and Ucal (30:4). These suggest that Ithiel and Ucal were among those who professed to have knowledge about what goes on *in heaven* (where divine beings and gods exist). Solomon himself became enamored of the mythologies and worldviews associated with other gods (1 Kgs 11:1-6). The questions posed by Agur give a rare glimpse into the way those loyal to God in the tradition of Moses challenged the intellectual pretensions of those who embraced these mythologies. The questions Agur poses in his oracle are designed to expose the lack of an empirical basis for knowing what goes on in heaven. *Who has gone up to heaven and come down?* (30:4a; cf. Deut 30:12). Obviously, no one has. So likewise, the remaining questions are really not answerable. *Who has established all the ends of the earth? What is his name, and the name of his son? Tell me if you know!* The expression *if you know* (30:4d) forms a counterpart to Agur's claim that *knowledge of the Holy One I know* in the preceding verse (30:3b, lit.). Agur's point is that what they do not *know* (the true *name* of the one who created *all the ends of the earth*) is the *Holy One,* about whom he (Agur) knows, even though he has not *learned wisdom* in the traditional way.

30:5-6 Statement of Principle

How then does Agur know? Agur too has not gone up to heaven and come down, nor can he. So what makes him so confident that he does *know the Holy One* (30:2)? Agur's words in 30:5-6 allude to the phenomenon of prophetic revelation (30:5-6). They presuppose that the One who created *all the ends of the earth* (30:4) has spoken: *Every word of God is flawless* [*refined*]; *he is a shield to those who take refuge in him* (30:5; cf. Ps 18:30). The *oracle* ends with a forceful admonition *not* to *add to his* [God's] *words* lest he *rebuke you and prove you a liar* (30:6; lest he "demonstrate the falsity of your opinions," Cohen: 202). The language of these closing lines of Agur's oracle (30:5-6) is strikingly similar to words that Deuteronomy reports Moses speaking in conjunction with giving the Ten Commandments: "Do not add to what I command you and do not subtract from it, but keep the commands of the LORD your God that I give you" (4:2; 12:32). Agur is a *man* who believes in the *word of God* revealed through Moses. This *word* is not in heaven, so that you need to ask, "Who will ascend into heaven to get and proclaim it to us?" On the contrary, "The word is very near you; it is in your mouth and in your heart so you may obey it" (Deut 30:12-14). It was *men* like this (with convictions like this) who produced the Hezekiah Edition of Proverbs (25:1).

Agur's Prayer   30:7-9

Agur's prayer (the only one of its kind in the book) is a model of simplicity. He begins by asking God for *two things* (as later he will comment on two, three, or four aspects of different subjects). God is addressed with a simple *you* (lit., *two things have I asked of you*; 30:7a; NIV added the invocation, *O LORD*). The words of 30:7b (lit.), *Do not deny me them before I die,* mean "for the rest of my life" (Cohen); they underscore the seriousness of his request. The petitions pertain to how he wants to live the totality of his life on earth. *Keep falsehood and lies far from me* (30:8a); this is his number one request. Above all else he desires to be a man of truth and integrity.

Agur's second request is more complex. He prays that God might grant him neither poverty nor riches, but *only my daily* [lit., *allotted*] *bread* (30:8), lest *I be full, and deny and say, "Who is Yahweh?" or lest I be poor, and steal, and dishonor the name of my God* (30:9, lit.). In this part of the prayer, he reveals the name of his God. It is *Yahweh*, the God of Israel. When reading this, one is reminded of Moses' warning to Israel not to forget Yahweh "when you eat and are satisfied, when you build fine houses and settle down" (Deut 8:12; cf. 32:15). Agur is a man who has taken this warning to heart. He is aware of human frailty. He knows how easy it is to forget Yahweh when one becomes wealthy, and when destitute how easy it is to steal and dishonor Yahweh's name by being careless about his laws (one of which is not to steal; Deut 5:19). For this reason he asks for just enough to live each day. Like the Lord's Prayer of Jesus (Matt 6:9-13, with which it may justifiably be compared), Agur's prayer speaks volumes as to the kind of man he was.

Agur's Poems   30:10-33

To his oracle and prayer Agur adds a selection of ten of his poems. These poems reveal him, if not as a professional sage (30:2a), surely as an astute observer of the human condition and an adroit poet. Other poems of his might well have been added elsewhere in the Hezekiah Edition (see notes on 5:15–6:19). Like the parables and teachings of Jesus, they are marked by a distinctive, identifiable style. They combine acute observations on daily life, spiced with a touch of hyperbolic humor and numerical tropes of one kind or another (*there are three, yes four . . .*). Most of Agur's ten poems in this section are simple observations, but the collection begins (30:10) and ends (30:32-33) with admonitions.

30:10 Beware of Slandering a Servant to His Master

In this verse an imperative not to do something is followed by a *lest* clause indicating what the consequence might be (for the same construction, see 30:6, 8-9). The imperative warns against slandering (lit., *wagging the tongue about*) a servant to his master. A servant (or slave) was vulnerable to false charges and had little recourse but to *curse* the one disparaging him in this manner. The saying alludes to the dire consequences such a *curse* might have on the one perpetrating a wrong of this kind.

30:11-14 "Those Who Curse Their Fathers"

The single Hebrew word *dôr* at the beginning of each of the four stanzas of this somber poem (30:11, 12, 13, 14) means *generation* ("a mass of people living in the same age," Toy: 527; cf. Matt 11:16). The portrait drawn is not of four generations but of four characteristics of a given generation. These four characteristics explain why the generation being described does the abominable thing described in the poem's final couplet: devouring *the poor from the earth, the needy from among mankind* (Prov 30:14b). This cruel disregard for the rights of others is traced first to a generational (culturally embedded) hatred of parents. That this generation *curses its father and does not bless its mother* (30:11, lit.) is just the opposite of what is called for in the Decalogue of Moses (Deut 5:16).

A second characteristic of a generation that cruelly devours the poor on earth is its self-righteousness: it is *pure in its own eyes and yet not cleansed of its filth* (30:12, lit.). That too is why it is proud (30:13) and prone to violence (30:14). Isaiah, living in the midst of the Hezekiah reforms, described the "generation" of his time in similar terms, as proud, violent, and disregarding of the poor (see Isa 3:8-17; 5:8-23). Here, however, Agur traces the general malaise and evil of this culture to deeper roots in a perversity that has corrupted the emotional space between children and their parents (see also the passionate outburst on this issue in Prov 30:17).

30:15-16 Three or Four That Never Say, "Enough!"

Most of the remaining poems highlight features of the human condition that are ordinarily overlooked or trivialized. Individually and together, they reveal Agur to be a poet of unusual sensitivities. The first is a seven-line poem on the theme of insatiability (30:15-16). It begins cryptically with an image of a voracious leech of a type that has a sucker at each end (Clifford); these are its two daughters who cry: *"Give! Give!"* (30:15a). In like manner there are *three things, yes, four,* that are *never satisfied,* never say *"Enough!"* They are *the grave* [šĕ'ôl], *a barren womb, land . . . never satisfied with water,* and *fire, which never says, "Enough!"* (30:16). Numerical sayings of this kind are a feature of Canaanite literary style (Clifford: 265; cf. 6:16-19; Amos 1:3–2:6; Eccl 11:2). The form itself is attractive, allowing the poet to make provocative comparisons in a brief, compelling way. Almost lost within this particular list of *things* never satisfied is the passing reference to an instance of *human* desire and longing: *a barren womb.* In contrast to the visibly voracious appetite of *grave,* parched *land,* or *fire,* the longing signified by the *barren womb* is hidden. Women who suffer in this way do so (mostly) in silence. Perhaps a goal of this subtle poem is to make this silent suffering a little more audible.

30:17 "The Eye That Mocks a Father"

In accordance with several ancient versions, the second line of this poem should be rendered, *and scorns an aged mother* (instead of *scorns obedience to a mother,* NIV). The *eye that mocks a father* and *scorns an aged mother* is pictured as being *pecked out* [at the time of death] *by the ravens* and *eaten by the vultures* (as they are wont to do in the case of unburied flesh). The saying is not just about individuals, but the attitude of a *generation* (as in 30:11). Neither here nor in 30:11-14 is it directly said that such attitudes are wrong. What is said is that they have horrific consequences—a society (*generation*) in which fathers are mocked and mothers scorned is headed for destruction. Implicit in the gruesome picture of the *eye* being *pecked out* is a military invasion that leaves behind dead corpses to be ravaged by birds.

30:18-19 "The Way of a Man with a Maiden"

Agur speaks again (as in his oracle and prayer in 30:2-9) in a personal voice: he speaks of three and four *things that are too amazing for me* (30:18a). Here too (as there), these are things that baffle and astonish him: the *way of an eagle* [lit., *the vulture;* cf. 30:17] *in the sky* [how effortlessly it manages to stay afloat]; *the way of a snake on a rock* [how effortlessly it slithers along without feet]; *the way of a* ship in the midst of [in the heart of] the high seas [how it stays afloat and glides through the water] (30:19, lit.). The fourth and climactic wonder (and the point of the poem) is the way of a man [geber, a strong young man] with a maiden ['almāh, a young woman of marriageable age] (30:19d). How naturally, effortlessly, and mysteriously they are drawn together into a loving intimate bond, one of life's supreme experiences (similarly depicted in Gen 2:19-25). What seems to tie these four phenomena together is the miraculous effortlessness of each one. The intent is to create a heightened awareness and contemplation of the mysterious dynamic involved in the way of a man with a maiden.

30:20 "The Way of an Adulteress"

This poetic vignette captures a revealing moment in the way of an adulteress (lit., adulterous woman). Agur pictures her right after one of her impersonal liaisons with men other than her husband. He says nothing about the rightness or wrongness of her behavior. Rather, with a sketch of her casually finishing off a meal (she eats and wipes her mouth), he creates a lucid image of her trivialization of what she has just done. I've done nothing wrong, she says. For a comparable portrait of the way of an adulteress, see Proverbs 7:10-20, possibly also from Agur's pen.

30:21-23 Three or Four Under Which the Earth Trembles

This is a third three-plus-four poem (a fourth is 30:29-31). The previous two were about insatiable passions (30:15-16) and things that amaze (30:18-19). The theme of this third poem is that under which the earth trembles (the word under appears in Hebrew at the beginning of lines one, two, three, and five). The earth trembling is a metaphor for psychological and social upheavals. Examples of things that produce such upheavals are drawn from the political and domestic spheres—two from the world of men, two from the world of women. There is a touch of hyperbole in the poem's opening two lines: Under three things the earth trembles, under four it cannot bear up (30:21). The poet is serious but also smiling a bit about the earthshaking havoc of the examples he cites: A slave wreaks harm when he becomes king. A fool (when intoxicated) can disrupt a party. A hated married woman has terrifying bitterness (referring perhaps to the less favored wife in a polygamous household). A maidservant who displaces her mistress displays disruptive arrogance (like Hagar in Abraham's household; Gen 16:1-5). A social world may appear to be tranquil but is often the opposite. Little things like these may have earthshaking consequences.

30:24-28 Four That Are Small but Extraordinarily Wise

This poem consists of a list of four examples of creatures *on earth* that are *small* but *wise*, as indicated by their uncanny ability to survive in the face of stupendous odds (30:24). First mentioned are *ants* (lit., *the ants*), described as *creatures of little strength* (lit., *people not strong*). Yet they display an uncanny ability to plan ahead, storing up food in summer that they will need in winter (30:25; for a comparable picture, see 6:6-8). Next mentioned are the *conies* (*rock badgers*, NIV note), a little animal common to the rocky heights of the region (30:26). They too are described as a *people not strong* (lit.), who yet manage to survive by making their homes in *crags,* where predators cannot find and destroy them. The description of the third example, the *locusts,* begins by observing that though they *have no king, yet they advance together in ranks* (30:27). The fourth example is either a *spider* or *lizard* (Cohen). What is emphasized is that even though it can be easily *caught with the hand* (and in this sense is extremely vulnerable), yet it manages to survive in *kings' palaces* (30:28). No obvious lessons for human behavior are drawn from these observations (in contrast to 6:6-8), except that there is a wisdom manifest in some of earth's tiniest creatures that is truly amazing (cf. 30:18-19).

30:29-31 Three or Four Pompous in Their Bearing

This fourth of the three-plus-four poems simply cites examples of three, yes, four animals that walk or go forth in *stately* manner. The first three examples are from the world of animals (a *lion,* a *rooster,* and a *he-goat*); the fourth is a *king with his army around him* (or *secure against revolt*, depending on how a key word of this line is understood). Only the lion and the king are fully described. However, what is said about the king is uncertain due to an ambiguous text. Uncertain too is the identity of the second animal mentioned (*rooster* is only one of several guesses). The comment about the lion, who is characterized as *mighty among beasts,* is that he *retreats before nothing* (lit., *does not turn away from any*). Nothing at all is said about the third animal mentioned, the *he-goat,* but maybe there was no need to do so. A he-goat is renowned for its haughty strutting mannerisms in the midst of the flock. Considering the examples chosen, the poem's intent might have been to poke a little fun at a king's analogous haughty, self-important bearing, especially when his army surrounds him and he feels impregnable.

30:32-33 "If You Have Played the Fool"

The final poem (in this list of ten) is again an admonition like the first one (see 30:10). It begins with an *if* clause, followed by an admonition (30:32), followed by a rationale for the recommended action (30:33). This is the form in which case laws were written (cf. 6:1-3, perhaps also a poem of Agur; Exod 21-22). The case described is a tense moment when *you* (the reader) suddenly realize that you have acted foolishly by exalting yourself (lit., *lifting yourself up*) or by plotting some evil or mischief against another. The advice is that as soon as you realize this, you should take swift and decisive action to rectify matters. The Hebrew in line 30:32c expresses the action to be taken in a terse, powerful image: *hand to mouth!* (lit.). Stop at once the *evil* coming from your heart and mouth. Alter course immediately! Why? The final lines of the poem give the answer in terse alliterative metaphors: *Squeeze milk, out comes curds; and squeeze nose [*'ap*], out comes blood; so squeeze anger [*'appayim*], out comes strife* (30:33, lit.). Pressing on in an evil, foolish action can quickly intensify hostile emotions and lead to an outbreak of strife and violence.

THE TEXT IN BIBLICAL CONTEXT

Agur and Jesus

This chapter affords a glimpse into the mind of one of the seminal figures of the Bible. To this point Agur has not been recognized as such due to an unfortunate mistranslation of a key line of his oracle, which made him out to be saying just the opposite of what he was meaning to say. Admittedly, he writes, he had not *learned wisdom* in the sense of not being a professional sage, but he *did* have *knowledge of the Holy One* by virtue of being part of a Levite guild that for centuries had cherished the revelation of God's word to Moses. Agur was also remarkably gifted in grasping how *knowledge of the Holy One* is congruent with (and an enrichment of) all that is wise and good, as this had become known in Israel through the legacy of Solomon.

As I have grown in my understanding of the book of Proverbs, I am increasingly awed by what I observe. Two worlds often kept apart (the world of faith and the world of reason) are here united in a synthesis so unique and strong that one senses that some gifted individual must have forged it. An achievement like this does not just happen, nor does a committee create a book like this. It requires a creative individual. I have come to believe that the creative individual behind the biblical book of Proverbs is the person named in the final chapter of the Hezekiah Edition of Proverb, Agur son of Jakeh.

All we know about this individual is what we can derive from the contents of this chapter, Proverbs 30—and the literary work he and his colleagues created, the Hezekiah Edition of Proverbs. But from these two sources alone, we can begin to sense a lot about him. Might he be thought of as a forerunner of Jesus Christ? Like Jesus, he was a man of integrity whose "yes" was "yes" and "no" was "no." Like Jesus, he did not aspire to wealth but prayed that he would have only what was needed day by day. Some think there is an echo of Agur's prayer for *daily bread* (30:8b) in the prayer for daily bread Jesus taught his disciples (Matt 6:11). Like Jesus, Agur was devoted to God and hoped above everything else to honor and hallow his name (cf. 6:9).

But also like Jesus, Agur was curious and insightful about the ways of human beings. Like Jesus, he had a way with words and could express his thoughts in memorable ways. So as Jesus also did, Agur left behind a legacy of poems and parables. Those poems, like the parables of Jesus, were not so much intent on admonishing and advising, as on provoking insights and reflection.

Agur—again like Jesus—was a man of courage who stood up to the elite of his time. He had a keen appreciation of nature—again like Jesus. He observed how God made the world and every tiny creature in it. Like Jesus, he believed we could learn from these creatures and from God's actions in the world he had created. He was in awe of the mystery of human love that draws a man and woman together in a bond stronger than death. Jesus was similarly awed (Mark 10:6-9).

If it is actually true that Agur was the moving force in the creation of the Hezekiah Edition of Proverbs, then our debt to him is great. It was through him that *wisdom* was embraced as a chief attribute of those who believe in God. In this respect too, he may have been a forerunner of Jesus Christ, who taught his disciples to strive to be among the "wise" who build their house on a rock (Matt 7:24-27).

THE TEXT IN THE LIFE OF THE CHURCH

Bearing Witness to the Holy One in a Scientific Age

In this commentary one of my goals is to restore Agur's voice to its rightful place in the traditions of synagogue and church. A key conviction of Agur was that *knowledge of Holy One*, which he knew (Prov 30:3b), *is* true *knowledge* (9:10b)—and it is not just knowledge, it is the *beginning of knowledge* (1:7). Agur was a pioneer in forging a seamless bond between religion and knowledge, knowledge of God and knowledge of all aspects of life. He was bold to challenge the religious cosmologies of the wise of his time. They did not acknowledge the God revealed to Moses as the Holy One. They were still enamored by other myths and deities (like most of their "wise" counterparts at the time in Greece and India, Mesopotamia and Egypt).

In his oracle Agur's challenge to them is one of the few examples in the Bible of what we might call "demythologizing." He pressed the question of what goes on in the heavens, and declared that so far as he was concerned, there is nothing to be known in that regard by means of human observation and intelligence. At the same time he testified of his belief that a *word* had been spoken from the Holy One, who created the world. Knowledge of the Creator is possible, his poem implies, but only if the Creator speaks, and he has spoken. His *word* is that which Israel heard at Horeb. What that *word* consists of is epitomized in *words* like those in the Decalogue (Deut 5).

The book of Proverbs exemplifies the way in which Agur believed words such as these could be brought together with Solomon's wisdom and also the wisdom of others. God has spoken. The world is not for that reason less mysterious, but we do know now that there is a Holy One, who is present to those who call on his name, like a father is present to his children. This too, I think, is in essence what the church is about: bearing witness to the unity of life under God. In an age awed by scientific knowledge, believers bear witness to the reality of a divine Being, who created the world and is present to those who seek him.

In our time the issues confronting us are not mythologies of the kind Agur had to confront, but the collapse of any belief in God at all—and the ascendancy of science alone as the dominant worldview. Sehdev Kumar, environmental studies professor at the University of Waterloo, has put the challenge we are now facing as follows:

> At the dawn of the Age of Reason, in the 17th century, Blaise Pascal had observed: "There are two equally dangerous extremes: to shut reason out, and to let nothing else in." But this is precisely what has happened. Refuting earlier Christian assertions of the presence of a designer, Dr. Dawkins [Oxford biologist] insists that "natural selection—the blind, unconscious, automatic process that Darwin discovered, that we now know is the explanation for the existence and apparently purposeful form of all life—has no purpose in mind. It has no mind, and no mind's eye." And Nobel Prize winning French biologist Jacques Monod echoed the existential despair when he wrote in Chance and Necessity that man "knows at last that he is alone in the universe's unfeeling immensity, out of which he emerged only by chance." (Kumar: R14)

From Agur's personal example, as well as Proverbs as a whole, the church can derive courage to continue its witness to the God who has spoken through Moses and the prophets, through Jesus Christ and his apostles. This is a revelation of God that is beyond reason but confirmed in the daily experience of countless people throughout the world and throughout human history.

Proverbs 31:1–31

Later Additions

The Book of Proverbs, Part 3: Supplemental Collections					
"Words of the Wise" 22:17–24:22	"Also Words of the Wise" 24:23-34	"Also Proverbs of Solomon" 25:1–27:27	Hezekiah Reform Manual 28:1–29:27	"Words of Agur Son of Jakeh" 30:1-33	Later Additions 31:1-31

PREVIEW

There are two distinct units in this final chapter: *the sayings of King Lemuel's mother* (31:1-9) and a poem praising *a wife of noble character* (31:10-31). In both cases the focus is on mothers as wise teachers of their own children. This is obviously a theme compatible with what is said elsewhere in Proverbs. In the opening poems of the book, a son is invited to listen to the teachings of his own father *and* mother (1:8; 6:20). However, in those poems there is no portrayal of the mother actually teaching her son or children. That they are represented doing so here is therefore something new and unique in the pages of this manual. Perhaps the poems were added to highlight the fact (presupposed elsewhere in the book) that women too play a vital role in transmitting wisdom. Even more, these poems challenge the men of the community (31:31) to be more appreciative of this fact and of other contributions women make to their own families and to the community at large.

As to when these poems were added, there are several reasons for regarding both units as later additions and not part of the Hezekiah Edition of Proverbs. One is the already-cited evidence that points to Proverbs 30 being the closing chapter of that edition (see Preview to the Supplemental Collections). Another is the fact that the heading of this chapter (31:1) is unlike any of the preceding headings (22:17; 24:23; 25:1; 30:1): it cites first the person's name *for* whom the following sayings were intended, rather than the person who composed them. Yet another reason is the use of Aramaic words in this section, notably the Aramaic word for *son*, "one of several indications in this section of late Hebrew usage" (Cohen: 209). There is also the matter of the unique content of these units. The specific, down-to-earth advice of a queen mother to her son—plus the acrostic poem, spelling out in detail a married woman's daily activities—are unlike anything else in the book. Finally, there is the research pointing to a remarkable "fit" between the portrait of the wife-mother in 31:10-31 with what is otherwise known about the entrepreneurial freedom and dignity of married women in the Persian period (Yoder).

OUTLINE

"Words for Lemuel King of Massa,
    Which His Mother Taught Him," 31:1-9
"A Wife of Noble Character Who Can Find?" 31:10-31
    31:10-31   An Acrostic and Its Themes
    31:10-31   Portrait of a Wife of Noble Character
    31:10-31   Deserving of Recognition and Praise

EXPLANATORY NOTES

"Words for Lemuel King of Massa, Which His mother Taught Him" 31:1-9

The heading to this unit does not state that the *sayings* (lit., *words*) that follow are words *of* Lemuel (as most translations render it), but that they are *words* addressed *to* him by his mother. When a name is given followed by the title *king*, it is customary to specify of what nation he is king (as in the case of *Solomon son of David, king of Israel,* 1:1; and *Hezekiah king of Judah,* 25:1). This leads us to expect that the Hebrew word *maśśā'* designates the country over which Lemuel reigned as king. Some, however, prefer to translate the world *maśśā'* as *oracle*, its meaning in Proverbs 30:1 (NIV's preferred reading). In the heading in 30:1, however, Agur is not identified as a king and *oracle* is appropriately descriptive of his initial poem (30:2-6). In the case of 31:1, "oracle" is not at all apt for designating what Lemuel's mother taught him. His mother's words are just that, a mother's words to her own beloved son (cf. 31:2). In this instance, therefore, it is much more likely that *maśśā'* refers to the territory over which Lemuel reigned, especially since a country by that name in that region is known from biblical sources (the people of Massa, [*maśśā'*] were descendants of Abraham through Ishmael; see Gen 25:14; 1 Chr 1:30).

The words of King Lemuel's mother for her son consist of four distinct admonitions, each four lines long (31:2-3, 4-5, 6-7, 8-9). The first two advise him what *not* to do (31:2-3, 4-5); the second two advise him what he *should* be doing (31:6-7, 8-9). The first set of admonitions begins on a very emotional note. Three times Lemuel's mother addresses her son with the single word "What!" (Heb.: *mah*), as if to say, "What are you doing? What is the matter with you?" In each instance this exclamation is followed by a reminder that he is indeed her son, *my son, son of my womb, son of my vows* (son for whom I prayed; like Hannah, 1 Sam 1:11). In each instance the word used for *son* is not the usual Hebrew term *ben* but the Aramaic *bar* (perhaps a term of endearment used in her home). To scholars the word *bar* suggests a postexilic period, when Aramaic replaced Hebrew as the lingua franca of this region. The emotionality of this address is meant to give weight to the admonition that follows. King Lemuel must not expend his *strength on women* [the women of his harem], *your vigor* [lit,. *your ways*] *on those who ruin kings* [lit., *that which destroys kings*] (31:3; for similar advice, see Deut 17:17). Ironically, King Solomon (in whose book this warning now appears) was led astray by a harem just like this (see 1 Kgs 11:1-6).

In her second teaching King Lemuel's mother addresses her son by name, but simply as *Lemuel,* as a mother would speak to her son (31:4a) and mentions yet another activity that is definitely not for kings. Three times she says, *not for kings . . . , not for kings . . . , not for rulers . . .* (31:4). What she is so concerned about is that her son might *crave* (be addicted to) *beer* and *wine*. What is so terribly wrong with an addiction of this kind for kings, she points out, is that it affects their memory and judgment. They tend to *forget* what is decreed (in *the law*) and hence deprive their subjects of their rights before the law (cf. 23:29-35; Isa 5:11-12; Amos 6:5-6).

After warning her son of what to avoid, the mother in her next two poems turns to advise him on what he should be doing instead. Interestingly, her first word of counsel in a more positive vein is to point out his responsibility for providing beer and wine to *those who are perishing* (31:6a). While not appropriate for *kings*, there are those for whom alcohol may be just what is needed. The more concrete examples given are those *in anguish*, a reference perhaps to the sick and dying (31:6).

The mother's final piece of advice is an admonition to take leadership in doing what was mentioned. This would be difficult to accomplish if he was intoxicated: *Speak up* [lit., *open your mouth*] *for those who cannot speak for themselves* [lit., *the dumb*], *for the rights of all who are destitute* [lit., *sons of passing*]. "The underlying subject of the poem is a king's duty to effect justice for the poor. How easy it is for a king to squander the authority God has given him to protect the weak!" (Clifford: 270).

"A Wife of Noble Character Who Can Find?" 31:10-31

31:10-31 An Acrostic and Its Themes

The form of this concluding poem itself attests to its importance. It is an alphabetic acrostic, one of the few in the Bible. Each of its twenty-two couplets begins with a word whose first letter is a successive letter of the Hebrew alphabet. Acrostics channel the poet's desire to be thorough about a given subject (from *A* to *Z*). Elsewhere this technique is used for reflecting on large, complex themes such as adoring and serving God (Pss 25, 34, 37, 111, 112). The poet's use of the acrostic form in praise of a certain kind of woman is all the more striking.

Some believe the woman in question is both the "portrait of an ideal wife (of a great house) and, on a metaphorical level, a portrait of Woman Wisdom and what she accomplishes for those who come to her house as disciples and friends" (Clifford: 274). However, personified wisdom in Proverbs 8 and 9 is a majestic queenlike figure, while the woman described here is a down-to-earth wife and mother of the kind referred to in the book's earlier teachings on this same subject (12:4; 14:1; 18:22; 19:14). Furthermore, the poem's opening and closing lines are quite explicit about its subject matter and purpose: a wife such as the one being described is *worth far more than rubies* (31:10b) and is worthy of *praise* (31:31b). *Who can find* such a wife? (31:10a).

In the poem's opening line (31:10), a single word is used to characterize her: she is *a woman of . . . character* (Heb.: *ḥayil, valiant*); this word appears again in the latter part of the poem: *Many women do noble things* (31:29a; lit., *many daughters act valiantly* [*ḥayil*]), creating a frame for the portrait. Elsewhere in the Bible the word *ḥayil* is mostly used for men of exceptional strength, skill, and fortitude (1 Sam 14:52; Gen 47:6; Exod 18:21, 25). Only here and in Proverbs 12:4—and then one more time in Ruth 3:11—is it used of a woman. The word's core meaning is "strength" or "competence." In this context (and in Ruth), however, it is used to characterize women who are not just strong but wise and deeply caring for those around them in their families and the wider community. So the full meaning of this word in this setting is best defined by what is actually said about this *valiant* woman in the poem that follows. The poem itself defines what is meant when she is said to be a woman of *character* who is *worth far more than rubies* (31:10).

In addition to an acrostic structure, the poem has a thematic structure consisting of two equal parts of eleven two-line couplets each (31:10-20, 21-31). Each part has three stanzas (the first with three couplets, the second and third with four couplets). The opening stanza in part 1 (31:10-12) introduces the woman being praised in general terms. This is followed by a detailed picture of her at work, from early morning (four couplets, 31:13-16) to late into the evening (four couplets, 31:17-20) on a typical day. In the poem's second half, some of her wintertime activities are first described (31:21-23, 24-27). The poem concludes with the praises of her children and husband and a call for *her works* to be praised by still others *at the city gate* (31: 28-31).

31:10-31 Portrait of a Wife of Noble Character

The poem opens with a rhetorical question implying that it is beyond human wisdom to find a wife of the kind described: *A wife of noble character who can find?* (31:10). A teaching in the Main Collection makes the same point (*Houses and wealth are inherited from parents, but a prudent wife is from the LORD;* 19:14); see also the story in Genesis 24 of such a wife being found for Isaac, but only with God's help and guidance. Men who have found such wives are not loath to testify that such a wife (as described in this poem) is *worth far more than rubies* (31:10b; this is what is said about *wisdom* in Prov 3:15; 8:11).

The first more-specific thing mentioned about her is that *the heart* [*lēv*] *of her husband* [*ba'al, lord*] *trusts in her* (31:11a, lit.). This is because *she brings him good, not harm, all the days of her life* (31:12). In this general introduction the emphasis falls on the way she enhances the life and well-being of her husband during their entire life together. She is "a helper suitable for him" (Gen 2:18b). The perspective is that of the husband: "It is not good for the man to be alone" (2:18a). The *good* that she brings her husband (31:12a) is exemplified in the list of things she is said to do, morning and evening, summer and winter (31:13-27).

On a typical day, she rises early, *while it is still dark,* and begins preparing *food,* not just *for her family,* but also for the servants (31:15). During the course of the day, she may go to market, where she purchases items like wool and flax (31:13) and brings them home. She is *like the merchant ships, bringing her food from afar* (31:14). She may even, on certain days, *consider* [examine] *a field,* decide upon its purchase (lit., *take it*), and then with *her earnings* (lit., *the fruit of her hands*) make arrangements to *plant a vineyard* (31:16). She is so energetic and strong (31:17) that she continues working into the night with the help of *her lamp* (31:18). As the last activity of the day, she may weave linen cloth from the flax and wool purchased earlier (31:19; cf. 31:13). And most remarkable of all, in the midst of everything else, she finds ways of sharing with those less fortunate. *She opens her arms to the poor and extends her hands to the needy* (31:20).

As a consequence, when winter comes (*when it snows*), as it sometimes does in the highlands of Judea, she has no anxiety, for she is well prepared, having made the clothing and *bed coverings* that will now be needed by her family and herself (31:21-22). Indeed, *she can laugh at the days to come* (feel utterly confident about the future, 31:25) because *she makes linen garments* not just for herself and her family, but also for sale to *merchants* (31:24). She is justifiably proud of her accomplishments, and it shows: *She is clothed with strength and dignity* (31:25). Yet she is not domineering, for *she speaks* [lit., *her mouth she opens*] *with wisdom* [ḥokmāh], *and faithful instruction* [tôrat-ḥesed] *is on her tongue* (31:26). In summary, she *watches over* her household (attends to all the minute details involved) and thus embodies the essential qualities of a *wise woman. The wise woman builds her house, but with her own hands the foolish one tears hers down* (14:1).

31:10-31 Deserving of Recognition and Praise

The *husband,* whose trust in his wife was mentioned in the poem's opening stanza (31:11), is referred to again in the opening stanza of the poem's second half (31:23), and then again at the beginning of the final stanza (31:28). He is portrayed as a respected member of *the elders of the land* who meet at *the city gate*, the place where the elders gather to transact community business (31:23; cf. Deut 21:19; 22:15; Ruth 4:1-12). In the poem's concluding stanza the woman's husband is said to honor and bless her along with his children, but also *he praises her* in words spoken directly to her (31:28). *Many women act worthily*, he says, *but you surpass them all* (31:29, lit.).

"The concluding verses [31:30-31] are the poet's reflection upon the picture he has drawn and the lesson he wishes to impress upon the reader" (Cohen: 215). *Charm* and *beauty* are not disparaged but viewed realistically: the one (*charm*) is *deceptive* (misleading as to the true worth of a given woman), the other (*beauty*) *fleeting* (lit., *a breath*, soon gone as old age approaches). The woman to be praised is one *who fears the LORD* (31:30). With this comment the portrait is linked to the core ideals of the Hezekiah Edition of Proverbs (1:7). The poet's final comment reveals his motive for writing a poem like this. A woman such as the one just described merits being given *the fruit of her hand* (lit., merits enjoying the rewards of her labors). She deserves that *her works* be recognized and praised by other men (like her husband) who govern the community *at the city gate* (31:31).

Thus, in the end this poem is not only about the miracle of finding a wise, strong, and competent wife of the kind just described. It is also about the recognition such a wife deserves in her family and in the wider community, especially among men. Taken as a whole, the poem is an encouragement to husbands to honor their wives and praise them for the tremendous amount of good they do for them and for *the needy* in the community (31:20). This in fact is how the poem later came to be used. It is a tradition in Jewish households for this poem to be recited by the husband to his wife as part of the Sabbath evening ritual (Cohen: 211).

THE TEXT IN BIBLICAL CONTEXT

Two Portraits of Women

The two portraits of women in the texts of Proverbs 31 are different, yet overlapping. The mother of Lemuel is an actual mother, in this case, a queen mother. Her son was an actual king over an actual country or territory. In this respect she may be compared to Bathsheba, queen mother of Solomon, to whom reference is made in 4:3. In Jewish tradition King Lemuel came to be interpreted as another name for Solomon. Then as now, queen mothers were influential in the lives of their sons. Bathsheba's intervention secured the throne for her only son Solomon (1 Kgs 1:11-31). King Lemuel's mother is likewise invested in her son's success. When he was a newborn infant, she dedicated him to God (31:2), as Hannah did for her son (1 Sam 1-2). But her chief distinction is that her words of wisdom for her son, though brief, were deemed valuable enough to be preserved and eventually added to the teachings of Proverbs. There are examples of other wise women in the Bible: the "wise woman" of Tekoa (2 Sam 14:1-24); Abigail, who acts wisely (1 Sam 25); the Syro-Phoenician mother whose sharp repartee took Jesus by surprise (Mark 7:24-30). But there are no other women elsewhere in the Bible to whom a collection of wise words is attributed. In that regard, King Lemuel's mother is unique.

The other portrait of a woman is imaginary. The picture of her and her activities is idealistic, although not a fantasy. It is the portrait of a beloved wife as seen through the eyes of a grateful and admiring husband. There is nothing quite like it anywhere else in the Bible. The point at which this portrait overlaps that of King Lemuel's mother is that in both cases women are shown teaching their own children. In the case of the second portrait, however, this aspect of her role is only one of her many activities during a given day or year. A prominent feature of this portrait is how strong this woman is and how large the scope of her activities. These extend from the heart of the home to the most pressing needs of the wider community. The portrait as such is not just of a wife and mother in her domestic role, but of the way a woman like this contributes to the welfare and happiness of the whole society of which her home is a part.

The poem ends by calling upon the men of the community to recognize this contribution and see to it that a woman like this is duly honored for it. In the fifth commandment of the Decalogue, children are told to honor their fathers and mothers (Deut 5:16). And in 1 Peter 3:7, husbands are instructed to treat their wives "with respect as the weaker partner and as heirs with you of the gracious gift of life." But Proverbs 31:28-31 is the only place in the Bible where it is explicitly said that husbands should recognize and honor their wives for their many contributions to the family and the wider community.

"Charm Is Deceptive, and Beauty Is Fleeting" (31:30)

In the story of Ruth, nothing is said about her charm or beauty. We only conclude that she was beautiful because of the sheer beauty of her ways as described by the narrator. Next to the portrait in Proverbs 31:10-31, the literary portrait of Ruth in the book of Ruth is the most fully developed picture of an ideal woman in the Bible. The narrative in which this portrait is found is a literary gem. The book itself was originally the first of the Writings (Babylonian Talmud, *Baba Bathra* 14b). As such, it introduced the entire body of books in this section (Psalms, Job, Proverbs, Ecclesiastes, et al.).

Ruth is described in a way that resonates with the description of the ideal woman in Proverbs 31. "All my fellow townsmen," her future husband says to her, "know that you are a woman of noble character" (Ruth 3:11). The Hebrew term translated "noble character" is *ḥayil*, and this is the only place in the Bible where it is used of a woman apart from its use in Proverbs (12:4; 31:10, 29). Why does Boaz speak of Ruth in this manner? At the moment Boaz described her this way, she was not yet married to him. Her first husband, an Israelite whom she had married when his parents had come to Moab during a famine in Judah, was deceased (Ruth 1:1-5). She herself was a foreigner, a Moabitess, and hence from a people despised by Israelites for the way they had treated them on their way from Egypt to Canaan (Deut 23:3-6; Neh 13:1-3).

Yet Ruth was so deeply loyal to her husband and mother-in-law that when she, Naomi, decided to return to her Judean homeland, Ruth insisted on going with her. She was not only attracted to Naomi but to Naomi's God and people. She wanted to be where people worshipped Naomi's God, in the land of her deceased husband (Ruth 1:6-22). Upon arriving in Judah, she helped support Naomi and herself by working among the women who were gleaning. Boaz, who saw her there, was a relative of her husband, so in line to marry her and perpetuate the family of her deceased husband, in accordance with the traditions of the time (Ruth 2; Deut 25:5-10).

It was at the point in the story where Ruth indicated her readiness to marry Boaz that he praised her as he did for being a "woman of noble character," respected as such by all in the wider community (Ruth 3:11). She was such a woman in the eyes of the community for all the reasons for which the poem in Proverbs praises this kind of woman: for her respect for God, for the way she supported her husband's widowed mother, for her attitude toward work and marriage. Boaz praised her in a special way for not running "after the younger men, whether rich or poor" (3:10). Instead, she was conducting herself in a manner that showed respect for her deceased husband. The story ends on an exuberantly joyful note when she becomes wife to Boaz and gives birth to her firstborn child, a baby boy named Obed (4:13-16). "He was the father of Jesse, the father of David" (4:17). *Charm is deceptive, and beauty is fleeting; but a woman who fears the LORD is to be praised* (Prov 31:30).

A Mother's Advice for Her Son About Women and Beer

The teachings of King Lemuel's mother stand out in the Bible because of her passionate desire that her son conduct his royal office to the maximum benefit of his people. At that time (and since) kings tended to be autocratic, doing what they pleased. Yet there was the widespread ideal in this part of the world, ever since the days of the Mesopotamian lawgivers like Hammurabi, that kings should use their office to protect the rights of the oppressed (Weinfeld, 1995). King Lemuel's mother pleads with her son that he not be delinquent in this regard through selfish indulgence in women and strong drink. She knows how these can rob him of his strength and clarity of mind and divert him from his primary responsibilities. Her passion in this regard is the most notable thing about her sayings. She wants him to speak up for those who cannot speak for themselves: *Speak up and judge fairly* (31:9). The prophets of the Bible say something similar to the kings of their time (Jer 22:1-3, 13-17; cf. Ps 72), but here a king's mother urges her own son to live up to such standards. This is quite exceptional.

But then she does something else. She speaks to her royal son about a need in his kingdom that is not otherwise discussed in the Bible. She calls his attention to those of his subjects who are suffering and poor, not because they are oppressed, but because they are sick or dying. She tells him in no uncertain terms that he should provide them with *beer* (31:6) so that they might forget their poverty and their misery (31:7). In other words, the same compassion that prompted King Lemuel's mother to be concerned about the oppressed prompted her to be concerned for the sufferings of the sick and dying. In her wisdom she saw that although too much beer was unwise for her son, it was just what those ill or dying might need, and need desperately.

THE TEXT IN THE LIFE OF THE CHURCH

Caring for the Sick and Dying

The concern of King Lemuel's mother that her son provide beer to help those in his kingdom who were needing it to cope with the pain of serious illnesses anticipates the role that modern nations play and ought to play in providing medical services for their citizens. It also touches on issues related to the sufferings many continue to experience, especially as they approach the end of their lives. The alleviation of pain remains a challenging one in modern medical practice. I became aware of this recently in my weekly conversations with an elderly friend suffering the final ravages of an untreatable skin cancer. I mention this here because readers of the Bible may have overlooked this bit of ancient wisdom and encouragement pertaining to a still-pressing human problem.

Finding a Wife and Building a Home—Then and Now

Like the rest of the book, the final poem of Proverbs is directed to young men (see Introduction, "Why the Gender-Specific Focus"). It ends with a challenge to the men of the community (young and old) to be more affirmative of the role their wives and mothers play in their homes and in the wider community. The poem begins with a rhetorical question of special relevance to unmarried youth in particular: *A wife of noble character who can find?* (31:10a). As noted, the implied answer to this question is that no one can find such a woman without God's help. Yet the poem was undoubtedly written to evoke reflection about the kind of wife young men should be looking and praying for. As such, it evokes ideals and thoughts. It is an invitation for young men and their families (and anyone else concerned with creating good marriages and homes) to do some serious thinking about their ideals and aspirations in this regard.

How relevant is the picture it presents for modern thinking about these matters? Although coming from an ancient time and place quite different from that of most Bible readers today, the portrait is remarkably provocative. It is not assumed, for example, that one finds a wife in any prescribed way. In this sense it is open to various courtship and marriage traditions. In the culture of the time, parents played a bigger role than today, but it is clear from various proverbs that they were not the ones who made the decisions in this regard. In this sense, neither this poem nor other teachings of the book validate or reject so-called arranged marriages. What the one saying on this subject does emphasize (as implied here) is that finding a wife is one of those decisions where human reason alone is not enough. Young men should be thoughtful in this as in other decisions of their lives, and not be swept off their feet by a woman's charm. Finding a truly prudent wife who will be a true companion and helper *is from the LORD* (19:14). How young women should approach a momentous decision of this kind is not said, but it can be inferred.

Though the text at hand is somewhat vague regarding the steps to be taken in finding such a wife, it is very forthcoming in picturing what this idealized woman does, once married. Her base is her home. She has children. She is secure in the affection and esteem of her husband. From that base she operates with tremendous freedom in a number of spheres. It also paints a picture of the kind of person this idealized woman becomes. She fears God and speaks with wisdom. She dresses well and moves with a certain inner dignity and grace. The portrait contradicts the stereotypes some have of biblical attitudes toward women. She is not bound to the domestic sphere only. Her husband is not jealously watching over her as though she were some kind of possession that must do his bidding. We do not know what her husband does, but she, in any case, is seemingly involved in all aspects of the household activities, including buying and selling.

Most modern couples do not live on farms, but in houses or apartments in towns or cities. As the industrial revolution came, the husband typically went off to work in some factory or office, and the wife stayed at home and cared for the children. This produced an unnatural environment in which men and women were less involved together in the care of their children and in the total activities of the household economy. With the advent of birth control, a revolutionary change has occurred in many modern societies. This allowed women to become more involved in the world of work and men more involved in the life of the family. But still there are problems and challenges in finding a right balance. A text like this, even if from a distant time and culture, can lead us to reflect on our present circumstances and to decide whether the ideals it evokes are those we still believe in and want to realize in one way or another, with God's help.

Outline of Proverbs

PART 2: THE MAIN COLLECTION (THEMES)   10:1-22:16

To identify which section discusses a proverb in the Main Collection,
see the "Thematic Index for Poems of the Main Collection," on
pages 114-15.

**Wisdom: What It Is, Its Value, and How
   to Get It   10:1-22:16**

Wisdom: What Is It? 13:16; 14:8, 9, 15, 16; 15:2, 7; 16:21;
   18:4; 19:2; 20:1, 5; 21:24; 22:3
Wisdom: Its Value 11:22; 12:8; 13:14, 15; 15:10, 24; 16:16, 22;
   17:12; 19:8; 20:15, 16; 21:16, 22

Wisdom: How to Get It   10:8, 10, 13, 14, 17, 23; 11:2, 30;
  12:1, 15; 13:10, 13, 14, 18, 20; 14:6, 7, 17, 18, 29, 33;
  15:12, 14, 21, 31, 32; 16:25; 17:10, 16, 24; 18:2, 15;
  19:16, 20, 23, 25, 27, 29; 20:1, 12; 21:11, 24, 29

Nationhood: Kings, Courts of Law, and Civil Servants   10:1–22:16

Kings and Their Courtiers or Servants   13:17; 14:35; 15:22;
  16:10, 12, 13, 14, 15; 17:8, 11, 23; 19:6, 10, 12, 19; 20:2,
  8, 18, 26, 28; 21:1; 22:11
Courts of Law   11:10; 12:5, 17, 28; 14:5, 25; 16:33; 17:15, 23,
  26; 18:5, 17, 18; 19:5, 9, 28; 21:8, 12, 28
Qualities That Make a Nation Great   11:10, 14; 14:28, 34; 15:22;
  20:18; 21:15

Speech: Tongue, Lips, Mouth, and Words   10:1–22:16

Benefits of Knowing How to Speak Well   10:10, 11, 20, 21;
  12:14; 13:2; 16:23, 24; 18:20, 21; 22:11
Disciplined, Restrained Speaking   10:11, 19, 31, 32; 12:13, 23;
  13:3, 5; 14:3; 15:28; 16:23; 17:27, 28; 18:13; 21:23
Harmful Speech   10:18; 11:9, 11, 12, 13, 19; 12:6, 19; 16:27,
  28, 29, 30; 17:4, 7, 20; 18:6, 7, 8; 20:19
Healing Words, Wounding Words 12:18; 15:1, 4, 23; 16:24

Family: Husbands and Wives, Parents and Children   10:1–22:16

Husband-Wife Relations: Finding a Wife and Remaining
  Faithful 12:4; 14:1; 18:22; 19:13, 14; 21:9,19; 22:14
Parent-Children Relations: Having Children and How to Raise
  Them 10:1; 11:29; 13:1, 24; 15:5, 20; 17:2, 6, 21, 25;
  19:13, 18, 26; 20:7, 11, 20, 29, 30; 22:6, 15

Economics: Wealth and Poverty   10:1–22:16

Core Economic Values 10:2, 15; 11:1; 13:8, 23; 14:20, 24, 31;
  15:27; 16:11; 17:5; 18:16, 23; 19:4, 6, 7; 20:10, 23, 25;
  21:6, 14; 22:7, 9
Values of Greater Worth than Wealth 11:4; 15:16, 17; 16:8, 19;
  17:1; 19:1, 22; 22:1, 2
The Faith of Those Who Do Right 10:3, 16, 22; 11:4; 13:21, 22,
  25; 15:6; 22:4, 5

Thoughts About Making a Living 10:4, 5, 26; 11:15, 24, 25, 26,
    28; 12:11, 24, 27; 13:4, 11; 14:4, 23, 31; 15:19, 27; 17:18;
    18:9, 11; 19:15, 24; 20:4, 11, 13, 16, 17, 21; 21:5, 14, 17,
    20, 25-26; 22:2, 13, 16
Random Observations 13:7; 16:26; 20:14

Personal Relations   **10:1–22:16**
Relations Among Friends and Brothers 10:12; 12:26; 16:28; 17:9,
    13, 14, 17; 18:1, 19, 24; 20:6, 22; 21:10
Relations Among Neighbors 11:16, 17, 27; 12:10; 14:21
Relations in the Wider Community 12:16, 20; 14:9, 22; 15:18;
    16:32; 17:13, 14, 15, 19; 19:11, 19; 20:3, 22; 21:10, 21,
    24; 22:10
Treatment of Animals 12:10

Matters of the Heart   **10:1–22:16**
The Mystery of the Heart 14:10, 13; 20:27
The Heart's Impact on Health 12:25; 13:12, 19; 14:30; 15:13,
    15, 30; 17:22; 18:14
A Proud, Self-Righteous Heart 14:12; 16:18, 25; 18:12; 19:3;
    20:9; 21:4

Knowledge of the Holy One   **10:1–22:16**
God's All-Seeing Providence and Power, His "Loves" and
    "Hates" 11:20; 12:2, 22; 15:8, 9, 25, 26, 29; 14:2; 15:3, 11,
    20, 25, 33; 16:1, 2, 3, 4, 5, 7, 9; 17:3; 19:17, 21; 20:23, 24,
    25; 21:2, 3, 7, 13, 27, 30, 31; 22:12
The Contrasting Fate of Those Who Do or Do Not Serve God (the
    Upright and Wicked) 10:6, 7, 9, 24, 25, 27, 28, 29, 30; 11:3,
    5, 6, 7, 8, 18, 19, 21, 23, 31; 12:3, 5, 7, 12, 21, 28; 13:6, 9;
    14:11, 14, 19, 26, 27, 32; 16:6, 13, 17, 20, 31; 18:3,10;
    19:23; 21:7, 18, 21; 22:8

PART 3: SUPPLEMENTAL COLLECTIONS   22:17–31:31

"Words of the Wise"   **22:17–24:22**
Title and Prologue   22:17-21
For Civil Servants (the Initial Ten Teachings)   22:22–23:11
    Organization   22:22–23:11

Essays

A DISTINCTIVE APPROACH TO THE BOOK OF PROVERBS A basic thesis of this commentary is that there was an original Solomon Edition, which was substantially enlarged by the *men of Hezekiah*, mentioned in Proverbs 25:1. The idea itself is not new. The book itself alludes to just such a second edition (25:1), and in the Jewish Babylonian Talmud, Proverbs is attributed—not to Solomon—but to "Hezekiah and his colleagues" (*Baba Bathra* 15a). There are also shorter studies in which an enlarged Hezekiah Edition of Proverbs is hypothesized (Estes: 17) or explored (Bullock). In addition, the innovative commentary by McKane suggests that an older manual from the Solomon period was supplemented in the late kingship period by "biblical scholars devoted to sacred learning" (19).

What is new in this commentary is the detailed investigation of the entire book of Proverbs in the light of its Hezekiah Edition. In the course of carrying out this investigation, I made numerous corroborating observations, some of which I will highlight in the following synopses. I am doing this to aid readers and in a spirit of openness to assessment by colleagues and all who cherish these Scriptures. It should be kept in mind, however, that synopses are blunt instruments. I came to this thesis late in my research as it began to clarify textual details that had previously baffled me. The following is only a selection of these clarifications.

Clarification 1. The *men of Hezekiah* of whom we read in Proverbs 25:1 were "Levites," not "scribes" or "sages," as generally assumed *[Modern Study]*. The Levites were a priestly guild that had been set apart by Moses to be the custodian of his teachings (Deut 10:8; 33:8-11). But then Solomon dismissed them from priestly duties at Jerusalem (1 Kgs 2:26-27). They were also excluded from service at the shrines of the northern kingdom when it was founded (1 Kgs 12:31). This exclusion of the Levites from the shrines of both Israelite kingdoms had serious consequences since the priests appointed to replace them had little or no knowledge of Moses or his teachings (Miller, 1994:31-48). It was this deficit that King Hezekiah was seeking to address when reinstalling the Levites in Jerusalem at the beginning of his reforms, as we are told he did in the account in 2 Chronicles 29-31 of what transpired in these reforms.

Clarification 2. Agur son of Jakeh (30:1) was also a Levite and not a sage or skeptic, as traditionally thought. A key insight leading to this conclusion was the realization that a pivotal line in Agur's "oracle" (30:3b, *knowledge of the Holy One I know*) has been wrongly translated in modern versions. In this line (30:3b) Agur is not confessing that he *lacks knowledge of the Holy One* (as usually translated) but just the opposite; he is declaring that he has such knowledge despite the fact that he has not studied wisdom (30:3a). Agur was deeply devoted to the *words* of God revealed through the prophet Moses (30:5).

Clarification 3. Agur may have been the editor in chief of the Hezekiah Edition of Proverbs. It was for this reason that his oracle and poems were placed at the end of this edition. This was the traditional way of identifying the author or editor of a scroll. If he was editor in chief, one might expect to see links between Agur's *words* in Proverbs 30 and the rest of the book. In this commentary I try to indicate that such "links" do exist. The most obvious and important are the way the second line of the watchword in 9:10 (*knowledge of the Holy One is understanding*) matches the pivotal line of Agur's oracle in 30:3b (*knowledge of the Holy One I know*).

Clarification 4. The *men of Hezekiah* designed their new edition of Proverbs with meticulous care in order to highlight key convictions. The supplements they added within the Introductory Collection in chapters 1-9 expanded it to the point where it was virtually equal in size to the Supplemental Collections they added in 22:17–30:33 at the end of the Main Collection. I conjecture that their purpose in doing this was so that the Main Collection in 10:1–22:16 would be at the exact center of their new edition. And then, in addition, the Main Collection was also designed so that a series of profound statements about Yahweh, the God of Israel, would be at the exact center of that collection (16:2-6). My hypothesis is that scrolls were kept rolled up from both ends and therefore, when opened, the words at the exact center would be the first to be seen.

Clarification 5. The *men of Hezekiah* added all the appendixes in 22:17–31:31 except for the final poems in Proverbs 31. The manner in which they appended these Supplemental Collections in this third part of the book is more or less apparent from an analysis of the editorial markers used to head each added collection. The clarification in this instance is that all these supplements (22:17–30:33) were added at the time the Hezekiah Edition was created. Viewing them with this in mind sheds light on why they were added and why the individual collections themselves were edited and supplemented as they seemingly were.

Clarification 6. The *men of Hezekiah* also supplemented the Introductory Collection in Proverbs 1-9 and did so in ways that can be readily identified. There is no consensus as to compositional profile or history of these chapters. The thesis presented in this commentary is that blocks of poems belonging to the original Solomon Edition can be readily identified once the distinctive linguistic and theological "fingerprints" of the Hezekiah Edition supplements are recognized *[Solomon Edition].*

Clarification 7. When we become acquainted with the extent to which the *men of Hezekiah* supplemented an initial Solomon Edition of Proverbs, we can compare the two editions and thereby get a sharper focus on what the purposes of each edition was. Then we see how the Hezekiah Edition editors interacted with the contents of the older edition. An example is the watchword that now frames the Hezekiah Edition of this book: *the fear of Yahweh is the beginning of knowledge/wisdom* (1:7; 9:10; 30:3). This watchword appears to be a deliberate attempt on the part of the Hezekiah Edition editors at qualifying (without negating) the watchword of the Solomon Edition in 4:7 (lit.): *Wisdom is the beginning*. When comparing the two editions, one becomes aware of many instances of this kind where the Hezekiah Edition editors seem to be interacting with the legacy of the Solomon Edition poems.

Clarification 8. Recovering the contours of the original Solomon Edition has made it possible to examine that version of the book in its own right. When we realize, for example, that the poems in 4:1–5:14 (followed by most of the poems in 7:24–9:18) might have constituted the introductory poems of the Solomon Edition, we begin to recognize both the form and content of these chapters *[Solomon Edition]*. In that light it becomes apparent that the "voice" in that original edition is that of Solomon himself (4:1-3). As well, the reference at the end of this set of poems to *teachers* and *instructors* (5:13) can be taken at face value. There has been a great deal of discussion about whether there were royal schools at the time of Solomon where instructions of this kind were utilized. When we realize that the poems in 4:1–5:14 might have served to introduce the Solomon Edition of Proverbs, it seems all the more evident that there were, and that the original manual was created for the students of these schools.

Clarification 9. Being able to identify what the *men of Hezekiah* added enables us to see that their edition was created, not just for the royal schools, but also for a type of homeschooling in wisdom in which both parents played key roles. In fact, this seems to have been one of the pedagogical strategies of the Hezekiah reformers. There is striking parallelism in what is intimated in this regard in Proverbs and what is advocated in Deuteronomy with respect to parents homeschooling their children in the "words" of God in the teachings of Moses (Deut 6:6-9; 11:18-20). Since Deuteronomy is an edition of Moses' words that was likely published in its present form during Hezekiah's reforms *[Hezekiah Reform Literature]*, it may be that the Hezekiah Edition of Proverbs was meant to be a companion volume to Deuteronomy in a curriculum for homeschooling.

Clarification 10. It is enlightening to read Proverbs not just as a companion of Deuteronomy but also of other books produced in the period of Hezekiah's reforms *[Hezekiah Reform Literature]*. These books have many things in common: the same historical background, the same momentous goal of reforming the Judean kingdom, the same monotheistic ideals, and the same hope for the wider world (Miller, 2004:19-25). Keeping this in mind sensitizes readers to the unique place Proverbs has within this reform literature and within the Bible as a whole—and within the unfolding drama of world religions *[Proverbs and the Birth of Ethical Monotheism]*.

GENRE ISSUES IN PROVERBS The *proverbs* in the book of Proverbs are sometimes likened to "folk sayings" and viewed as having their closest parallels in an "indigenous wisdom" that goes back "to the early history of the [Israelite] tribes" (Golka: 15). Those who espouse this perspective view wisdom as "a human trait, an element of our createdness" (Westermann: 1).

They note the many "correspondences" that exist "between the sayings of Proverbs 10-31 and the proverbs of diverse peoples," especially folk sayings from Africa (Westermann: 140; Golka). There are folk sayings in the OT, such as the following: "As is the man, so is his strength" (Judg 8:21). "From evil-doers come evil deeds" (1 Sam 24:13). "One who puts on his armor should not boast like one who takes it off" (1 Kgs 20:11). And there are similarities between sayings of this kind and those in Proverbs 10:1–22:16. In both instances the sayings are terse and allusive and formulate down-to-earth truths about life.

Nevertheless, there are also marked differences. Folk sayings are generally shorter than the sayings in Proverbs and are transmitted orally. No one knows who their authors are or when or how they originated. They are not usually assembled and studied. This is not the case with the sayings in Proverbs 10:1–22:16 or the sayings and poems elsewhere in Proverbs. All are attributed to some author or source. They are assembled in a book whose stated purpose is the instruction of young men. When contemporary literary scholars study these "proverbs," they characterize them as carefully crafted "poetic compositions" that are marked by "elevated speech" and "features of special linguistic order." This is not to say that all of them are poetic master-pieces, but "some of them are artful to the point of being real literary art." There is a basic literary pattern, that of "the binary proverb, which is composed of two members or phrases drawn together into a sort of parallelism" (Williams: 270).

The 375 "bicolon proverbs" of the Main Collection (10:1–22:16) have been characterized as a unique "subgenre" in the literature of the time (Clifford: 19). Von Rad refers to them as "thought rhymes," their aim being not as much "conceptual precision as . . . precision in the reproduction of the subject matter, if possible over its whole range" (1972:27). The precise genre of the poems in the Supplemental Collections (22:17–31:31) varies from collection to collection. The first of these collections (22:17–24:23) is strikingly similar to the instruction literature of Egypt, "a popular genre throughout the entire history of ancient Egypt" (Clifford: 14). In the Introductory Collection (chs. 1-9) the two-line sayings have been combined into longer poems of varied length and sometimes exquisite design (see notes). In my opinion it is a mistake to call them "lectures," as does Fox (45); instead, they are intricate didactic poems.

The oldest poems are ascribed to the historical Solomon [Solomon Edition]. His reign has been described as an "enlightenment" during which a "creative upsurge" occurred that left its mark on the whole subsequent history of Israelite thought and culture (von Rad, 1962:51). Such an epoch-making "upsurge" does not occur in a vacuum. I see no reason to deny Solomon his rightful role in this "upsurge." His poems personifying wisdom are unique in the literature of the time [Personified Wisdom]. Many of his poems bear the stamp of a gifted poet. Although the focus of this commentary is on the Hezekiah Edition of Proverbs, it is important to give credit where credit is due and not fail to honor the literary legacy of Solomon, Israel's most prolific poet-king (1 Kgs 4:29-34).

"HEART" IN PROVERBS The Hebrew term "heart" (lēb) is not simply a metaphor for feelings or emotions but also refers to the actual place in the body where thinking occurs and wisdom is born. How the heart was viewed at the time is spelled out in a lucid text from ancient Egypt, which describes how the heart is related to other bodily organs in performing its task:

> The sight of the eyes, the hearing of the ears, and the smelling the air by the nose, they report to the heart. It is this [the heart] which causes every completed (concept) to come forth, and it is the tongue which announces what the heart thinks. ("The Theology of Memphis," Pritchard: 5)

In other words the heart receives factual knowledge from the surrounding world, reflects on it, and then, through speech, expresses the conclusions drawn. The heart is the bodily organ by means of which the raw data of experience is shaped into thoughts, concepts, or judgments.

This will explain why the poem in Proverbs 4:20-27 describes the *heart* as *the wellspring of life* (4:23b). The thoughts of the heart are vital to the health and vitality of the whole body. That too is why those who lack wisdom are spoken of in Proverbs (and in Egyptian literature) as *lacking heart* (7:7; NIV: *judgment*). They lack the capacity or willingness to think things through and come forth with realistic judgments or thoughts *[Words for Wisdom and Folly]*. In his *Anthropology of the Old Testament,* Hans Walther Wolff has shown that in most cases in the Bible where the term "heart" is used, "intellectual, rational functions" are ascribed to it, "precisely what we ascribe to the head and, more exactly, to the brain" (1 Sam 25:37).

For this reason it is no accident, Wolff continues, that the term *heart* "occurs by far the most frequently in the wisdom literature of the Bible—99 times in Proverbs alone, 42 times in Ecclesiastes, and in the strongly didactic Deuteronomy 51 times" (Wolff: 46-47; see also proverbs on the theme "Matters of the Heart," in the Main Collection). That too is why the admonition to *guard your heart above all else* (4:23) may be thought of as one of the core challenges of the book of Proverbs. To *guard your heart* is "a fundamental precept, like Socrates' 'know thyself'" (R. Van Leeuwen, 1997:61).

HEBREW AND GREEK TEXTS   The standard Hebrew text of Proverbs (on which this commentary is based) is one that first-century rabbis chose for transmission; it is best preserved in the Leningrad Codex (AD 1008/9). The only other Hebrew texts of this book are mere fragments that were found among the manuscripts in Cave 4 at Qumran. These date to the first century AD and are similar to the standard Hebrew text, except for a few "inadvertent" variants (Abegg, Flint, and Ulrich: 594).

A Greek translation of the Hebrew Scriptures was made in the third century BC (the so-called Septuagint version). In some instances this can be helpful in reconstructing or interpreting the Hebrew text. However, this is not as much the case with Proverbs because of the "creativity" of the translators in this instance (McKane: 33-35). A notable example is the way they sequenced the book's appended collections in Proverbs 22:17–31:31, in a different order: 22:17–24:22; 30:1-14; 24:23-34; 30:15-33; 31:1-9; 25:1–29:27; 31:10-31. The Greek translators were either working with a different Hebrew text of the book than the one the first-century rabbis chose or were rearranging its appendices as they saw fit. The latter seems to be the case, since the arrangement of these appendices in the standard Hebrew version is meaningful (see notes).

Students of this Greek version cite many similar examples of freedoms taken by its translators (Clifford: 28-29). There is general agreement that the Greek version of Proverbs "can only be used with great caution" (Whybray, 1994:19).

HEZEKIAH REFORM LITERATURE There is a growing recognition that the period of Hezekiah's reforms was a time of intense literary activity in Judah, during which key biblical books were produced in the approximate form we still have them (Schniedewind, 2000:330; 2004:64-117). This period therefore qualifies as the first of three major canon-forming epochs, during which the books of the Bible were assembled and became authoritative. The other two were the aftermath of the second temple reforms of Ezra and Nehemiah and the period several centuries later (in the second century AD) when the church added a collection of Christian Scriptures to the Scriptures of Judaism and published them in a single codex (Miller: 2004).

Among the books produced in the period of Hezekiah's reforms, Proverbs is the only one explicitly identified as belonging to this epoch (25:1). However, there are compelling reasons for thinking that a version of Deuteronomy ("words of Moses") was published at this time to serve as the state constitution for the reformed kingdom. It is the only law code that specifies what the king should do in his governance of the nation (Deut 17:14-20). A century after the collapse of Hezekiah's reforms, it was rediscovered during the reign of King Josiah and served as the state constitution for his reformed kingdom (2 Kgs 22:1–23:25).

One of the most ambitious literary productions of this period is a history of Israel's sojourn in Canaan, as set forth in Joshua, Judges, 1 and 2 Samuel, and 1 and 2 Kings. Close to the end of this multivolume work, we learn of Hezekiah's reforms and what led up to them. Some believe an initial edition of this history ended with the dramatic story in 2 Kings 18-19 of how God vindicated Hezekiah's faith and reforms by delivering Judah from the Assyrians. Indeed, this may have been a major reason why this history was compiled: to provide a rationale for Hezekiah's bold actions. At the time Judeans must have faced an urgent question: What gave Hezekiah the right to rescind the policies toward worshipping "other gods" that the renowned Solomon had put in place? This history gives a clear and forceful answer. It relates how Solomon's policies toward other gods not only violated those of his father, David, but also the teachings of Moses and Joshua, the nation's founding leaders. It also tells in graphic detail how disastrous were the consequences of Solomon's more lenient policies—the destruction of the northern kingdom (Israel) by the Assyrians was seen as a direct result of worshipping other gods (2 Kgs 17). By simply relating this story and then adding the story of Hezekiah's reforms and their miraculous aftermath (2 Kgs 18-20), the authors of this history conveyed a vital message: these reforms were essential for Judah's survival.

In the years leading up to and during these reforms, a cluster of prophets were speaking: Amos, Hosea, Micah, and Isaiah. It is highly probable that first editions of their oracles were published at this time as well, to serve as warnings to the nation of what would happen if the reforms were unsuccessful, and to envision what to hope for if they were successful. There is much to suggest that Book 1 (Pss 1-41) and 2 (Pss 42-72) of the Psalter were also published at this time. This amounted to an expanded edition of "the prayers of David"

(Ps 72:20), somewhat like the enlarged edition of *the proverbs of Solomon* (Prov 25:1). The diversity and depth of the Hezekiah reform literature is truly amazing. A broad range of needs and concerns are addressed, from educating youth to issues involved in the governance of a nation, from understanding the past to envisioning the future, from personal prayers to public worship.

IDENTITY OF THE FOREIGN SEDUCTRESS There are repetitious warnings against the solicitations of a certain kind of woman in the introductory poems of Proverbs (2:16-22; 5:1-14, 15-23; 6:20-29, 30-35; 7:1-23, 24-27). Since the Hebrew terms used to identify her (*zārāh* and *nokriyyāh*) are ambiguous, debates rage over precisely what type of woman she is. They are variously translated as "foreigner," "stranger," "outsider," or with the presumption that she is married, some translate "adulteress." She has been understood in no less than six different ways (Fox: 134): as (1) a foreign and secular harlot, (2) a foreign devotee of a foreign god, (3) a foreign goddess, (4) a social outsider, (5) a native prostitute, and (6) another man's wife.

In the opinion of Fox, only the sixth of these options is credible. This assessment is supported by the way Egyptian manuals describe the same type of woman. There she is said to be "a woman from abroad, who is not known in her (own) town, . . . a woman who is far away from her husband" (The Instruction of Ani, Pritchard: 420). She therefore is, strictly speaking, not a "foreigner" but a married woman away from home in search of an affair with a man other than her husband. This too is the picture of her in the one place in Proverbs where she is more fully described, the story told in 7:10-23. However, in the picture drawn of her there, her husband is the one who is away from home, so that in this case she feels free to invite a gullible young man to her own home for the night without fear of being discovered.

Prior discussions of this "seductress" have not differentiated between the way she is described in the Solomon Edition poems in 5:1-13 and the way she is described in the Hezekiah Edition supplements *[Distinctive Approach]*. In the Solomon Edition poems, she is portrayed as a seductive woman away from home, exactly as in the manuals of Egypt. In the Hezekiah Edition supplements, she is referred to as the wife of a neighbor (Prov 6:29; Deut 5:21). In describing her actions, the terms for adultery in the Decalogue are used (Deut 5:18; cf. Prov 2:17; 6:32). Moreover, the son is warned not just against spending a night with her but also against "lusting" after her, also as in the Decalogue (Deut 5:21; cf. Prov 6:25). In this instance the Solomon Edition poems provided the Hezekiah Edition editors with a theme that could be readily adapted and developed along lines indicated in the "words" of God revealed at Horeb and now recorded in Deuteronomy (ch. 5).

MIDDLE POEMS OF THE MAIN COLLECTION Most agree that the poems of the Main Collection of Proverbs (10:1–22:16) are made up of two distinct sub-collections (10:1–15:33; 16:1–22:16), and that the poems in the middle (15:33–16:7) function in some sense as a suture (see Overview to the Main Collection). There is otherwise no consensus as to why they are arranged as they are. My own analysis has led me to think that its 375 poems might have been compiled to be studied five poems at a time, and that there are 37 five-poem panels in part 1 and 37 five-poem panels in part 2, with a five-poem panel at the center (16:2-6). My thesis is that this symmetrical design is related to the fact that larger scrolls of this kind were kept rolled up from both ends. When opened for reading, therefore, their middle columns would be the first to be seen (see Introduction, "Purpose and Design of the Hezekiah Edition").

This being the case, the five poems in the middle merit special attention. I conjecture that they were inserted here for the purpose of being seen and pondered every time the scroll was opened. A closer analysis suggests that these five poems are the middle section of an eight-verse poem. The poem begins in 15:33 and ends with 16:7. Each of its verses mentions *Yahweh* by name. These eight two-line verses are grouped in two stanzas of four verses each (stanza 1 is 15:33–16:3; stanza 2 is 16:4-7). Each of the two stanzas has a distinct theme. As such, it resembles the poem in Proverbs 3:1-12, which also has two-line verses grouped into stanzas of four verses each (3:1-4, 5-8, 9-12). The contents of these two poems overlap as well: at the center of each is an invitation to put one's trust in *Yahweh* (3:5; 16:3).

When we take a closer look at this eight-verse poem inserted in the middle, we observe that the poem's first stanza (15:33–16:3) begins with a statement of principle: *Fear of Yahweh is instruction in wisdom* (15:33a, lit.). Next is a line stressing the importance of *humility* for instruction of this kind (15:33b). This opening verse thus closely resembles the watchwords that frame the Introductory Collection of the Hezekiah Edition (1:7; 10:9). Verses 2 and 3 of the first stanza of this poem (16:1-2) dissect the intricate ways in which those who actually do fear Yahweh go about pursuing their studies. This poet realizes that thinking and planning are aspects of being human (*To man* [*'ādām*] *belong the plans of the heart;* 16:1a). But he is also conscious of the mysterious ways in which God is present to aid and help: *but from the LORD comes the reply of the tongue* (16:1b). For this reason the poet is on guard against the human inclination to be smug and self-content (*All a man's ways seem innocent to him;* 16:2a), knowing that even the innermost *motives are weighed by the LORD* (16:2b). The climactic line of the poem's first stanza is a bold invitation to the book's reader (*you*) to make a decision with regard to these matters. *Commit to the Lord whatever you do* (16:3a), literally, *Roll onto* [*gō'el*] *the LORD whatever you do*, in the sense of turning over to him *your plans* and projects for appraisal and help in establishing them (16:3b; cf. 3:6; Ps 90:17).

The poem's second stanza (Prov 16:4-7) begins with the verse that is at the exact center of the Main Collection (16:4). Through the placement of the word *everything* at the forefront of its first line (in Heb.), it emphasizes that *everything* created by Yahweh is according to his purpose—*even the wicked for a day of disaster* (16:4, lit.). The point being made is that Yahweh is sovereign everywhere. "There is nothing aimless in the world" (Cohen: 103). This point is clarified in the following three verses (16:5-7). Because *everything the LORD created is according to his purpose,* the *proud in heart* should be sure of this: *They will not go unpunished* (16:5). On the other hand, through *love and faithfulness* [devotion to God] *sin is atoned for* (16:6a; cf. Hos 6:6). *Through fear of the LORD a man avoids evil* (Prov 16:6b; lit., *turns from evil*). And when that happens, miraculous things occur: *When a man's ways are pleasing to the LORD, he makes even his enemies live at peace with him* (16:7).

In brief, the second stanza of this two-stanza poem conveys an assurance of God's beneficent presence with those who pursue *wisdom* in the God-fearing manner described in the poem's first stanza (15:33–16:3). The middle poems of the Main Collection are a thought-provoking statement of the pedagogical perspectives of those who created the Hezekiah Edition of Proverbs.

MODERN STUDY OF THE BOOK OF PROVERBS In a major survey of the modern study of Proverbs in the twentieth century, Whybray writes that by "the mid-nineteenth century the critical study of Proverbs in the modern sense of that term was already well into its stride. The traditional view that Solomon was the author of the whole book was still a subject of discussion, but had in general given way to theories of multiple authorship extending over a considerable period" (1995:1). An overriding question of that initial period was why Proverbs, as well as Job and Ecclesiastes, differed so markedly from other books in the Hebrew Bible in their lack of concern with Israel and the Israelites. This lack made it problematic to place Proverbs "in the history of Israelite thought and religion." A proposed answer was that Proverbs in its final form is "a product of a very late stage in Israel's intellectual development" (Whybray, 1995:1).

Whybray notes that "the main cause of the difficulty faced by scholars of this period in finding a place for Proverbs and the other Old Testament wisdom books within their developmental scheme of the history of the religion of Israel was that there was no known literature with which these books could really be compared" (1995:2). For this reason, he suggests, "a new era in the study of the Book of Proverbs and indeed of Old Testament wisdom literature as a whole began with the publication in 1923 by E. W. Budge of an Egyptian 'wisdom' text which came to be known as The Instruction of Amenemope (Papyrus 1047 in the British museum)." It was only in the light of this discovery that the book of Proverbs "was now seen to belong to an age-old international tradition and to be the product of a particular social and professional class—that of the scribes" (1995:6).

This discovery alone "removed the book from the unsatisfactory classification of post-exilic manual of morals to which it had previously been consigned, . . . making it possible to see it for the first time as an example of an international current of thought and literature which was of great antiquity but was still actively flowing in Israel's own time." Whybray observes that "this led in turn to a virtual consensus about its provenance: on the analogy of Egyptian and Mesopotamian models, it was seen as an upper-class phenomenon, associated with the royal court, with school education and especially with the scribal profession" (1995:32-33).

However, noting the affinities of Proverbs with the literature of other peoples did not resolve earlier questions about how the teachings of this book relate to the theological perspectives of most other writings in the Hebrew Bible. At first the book's teaching "was widely taken to be purely human and its tone purely utilitarian or eudaemonistic—concerned only with inculcating useful advice on how to achieve material success, with no real ethical content. Subsequently, however, as the nature of the Egyptian Instructions was more fully understood, this view came to be seen as mistaken: the Egyptian literature itself in fact had significant religious and ethical features and was not purely utilitarian in intention. There [in Egypt] as well as in the ancient world in general, there was no notion of a distinction between the secular and the religious" (Whybray, 1995:147).

Thus, at the end of the period surveyed by Whybray, scholars' attitudes toward the book of Proverbs are quite different from what they were before 1923, when realization dawned that the book was related to a wider body of literature in the ancient Near East. Now there is an almost universal recognition that the teachings in the book are from Israel's kingdom period. But regarding how or why the book was created in the first place, or how it achieved its present form, there is still no consensus apart from vague suggestions that "the book is the work of a number of different authors of different periods" (Whybray, 1995:150).

Whybray's concluding reflections on the reasons for this impasse are indicative of the present state of scholarship on Proverbs. It is "undeniable," he writes, that the book of Proverbs "contains almost no obvious links with the normative faith of Israel: there are no references to Israel and its political or religious history, and few to its institutions; no Israelite proper names occur in it apart from those of Solomon and Hezekiah. Moreover, although it knows of only one God, Yahweh, it presents that deity in terms that may not appear to permit a specific link with the Yahweh of the rest of the Old Testament." Whybray concludes, "It may be correct, as some writers have suggested, to regard it as expressing a faith *parallel* with or, in a sense, *alternative* to the more traditional forms of Yahwism." Yet, he says, "it is difficult to pinpoint its religious thought in the context of any particular stage in the development of Yahwistic theology" (1995:150).

It is the opinion of Roland Murphy, in a series of more recent surveys of the pertinent literature, that not much has changed in the study of Proverbs since 1995, when Whybray's overview was published. There is still generalized uncertainty about the book's compositional history, and hence also about where it fits into the spectrum of biblical traditions and theology. No one doubts that the book was formed in stages, nor that, "sages" (or "scribes") had a hand in its transmission. But who these sages were, Murphy admits, is still unanswered (2002:231). In his opinion, this might be the wrong question: instead of asking who the sages were, perhaps we should be asking, "What is Wisdom?" The term "sage," he writes, "is more applicable to the traditional 'Solomonic' works," but wisdom in Proverbs is obviously multifaceted (Murphy, 2002:231-32). However, without knowing who the "sages" were who transmitted this book—or what their goals were in producing it in its present form—it is difficult to pin down exactly what the multifaceted *wisdom* is that is being promulgated. So the uncertainties that have plagued the study of this book over the past century continue to the present time. In this context the "distinctive approach" advanced in this commentary seeks to make a clarifying contribution *[Distinctive Approach]*.

PERSONIFICATION OF "WISDOM" IN PROVERBS   Scholars have searched in vain for a cultural background that might illuminate the vibrant personification of wisdom in the poems in Proverbs 8 and 9. As do many, Bruce Waltke believes the strongest parallels are with the Egyptian concept of a "fixed, eternal righteous order" that manifests itself in human society as justice and truth (61). He points out that the Egyptian term for wisdom, *ma'at*, like Hebrew *ḥokmāh,* lies at the heart of the instruction manuals of Egypt. In Egyptian mythology, *ma'at* is personified as the daughter of Re, the sun-god. But in the opening section of the oldest manual of this kind from that region, The Instruction of the Vizier Ptah-hotep, she is described in the following terms: "*Ma'at* (justice) is good and its worth is lasting. It has not been disturbed since the day of its creator, whereas he who transgresses its ordinances is punished. It lies as a path in front even of him who knows nothing" (cf. Pritchard: 412).

These sentiments regarding *ma'at* in Egyptian instruction do not begin to approach the vibrancy with which wisdom is personified in the poems of Solomon. In Solomon's poems *wisdom* is fully alive. She speaks in a personal voice so powerful and appealing that we forget that she is a literary fiction. Roland Murphy is of the opinion that "research [on this subject] has been more successful in devising theories than in proposing a convincing explanation for the origin of the personification of Woman Wisdom." He adds that this assessment "by no means" excludes the possibility of "outside influence upon the figure of Wisdom, but it should be recognized that there is great uncertainty on this score." In other words, he adds, the biblical presentation of *wisdom* in these texts is "independent enough to be heard largely on its own as something new and unique" (1998:279). Clifford seems to agree: "Some influence is certainly possible, but personified Wisdom in Proverbs has a vigor and personality that goes far beyond the abstract Egyptian goddess" (14).

This conclusion is consistent with the representation of the texts themselves. It is the thesis of this commentary that the poems in Proverbs 8 and 9 in which *wisdom* is personified so majestically (minus a few inserts) were the climactic poems of the introduction to an original Solomon Edition of Proverbs. I have concluded that these poems were authored by Solomon himself *[Solomon Edition]*. If correct, this would mean that in these texts wisdom is personified in such a vibrant, powerful way because it was in precisely these terms that the historical Solomon imagined her. They reflect his unique and extraordinary poetic imagination. They are a window as well into his worldview, one in which God is gloriously mysterious (Prov 25:2) and *wisdom* plays the paramount role in instructing humanity about how to find life and avoid death (8:32-36).

PROVERBS AND THE BIRTH OF ETHICAL MONOTHEISM The literature of King Hezekiah's reforms *[Hezekiah Reform Literature]* marks a momentous new development in the life of Israel and the world. As never before, this literature challenges the state policies begun by Solomon of allowing "other gods" besides Yahweh (God of Israel) to be worshipped (1 Kgs 11:1-10). For this reason the historians of the period wrote of Hezekiah himself that "there was no one like him among all the kings of Judah, either before him or after him" (2 Kgs 18:5). Readers do not always realize how deeply mired in the cults of these other gods the Israelites had become in the intervening centuries, even though the histories of the period recite their names. They included "Ashtoreth the goddess of the Sidonians, and Molech the detestable god of the Ammonites"; "Chemosh the detestable god of Moab" (1 Kgs 11:5, 7; 2 Kgs 23:13); and "Baal and Asherah and all the starry hosts" (2 Kgs 23:4-7; 18:4). Most were personifications of nature (fertility, death, wind, storm, sun, moon, or stars). They required of their worshippers not basic goodness but "incense" or breads or animal sacrifices (Jer 7:17-19), or even children (1 Kgs 11:5, 33; 2 Kgs 16:3; 23:10; Jer 19:1-6; Ezek 16:20), or consorting with sacred prostitutes (Amos 2:7-8; Hos 4:10-14; 2 Kgs 23:7).

Only in divine "words" revealed to Moses (words that were carefully transmitted through the centuries by his Levite followers) was there a compelling religious alternative. But before Hezekiah's reforms this option was unknown in the wider world and only intermittently within the Israelite kingdoms themselves. One reason was Solomon's dismissal of the Levites from the Jerusalem temple (1 Kgs 2:26-27) and their exclusion as well from the shrines of the northern Israelite kingdom when it was founded (1 Kgs 12:31; Miller, 1994:47-48). The result was that, at the time of Hezekiah's reforms, both Israelite kingdoms were awash in the worship of other gods to such an extent that Israel's historians identify this as the chief reason for their nearly total destruction by the armies of Assyria (2 Kgs 17:18-20).

It is against this background that we can take full measure of the place of the Hezekiah Edition of Proverbs within the religious history of Israel, the church, and the world *[Hezekiah Reform Literature]*. The innovative literature of Hezekiah's reforms functioned in diverse ways in support of a radical new approach to the religious life of Judah. It adopted the "words" of Moses in Deuteronomy as the state charter and guide (Deut 17:14-20). It took the account of Israel's history in Canaan in Joshua, Judges, Samuel, and Kings as an explanation of why Hezekiah's reforms were so urgently needed. It claimed the God-centered "prayers of David" (Pss 1–72; 72:20) as a devotional resource for a renewed personal and corporate worship. It accepted the oracles of certain prophets as additional sources of guidance and hope (Hosea; Amos; Mic 1-3; Isa 1-39). And last but not least, the Hezekiah Edition of Proverbs was produced to serve as a resource for inculcating in the minds and hearts of young men the monotheistic God-centered wisdom needed for building thriving peaceful households and societies *[Distinctive Approach]*.

Thus, in Proverbs the foundations were laid for what Jewish and Christian scholars have sometimes termed "ethical monotheism" (Vial and Hadley). This is a way of viewing the world and the whole of life from the carefully thought through perspective of a single holy God (Prov 9:10; 30:3, notes), who is involved in everything that happens (16:4). This Deity (*Yahweh*) is no mere personification of this or that aspect of nature, but as Creator of all that exists (3:19-20), he belongs to an invisible realm beyond imagination (Deut 5:8). Yet he has spoken and in speaking revealed his name and his will (Deut 5:1-21). Furthermore, in his dealings with Israel, Yahweh has proved himself to be fatherlike in his compassion and guidance (Prov 3:12). He can be called upon and trusted; he is personally present to everyone everywhere (3:5; 16:1, 2) and attentive to their prayers (15:29). His supreme desire is that human beings "enjoy the good life," which is why he led Israel into such a good land (Martens: 19). Revering him *teaches a man wisdom* (15:33a), and *from his mouth come knowledge and understanding* (2:6b). The *fear* of him is the *beginning of wisdom* (9:10) *[Middle Poems]*.

To have grasped this truth about God's universal sovereignty, love, and concern for humanity so firmly and integrated it with the rich legacy of Solomon's wisdom about life so seamlessly (in their version of the book) is the great gift to humanity from those who created the Hezekiah Edition of Proverbs.

SOLOMON EDITION OF PROVERBS *Contents.* One of the theses of this commentary is that the blocks of poems remaining in the book of Proverbs after the Hezekiah Edition supplements are identified and removed belong to an older Solomon Edition of Proverbs. When this separation is done, most of the poems remaining in Proverbs 1-9 are those that served as an introduction to the original Solomon Edition of Proverbs (see chart below).

Just how many poems were added to the Main Collection (10:1–22:16) is less clear, but it might be conjectured that since more Solomon poems were added in chapters 25-27, few if any of his poems in the Main Collection would have been deleted. Except therefore for the poems in this section with the earmarks of the Hezekiah Edition editors (about a third of them allude to fearing or serving Yahweh), it may be assumed that the rest are Solomon Edition poems. So we can imagine that the Main Collection of the Solomon Edition was fairly large. But that was it—there were no appendixes.

Solomon Edition Poems	Hezekiah Edition Inserts and Supplements
Prologue (1:1-7) 1:1-4, 6	**Prologue (1:1-7)** 1:5, 7 (inserts)
Introductory Collection (1:8–9:18) 4:1–5:14 7:24–8:12 8:14–9:6 9:13-18	**Introductory Collection (1:8–9:18)** 1:8–3:35 (supplements) 5:15–7:23 (supplements) 8:13 (insert) 9:7-12 (supplement)
Main Collection (10:1–22:6)	**Main Collection (10:1–22:16)** 10:1–22:16 (many supplemental inserts) 22:17–30:33 (supplemental collections) 31:1-31 (later post-Hezekiah additions)

Description. The characteristics of the Solomon Edition of Proverbs may be derived not only from its preface and its introductory poems in chapters 1-9, but also from the added poems of Solomon in chapters 25-27, since they too reflect its values and worldview (see notes). When we read the Solomon Edition poems in chapters 1-9, it immediately becomes apparent to us that this initial manual originated with Solomon himself, and that he is the one speaking in its opening verses in 4:1-3. Evident as well is that the *sons* Solomon addresses in this part of the book are not *his* sons but students in the royal schools (5:7-14).

The worldview enunciated is that *wisdom is supreme* [the beginning or starting point]; *therefore get wisdom* (4:7). Wisdom is personified as a powerful queenlike figure, with Yahweh from the dawn of creation and present throughout the universe (Prov 8). It is wisdom, therefore, who dispenses life and blessing to those who watch daily at the doors of her house (8:32-36). Yahweh is seldom mentioned—not because he is forgotten or unimportant, but because of a philosophical premise: *It is the glory of God to conceal a matter; to search out a matter is the glory of kings* (25:1). While Yahweh is the Creator of the universe, wisdom is the life-giving force that reveals itself to the inquiring minds of kings (25:2b-3) and all who follow their example by watching *daily* at wisdom's *doors* (8:34; NRSV: *gates*).

TRANSLATION ISSUES IN PROVERBS There is a tendency among translators of the book of Proverbs to "improve" the Hebrew text when translating it into English. An especially striking example is the manner in which the NRSV has chosen to change the book's masculine nouns and pronouns. Thinking (presumably) that a book addressed to young men is prejudicial to women, the NRSV replaces words like *son* or *sons* with gender-neutral terms like *child* or *children*. It dispenses with gender-specific pronouns like *his* or *him* through paraphrases that allow for it to use gender-neutral pronouns like *their* or *them*. On the face of it, this is misleading and, in my opinion, unhelpful (see Introduction, "Why the Gender-Specific Focus").

Not all translations have gone this far, but most of them quite regularly insert words and phrases that are missing in the Hebrew text in order to make a smoother, more understandable, or more compelling sentence. For the most part, the Hebrew poems of the book are terser and more enigmatic than their English versions would suggest. Ideas are presented in subtle, thought-provoking ways. More often than not, nouns are juxtaposed without intervening verbs.

A simple example is Proverbs 10:1, which literally translated reads: *Wise son, glad father; but foolish son, grief of his mother* (10:1). There is no verb between *glad father* and *foolish son* or between *foolish son* and *grief of his mother*. By thus juxtaposing them (without verbs), the poem challenges the reader to think about the relationship between these phenomena. Why are these realities juxtaposed in this way? What does a wise son have to do with a glad father? What does a foolish son have to do with a grieving mother? Translators customarily answer these questions by supplying the missing verb, as does the NIV: *A wise son brings joy to his father, but a foolish son grief to his mother* (10:1). The added verb *brings* turns a terse set of juxtaposed terms into a straightforward (rather mundane) observation. A wise son does bring joy to his father, and a foolish one does bring grief to his mother, but there is more to it than that. The translator in this instance has preempted the discussion of the varied and profound ways in which a son's foolish or wise conduct affects the emotionality of his parents.

In his commentary on Proverbs, Roland Murphy has argued for a more literal style in translating the poems of Proverbs. He wants one that will do "justice to the ambiguity of a saying, an ambiguity that might be eliminated if the saying were translated in too bland a fashion" (1998:622). It is his point of view that while "most translators feel bound to a smooth and perfectly clear rendering, the format of a detailed commentary provides an opportunity to depart from this traditional style" (1998:623). In my opinion such a more literal translation would be a helpful resource for any serious student of the book of Proverbs.

WISDOM IN PROVERBS IN BIBLICAL TRADITION

Wisdom in Proverbs in the Old Testament. Hezekiah's reforms were short-lived. Upon Hezekiah's death in 687 BC, the Israelites reverted to worshipping "other gods" (2 Kgs 21). Two generations later, in 621 BC, Hezekiah's great-grandson attempted similar reforms (2 Kgs 22-23), but these were also unsuccessful. In 586 BC the kingdom of Judah was destroyed and most of its surviving population deported to Babylon. It was not until a century later, in the wake of the conquest of this region by Persia in 539/538 BC, that events transpired leading to the return of Israelites to their Judean homeland and the rebuilding of the temple (Ezra 1-6).

Following this came new and more enduring reforms led by Ezra and

Nehemiah, the climax of which was a covenant renewal experience different from any heretofore. Older Scriptures were read and interpreted so that the people understood (Neh 8). Those willing to live in the light of these Scriptures freely pledged to do so (Neh 9-10). An existing collection of scrolls created in support of Hezekiah's reforms was revised and republished with many additional scrolls added, to create a body of Scripture that would meet the needs of Israelites at home and abroad in this very different period of history (Miller, 2004:26-38). Master copies of the scrolls in this growing collection were housed in a library in Jerusalem, and duplicates were made and distributed to those who requested them (2 Macc 2:13-14).

Eventually these scrolls were organized (as in Jewish Bibles today) into three major sections called "Law," "Prophets," and "Writings" (cf. Luke 24:44). The scroll of Proverbs was placed in the Writings section after Ruth, Psalms, and Job (see Babylonian Talmud, *Baba Bathra* 14b). This location is indicative of the importance accorded it at this time. The books added in the "Writings" section were those deemed helpful for strengthening Israel's faith in the God who had revealed himself in the many and various ways set forth in the preceding sections of this collection (the Law and the Prophets).

One of the major challenges Israelites *now* faced in this postexilic period was knowing God's will for them in their quite different circumstances. The Persian monarch Cyrus had liberated them from Babylonian captivity, their temple had been rebuilt, but their kingdom had not been restored. Moreover, many Israelites were still living in various places throughout the vast Persian Empire. What was God's will for them now, with a temple but not a kingdom of their own, and with their people living in so many regions of the world side by side with other very different peoples?

One of the conclusions arrived at is set forth in the books of Ezra and Nehemiah. Right off, Ezra 1:1 declares that the decree of Cyrus authorizing Israel's release from captivity and the rebuilding of the temple was an act of God in fulfillment of his word a generation earlier to the prophet Jeremiah (29:10). Jeremiah had prophesied that after seventy years events would transpire matching those they had just experienced. He also said that at this time Israel's bond with God would be renewed and his laws would be written on their hearts (29:10-14; 31:33-34). Other prophets too had spoken of these developments and this period as a time when Israel would be renewed spiritually. Israel was to become "a light for the Gentiles" (Isa 42:6), their temple "a house of prayer for all nations" (56:7), so that God's "glory" might shine forth for the whole world to see (40:5).

To equip their people for this calling to make God known to the whole world, the Jews began to assemble the Jewish Scriptures (the OT of Christian Bibles). In that context the Jews valued the Hezekiah Edition of Proverbs as never before, and they added a final chapter highlighting the vital role wives play in fostering the well-being of their families and the whole society. The book's affirmation of wisdom and God's sovereignty in every aspect of life (and in the life of all peoples) must have afforded a way for Israelites to build bridges of understanding between themselves and their culturally diverse neighbors (Clements: 18). Now that they no longer lived in a kingdom of their own, they recognized the importance of the book's emphasis on home-schooling.

The teachings of the book of Proverbs were not without problems. The book emphasizes that it is by wisdom that God created the universe (3:19-20), and everything that happens is under his care (16:4). If so, how are life's obvious inequities, cruelties, and irrationalities to be explained? Do the wicked always suffer? Are the upright always blessed? Is there a rational explanation for everything that happens? Questions of this kind were pressing ones for those wanting to "trust in the LORD with all their heart" (Prov 3:5) in the postexilic period. This is evident in books added to the Jewish Bible at this time, notably Job and Ecclesiastes. For the most part this added "wisdom literature" (as it is sometimes called) testifies to the enduring strength of the synthesis wrought in Proverbs between respect for God and wisdom. It is true that Job's quest for understanding of the inequities of life did not get him very far; in the end he simply had to put his trust in God (42:1-6). And Ecclesiastes also comes to the conclusion that there is a great deal that we do not and cannot know about life (8:16-17). Nevertheless, the authors of these books do not give up the quest for knowledge and wisdom. In these books, as in Proverbs, respect for God (*fear of Yahweh*) and the quest for *wisdom* are harmonious and complementary endeavors.

Wisdom in Proverbs in Early Judaism. This is not the case, however, with a series of pivotal texts that were to have a profound effect on the thinking about *wisdom* in Early Judaism. The first of these is a poem inserted in the book of Job, in chapter 28, that openly questions whether wisdom can be found anywhere except in "the fear of the Lord" (28:28). In Proverbs, *the fear of the LORD is the beginning of knowledge/wisdom* (1:7; 9:10), *not* the only place where wisdom can be found. But the latter seems to be the point of view being introduced in Job 28, when it raises the question, "But where can wisdom be found? Where does understanding dwell?" (28:12, 20). The book answers by stressing that "it is hidden from the eyes of every living thing, concealed even from the birds of the air" (28:21). Even "Destruction and Death say, 'Only a rumor of it has reached our ears'" (28:22).

A similar point is made in a famous poem in the book of Sirach (Ecclesiasticus). The book's author, Jesus ben Sira, was a renowned teacher in Israel in the second century BC. In chapter 24 of his book, he imagines "Wisdom" speaking in her own voice, as in the poems of Solomon in Proverbs 8 and 9. In Ben Sira's poem "Wisdom" is pictured, not speaking to the whole world, but "in the assembly of the Most High" (24:2, NRSV). In her address to that assembly, she tells of how she "came forth from the mouth of the Most High" and "covered the earth like mist" (24:3, NRSV). Wisdom explains, however, that at first she did not see where she might dwell on earth, so she built her tent in the heights and began searching for a place on earth where she might "pitch camp" (24:4-7, NJB). Then it was, she continues exuberantly, that a momentous event occurred. "The Creator of all things instructed me and he who created me fixed a place for my tent. He said, 'Pitch your tent in Jacob, make Israel your inheritance'" (24:8, NJB). Wisdom was forthwith "established in Zion, in the beloved city he [the Creator] has given me rest, and in Jerusalem I wield my authority. I have taken root in a privileged people" (24:10-12, NJB). "All this," the poem concludes, "is no other than the Book of the Covenant of the Most High God, the Law that Moses enjoined on us, an inheritance for the communities of Jacob. This is what makes wisdom brim over like the Pishon" (24:23-25, NJB).

The question posed in Job 28, "Where can wisdom be found?" is here given a fuller, more dramatic answer. The wisdom that comes forth from the mouth of God is nowhere to be found except in "the Law that Moses enjoined on" Israel. From being thought of in the Hezekiah Edition of Proverbs as *the beginning of wisdom*, the *fear of the LORD* (which implies reverence for "the Law of Moses") is now thought of as the beginning and end of wisdom.

This developing regard for "the Law of Moses" as the sole source of wisdom is spelled out with utmost precision in the apocryphal book of Baruch, an influential Jewish writing of the first century BC. In Baruch 3—when trying to explain why Israel was defeated and in captivity—the author forthrightly declares: "It is because you have forsaken the fountain of wisdom!" (3:12, NJB). What fountain is Baruch referring to? Echoing the poems in Job 28 and Sirach 24, the poet asks, "Who has found out where she [wisdom] lives, who has entered her treasure house?" (3:15, NJB). Then he replies (as do Job 28 and Sir 24) that wisdom is inaccessible to every people on earth with one exception (Bar 3:15-31). The God who created the universe (3:32-36) "has uncovered the whole way of knowledge and shown it to his servant Jacob, to Israel his well-beloved; only then did she [wisdom] appear on earth and live among human beings. She [wisdom] is the book of God's commandments, the Law that stands for ever; those who keep her shall live, those who desert her shall die" (3:37–4:1, NJB).

This point of view (in which "wisdom" and the "Torah of Moses" are equated and said to be the *only* source of wisdom) became increasingly powerful and pervasive in the Judaism of the first centuries AD as reflected in the teachings of the Jewish sages of the Talmud. For them, it was a given that in the Law of Moses a wisdom about God and life had been revealed that was not just superior to that of other nations but for the most part was absent everywhere else (Schäfer: 34-42). The Talmudic rabbis discussed why this was the case. Their speculations were that God had offered his laws to other nations first, but they all refused them, and so God turned to Israel and gave his laws to them (Urbach: 533). In the course of time, the teachings of Proverbs were themselves viewed in this light. In a recently translated tenth-century Jewish commentary on Proverbs, "Lady Wisdom" (in Prov 8–9) is regarded as a symbol of the Torah of Moses. Thus, when the poem states that *wisdom* was with God from the beginning, this is interpreted to mean, "At first Torah was in heaven," but then "later on Moses arose and brought it down to earth to give it to humanity" (Visotzky: 46).

Wisdom in Proverbs in the New Testament. A similar set of ideas about wisdom entered Christianity through the writings of the apostle Paul. In 1 Corinthians he draws a stark contrast between the wisdom manifest in Christ and human wisdom similar to that drawn in Jewish writings of that period between human wisdom and the wisdom revealed in the Torah of Moses. Especially notable are the verbal links that exist between Paul's discussion of these matters in 1 Corinthians 1:10–4:21 and the previously discussed poem in Baruch 3. According to Pearson, the poem in Baruch states "that God has hidden Wisdom from the 'rulers of the nations' (3:16) and the mighty, but has given it in the form of his Torah to Israel, his elect." "Paul uses a similar terminology (he probably knows the Baruch passage)—but for him the 'Wisdom of God' is not Torah, but Christ crucified (1 [Cor] 1:23f., 30). This Wisdom of God stands over and against all forms of human wisdom and self-assertion" (48-49).

Drawing this kind of stark contrast between revealed wisdom and human wisdom poses difficult issues. If the Torah of Moses is humanity's only source of wisdom—or if Christ is that sole source of wisdom instead of the Torah of Moses—what shall we do with human wisdom? What shall we do with the book of Proverbs, which makes the point that the wisdom the Law reveals is the *beginning* of wisdom, not its sole source? How did Paul himself resolve this issue? In explaining Paul's warrants for ethical conduct, Richard Hays (in a highly regarded study of these issues) identifies three reference points: union with Christ, a sense of being liberated from the power of sin, and the Holy Spirit at work in the community of faith (1996:39). As to the "shape of obedience" in Paul's writings, Hays observes, "there are many clear instances where his ethical categories and vocabulary are drawn from his Jewish and Hellenistic cultural backgrounds." But the "two fundamental norms" to which Paul points repeatedly, states Hays, are "the unity of the community and the imitation of Christ" (1996:41). It seems that the values of his Jewish heritage were influential for Paul, but after his conversion these were (so far as he was concerned) replaced by and channeled through "the mind of Christ" (1 Cor 2:16; Eph 1:7-10).

Do other NT writers and writings share Paul's views in this regard? The Gospels portray Jesus as bringing a message of hope for the world through his proclamation of the nearness of God's kingdom (Mark 1:14-15). In this context his teachings are accorded a prominent place, especially in Matthew's Gospel. When assembled—as in the Sermon on the Mount (Matt 5-7)—these teachings resemble those in Proverbs in form and content. They (like the teachings in Proverbs) are referred to as the gateway to life (7:14). Those heeding them are identified as being wise because they have enough sense to build their houses on the rock (7:24). Furthermore, in this instance the teachings are said to be, not a replacement for the law but a "fulfillment" of the Law and the Prophets (5:17) in such matters as control of anger, fidelity in marriage, truthfulness, and goodwill toward enemies (Matt 5:21-48). As does the book of Proverbs, the teachings assembled here foster trust in God as caring Father (Matt 6) and regard for others (Matt 7). The wisdom of faithful disciples is also (as in Proverbs) viewed as relevant for the whole world (28:19). Matthew's Jesus speaks of the good fruits of those who do right regardless of where they live. He encourages thought and reflection, a human capacity shared by every people on earth. Those who heed Jesus are said to be the light and the salt of the earth (Matt 5:13-15). In Jesus's final words to his disciples, he commissions them to teach the nations what he has commanded (28:16-20). His wise words convey "new treasures as well as old" about God's coming kingdom (13:52) by one "greater than Solomon" (12:42; cf. 11:19; 13:54). The basic outlook and terminology of the teachings of Jesus in Matthew's Gospel appear to be more affirmative of the kind of wisdom we find in Proverbs than Paul's teaching seems to be at points.

The language of John's Gospel also differs from that of Paul in his letters. Its very first words characterize Jesus as the incarnation of the "word" that was with God from the beginning (1:1). This text recalls what is said about "wisdom" in Proverbs 8:22. In Jewish theology the "word" and "wisdom" of God are synonymous terms (Charlesworth: 121). In other words, what John's Gospel suggests is that in Jesus's life, death, and resurrection the kind of wisdom spoken of in Proverbs is manifest in a powerful new way. The prologue further explains that this incarnate "word" was "the true light that gives light to every man" (John 1:9). In this way a connection is drawn between the "wisdom" revealed through Jesus Christ and wisdom elsewhere in the world. "Like Jewish Wisdom literature, Jesus calls all to him and instructs them concerning the way, the truth, and the life. Like Wisdom he personifies these virtues. Like Wisdom he brings joy to those who know him and offers them life, indeed eternal life" (Charlesworth: 127). The wisdom revealed through Jesus Christ is summed up in the love Jesus showed toward his disciples when going to the cross, a love that he wants them to show for one another (15:12-17).

The book of James is yet another powerful example of Proverbs-like teachings in the NT. Scholars have noted over thirty parallels between the teaching legacy of Jesus and that of James (Painter: 361-62). In a key statement on the nature of God, James writes that "every good and perfect gift is from above, coming down from the Father of the heavenly lights, who does not change like shifting shadows" (1:17). This "affirmation is rooted in the understanding of the goodness of the creation and thus, by implication, of the creator, who is described here as 'father of lights'" (Painter: 252). This view of the world is similar to the one conveyed in Proverbs 3 and Genesis 1. In Proverbs 3 God is referred to as father and Creator of the world (3:5-8, 12, 19-20); in Genesis 1 he is described as Creator of the "lights in the expanse of the sky" (1:14). Many themes touched on in James are also similar to those in Proverbs, such as the "belief that true religion involves caring for the poor, sick and needy, correcting those who err, treating all people with fairness, gentleness, peaceableness, self-control especially in relation to speech" (Painter: 252). Perhaps James is taking issue with Paul when he writes, "What good is it, my brothers, if a man claims to have faith but has no deeds? Can such a faith save him? Suppose a brother or sister is without clothes and daily food. If one of you says to him, 'Go, I wish you well; keep warm and well fed,' but does nothing about his physical needs, what good is it? In the same way, faith by itself, if it is not accompanied by action, is dead" (2:14-17).

WORDS FOR WISDOM AND FOLLY IN PROVERBS The book of Proverbs contains a variety of words to convey what it means by *wisdom* and its opposite. A respected linguist, Michael Fox, has made an especially thorough study of this "rich vocabulary" (28-43). In it he notes that "precise distinctions between terms for wisdom" are often not essential for understanding a given verse, nor is the book itself much concerned "with drawing fine distinctions among the types it condemns" (28). He also cautions that it is often "impossible to find a single English equivalent for each Hebrew term." Moreover, it is "important to distinguish between lexical and contextual meaning, which is to say, between the nuclear meaning a word contributes to the new context and the enriched meaning it receives by interaction with its new environment" (28). Still, he insists, knowing what a given word brings to a text is important, and dictionary meanings are helpful.

The following is a selected list of terms for wisdom and folly in Proverbs. In each instance a transliteration of the selected Hebrew term is cited first, followed by the word used to translate it in the NIV. This is followed by a verse where it is so translated, and then by a quote or two from the analysis of this word by Fox.

bînāh = insight (for understanding words of insight [bînāh], Prov 1:2b). "The raw faculty of *bînāh* . . . is similar to the modern concept of intelligence, except for the modern assumption that intelligence is innate" (Fox: 30).

da'at = knowledge (for giving . . . knowledge [da'at] and discretion to the young, 1:4). "*Daʿat* is the broadest of the wisdom words. It appears that everything designated by any of these words could also be called *daʿat*. It is broader even than English 'knowledge,' in so far as it includes minimal acts of awareness and innate intellectual capacities apart from learned information and skills" (31).

ʿēṣāh = *purpose* (*The purposes* [*ʿēṣāh*] *of a man's heart are deep waters;* 20:5a). The *ʿēṣāh* "is essentially *deliberation*: careful thinking and planning, the resolution arrived at by such thinking, and the capacity for such thought" (32).

ḥokmāh = *wisdom* (*for attaining wisdom* [*ḥokmāh*], 1:2a). This *ḥokmāh* "is essentially a high degree of knowledge and skill in any domain. . . . The nearest English equivalent that encompasses its semantic range is expertise" (32).

mûsar = *discipline* (*for attaining wisdom and discipline* [*mûsar*], 1:2a). "The core notion conveyed by *mûsar* is the teaching of avoidance of faults. . . . *Mûsar* is basically correction, whether by verbal rebuke or by physical punishment" (34).

śēkel = *understanding* (*Good understanding* [*śēkel*] *wins favor;* 13:15). "When *śēkel* refers to a kind of wisdom, its core meaning is 'insight,' the ability to grasp the meanings or implications of a situation or message. *Śēkel* is consequently discernment or prudence, the ability to understand practical matters and inter-personal relations and make beneficial decisions. It later comes to include intellectual understanding and unusual expertise" (36).

bāʿar = *stupid* (*He who hates correction is stupid* [*bāʿar*]; 12:1b). "The *bāʿar* is an ignoramus. Animal-like brutishness is his earmark. . . . The term *bāʿar* does not necessarily denote a pernicious defect" (39).

ḥăsar-lēb = *lacks judgment* (*I noticed . . . a youth who lacked judgment* [*ḥăsar-lēb*]; 7:7). The expression "means the same as the English 'empty-headed.' It has a precise equivalent in Egyptian, . . . 'one who lacks a heart,' which refers to the senseless, imprudent person rather than the arrogant or wicked fool. . . . Since the Hebrew expression is found only in Wisdom literature, it is likely an Egyptianism" (39-40).

ʾĕwîlîm = *fools* (*Fools* [*ʾĕwîlîm*] *despise wisdom and discipline;* 1:7b). The *ʾĕwîlîm* "are not idiots or madmen, for these would not bother either to esteem or to despise discipline. Rather . . . [folly] is the willful refusal to make moral choices" (40).

kĕsîlût = *folly* (*The woman Folly* [*kĕsîlût*] *is loud;* 9:13a). "*Kĕsîlût* is smug mental sloth with respect to its impact on judgment and reason. It is stupidity that comes from obtuseness and complacency, not merely from inadequate intelligence" (41).

lēṣ = *mocker* (*The mocker* [*lēṣ*] *seeks wisdom and finds none;* 14:6). The *lēṣ* "is both arrogant and scornful." Such people's "words do not express mockery so much as cynicism and insolence. In their audacity, they imagine themselves immune from punishment" (42).

pĕtāʾîm = *simple* (*for giving prudence to the simple* [*pĕtāʾîm*], 1:4a). The root meaning is to "be gullible." The "malleability" of the simple "leaves them open to learning and improvement (8:5; 9:4, 6; 19:25; 21:11). Indeed, according to the Prologue the *pĕtî* [simple] is the primary audience of Proverbs' instruction (1:4)" (43).

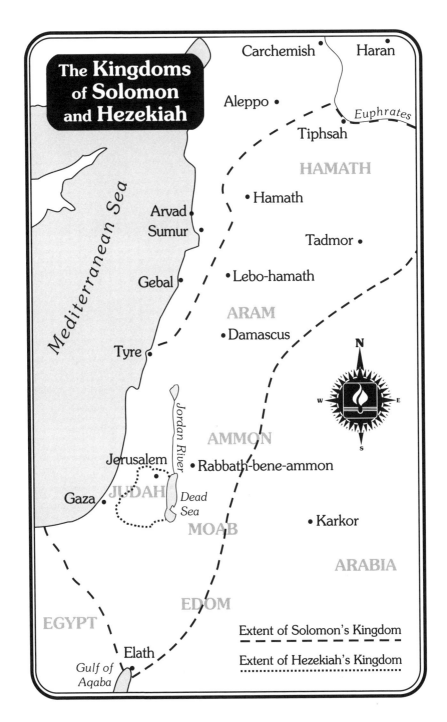

The Kingdoms of Solomon and Hezekiah

Carchemish
Haran
Aleppo
Euphrates
Tiphsah
HAMATH
Hamath
Arvad
Sumur
Tadmor
Lebo-hamath
Gebal
ARAM
Damascus
Mediterranean Sea
N
W E
S
Tyre
Jordan River
AMMON
Jerusalem
Rabbath-bene-ammon
Gaza
JUDAH
Dead Sea
Karkor
MOAB
ARABIA
EDOM
Extent of Solomon's Kingdom
EGYPT
Extent of Hezekiah's Kingdom
Elath
Gulf of Aqaba

Bibliography of Works Cited

Abegg, Martin, Jr., Peter Flint, and Eugene Ulrich
    1999   *The Dead Sea Scrolls Bible: The Oldest Known Bible Translated for the First Time into English.* New York: HarperCollins.

Alcorn, Randy C.
    1985   *Christians in the Wake of the Sexual Revolution: Recovering Our Sexual Sanity.* Portland: Multnomah.

Alden, Robert L.
    1983   *Proverbs: A Commentary on an Ancient Book of Timeless Advice.* Grand Rapids: Baker.

Aristotle
    1953   *The Ethics of Aristotle: The Nicomachean Ethics.* Translated by J. A. K. Thomson. Harmondsworth, Middlesex, UK: Penguin.

Bender, Harold S.
    1955   "Church." In *The Mennonite Encyclopedia,* 1:594-97. Scottdale, PA: Mennonite Publishing House.

Bennett, William J.
    2001   *The Broken Hearth: Reversing the Moral Collapse of the American Family.* New York: Doubleday.

Blakney, Raymond Bernard
    1941   *Meister Eckhart: A Modern Translation.* New York: Harper & Brothers.

Boadt, Lawrence E.
    1986   *Introduction to Wisdom Literature: Proverbs.* College Bible Commentary 18. Collegeville: Liturgical Press.

Brown, William P.
1996   *Character in Crisis: A Fresh Approach to the Wisdom Literature of the Old Testament.* Grand Rapids: Eerdmans.

Bullock, C. Hassell
1995   "The Book of Proverbs." Pages 19-33 in *Learning from the Sages, Selected Studies on the Book of Proverbs.* Edited by Roy B. Zuck. Grand Rapids: Baker.

Charlesworth, James H.
2003   "Lady Wisdom and Johannine Christology." Pages 92-133 in *Light in a Spotless Mirror: Reflections on Wisdom Traditions in Judaism and Early Christianity.* Edited by James H. Charlesworth and Michael A. Daise. Harrisburg: Trinity.

Clements, Ronald E.
1990   *Wisdom for a Changing World: Wisdom in Old Testament Theology.* Berkeley Lectures 2. Berkeley: BIBAL Press.
1992   *Wisdom in Theology.* The Didsbury Lectures, 1989. Carlisle, UK: Paternoster.

Clifford, Richard J.
1999   *Proverbs.* Louisville: Westminster John Knox.

Cohen, Abraham
1952   *Proverbs: Hebrew Text and English Translation with an Introduction and Commentary.* London: Soncino (see verse in question).

Cunningham, David S.
2003   "The Way of Wisdom: The Practical Theology of David Ford." *The Christian Century,* May 3, 30-37.

Delitzsch, Franz
1872   *Biblical Commentary on the Proverbs of Solomon.* Reprint, 1986. Grand Rapids: Eerdmans.

Dobson, James
2001   *Bringing Up Boys.* Wheaton: Tyndale.

Dodd, C. H.
1961   *The Parables of the Kingdom.* Rev. ed. New York: Charles Scribner's Sons.

Donin, Hayim Halevy
1977   *To Raise a Jewish Child: A Guide for Parents.* New York: Basic Books.

Eaton, John H.
1989   *The Contemplative Face of Old Testament Wisdom in the Context of World Religions.* London: SCM.

Estes, Daniel J.
1997   *Hear, My Son: Teaching and Learning in Proverbs 1-9.* New Studies in Biblical Theology 4. Downers Grove, IL: InterVarsity.

Fackenheim, Emil L.
1989   *To Mend the World: Foundations of Post-Holocaust Thought.* New York: Schocken Books.

Franz, Günther, et al., eds.
1951   *Wiedertäuferakten, 1527-1626. Veröffentlichungen der Historischen Kommission für Hessen und Waldeck 11.4.* Marburg: Elwert.

Fox, Michael V.
2000   *Proverbs 1-9: A New Translation with Introduction and Commentary.* Anchor Bible 18A. New York: Doubleday.

Gamble, Harry Y.
1985   *The New Testament Canon: Its Making and Meaning.* Philadelphia: Fortress.

Gilmore, David G.
1990   *Manhood in the Making: Cultural Concepts of Masculinity.* New Haven: Yale University Press.

Golka, Friedemann W.
1993   *The Leopard's Spots: Biblical and African Wisdom in Proverbs.* Edinburgh: T & T Clark.

Goldingay, John
2003   *Old Testament Theology,* Vol. 1, *Israel's Gospel.* Downers Grove: InterVarsity.

Harris, R. Laird, ed.
1980   *Theological Wordbook of the Old Testament.* Chicago: Moody.

Harrison, Carol
1999   "Augustine, Wisdom and Classical Culture." In *Where Shall Wisdom Be Found?* Edited by Stephen C. Barton. Edinburgh: T & T Clark.

Hays, Richard B.
1996   *The Moral Vision of the New Testament: Community, Cross, New Creation.* San Francisco: Harper Collins.
1999   "Wisdom According to Paul." Pages 111-24 in *Where Shall Wisdom Be Found? Wisdom in the Bible, the Church and the Contemporary World.* Edited by Stephen C. Barton. Edinburgh: T & T Clark.

Heaton, E. W.
1974   *Solomon's New Men: The Emergence of Ancient Israel as a National State.* London: Thames & Hudson.

Hoksbergen, Roland, and Lowell M. Ewert
2001   *Local Ownership Global Change: Will Civil Society Save the World?* Monrovia, CA: World Vision.

Horst, Irvin B.
1988   *Mennonite Confession of Faith, Adopted April 21st, 1632, at Dordrecht, the Netherlands.* Newly translated and edited with prefatory materials in English. Lancaster: Lancaster Mennonite Historical Society.

Hugenberger, Gordon P.
1994   *Marriage as a Covenant: Biblical Law and Ethics as Developed from Malachi.* Grand Rapids: Baker.

Johnson, Luke Timothy
1995   *The Letter of James: A New Translation with Introduction and Commentary.* Anchor Bible 37A. New York: Doubleday.

Kumar, Shedev
2000   "Why Science Alone Cannot Satisfy the Soul." *The Globe and Mail,* January 17, R14.

Landes, David S.
1999   *The Wealth and Poverty of Nations: Why Some are So Rich and Some So Poor.* New York: Norton.

Lang, Bernhard
1986   *Wisdom and the Book of Proverbs: A Hebrew Goddess Redefined.* New York: Pilgrim.

Malchow, Bruce V.
1995   "A Manual for Future Monarchs: Proverbs 27:23–29:27." Pages 353-60 in *Learning from the Sages: Selected Studies on the Book of Proverbs.* Edited by Roy B. Zuck. Grand Rapids: Baker.

Malek, Jaromir
1986   *In the Shadow of the Pyramids: Egypt during the Old Kingdom.* Norman: University of Oklahoma Press.

Marshall, Christopher
2001   *Crowned with Glory and Honor: Human Rights in the Biblical Traditions.* Telford, PA: Pandora Press U.S.

Martens, Elmer A.
1981   *God's Design: A Focus on Old Testament Theology.* Grand Rapids: Baker. 3d ed., 1998. N. Richland Hills, TX: BIBAL Press.
2000   "The Way of Wisdom: Conflict Resolution in Biblical Narrative." Pages 75-90 in *The Way of Wisdom: Essays in Honor of Bruce K. Waltke.* Edited by J. I. Packer and Sven K. Soderlund. Grand Rapids: Zondervan.

Matzner-Bekerman, Shoshana
1984   *The Jewish Child: Halakhic Perspectives.* New York: Ktav.

McBride, S. Dean, Jr.
1993   "Polity of the Covenant People: The Book of Deuteronomy." Pages 62-77 in *A Song of Power and the Power of Song: Essays on the Book of Deuteronomy.* Edited by Duane L. Christensen. Winona Lake, IN: Eisenbrauns.

McKane, William
1970   *Proverbs: A New Approach.* Philadelphia: Westminster.

McNeill, John T.
1951   *A History of the Cure of Souls.* New York: Harper & Row.

Menno Simons
1956   *The Complete Writings of Menno Simons.* Edited by J. C. Wenger. Translated by Leonard Verduin. Scottdale, PA: Mennonite Publishing House.

Millar, Thomas P.
1983   *The Omnipotent Child.* (2d ed., 1989.) Vancouver: Palmer.

Miller, John W.
1973   *A Christian Approach to Sexuality.* Scottdale, PA: Mennonite Publishing House.
1981   *Step by Step Through the Parables.* New York: Paulist Press.
1987   *Meet the Prophets: A Beginner's Guide to the Books of the Biblical Prophets.* New York: Paulist Press.
1994   *The Origins of the Bible: Rethinking Canon History.* New York: Paulist Press.

1997   *Jesus at Thirty: A Psychological and Historical Portrait.* Minneapolis: Fortress.

1999   *Calling God "Father": Essays on the Bible, Fatherhood, and Culture.* 2d ed. New York: Paulist Press.

2004   *How the Bible Came to Be: Exploring the Narrative and Message.* New York: Paulist Press.

Montefiore, C. G., and H. Loewe.

1974   *A Rabbinic Anthology: Selected and Arranged with Comments and Introduction.* New York: Schocken.

Montgomery, David J.

2000   "A Bribe Is a Charm." Pages 134-49 in *The Way of Wisdom, Essays in Honor of Bruce K. Waltke.* Edited by J. I. Packer and Sven K. Soderlund. Grand Rapids: Zondervan.

Murphy, Roland E.

1981   *Wisdom Literature: Job, Proverbs, Ruth, Canticles, Ecclesiastes, and Esther.* Forms of the Old Testament Literature 13. Grand Rapids: Eerdmans.

1998   *Proverbs.* Word Biblical Commentary 22. Nashville: Nelson.

2002   *The Tree of Life: An Exploration of Biblical Wisdom Literature.* 3d ed. (1st ed., 1990; 2d ed., 1996.) Grand Rapids: Eerdmans.

2003   "Israel's Wisdom: Dialogue between the Sages." Pages 7-25 in *Light in a Spotless Mirror: Reflections on Wisdom Traditions in Judaism and Early Christianity.* Edited by James H. Charlesworth and Michael A. Daise. Harrisburg: Trinity.

Neff, Christian, and Bender, Harold S.

1959   "Oath." In *The Mennonite Encyclopedia,* 4:2-6. Scottdale, PA: Mennonite Publishing House.

Oesterley, W. O. E.

1927   *The Wisdom of Egypt and the Old Testament in the Light of the Newly Discovered 'Teaching of Amen-em-ope.'* London: SPCK.

Painter, John

1999   *Just James: The Brother of Jesus in History and Tradition.* Minneapolis: Fortress.

Pearson, Birger A.

1975   "Hellenistic-Jewish Wisdom Speculation and Paul." In *Aspects of Wisdom in Judaism and Early Christianity.* Edited by Robert L. Wilken. Notre Dame: University of Notre Dame Press.

Perdue, Leo G.

2000   *Proverbs.* Interpretation, a Bible Commentary for Teaching and Preaching. Louisville: John Knox.

Pipher, Mary

1994   *Reviving Ophelia: Saving the Selves of Adolescent Girls.* New York: Ballantine.

Pope John Paul II

1995   *Gospel of Life [Evangelium Vitae].* The Encyclical Letter on Abortion, Euthanasia, and the Death Penalty in Today's World. Toronto: Random House.

Pritchard, James B., ed.
1950   *Ancient Near Eastern Texts Relating to the Old Testament.* Princeton: Princeton University Press.

Ruffle, John
1996   "The Teaching of Amenemope and Its Connection with the Book of Proverbs." Pages 293-331 in *Learning from the Sages: Selected Studies on the Book of Proverb.* Edited by Roy B. Zuck. Grand Rapids: Baker.

Schäfer, Peter
2003   "Wisdom Finds a Home: Torah as Wisdom." Pages 26-44 in *Light in a Spotless Mirror: Reflections on Wisdom Traditions in Judaism and Early Christianity.* Edited by James H. Charlesworth and Michael A. Daise. Harrisburg: Trinity.

Schniedewind, William M.
2000   "Orality and Literacy in Ancient Israel." *Religious Studies Review* 26/4: 327-32.

Schrock-Shenk, Carolyn, ed.
2000   *Mediation and Facilitation Training Manual: Foundations and Skills for Constructive Conflict Transformation.* Akron, PA: Mennonite Conciliation Service.

Toy, Crawford H.
1916   *A Critical and Exegetical Commentary on the Book of Proverbs.* International Critical Commentary. New York: Charles Scribner's Sons.

Urbach, Ephraim E.
1986   *The Sages: Their Concepts and Beliefs.* Cambridge: Harvard University Press.

Van Buren, Paul
1980   *Discerning the Way, A Theology of the Jewish-Christian Reality.* New York: Seabury.

Van Leeuwen, Mary Steward
2002   *My Brother's Keeper: What the Social Sciences Do (and Don't) Tell Us About Masculinity.* Downers Grove, IL: InterVarsity.

Van Leeuwen, Raymond C.
1997   *The Book of Proverbs: Introduction, Commentary, and Reflections.* New Interpreter's Bible 5. Nashville: Abingdon.
2000   "Building God's House: An Exploration in Wisdom." Pages 204-11 in *The Way of Wisdom: Essays in Honor of Bruce K. Waltke.* Edited by J. I. Packer and Sven K. Soderlund. Grand Rapids: Zondervan.

Vial, Theodore, and Mark A. Hadley
2001   *Ethical Monotheism, Past and Present: Essays in Honor of Wendell S. Dietrich.* Providence: Brown University.

Visotzky, Burton L.
1992   *The Midrash on Proverbs: Translated from the Hebrew with an Introduction and Annotations.* New Haven: Yale University Press.

von Rad, Gerhard
1962   Old Testament Theology. Vol. 1, The Theology of Israel's Historical Traditions. New York: Harper & Row.

Waltke, Bruce K.
1972   Wisdom in Israel. London: SCM.
1997   "The Book of Proverbs and Ancient Wisdom Literature." Pages 49-65 in Learning from the Sages: Selected Studies on the Book of Proverbs. Edited by Roy B. Zuck. Grand Rapids: Baker.

Walton, John H.
1989   Ancient Israelite Literature in Its Cultural Context: A Survey of Parallels Between Biblical and Ancient Near Eastern Texts. Grand Rapids: Zondervan.

Washington, Harold C.
1994   Wealth and Poverty in the Instruction of Amenemope and the Hebrew Proverbs. Dissertation Series 142. Atlanta: Scholars Press.

Weinfeld, Moshe
1972   Deuteronomy and the Deuteronomic School. Oxford: Clarendon.

Westermann, Claus
1995   Social Justice in Ancient Israel and in the Ancient Near East. Minneapolis: Fortress.
1990   Roots of Wisdom: The Oldest Proverbs of Israel and Other Peoples. Louisville: Westminster John Knox.

Whybray, R. N.
1990   Wealth and Poverty in the Book of Proverbs. Journal for the Study of the Old Testament, Supplement Series 99. Sheffield, UK: JSOT Press.
1994   Proverbs. The New Century Bible Commentary. Grand Rapids: Eerdmans.
1995   The Book of Proverbs: A Survey of Modern Study. Leiden: Brill.

Williams, James G.
1987   "Proverbs and Ecclesiastes." In The Literary Guide to the Bible. Edited by Robert Alter and Frank Kermode. Cambridge: Harvard University Press.

Wolff, Hans Walter
1974   Anthropology of the Old Testament. Philadelphia: Fortress.

Yoder, Christine Roy
2003   "The Woman of Substance (אשת־חיל): A Socioeconomic Reading of Proverbs 31:10-31." Journal of Biblical Literature 122/3: 427-47.

Selected Resources

Commentaries in English

Aitken, Kenneth. *Proverbs.* Daily Study Bible. Edinburgh: St. Andrew, 1986. Views Proverbs as a textbook for educating young people; before commenting, rearranges the sayings of chapters 10-31 according to themes.

Alden, Robert. *Proverbs: A Commentary on an Ancient Book of Timeless Advice.* Grand Rapids: Baker, 1983. While recognizing the contents of Proverbs as stemming from an ancient culture, sees their relevance for today; verse-by-verse comments on the whole book.

Boadt, Lawrence. *Introduction to Wisdom Literature: Proverbs.* Collegeville Bible Commentary. Collegeville: Liturgical Press, 1986. Views the book as reflecting a long practice in Israel of instructing boys in schools; introduction; notes to printed text of the New American Bible.

Clifford, Richard J. *Proverbs.* Old Testament Library. Louisville: Westminster John Knox, 1999. Insightful textual analysis; sees 25:1 as a clue to the book's social location among scribes of the king charged with writing and recording.

Cohen, Abraham. *Proverbs: Hebrew Text and English Translation with an Introduction and Commentary.* Soncino Books of the Bible. London: Soncino, 1952. Sparkles with brief, insightful comments on each verse; sees the teachings of the wise as complementing the teachings of priests and prophets.

Delitzsch, Franz. *Biblical Commentary on the Proverbs of Solomon.* Commentary on the Old Testament. Reprint. Grand Rapids: Eerdmans, 1986; original German, 1873. Erudite interpretations of grammar and vocabulary from a respected biblical scholar of a previous century.

Farmer, Kathleen A. *Proverbs and Ecclesiastes.* International Theological Commentary. Grand Rapids: Eerdmans, 1991. Emphasizes reading the book in the light of its final form; pays special attention to "Feminist Concerns."

Fox, Michael V. *Proverbs 1-9, A New Translation with Introduction and Commentary.* Anchor Bible 18A. New York: Doubleday, 2000. Exhaustive analysis of the book's first nine chapters; sees the book as reflecting many facets of ancient Israelite society "through numerous generations" (11).

Hubbard, David. *Proverbs.* The Communicator's Commentary. Dallas: Word, 1989. Researched and written with contemporary preachers and teachers in mind; opens with six guidelines for a meaningful study of this book.

Kidner, Derek. *Proverbs: An Introduction and Commentary.* Tyndale Old Testament Commentaries. Leicester, UK: Inter-Varsity, 1964. Views the book as "a course of education in the life of wisdom" (22); offers terse discussions and commentary on the whole book.

McKane, William. *Proverbs: A New Approach.* Philadelphia: Westminster, 1970. In the verse-by-verse part of this commentary, seeks to distinguish an older secular wisdom from a later pious tradition; offers a comprehensive review of background literature from the ancient world.

Murphy, Roland E. *Proverbs.* Word Biblical Commentary 22. Nashville: Nelson, 1998. Sees the literature of this book as influenced by both family and "some kind of court school."

Perdue, Leo G. *Proverbs.* Interpretation, a Bible Commentary for Teaching and Preaching. Louisville: John Knox, 2000. Thinks the book developed from the early monarchy into postexilic times; sees "evidence of a later theological and literary polish and skill that came with the increasing education of sages through the generations of Israel's and Judah's schools."

Scott, R. B. Y. *Proverbs, Ecclesiastes: Introduction, Translation, and Notes.* Anchor Bible 18. Garden City, NY: Doubleday, 1965. Suggests the book was used in private academies in which professionals gave instruction to the sons of the wealthy; a fresh translation with notes.

Toy, Crawford. *The Book of Proverbs.* Critical and Exegetical Commentary. New York: Charles Scribner's Sons, 1916. Pays close attention to textual variations and problems; an older work whose opinions on specifics are still worth consulting.

Van Leeuwen, Raymond C. "The Book of Proverbs." *The New Interpreter's Bible* 5:17-264. Nashville: Abingdon, 1997. Believes differing groups produced independent sections and that final author-editors assembled the parts into a compendium of wisdom. Includes "reflections" on issues of contemporary relevance.

Whybray, R. N. *Proverbs.* New Century Bible Commentary. Grand Rapids: Eerdmans, 1994. Believes the book in its present form cannot be earlier than the early postexilic period, but that it shows no sign "of the emphasis on the Mosaic Law which developed during the latter part of that period" (7).

Monographs

Arnot, William. *Laws from Heaven for Life on Earth: Illustrations of the Book of Proverbs.* London: Nelson & Sons, 1857. From a previous century, insightful homilies on selected proverbs.

Blenkinsopp, Joseph. *Wisdom and Law in the Old Testament: The Ordering of Life in Israel and Early Judaism.* Oxford Bible Series. Oxford: Oxford University Press, 1983. Invites the reader "to think of wisdom and law as two great rivers which eventually flow together and find their outlet in rabbinic writings and early Christian theology" (130).

Bostrom, Lennart. *The God of the Sages: The Portrayal of God in the Book of Proverbs.* Stockholm: Almqvist & Wiksell, 1990. Proposes that although Israelite wisdom has an international flavor, it was integrated to the salvation historical approach of OT thought about God.

Brown, William P. *Character in Crisis: A Fresh Approach to the Wisdom Literature of the Old Testament.* Grand Rapids: Eerdmans, 1996. Seeks "to demonstrate that the idea of character constitutes the unifying theme or center of the wisdom literature, whose raison d'être is to profile ethical character" (21).

Brueggemann, Walter. *In Man We Trust: The Neglected Side of Biblical Faith.* Atlanta: John Knox, 1972. Views the resources and insights offered by the wisdom materials as important for coping with the problem of how to be persons of faith and persons of culture.

Bryce, Glendon E. *A Legacy of Wisdom: The Egyptian Contribution to the Wisdom of Israel.* Lewisburg: Bucknell University Press, 1979. Traces links between Israelite and Egyptian wisdom literature; argues that the pursuit of wisdom was never humanistic or secular, but had its own unique theological setting in the notion of a divine endowment for wisdom bestowed on the king.

Camp, Claudia V. *Wisdom and the Feminine in the Book of Proverbs.* Bible and Literature Series 11. Sheffield: Almond, 1985. Relates the predominance of female imagery in the final form of the book of Proverbs to the family's importance in Jewish communities after the exile.

Clements, Ronald E. *Wisdom for a Changing World: Wisdom in Old Testament Theology.* Berkeley Lectures 2. Berkeley: BIBAL Press, 1990. Believes the more universalistic approach to faith in Proverbs was fashioned with the needs of the scattered Jewish communities of the Diaspora in view.

———. *Wisdom in Theology.* The Disbury Lectures. Grand Rapids: Eerdmans, 1992. Develops further his thesis that the Israelite wisdom tradition was developed to meet the need for a more universalistic ethic and spirituality among Jews of the Diaspora.

Crenshaw, James L. *Education in Ancient Israel: Across the Deadening Silence.* New York: Doubleday, 1998. Believes there were schools in Israel from about the eighth century (if not earlier), but that little can be known about them.

Davidson, Robert. *Wisdom and Worship.* The Edward Cadbury Lectures 1989. London: SCM, 1990. Explores "the relationship between the wisdom thinkers in Israel and the shared approach to reality" reflected in the Psalms.

Estes, Daniel J. *Hear, My Son: Teaching and Learning in Proverbs 1–9.* Downers Grove, IL: InterVarsity Press, 1997. Discusses the worldview, educational values, goals, and methods implicit and explicit in the first nine chapters of Proverbs.

Eaton, John. *The Contemplative Face of Old Testament Wisdom in the Context of World Religions.* London: SCM, 1989. Views biblical wisdom literature as the fruit of a contemplative practice whose approach and themes are similar to those in other religions and peoples.

Murphy, Roland E. *The Tree of Life: An Exploration of Biblical Wisdom Literature.* 3d ed. Grand Rapids: Eerdmans, 2002. A study of the quest for wisdom in Israel as reflected in the major biblical writings; he is uncertain in what social setting this quest was pursued. Contains two comprehensive bibliographical overviews of recent research.

———. *Wisdom Literature. Forms of the Old Testament Literature 13.* Grand Rapids: Eerdmans, 1981. An introductory discussion of the literary genre of the book as a whole, followed by a running commentary on the form and purpose of individual units.

Perdue, Leo G. *Wisdom and Creation: The Theology of Wisdom Literature.* Nashville: Abingdon, 1994. Believes wisdom theology centers on creation and providence, and from Jesus ben Sira onward it provides the context for understanding Israel's election and story. Its social location was schools for administrators, scribes, lawyers, and teachers.

Sheppard, Gerald T. *Wisdom as a Hermeneutical Construct: A Study in the Sapientializing of the Old Testament.* Berlin: Walter de Gruyter, 1980. Through case studies from Sirach and Baruch and several OT texts, concludes that wisdom functioned as "a hermeneutical construct to interpret the Torah as a statement about wisdom" (118).

Von Rad, Gerhard. *Wisdom in Israel.* London: SCM, 1972. Identifies trends of thought and theological contexts in which Israelite wisdom functioned.

Whybray, R. N. *The Book of Proverbs: A Survey of Modern Study.* Leiden: Brill, 1995. Provides a comprehensive overview of scholarly studies of Proverbs during the twentieth century.

Index of Ancient Sources

The Author

John W. Miller has combined an active life of scholarship, writing, university teaching, and pastoral leadership. He is professor emeritus at Conrad Grebel University College, an affiliate of the University of Waterloo in Ontario.

The author of numerous articles and books, his titles include *The Origins of the Bible*, *Rethinking Canon History* (1994), *Jesus at Thirty: A Psychological and Historical Portrait* (1997), *Calling God "Father"; Essays on the Bible, Fatherhood & Culture*, (1999), and most recently, *How the Bible Came to Be, Exploring the Narrative and Message* (2004).

Miller is a graduate of Goshen College (1948), Princeton Theological Seminary (B.D. 1951), New York University (M.A. English Literature, 1951) and the University of Basel (Th.D. Old Testament, 1955). After completing his doctoral studies, he taught Bible at Goshen College Biblical Seminary and several colleges and seminaries in the Chicago area before moving to Canada in 1969 to join the Religious Studies faculty of Conrad Grebel College.

In 1957 John and his wife Louise were founding members of the Reba Place Fellowship, an urban church-community in Evanston, Illinois. While in Evanston, John worked for nine years in psychiatric rehabilitation at the Chicago State Hospital. Since coming to Canada the Millers have been active in Mennonite affiliated house churches. In 1992 John was ordained as pastor for a house church that became responsible for the Blenheim Retreat and Bible Study Centre.

Miller was born in Akron, Pennsylvania, in 1926. In 1949 he married Louise Heatwole from Virginia. The Millers currently reside in Kitchener, Ontario. They have a son Christopher Miller and two daughters Jeanette Miller Ewert and Karen Miller Bearinger and grandchildren (listed in the dedication).